MIRRORS OF SELF

Mirrors of Self

HUMAN PERSONHOOD
IN CHRISTOLOGICAL PERSPECTIVE

Jonathan P. Badgett

PICKWICK *Publications* · Eugene, Oregon

MIRRORS OF SELF
Human Personhood in Christological Perspective

Pickwick Publications
An Imprint of Wipf and Stock Publishers
199 W. 8th Ave., Suite 3
Eugene, OR 97401

www.wipfandstock.com

PAPERBACK ISBN: 978-1-7252-6878-4
HARDCOVER ISBN: 978-1-7252-6879-1
EBOOK ISBN: 978-1-7252-6880-7

Cataloguing-in-Publication data:

Names: Badgett, Jonathan P., author
Title: Mirrors of self : human personhood in christological perspective / Jonathan P. Badgett.
Description: Eugene, OR: Pickwick Publications, 2021 | Includes bibliographical references.
Identifiers: ISBN 978-1-7252-6878-4 (paperback) | ISBN 978-1-7252-6879-1 (hardcover) | ISBN 978-1-7252-6880-7 (ebook)
Subjects: LCSH: Psychology and religion | Theological anthropology—Christianity | Personhood | Jesus Christ—Person and offices | Self—Religious aspects—Christianity | Mind and body | Theology of the body
Classification: BT713 B33 2021 (print) | BT713 (ebook)

To Alison, whose beauty reflects to me Christ's own

Table of Contents

Preface

THIS WORK REALLY STARTED as two projects—one personal and the other professional. Both, as it happens, have spanned at least a decade and, as of today, are still ongoing. As to the latter, my calling is as a pastor. A little over twelve years ago, I stepped into pastoral counseling relationships with several individuals and families who had been severely underserved by the mental health system. A few had spent time in inpatient institutions that had since closed. Several bore physical scars from ongoing self-harm. Many were suffering from various mental disorders that had either been misdiagnosed or under-diagnosed. And then there were a few who showed signs of something I did not understand at the time but would later come to recognize as pathological dissociation.

Now, ethical counseling standards demand that caregivers not extend themselves beyond their training and expertise. This is for the protection of both counselee and counselor. I have no compunction against acknowledging my own limitations. My initial efforts respective to these parishioners was to refer them. For more than a year I labored with a number of individuals to no avail trying to find licensed mental health professionals who grasped their respective conditions and would honor their Christian faith. For those suffering from pathological dissociation, I personally consulted with psychiatric and psychological services in the surrounding region to try and find providers who met these basic criteria. All with no luck.

You see, where I served in ministry at the time, on Long Island in New York, there is a dearth of principled Christian counseling. Dissociative disorders, as I was soon to discover, require a particular knowledge base and skillset that relatively few licensed professionals undertake. Though in hindsight I should have guessed as much, it would take some time for me to come to the conclusion that not all mental health service providers are created equal. As it happens, much of what passes for care is far from it.

Eventually I would agree to serve as a consulting pastoral counselor to several individuals with diagnosed dissociative disorders with the condition they remain under the care of their licensed caregiver. I made this arrangement with the licensed mental health service providers. For each counselee, I required signed consent forms indicating that they understood and agreed to the limits of the care I could provide. I further informed them that, should they discontinue care with their licensed professionals, I would no longer work with them.

This arrangement lasted for a number of years, during which time I read extensively on the nature and treatment of dissociative disorders. I attended conferences, met with experts in the field, and returned to school under a trained psychologist, all in the interests of better serving these individuals. I have also published on the subject of dissociative disorders and presented at professional conferences. My doctoral dissertation, the kernel from which the present work grew, included a host of material developed in both academic and caregiving contexts. Much of what I now know of dissociative disorders, however, I learned in the trenches.

Dissociative disorders form in chronically aversive relational environments. The cure for the loss of subjective unity is relational integrity: a relational secure base within with genuine compassionate care, over time, mitigates the damage of interpersonal abuse and neglect. *Mirrors of Self* is, in part, an attempt to frame the care and cure for pathological dissociation through faithful application of the Christian gospel. At least, that is what I first set out to achieve.

As I mentioned, the second project is more personal in nature. At about the same time I began to discover the signs of psychopathology in the broken, I came to be confronted with my own garden-variety nonpathological (but ever-so-sinful) self-blindness. The details of my coming to see myself matter little; the outcome, on the other hand, could accurately be called a conversion. There was no blinding Damascus-road light. I heard no child's distant voice admonishing me to "Take up and read." Yet the result was every bit as upending and disorientating as those others'. I came to the end of my self-delusions and discovered I was not who I thought I was. His decision to use my wife, who has contributed more to the present work than appears on the page, got me thinking about how God works. He uses others as mirrors to show us who we are. He does the showing. We the reflecting. That's what being a self-in-relation is all about. And why reconciliation is the heart of the gospel.

The present work is not strictly theological, anthropological, or psychological, but entails all three disciplines. Avowedly christocentric, *Mirrors of Self* is nevertheless "about" me. I do not mean to say that it is autobiographical, at least not in the technical sense. Rather, what I aim to accomplish is a demonstration that true self—*my* self, *your* self—is finally discoverable and veridically knowable only in right relationship to Christ. All this is entailed in the gospel, of course. What is unique about the present work is its transdisciplinary scope, along with the christological linkages I endeavor to build with epistemology, hermeneutics, and ethics.

Applied Christology is, finally, psychotherapeutic. So, while I spend considerable time working through the minutiae of historical Christology and anthropology, the intended end of all this effort is to bring you closer to who you really are *in him*, dear reader. I suppose that's the pastor in me coming out. While you may find it tempting to skip to whichever chapter you find your own disciplinary interests reflected, I encourage you to rightly identify this as the causata of your own post/modernist indoctrination. You may see how much you are beholden to and trapped within your specialization once you've strayed outside your intellectual comfort zone.

Finally, let me say a few words about my use of terms. Throughout the work your grasp of two terms in particular will prove critically important. For the sake of clarity, I define these here:

Dissociation. As a descriptor of psychological phenomena, dissociation is notoriously resistant to definition (see Carlson, Yates, & Sroufe, 2009; Howell, 2005; van der Hart, Nijenhuis, & Steele, 2006). I will employ the term at different times in a non-technical sense to refer generally to the means by which individuals distance themselves from awareness (Lat. *dissociare*; to separate) of some aspect of self- or other/Other-knowledge. More precisely, dissociation is descriptive of a primarily cognitive process (or processes) by which the human subject avoids conscious mentation concerning that which might trigger unpleasant feelings or associations.

Dissociation is neither necessarily pathological nor morally problematic. An individual who dissociates from full awareness of some traumatic event can hardly be sinning. A soldier while advancing into enemy fire may unconsciously dissociate from full awareness from the reality of his comrades falling around him. A child enduring unspeakable abuse at the hands of a close relative may experience dissociative amnesia after the fact. Our ability to dissociate from trauma is a God-given mercy in the face of what would otherwise overwhelm us (Badgett, 2018a; Gingrich, 2013; Langberg, 2015).

Nevertheless, dissociation becomes morally problematic when it occurs in a mature agent with the result that the individual persists in a state of self-deception (see Badgett, 2018b; cf. Matt 7:3; Gal 6:3). When we dissociate from what is evident yet unpleasant, it becomes possible for us to concoct a comforting yet false view of the way things are, including the nature and moral quality of self, God, and others. Dissociation, when it serves our conscience-placating agendas, can lead to real harm. This is apparently how otherwise good German citizens in World War II allowed the heinous Nazi regime to murder countless innocents (see Howell, 2005).

Self. If convention is any indication, self, as an object of epistemic concern, should be accompanied by the definite article: *the* self (see, e.g., Baumeister, 1998; Grenz, 2001; Harter, 2015; Strauss & Goethals, 1991; Vitz & Felch, 2006). I have resisted this convention throughout. My concern is to avoid what I believe to be a post/modernist impulse out of concern that selfhood not be abstracted or objectified as a segment, attribute, or form somehow distinct from or contained within whole persons. A person is a self, though the two are not equivalent. A self is a whole person bearing an individuated, idiosyncratic identity. You and I are both persons; but only I am myself. So, throughout, "self" may be understood to be in close semantic relationship with "person," but with the suggestion of particularity. In other words, self is *me—my*self. As you proceed, I invite you, dear reader, to apprehend and assert the same: *you* are *your* self.

In addition to these two, I have employed a number of descriptive terms intended to foster semantic linkages with theological and/or biblical concepts. Readers with some theological training that included biblical Greek will readily grasp the meaning of most of these. My intended audience, which includes those working in theological, pastoral, psychological, and applied philosophical fields, may nevertheless benefit from a quick reference list:

Agapic. Bearing the character of love or a disposition toward the good of another.

Agapist. Pertaining to the field of ethics, suggestive of love for others as the supreme ethical aim or moral good.

Eudaimonist. Pertaining to the field of ethics, suggestive of individual wellbeing as the supreme ethical aim or moral good.

Kenotic. Having a disposition toward self-denial in the interest of another's good.

Ontic. Pertaining to existence or being.

Perichoretic. Characterized by interpersonal communion analogous to the metaphysical relationship of Christ's two natures; respective to human-divine relationality, accomplished through the indwelling of the Holy Spirit; respective to human-human relationality, accomplished by a shared experience of the Spirit's presence.

Pistic. Bearing a disposition toward confidence or faith in the word of another.

Theanthropological. Pertaining to the transdisciplinary study of human nature through the lens of theological truth as revealed in Christian Scripture.

Acknowledgements

THIS PROJECT HAS BEEN a passion of mine for a number of years. As passions go, however, it has periodically ebbed and flowed. This year, as you have no doubt experienced, has been especially challenging. For several months I had to put aside my editing work to manage the affairs and needs of the congregation I serve. I am grateful that my wife kept after me all during this season of struggle to return to the work and finish well. In fact, she has been both my biggest cheerleader and most-faithful editor since I first set out to write not just an academic treatise but a work with pastoral and psychotherapeutic applicability. I have dedicated *Mirrors of Self* to her. I hope any beauty within these pages reflects on her. To be sure, the shortcomings are all mine. Thank you, Alison, for your unflagging support every time I needed it most.

I must also take a moment to give credit to those who read and offered feedback at various stages of the work. Eric Johnson has been a tremendous help from its inception. He is a dear friend and mentor, but he didn't let that prevent him from offering much needed, yet always constructive, critique. His keen insight stands behind many of the seminal turning points in the development of this project. He was the one who suggested Christology as my conceptual jumping-off point. I cannot say how important his suggestion proved to be. In addition, I must also thank Prof. Andrew Purves, who interrupted his retirement to read and respond to what I have written, and Dr. Todd Wilson from the Center for Pastor Theologians for offering such strong affirmation of the work. They do me much honor. Respectively, Prof. Jeremy Pierre's and Prof. Michael Haykin's early feedback substantially strengthened my thesis and historical background sections.

Finally, I am very grateful to Wipf & Stock and especially the team at Pickwick Publications for seeing this project to completion. Rev. Dr.

Robin Parry in particular gave special attention to the concerns I had about publishing a transdisciplinary work. His assistance came at exactly the right time and to the best effect.

Part I

Knowledge of Self
in Historical Christian Perspective

1

Introduction and thesis

JOHN CALVIN (2008) FAMOUSLY opened his great theological treatise by positing not one but two epistemological poles, which together comprise "the sum of true wisdom" (p. 4). These two, the knowledge of God and the knowledge of oneself, he regarded as equally and integrally foundational to all human knowing. Calvin, it should be noted, eschewed any willingness to resolve the dialectical tension inherent in this dipolarity. As human beings come to know themselves more fully, he believed, they discover a need within themselves to know God more fully; yet to know themselves, they may see truly only when illuminated by the revelation of his goodness and glory. "The knowledge of God and the knowledge of ourselves," he concluded, "are bound together by a mutual tie" (p. 6). Neither, in other words, is dispensable.[1]

---

1. Calvin's epistemology and his soteriology are inseparable. So for example, he understands personal knowledge of God-as-holy and self-as-sinful to be indispensable for salvation (see Hos 6:6; Luke 5:8; 1 Cor 15:34). This is not to say Calvin believed knowledge of self *effects* salvation. Rather, Calvin held to a strict view of salvation by the electing will of a gracious God. Yet, according to Calvin, self-knowledge is indispensable for salvation precisely because of the mutuality of the knowledge God and of self—what throughout Christian history has been called the "double" knowledge that leads to true wisdom (Houston, 2000). From the standpoint of human experience, salvation comes to those who have first recognized their need for God's grace and have thrown themselves upon his mercy. This recognition of human sinfulness is made possible through divine revelation. It should be further noted that Calvin's approach defends the Creator-creature distinction against the modernist error of objectivism, wherein God and self become discrete objects of inquiry. Calvin rejects the notion that God can be known if self is wholly unknown. Before we can know God, we must know that *we* are not.

3

Moreover, self-knowledge, according to Calvin, makes possible our knowledge of God:

> [T]he infinitude of good which resides in God becomes more apparent from our poverty. In particular, the miserable ruin into which the revolt of the first man has plunged us, compels us to turn our eyes upward. . . . [E]very man, being stung by the consciousness [*conscientia*] of his own unhappiness, in this way necessarily obtains at least some knowledge of God. . . . [I]ndeed, we cannot aspire to him in earnest until we have begun to be displeased with ourselves. For what man is not disposed to rest in himself? Who, in fact, does not thus rest, so long as he is unknown to himself; that is, so long as he is contented with his own endowments, and unconscious [*inscius*] or unmindful of his misery? Every person, therefore, on coming to the knowledge of himself, is not only urged to seek God, but is also led as by the hand to find him. (p. 4)

For Calvin, awareness (*conscientia*) of self impels human beings on a quest for a greater knowledge of the divine. As we come to the truth about ourselves—though what we find be little more than spiritual poverty and misery—the more sensible of the benevolence and mercy of God we may become. Whereas, when we are ignorant (*inscius*) of our condition, our appropriation of the knowledge of God is impeded, our epistemic capacity having been constrained, as it were, by lack of self-knowledge (see Hoekema, 1994). According to Calvin, knowledge of God can only be sought "in earnest" as we become aware of ourselves.

Nevertheless, Calvin also believed that we are fundamentally incapable of overcoming our hereditary and congenital self-blindness without divine assistance—that is, through God's disclosure of himself to us. Though he argues that human beings have some innate sense of their creaturely contingency within the cosmos, sin causes us to mistrust that sense. This inescapable impression of God's existence and our answerability to him, Calvin (2008) holds, God himself "has endued" in every one of us "to prevent [us] from pretending ignorance" (p. 9). Whereas, to forswear pursuit of the knowledge of God, directing anything less than "the whole thoughts and actions of [our] lives to this end," is to "fail to fulfill the law" written in our very being (p. 11). Yet, somehow, the truth of this law manages to elude us. Due to our fallen condition, we inevitably place our confidence in an erroneous and sinful autonomy instead, until and unless the Spirit of God reveal himself to us in his word and, ultimately, in the person of Christ.

Though Calvin never considered the psychological means—i.e., dissociation[2]—by which we conceal from ourselves this innate sense of God, he nevertheless held that such was the case.[3] Human beings, so it seems, are capable of dissociating from their God-given sense of his existence and deceiving themselves in regard to his glorious nature and his gracious disposition toward them, in spite of our sin. Whatever the means, Calvin held the result of this tendency to be tantamount to denying ourselves inasmuch as we have been created according to his image and likeness (see Gen 1:26–27). Finally, notwithstanding the ontological and axiological disparity between these two objects of knowledge—God and self—Calvin considered that they function epistemically for human beings as inseparable, complementary, mutually-entailing, dialectically-conjoined poles.

Calvin is hardly the first within the Christian tradition to propose a dipolar self-knowledge that mutually entails the knowledge of the triune God. Discussions of Christian self-knowledge begin in earnest with Augustine's appropriation and reformulation of Socratic self-knowledge in the fourth century (Warfield, 1956; see, e.g., Augustine, 2002, Books 9–11). Nevertheless, it was Calvin (2008), drawing in large measure on Augustine, who bequeathed to Reformed theological anthropology the notion that self-knowledge, along with the knowledge of God, is critical to the human pursuit of wisdom. Referencing the pre-Christian admonition, "Know thyself," he remarks,

> It was not without reason that the ancient proverb so strongly recommended to man the knowledge of himself. For if it is deemed disgraceful to be ignorant of things pertaining to the business of life, much more disgraceful is self-ignorance in consequence of which we miserably deceive ourselves in matters of the highest moment, and so walk blindfold. (p. 147)

In contrast to pagan philosophy, Calvin insists, along with Augustine before him, on the dialectical contingency of human self-knowledge.

---

2. See my brief discussion of dissociation in the Preface.

3. "[The elements of Calvin's thought] include the postulation of an innate knowledge of God in man," notes Warfield (1956), "quickened and developed by a very rich manifestation of God in nature and providence, which, however, fails of its proper effect because of man's corruption in sin" (p. 31).

Self cannot see itself properly without an Other—a "mirror," as it were.[4] For Calvin the only mirror that reflects not only us-as-we-are, but also us-as-we-ought-to-be, is God. Without a proper view of ourselves as created in the image of God—response-able to and dependent on his divine power and love even for our very existence—we will fail the crucial test of self-knowledge. If we do not know God, we cannot know self truly. If we are ignorant of self, God will remain unknown. Wisdom demands that we know both (Houston, 2000; cf. Prov 4:7). Yet neither, according to Calvin, is possible without the other.

An ancient quest

Our epistemic quest to know self began long before Calvin. As early as the fifth century BC, the Delphic maxim, "Know thyself," captured this impulse in human beings. For the ancients this quest was part of a greater agenda of characterological growth (Wilkins, 1979; see Baumeister, 1999). Greek thought in particular held self-improvement through self-knowledge, enacted through virtuous activity, to be the ultimate aim of philosophy (Renz, 2016). For the ancient philosophers the path of self-knowledge would lead them to wisdom. Wisdom, then, would be their gateway to eudaimonia—a happy and virtuous life.[5] A presumptive belief in the perfectibility of the human condition was the necessary prerequisite for their confidence.

Greek thought conceived of this pursuit of "perfection" as a quest for wisdom and virtue made possible through self-understanding. So, Stoic philosopher Epictetus would write in the first century, "The beginning of philosophy to him at least who enters on it in the right way and by the door, is a consciousness of his own weakness and inability about necessary things. . . . [I]f they possessed this, . . . what would hinder them from being perfect?" (*Discourses*, II.11.i).[6] For the ancient Greeks, the epistemic gains necessary for wisdom were knowledge of self and virtue.

---

4. More properly, Calvin holds that humanity, indeed all of creation, serves as a mirror in which God beholds his own divine glory (see Torrance, 1957). Thus, human beings come to know themselves truly as they actively participate in reflecting the glory of God.

5. See Annas (1993) for a thorough discussion of ancient eudaimonism.

6. His language here is redolent of Christ's parable of the narrow gate and narrow road (Matt 7:14), a fact that bears on recent efforts to link Greek philosophy and the ethics of Jesus' Sermon on the Mount (see Pennington, 2017).

When grasped, these two would serve to draw the wise on to perfection. As Epictetus, suggests, autonomous self-reflection discloses the degree to which one's character conforms to virtuous ideals. Any reasonable lover of wisdom will respond accordingly.

In contrast to Calvin's "double" knowledge of self, Hellenist ideals were discoverable by human effort alone, rather than through divine self-disclosure. Wisdom would come, they believed, through strictly earth-bound self-reflection and self-awareness. Although different schools of thought propounded disparate visions of the happy life,[7] all allowed that self-knowledge was the beginning of wisdom through which eudaimonia was possible (cf. Prov 9:10). Furthermore, various intramural distinctions notwithstanding, they held the entire pursuit to be wholly anthropogenic. God, in other words, was dispensable.

Greek thought held human effort in high esteem when it came to the means and end of self-knowledge. Nevertheless, subtle distinctions did arise around the question of how *many* human beings might be necessary. Concerning this question, modern scholars (Annas, 1985; Shields, 2016) have pointed to a key distinction in Platonist and Aristotelian thought. Put simply, Plato held that individuals could grow in self-knowledge by strictly reflexive means. Spend enough time with yourself, he considered, and you will get to know yourself better. According to Kametkar (2016), this emphasis on reflexive self-knowledge permeates Plato's thinking. Individual human beings improve themselves, in the words of Socrates, "by attending, caring for, and being guided by the part of the soul in which wisdom, which makes the soul good, comes to be" (*Alcibiades I* 133b). Self can be known and improved all by one's self, so to speak. Not only is God dispensable, so is everyone else.

This so-called "Socratic" self-knowledge grants self considerable epistemic sovereignty. The degree of autonomy implied by Plato's formulation has led some modern readers to observe that it makes self "the ultimate reality." Annas (1985) observes that the Socratic/Platonist self "turns out to be God" given its ability to autonomously self-perceive and self-improve (p. 133). Socratic self-knowledge presumes an unrestricted sufficiency for the self's pursuit of wisdom. Whether this sanguine view of human epistemic freedom is justified seems to have been the concern

---

7. For the Stoics the axiological telos of wisdom was ethical perfection (Wilkins, 1979). In contrast to this, Plotinus, the founder of Neoplatonism suggests that wisdom leads to more than mere "happiness" (contra Wilkins, p. 66); rather, perfect self-knowledge would result in "god-likeness" (Remes, 2007, p. 125; see Long, 2001).

of later Greek thought, at least as evidenced in Aristotle's discussions of self-knowledge.[8]

In a departure from Plato's ideal for Socratic self-knowledge, Aristotle would argue, albeit inconsistently, against the possibility of strict autonomy (Shields, 2016). Though he maintained many other Platonist notions, Aristotle nuanced his understanding of human self-sufficiency to allow for the contingency of relationship. In doing so he brought Socratic method into contact with empirical reality. Human beings, he observed, all too often perceive the faults of others while remaining ignorant of their own moral failings. In his view, friendship was not dispensable for self-knowledge in at least some matters:

> But the self-sufficiency about which we are conducting our inquiry is not that of god but of humans, the question being whether the self-sufficient human will require friendship or not. If, then, when one looked upon a friend one could see the nature and attributes of the friend, . . . such as to be a second self. . . . [A]s we are, we are not able to see what we are from ourselves (and that we cannot do so is plain from the way in which we blame others without being aware that we do the same things ourselves). (*Magna Moralia* 2.15)

Aristotle, it seems, knew better than Plato that we human beings tend to think the best about ourselves despite evidence to the contrary. He recognized that what remains an essentially individual quest—for knowledge of oneself—may benefit from the insights and input of others.[9] A friend, as "a second self," serves to reflect back what we might otherwise never see in ourselves.[10]

Unlike Plato, Aristotle held that eudaimonia—a happy, virtuous life—was more likely with the help of others.[11] Along these lines, Shields (2016) concludes that Aristotle "envisages subjects knowing themselves, mirroring one another in a shared subjectivity presupposing the kind of

8. Philosophical skepticism regarding the self's ability to reflexively attain self-knowledge has flowered in the modern age (see Ryle, 1949).

9. In allowing that individuals may not always be able to reflexively self-perceive, Aristotle qualifies "self-sufficient" to entail relationship as a *possible* contingency (Shields, 2016). In order to attain veridical self-knowledge, individuals *may* require the presence of a mirroring other.

10. The parallel between Aristotle's proposal for contingent self-knowledge and Jesus' parable of the plank and the speck (Matt 7:3–5) is noteworthy.

11. Plato did value the dialogical role of the philosopher and the *polis* as well, which, perhaps, mitigates his emphasis on the autonomy of the individual.

self-knowledge reflected in mutual knowledge and perception" (p. 59).[12] Aristotle's emendation of Plato entails the possibility of both reflexive *and* reflective self-perception. Nevertheless, according to Aristotle, a truer, fuller self-knowledge is more reliably obtainable when it is contingent on relationship to others. Aristotle defends his view of contingent self-knowledge by pointing out the tendency in human persons toward unjustifiably favorable self-appraisal, though he never postulates the internal, subjective means by which this happens. Why, in other words, do we so often struggle to see ourselves as we are?

A modern pursuit

Modern secular philosophy owes a great deal to the ancient Greeks (Gertler, 2011; see also, Frame, 2015). Among nontheists, philosophical inquiry into the nature of "the self" and self-knowledge rely on many similar presuppositions.[13] That being said, the questions and considerations of secular philosophy have shifted markedly from their putative foundations (see Goethals & Strauss, 1991).[14] For Renz (2016), a major casualty of modern philosophy is the ancient link, common to Greek and premodern Christian thought, between self-knowledge and self-improvement.

12. Despite Shield's optimism, Aristotle's trenchant eudaimonism—the *individual* pursuit of happiness—nevertheless runs the risk of objectifying the mirroring other by essentially co-opting him or her into the service of individual wellbeing. Christian philosopher Nicolas Wolterstorff (2015) has noted the inherent individualism of the ancient paradigm and offered a counterproposal that elevates love, rather than happiness/wellbeing, as humanity's primary ethical aim (see esp. Chapter 1).

13. On particular note in this regard, Gertler (2011) outlines a history of philosophical thought beginning with the ancient Greeks. She then skips 1,600 years of Christian thought before picking up with Descartes, Locke, and Kant. Thus, she omits approaches to self-knowledge that include such notable figures as Augustine and Calvin. In what may be seen as a providential gain of postmodernity, Renz (2016) includes brief chapters on self-knowledge in Augustine and Kierkegaard, including making clear reference to the Danish philosopher's essentially Calvinist paradigm.

14. Recent philosophical explorations of self-knowledge have followed an essentially Cartesian epistemology being occupied in the main with the nature of human subjectivity. Of particular interest seems to be the question of whether and how humans have privileged access to their own mental states (see Cassam, 1994; Gertler, 2011; Moran, 2001; O'Brien, 2010). In other words, some philosophers are asking whether we can know anything about what we know. What the ancients assumed, however ironically, contemporary philosophy now holds in doubt.

From the time of the ancient Greeks until the advent of the modern era, self-knowledge was vital for wisdom, the path to eudaimonia. Never an end in itself, classical Western thought held self-knowledge to be a crucial means of self-improvement. Knowing oneself was an essential aspect of the human telos. Calvin and Augustine may have differed with the Greeks over the role of divine discourse for true wisdom and virtue, yet they largely accepted the latter's essentially eudaimonistic framework for self-knowledge. One's growth in self-understanding, they maintained, would result in happiness and virtue. Modern philosophical perspectives on self-knowledge have, for the most part, lost their telic urgency.[15]

The ancient Socratic pursuit of wisdom as the means of achieving eudaimonia has largely been abandoned as philosophical inquiry has become increasingly analytical and abstracted from everyday life. Along these lines, Renz (2016) confesses,

> One might regret that [the] moral or wisdom-related aspect of self-knowledge, which was quite important for the history of the concept, is largely absent in contemporary discussion. One reason for this shift in emphasis is obviously that philosophy has become an academic discipline hosted at research institutions. In antiquity, in contrast, philosophy was practiced at schools that conceived of it as a way of life. And it was as a way of life that philosophy was also regarded in the monastic culture of the early Middle Ages, where self-knowledge was often discussed in connection with the question of our distinction from and relation to God. (p. 3)

In contrast with its ancient antecedents, with few exceptions modern philosophy has not concerned itself with the benefits of self-knowledge. Knowing oneself, as with so much else in modern philosophy, has been reduced from a *how* to a mere *what*.

This is not to say, however, that the pursuit of self-improvement through self-knowledge has been entirely discarded in the modern era. To the contrary, C. Taylor (1989) notes that the ancient quest for happiness through self-improvement remains a paradigmatic pursuit of Western culture and morality. Indeed, notions of personal growth, wellbeing,

---

15. One exception to the rationalist mainstream can be found in Cassam (2014), who argues for "substantial" self-knowledge, or what he calls the "low road" approach. He endeavors to shift the conversation toward the benefits of knowing oneself and away from modern philosophy's preoccupation with what he calls "trivial" self-knowledge (p. 29). He includes among his examples of substantial self-knowledge: knowing one's character, values, abilities, aptitudes, emotions, etc.

and the pursuit of individual happiness pervade Western society. According to Brennan (2014), the principal disciplinary framework and "scientific" system within which self-knowledge has found a home is no longer philosophy, but modern psychology and psychotherapy.

As Anglo-American philosophical inquiry became an increasingly abstract enterprise, rationalistic and displaced from the world of everyday experience, early psychologists mounted something of a disciplinary "revolt" (Allport, 1968, p. 104). Browning & Cooper (2004) note that secular psychologists, concerned with the improvement of the human condition through "scientific" means, occupied themselves with explaining the internal workings of the human psyche in order to "provide concepts and technologies for the ordering of the interior life" (p. 2). As modern philosophy shifted its focus elsewhere, psychology took up the mantle of improving the human condition.

This is not to say that the knowledge of self has served as a crucial aspect of all modern psychotherapeutic models. Within the larger discipline of modern psychology and psychotherapy, approaches that offer wellbeing through self-knowledge trace their theoretical provenance to the work of Sigmund Freud and psychoanalytic psychotherapy (Prochaska & Norcross, 2014).[16]

Whereas all psychotherapeutic models concern themselves, by definition, with the mental health and wellbeing of human beings, not all approaches prioritize growth in self-knowledge as foundational. The fundamental psychotherapeutic basis for at least one early theorist, Sigmund Freud, might be summarized as wellbeing through self-knowledge.[17]

---

16. Chronologically, Pierre Janet's "psychological analysis" precedes Freudian psychoanalysis and appears to have provided Freud with a substantial conceptual basis for his more historically prominent contribution (Ellenberger, 1981).

17. Psychoanalysis, like other modern psychotherapeutic systems, competes both implicitly and explicitly with the Christian worldview generally, and with the gospel of Jesus Christ in particular. In unambiguous terms Bucci (1997) holds that "[p]sychoanalysis offers its patients a way to transform themselves and to gain a second life" (p. ix). Psychoanalysis, as a secular psychotherapeutic system, discounts the significance of divine revelation and the grace of God. In spite of this, Christians need not deny the possibility of gaining valid anthropological insight from secular systems like psychoanalysis. In considering the potential gains of a Christian psychodynamic psychotherapy, a theoretical descendant and close cognate of classical psychoanalysis, Jones and Butman (2011) conclude, "In order to make sense of a person's current behavioral patterns, it is necessary to understand the behavior's roots in largely unconscious conflicts and motives. . . . Only through greater self-knowledge and self-regulation can mature adults increase their capacity to love and work effectively" (p. 95). Edwards and

More to the point, Freud (1940) grounded his theoretical and therapeutic method in processes designed to overcome *resistance* to self-discovery (see Eagle, 2010).

Freud held, more strongly to be sure than Aristotle, that human persons persist in self-ignorance and self-deception due to intrapsychic conflict. This unconscious conflict leads to mental distress in varying degrees. On account of his infatuation with evolutionary theory, Freud (1940) concluded that primal drives and animalistic impulses impel otherwise well-socialized individuals to instinctually to pursue "pleasure" and "avoid unpleasure" (p. 16). Unconscious resistance to acknowledging socially unacceptable thoughts and associations resulted in a robust system of mental defenses. These mental operations, or "defense mechanisms," are initiated, he argued, outside the conscious awareness and control of the individual (see A. Freud, 1977).[18]

According to classical psychoanalytical theory (S. Freud, 1940; see Howell & Itzkowitz, 2016), a "repressed" individual could be cured from her "neurosis" with the help of a reflective other. The psychoanalyst, then, works to bring to light "truth"[19] that has become dislocated within her psyche. By means of slow, painstaking work, the analyst identifies mental defenses deployed to ameliorate psychic distress. Once acknowledged, these defenses can be deactivated over time, leading to what Freud described as "favorable modification of the ego" (S. Freud, 1940, p. 74). Ellenberger (1981) summarizes efficacious psychoanalytic treatment as "a journey through the unconscious" mind from which the individual eventually "emerges with a modified personality" (p. 524). Growth comes through self-discovery.

Davis (2013) offer numerous helpful distinctions for the appropriation of psychodynamic therapeutic processes within a Christian edification framework. See Chapter 6 for a more thorough evaluation of psychodynamic theory.

18. In examining the possible roots of Freud's atheism, Vitz (1993) argues with no small irony that Freud's belief in the non-existence of God amounted to a unconscious rejection of his own father.

19. Fromm (1980) argues that Freud's "greatest achievement" was his expansion of "the concept of truth" "beyond that which an individual believes to be the truth" (pp. x–xi). This assertion has some basis in fact. Yet, Freud (like Fromm) was a secular humanist so, as with the ancient Greeks, his quest for "truth" was a strictly empirical and intrasubjective affair. To wit, he held belief in God to be delusional—a "universal obsessional neurosis" (S. Freud, 1927, p. 117). As a result, Freud's contribution to a broader concept of truth demands considerable qualification.

Many of Freud's theoretical contributions have been challenged and critiqued on both philosophical (see, e.g., Ricoeur, 1977) and empirical grounds (Fisher & Greenberg, 1996) over the last century. In that time the field of psychoanalytical psychology has also evolved considerably. Contemporary psychoanalysis (see Bucci, 1997; Eagle, 2010; Mitchell & Black, 2016; Safran, 2012; cf. Jones & Butman, 2011; Tan, 2011) has abandoned his mechanistic model of the personality—along with other embarrassing notions, such as his theory of infantile sex drives—in favor of a more scientifically robust, empirically grounded framework. Nevertheless, the modern, secular pursuit of wellbeing through self-knowledge has flowered in no small measure due to his pioneering work.

Ancient and modern frameworks for wellbeing through wisdom are, of course, distinct in manifold ways. So, for instance, Hellenistic approaches emphasized the sufficiency of human persons to pursue self-knowledge for wisdom and virtue; the telos of that ancient quest was "happiness," eudaimonia. Freud, on the other hand, had little concern over the ancient pursuit of any so-called virtue, but rather the resolution of intrapsychic conflict through insight. Self-discovery was key to his psychotherapeutic process. Nevertheless, for both ancient and modern frameworks alike, self-knowledge was esteemed as a means to a favorable end. Good comes, in either framework, to those who knows themselves better. From this vantage point, psychoanalysis and its theoretical descendants, broadly known as depth or dynamic psychologies, can be viewed as modern psychotherapeutic attempts to systematize the pursuit of wellbeing through self-knowledge.

In a rejection of Platonist optimism, Aristotle came to question the former's doctrine of anthropocentric "self-sufficiency." Freud would carry Aristotelian skepticism to its zenith (see Ricoeur, 1977). Thus, in both systems, though to varying degrees and with disparate conclusions, suspicion surrounds any notion of strictly reflexive, intrasubjective self-discovery.[20] Some aspect of human nature or experience, both agree, restricts our ability to readily and accurately self-perceive. For Aristotle, it was enough to have friends to foster honest self-reflection. In the

---

20. The muted emphasis on relationality in early psychoanalytical theory has been replaced with a much stronger accent in latter-day iterations. Reflecting on the "relational turn" that has occurred in contemporary psychoanalysis, Mitchell (2000) remarks on the degree to "which mind has increasingly been understood most fundamentally and directly in terms of self-other configurations, intrapsychically and interpersonally, present and past, in actuality and in fantasy" (p. xiii).

modern age, the "friend" would become an expert professional offering exclusive access to the deep reaches of the psyche. Either way, within both ancient Greek eudaimonistic and modern psychoanalytic frameworks, self-knowledge is central to the project of self-improvement with human wellbeing, broadly construed, as its axiological aim—its ultimate benefit.

Contrasting paradigms

In light of the preceding discussion, the incompatibility of secular and Christian frameworks for self-knowledge should, by now, be evident. According to both the ancient Greeks and modern psychoanalytical theory, knowledge of self needs for no divine assistance. What Calvin holds as both the means and end of self-knowledge—the knowledge of God—is absent in Aristotle and Freud. For ancient Greek philosophy as well as classical psychoanalysis, human beings are basically self-sufficient. We do not need God, even if at times we are prone to overly favorable self-evaluation and self-deception. We possess a capacity for reflexive and reflective self-perception along an exclusively horizontal axis. This is to say that a friend or psychotherapist, perhaps, can be instrumental in helping to identify thoughts, associations, and dispositions by which we obfuscate truth. We may, and often do, find ourselves evading less favorable self-perception. Yet, a mirroring other can foster self-discovery, allowing us to recognize and resolve inclinations toward self-blindness.

As with all secular approaches to self-knowledge, divine self-disclosure is excluded as epistemically invalid. For ancient and modern humanists, the basis of self-knowledge is autonomous human ability. This holds true, even when some mirroring relationship is entailed. The knowledge of God, as revealed in the Scriptures and in the person and work of Christ, has no bearing on their project. Whether the end of such pursuits is described as eudaimonist "happiness" or psychotherapeutic wellbeing, the respective benefits of *secular* self-knowledge are treasures within our terrestrial reach. On our quest for wisdom and virtue or, alternately, through resolution of intrapsychic conflict, *true* self-knowledge and its benefits lay within our grasp.

By way of contrast, Calvin considered the knowledge of self to lay beyond the grasp of human ability. Self-knowledge, as Calvin understood it, is dipolar or "double" knowledge, and thus contingent on our coming to know God. Moreover, created as we are in the image of God, we come to know ourselves *as we are* before God, which is to say, as we are known by God. So, Calvin held self-knowledge and the knowledge of God to be dialectically conjoined epistemic poles. To remove one or the other from the equation is to remain finally ignorant of both. This means that the pursuit of self-knowledge without the knowledge of God is, for Calvin, an exercise in futility—a road that goes nowhere. Without God, knowledge of self is fatally truncated, finally false. What is known of self is not self-as-self-is before God.

The benefits of a truncated self-knowledge, as we might expect, are likewise limited. To remain ignorant of one's standing before God, for Calvin, is to remain separated from one's ultimate happiness and the Source of all wellbeing. Whatever growth or healing we might come to experience will prove inconsequential next to the promise of knowing and being known by God. Autonomous self-knowledge looks more like Babel's tower—a vainglorious and ill-fated attempt to ascend heaven's heights. Devoid of the wisdom gained in knowing God, self-knowledge is self-deceiving and self-defeating. For Calvin, then, self-knowledge may be necessary for wisdom, but secular approaches to "wisdom"—whether ancient or modern—are built on faulty foundations offering only pyrrhic gains. So long as we are bereft of the light of divine revelation, we remain fundamentally self-blind.

Beyond eudaimonist perspectives

Calvin is a useful foil when considering certain secular approaches to self-knowledge. His was not, however, the first or even the finest treatment of the subject of Christian self-knowledge.[21] As Warfield (1956) observes, Calvin drew on the writings of the early church father, Augustine. Indeed he follows an essentially Augustinian track (see Niesel, 1956), the latter also holding to the necessity of a dipolar knowledge of self and God. For both, the ancient Greeks had most of the story right: self-knowledge leads to wisdom leads to happiness—what the Bible calls, "blessedness" (see, e.g., Ps 1:1; Matt 5:3–12). What the ancients got wrong was they didn't know God. Had they grasped their need to know God, the rest of

21. This is not imply any deficiency in Calvin's thinking! To the contrary, his intellectual project entailed another worthy end: the reformation of Christian theology and ecclesial praxis.

their formula might have held up better. Put another way, the premodern perspectives of Augustine and Calvin rely heavily on Hellenist thought.

According to Grenz (2001), Christian thinking since the early, classical approaches of Augustine and Calvin has developed along a number of significant lines. One of most significant developments has been an increasing emphasis on human relationships. Augustine and Calvin were reacting against a secular understanding of self-knowledge that omitted God from the pursuit. As a result, they downplayed the role of other human beings as instruments of self-knowing. In addition, the putative benefits of self-knowledge in classical Christian thinking tended, as with the ancients, toward the individual. Less clear, then, are questions relating to any social benefit. How might *others* benefit, for instance, from *my* growth in self-knowledge?

The horizontal or "social" dimension of self-knowledge, including the ethical entailments of self–other interactions, plays little role in both Augustine and Calvin. The ancients believed that wisdom would redound to the individual's "happiness"—a theme clearly enunciated in the Scriptures (e.g., Prov 8:35; Jas 1:4–5). For Augustine, then, the gain that follows from self-knowledge is eudaimonia—for the knowing *self*. Less clear was what personal growth would mean for others. Rist (1996) concludes that, while Augustine differed from the ancient program of self-knowledge divorced from divine revelation, he wrestled over what to make of its axiological emphasis.[22] If the ancients were correct, a just and equitable society might well be possible when every individual pursued virtuous eudaimonia (see Annas, 1993).

Eudaimonist ethics, according to Wolterstoff (2015) holds that a society sufficiently full of eudaimon individuals will accomplish this very thing. Yet, he further notes, eudaimonist ethics does not go far enough to fulfill the high ethical calling of Scripture: to love God supremely and neighbor as self (Matt 22:36–40). For this reason, the ethics of eudaimonist self-knowledge is problematic. This is not to say that Calvin was entirely credulous toward Augustine's early appropriation of ancient

22. Wolterstorff (2008) argues that Augustine appears to have broken with eudaimonism in his later writings (see Chapter 8). Clearly, Augustine's eudaimonist formulations differ from ancient philosophical eudaimonism at least in their being theocentric and, for the most part, eschatological; to wit, "It is characteristic of all men to will to be happy [*beati*], but yet the faith, by which the heart is purified and arrives at happiness, is not characteristic of all. And thus it comes about that one must strive through faith, which all do not will for the happiness which no one cannot but will" (Augustine, 2002, XIII.xx.25; p. 133).

philosophical eudaimonism. Yet, a decidedly Hellenist emphasis on the individual as both the principal means and beneficiary of self-knowledge would continue to influence Christian formulations for over a millennium (see also, C. Taylor, 1989). Not until a so-called "relational turn" articulated in the theological anthropologies of Barth, Bonhoeffer, and others would Christian perspectives on the means and end(s) of self-knowledge come to be articulated with a clear social emphasis (Grenz, 2001; see Shults, 2003).

For the ancient Greeks, the telos of self-knowledge was eudaimonia, "happiness," the blessedness of a "well-lived life" (Wolterstorff, 2010, p. 149; see Annas, 1993).[23] By contrast, as philosophical historian Charles Taylor (1989) observes, the ultimate aim of the contemporary Western self and its knowledge is self-realization: "[S]ubjectivist expressivism has won its way into contemporary culture. . . . The goals are self-expression, self-realization, self-fulfillment, discovering authenticity" (pp. 506–507). With little qualification, Grenz (2001) finds modern, secular psychological theory and psychotherapeutic practice complicit in this inimitably anthropocentric paradigm. But what of *Christian* self-knowledge? How might a Christian pursuit differ, not just in means but in axiological end—what good might it do?

To return again to Calvin (2008) and faithful Christian writers down through the ages (see, e.g., J. Edwards, 1998), we conclude that the highest aim and ultimate telos of all things is the glory of God. We exist as signposts directing every watchful eye to our glorious Creator. Surely then, the telos of human self-knowledge must also be God's glory. If true, then coming to know ourselves in relation to God allows us to better behold his glory and bear out the reality of his infinite beauty and worth. To be sure, the New Testament also speaks of an eschatological happiness— or blessedness, flourishing, wellbeing, etc.—that God has promised to all who pursue these gifts in Christ (Matt 24:46; Luke 6:21; 14:14; John 13:17; Rom 2:7; Gal 3:9; Jas 1:12; 1 Pet 3:14; Rev 14:13; 22:14). Whether in this life or the next, God pledges to reward those who faithfully seek him. So, while the offer to believers is eternal happiness, our ethics must be properly balanced, as was Christ's, by the call to love and self-sacrifice (see Matt 20:28; Luke 14:27; Eph 4:2–3; Phil 1:21). By balancing joy and

23. Another term for eudaimonia that also reflects contemporary efforts to link ancient and modern ethics is "flourishing" (Cooper, 1986; see Pennington, 2017). Wolterstorff (2010) finds this modern gloss unconvincing.

suffering, benefit and sacrifice, we exemplify the one who suffered, died, and rose again, all to God's glory.

The life of Christ was bound up in love—above all for the Father, yet also for human beings and especially his own people, the church. So too, he calls us, at times, to forestall, for his sake, our direct, individual pursuit of "happiness." By faith in his promises, we can rest assured that the God who raised Jesus from the dead will also grant us joy and peace in the age to come (see Heb 12:2).

A christological ethics of self-knowledge is one that emphasizes love for God and others as its aim.[24] This is not to say, let's be clear, that Christians should eschew their hope in God's promises of eschatological wellbeing (see Rev 21:4).[25] Yet, the source of this blessed hope is the God who calls us to lay down our lives in order to find them (Matt 10:39), to "deny" self, to pick up our cross and follow Christ (Luke 9:23), and to embody his cruciform demonstration of love for others (John 15:12). In the end, an eudaimonist ethics, while not wholly incompatible with Christianity, nevertheless demands careful qualification in light of the agapic imperative of self-denying, kenotic concern for others (Phil 2:3–11).

Furthermore, as believers, we would do well to consider the example of the one who, though he eternally possesses exhaustive self-knowledge as the divine Son in triune communion, entered into our finite, noetically constrained existence as the incarnate Son of man in order to reconcile us to the Father. He set aside his divine goods and prerogatives, for a season at least, in order to seek and save that which was lost. This Jesus, I conclude, was no philosophical eudaimonist.

Toward a comprehensive Christian framework

Before constructing a framework for thinking Christianly about self-knowledge, we should reflect on Calvin's essentially Augustinian conception. The Swiss Reformer, it bears observing, rightly identified a dialogical relationship between the twin poles of self-knowledge: God *and* self. Much more needs to be said about this. For now, however,

24. Cf. Wolterstorff's (2015) "agapist ethics."

25. I find that Christian eudaimonism is best cast in an eschatological light. True, perfect happiness is a promise held up in heaven for God's people, yet to come "on the clouds" when Christ returns. For an eudaimonist reading of Jesus' Sermon on the Mount that carefully notes an already/not yet perspective on human flourishing, see Pennington (2017).

this presupposition stands as paradigmatic for any putatively Christian framework. It is, in other words, a helpful foundation to build on.

Calvin did not develop his dialogical approach to self-knowledge much past this point. His conclusions concerning human nature tend toward the general and universal. His intellectual project stops far short of considering *individual* selves. Nor did Calvin extend the purview of his theological anthropology to the development of practical and pastoral implications of self-knowledge. Unlike Augustine before him and Bonhoeffer much later, Calvin leaves relatively unaddressed the means and processes by which growth in self-knowledge affects (and effects) spiritual growth. That being said, his rationalistic bent has been outmatched by many who claim allegiance to his theological legacy.

Numerous classical and modern Christian writers have concluded, with Calvin, that knowledge of God and knowledge of self are linked. Yet, a broad survey of the history of Christian self-knowledge demonstrates the relative dearth of contemporary efforts to apply this premise. Christian theology, in apparent imitation of modern secular philosophy, has grown increasingly "speculative, abstract, rationalistic" (Houston, 2000, p. 323). Knowledge of self, some would have us believe, is an inherently misbegotten, and quite possibly sinful, enterprise. To seek knowledge of oneself is somehow to rob God of his glory. Doesn't our faith require us to hold the knowledge of God alone to be epistemically sufficient, whatever Calvin may have said?

As we will see, the Christian pursuit of dipolar self-knowledge—coming to knowing self and God mutually, dialogically—has fallen on hard times. At the edge of theology since the Reformation there exists a cliff, a chasm, and then another cliff upon which sits a diversity of Christian "psychologies." This gap is the result of an epistemic and disciplinary divorce wrought by modern objectivism. On the one side we find what bears resemblance to what Calvin meant by "the knowledge of God," that is, theology. On the other, psychologists delve the human condition to discover something amounting to a "knowledge of self." This bifurcation has stricken Christianity as well, though it can hardly be what Calvin had in mind.

A preliminary objective of the present inquiry is bridging the gap, reconciling theology and psychology at the epistemological level. I will argue that this is only possible through the person and work of Jesus Christ—the one who alone has reconciled God and humanity. With the help of Christology, I will proceed across this epistemological bridge toward my primary objective: to define self, and more than that, to uncover the subject of self-knowledge—the "me" of veridical self-knowledge. My primary aim, then, is not merely to better grasp at the nature of our shared human personhood through inquiry into the person and work of Christ. Rather, I intend to set a course for *self*-discovery in light of who Christ is and what he has done. As we come to know self-as-self-is-known, by means of Christ and in relationship to him, we take his nature for ourselves. So, this project has as its final objective outlining the pastoral and psychotherapeutic applications for Christian self-knowledge.

Any practicable framework for self-knowledge must include two key aspects: means and ends. My approach presumes a christological basis for questions of theanthropological and psychological concern. So, for instance, What can we know about who and what Christ is, in particular as we consider the theological implications of his human self-knowledge? How has his atoning work brought about reconciliation between God and humanity, and to what degree does this work fundamentally alter our human nature? Furthermore, what does the believer's union with Christ suggest to us in regard to who and what we are?

From a psychological vantage point, we may ask: How does Christ's human nature function respective to our own and to what degree is he like us? What is a human self and where is it "located" in individual human beings? And further, how can we know when the constraints of self-knowledge are defined by our finiteness as opposed to our fallenness? In other words, can we expect Christ to grant us sufficient healing from dissociation and self-deception in order that we might see ourselves as he does? And finally, what ethical and subjective benefits are entailed in the Christian pursuit of self-knowledge?

It may be helpful at this point to briefly consider Christ's most poignant and powerful lesson on self-knowledge, his parable of the plank and speck in Matthew 7. According to Jesus, we all bear a fallen tendency to dissociate from unpleasant truths about self and so deceive ourselves. By unspecified means, we possess the ability to see around planks in our own eyes in order to identify specks in others' eyes (v. 3). Jesus decries our hypocritical predilection for self-blindness and offers a solution: we must overcome this tendency in ourselves before helping others to do the same (vv. 4–5). As Jesus suggests in his parable, growth in self-knowledge follows only when we overcome our innate disinclination toward accurate self-perception. If as believers we hope to assist others in this vital task, we must first uncover the ways dissociation and self-deception have

locked away the truth of who we are. In this short passage, Jesus sketʟ
for us an ethics of Christian self-knowledge!

To return to establishing our Christian framework: I argue that it is
axiomatic that Christ is the means by which we come to know God and
self. The knowledge of God and of self are mediated to us by the Logos.
This is to say that God speaks to us authoritatively through both his written revelation in the Scriptures and, ultimately, in the person and work
of Jesus Christ. He is the Son who perfectly reveals the Father (Heb 1:3;
John 14:7). Additionally, according to the gospel of God's atoning love
in Christ, barriers to self-knowledge become deactivated only through
fellowship with Christ. Sinful resistance to self-knowledge leads to self-
blindness and self-deception. Christ overcomes our sin by means of his
grace and truth.

Orthodox Christian doctrine has ever held that knowledge of self-
as-sinful before a holy God is prerequisite to receiving God's mercy and
forgiveness. We may only be saved from sin's consequences once self-
knowledge and the knowledge of God enter into dialogical relationship.
God has made himself known through his Logos. When he is truly
known, we know ourselves. Our subjective response inescapably includes
awareness of sinfulness and a commensurate fear of God (Rev 1:17; 6:16;
cf. Ps 111:10).[26] In this light, awareness of self-as-sinful is one of the first
"benefits" of the knowledge of God, allowing for healthy expressions of
subjective shame, sorrow, and contrition. Without these, there can be no
repentance leading to life (2 Cor 7:10). But while this awareness may be
the first and most significant epistemic gain of the Christian life, it is
hardly the last. To the contrary, God's ultimate gift to us, as Jesus discloses, is that we should come know the one true God and the Son whom
he has sent (John 17:3; cf. Isa 11:9; Hab 2:14). This is, as he says, "eternal
life"—the telos, the ultimate end, to which God is working to bring his
people.

As we might imagine, "eternal life" entails numerous benefits,
among which individual eudaimonia—personal wellbeing—is certainly
one (see Matt 11:28; 2 Cor 1:4; Rev 21:4). Yet, the implication of Jesus'

26. There is a close association in Old Testament wisdom literature between the
"fear" of the Lord and the "knowledge" of God (Prov 9:10; see Longman, 2015, pp.
100–1.; Packer, 2000). The sort of fear that redounds in genuine knowledge of God,
as Calvin (2008) clarifies, is "the voluntary fear flowing from reverence of the divine
majesty" rather than a "forced and servile fear which divine judgment extorts" (pp.
13–14).

le knowledge *of* God amounts to fellowship *with him*
evers in the same sort of perichoretic communion he
Father (John 1:18; 10:15). Thus, the ethical telos of
ledge, when considered christologically, should en-
hat believers participate actively and corporately in
...c of perichoretic love shared between the Father and the Son
(John 17:20–23).

The knowing Christ speaks of does not erase the limits and distinctions of individual personhood. We do not, through communion with Christ, become God (nor do we cease to be ourselves).[27] Nevertheless, Christ offers means by which believers may enter into the same dynamic of the mutual self-giving eternally shared within the Godhead (John 14:6, 11; cf. 1 John 5:20). Moreover, Christ also works through the Spirit to allow individual believers to enact this dynamic relationally, albeit analogically, within the body of Christ (see Bonhoeffer, 2005; McFadyen, 1990).

The knowledge of God Jesus speaks of in John 17:3 is existential and interpersonal, not merely cognitive and propositional (R. E. Brown, 1982).[28] Christ prays that believers, through their union with him, would

27. Drawing on a Hegelian conception of personhood, Pannenberg (1977) suggests a limited anthropological application of the patristic doctrine of *perichoresis* (pp. 182–83). I have not attempted here to promulgate a Trinitarian anthropology in which human persons mirror the divine being through their relatedness to God and others (contra Moltmann, 1981; cf. Grenz, 2001; Schwöbel & Gunton, 1991). I do, however, intend to draw on the concept of "nature-perichoresis" to explain Christ's prayer in John 17:20–23. He asked God to unite believers to him and through him to the Father in some way analogous to his own Spirit-mediated union with the Father: "I in them and you in me" (v. 23). This is not a type of "person-perichoresis" like that which John of Damascus first suggested characterized intratrinitarian relations in his *De fide orthodoxa* (Crisp, 2007; see Otto, 2001). More will be said later on the nature of the perichoretic relationality between God and human beings and between human beings.

28. Brown (1982) explains, "In the Semitic understanding, knowledge is more than intellectual, for it involves an experience of the whole person—that is why 'knowledge' can be used for sexual intimacy. To know God means to share His life" (p. 279). In one memorable passage in 1 John, the writer clearly distinguishes between the two kinds of knowing—the cognitive/objective and the experiential/subjective—with two different forms of the verb stem, γινώσκ- (*ginōsk-*). In the four instances of "to know" that occur in the following pericope the writer employs the present active to denote propositional knowledge, and the perfect to denote intersubjective knowing: "He is the propitiation for our sins, and not for ours only but also for the sins of the whole world. And by this *we know* [γινώσκομεν, *ginōskomen*] that *we have come to know* [ἐγνώκαμεν, *egnōkamen*] him, if we keep his commandments. Whoever says '*I know* [ἔγνωκα, *egnōka*] him' but does not keep his commandments is a liar, and the truth is not in him, but whoever keeps his word, in him truly the love of God is perfected.

partake analogically in this interpersonal perichoretic knowing with God and others within the body. Clearly Jesus has much more than eudaimonia in mind in his prayer. From this I conclude that any ethics of Christian self-knowledge should entail more than individual wellbeing, though it is certainly not excluded. The telos of Christian self-knowledge is love. More precisely, the triune God offers human persons access to the divine love of Father and Son and, through the Spirit, individual and corporate experience of that love through our shared union with Christ.

Christ, the key of keys

Self-knowledge, Christianly conceived, is a massive project. The scope of the present work is, therefore, broad. The apostle's claim, however appalling to modern, secular sensibilities, bears tremendous import for what lies ahead: that in Christ "all things hold together" (Col 1:17). Christology, then, is both compass and map for the undertaking. In order to unlock that knowledge which is coordinated with the knowledge of self, whether epistemological, theological, anthropological, psychological, Christ is the key of keys. In order to know self truly, he is all in all.

God knows himself—and us—exhaustively. Further, this triune God desires that we should come to know him *and ourselves* to the end that we may love and glorify him accordingly. According to Scripture, nothing in God's nature or ways is hidden from his awareness, nor is his divine self-knowledge truncated or contingent in any way. Human self-knowledge, on the other hand, is wholly conditional: we know ourselves truly only as we come to know God. What we can know of ourselves may be limited by any number of factors. Yet God desires that we seek to know ourselves as we are known—created in the image of God for the glory of God so that we might come to know and love him as he is.

The highest gift God offers to human beings is "eternal life," which Christ himself describes as coming to know the Father through the Son. From the knowledge God gives of himself, knowledge of self grows instrumentally and contingently. To be clear, the degree to which we may know God and ourselves will always be less than infinite. We are limited by a finite human capacity. Furthermore, as fallen beings, we suffer from a congenital inclination toward estrangement from God. We are prone to

---

By this *we may know* [γινώσκομεν, *ginōskomen*] that we are in him: whoever says he abides in him ought to walk in the same way in which he walked" (1 John 2:2–6).

wander. In the same way, we are prone to dissociation and self-deception. Yet, as we pursue union with the true image of God, Jesus Christ, we encounter a Spirit-mediated agapic and perichoretic relationality with him. We enter into "union with Christ."[29]

The means by which God sets aside human sin and works out his redemptive plan for us is by bringing us into relationship with his Son. Through and in Christ, God reveals himself to us as he truly is so that we might see ourselves as we truly are. His aim for us includes reversing the relational consequences of the fall—our estrangement from him and from each other. To this end the Spirit of Christ works mysteriously within us, and instrumentally through others, to help us overcome subjective barriers to self-knowledge. Dissociation and self-deception, the means by which we evade and obfuscate our knowledge of God and self, are universal fallen tendencies. Jesus, on the other hand, was sinless. In his humanity his knowledge of self was just as truncated by his human finitenessas ours. Yet, as "he increased in wisdom and in stature . . . before God and man" (Luke 2:52), never once did he sinfully evade or obfuscate from the truth of himself. Veridical knowledge of oneself, therefore, is a divine gift whereby human beings come to image Christ's own sinless knowledge of self.

God's gift of himself in the person of Jesus Christ stands as the only final standard of truth to which all veridical knowledge of self relates. Consequently, overcoming dissociation and self-deception should be understood as a crucial means of believers' growth in conformity to the image of Christ. The Father's knowledge of and love for the Son and the Son's love for and knowledge of the Father are perfect and unchanging, yet dynamic and perichoretic. God's offer of eternal life amounts to his invitation to human beings to participate in this divine communion. Through the self-revelation of his Logos, God brings human beings into individual and corporate communion with himself.

As we grow in both love for and knowledge of God, we should expect our knowledge of and love for self and others to grow as well. The fruit of God's most precious gift—himself—is love. By means of his love we overcome estrangement from him and from others. As his love penetrates ever deeper, we find strength to overcome the fear of self-discovery. We grow beyond the dissociative and self-deceptive tendencies that formerly held us captive and cut off from others. Increasingly known

---

29. Murray (1955) calls this seminal Pauline doctrine, "the central truth of the whole doctrine of salvation" (p. 161).

and knowing, we come to enjoy and apply the benefits of "eternal life" in the here and now.

Perspective and method

In the half-millennium since John Calvin, the theanthropological landscape has transformed dramatically. Perspectives, both ancient and contemporary, abound. To say that the discipline of theological anthropology suggests a putatively *Christian* perspective on human nature and personhood, while accurate, does little to eliminate myriad other distinctions and differences. I dare say, if one ventured a look into such things, we might find more permutations of "Christian" anthropology than any other. Over the past few decades, a surge of scholarly interest on the subject has also occurred. A quick subject search for theological anthropology will yield a trove of publications, some helpful and others less so. Panning for gold can be quite tedious until one knows where to begin digging.

As is further implied in the label *theological* anthropology, the discipline seeks to understand human nature and personhood by referencing what we know of God's nature. This project may at first seem a bald and misguided enterprise, doomed to abstraction and incoherence; and yet, to do so is to take seriously the very word of the God who

> created mankind in his own image,
>   in the image of God he created them;
>   male and female he created them. (Gen 1:27 NIV)

Theanthropology looks for the footprints of humanity's Creator, traces his steps back to our beginning. It enters God's laboratory and studies his notes, his formulas, and marvels at his genius. At the same time, by doing the work of theological anthropology we also consider God's intent for humanity—his purposes and plans for us. If we want to know how human persons flourish best, we would do well to read the manual.

The present work answers both questions, of perspective and method, with one solution: the person and work Jesus Christ. Christology, in other words, will supply the map and compass for this journey. To a lesser yet significant degree, other considerations will figure prominently as well. For instance, the turn toward relationality evidenced in the theanthropologies of Bonhoeffer, Barth, and others I will regard as crucial to rightly applying Christology to human personhood. To some extent this trend has been mirrored in the modern disciplines of psychology and sociology as well. Taken as a single phenomenon, the turn to relationality in the modern age supplies the needed impetus to reevaluate premodern thinking regarding self-knowledge.

Paralleling the relatively recent (re)discovery of a biblical emphasis on relationality, theology and theological anthropology have followed suit. Trinitarian theology and trinitarian theanthropology, at least since Barth, have occupied the main stage in this unfolding drama. Augustine is something of a patron saint for those sharing trinitarian perspectives. In the last few decades, however, a quiet but growing dissatisfaction around trinitarian theanthropology has prompted some to regard Christology as a suitable alternative.

What I have set out to accomplish, however, is not merely to add another text to any already overcrowded shelf. What I seek to do is to advance and apply a christological perspective on human personhood in the field of Christian psychology. In short, I plan to start on one side of the chasm and end on the other. The bridge I intend to build, if rightly done, will be made of christological gold. That last sentence, I admit, sounds grandiose. Yet, only in undertaking such a project, with Christ deployed as our key of keys, can the worth of such a grand claim be evaluated. Mixed metaphors and grandiose claims aside, the work of applying Christology to the field of Christian psychology is, in the end, to exercise our faith in the redemptive work of God.

An epistemological aside

Christology suggests the interconnectedness of theology and anthropology. The mere existence of Jesus, the God–man—who, according to orthodox Christian doctrine, is the unique historical instantiation of the reconciliation between divinity and humanity—commends a careful consideration of the interactions between these two systems of thought and the disparate ontologies to which they point (see Tanner, 2010; *pace* Hunsinger, 1995). I will demonstrate in what follows that numerous points of connectivity have been made throughout Christian history between philosophical-theological discursive systems on the one hand and anthropological-psychological systems on the other. When considering the implications for human self-knowledge from a Christian perspective, we should expect the incarnation to suggest, and even demand, such discursive and disciplinary interactions. From Augustine and Calvin to Kierkegaard and Barth, orthodox Christian belief has rejected, if not universally, the notion of the irreconcilability of theology and anthropology. Epistemic hazards abound, to be sure. What is needed, I maintain, is not a ban on transdisciplinary dialogue, but rather more careful dialogue.

An aside on ethics

Arguably, the field of modern psychotherapy has done more to advance the ethical care of human persons in the last one hundred years than has the church. Although the church is now beginning to catch up, we have a lot of ground to make up. Still, much of what informs regnant paradigms for an ethics of Christian caregiving has been borrowed from secular theory. What I hope to contribute will advance a much-needed reevaluation of Christian ethics, at least as it pertains to pastoral and psychotherapeutic care.

Secular and Christian ethics alike suffer from an over-emphasis on eudaimonist outcomes. Unaccountably, individualist anthropologies and ethics have received more attention and affirmation in contemporary ecclesial contexts than can be biblically justified. A christological approach to human personhood, by contrast, prioritizes other outcomes as well, not to the exclusion of individual happiness and wellbeing, but with these held in proper dialogical balance. Since Bonhoeffer and Barth, Christian theanthropology has moved considerably beyond the ethical priority of the individual. A more relational perspective shifts the priority of ethical outcomes from a dyadic to a triadic ideal. Human persons flourish, in other words, not merely in right relationship with God, but rather in right relationship with God *and with others*. Both axes of human relating are christologically and ethically significant and, thus, binding on any putatively Christian caregiving model.

Hermeneutical aside

Christology bears on hermeneutics as well. Good reading demands a good hermeneutics, especially when handling different texts from disparate perspectives. In the present work, I follow two hermeneutical priorities when reading any text, whether sacred or secular, and whether imprinted or embodied. According to the first of these two priorities, sacred texts have epistemic priority over secular texts. Although all verid-ical knowledge comes from God, every epistemic schema is not equally valid and reliable. In the modern era numerous claims have been made about the nature of human beings that fall far outside of a biblical para-digm grounded in the revealed truth of the Scriptures and in the person and work of Jesus Christ. As such, the findings of modern psychology continue to provide, alternately, both a foil and an interlocutor for a thoroughgoing Christian psychology of the self and its self-knowledge. Yet, herein lies the kernel for my second hermeneutical priority, that of dialogue.

By referring to secular texts, both imprinted and embodied, as foils and interlocutors, I mean that they have something helpful to say as well. A foil, so-called, serves best when set in relief against the main character. So, fallen human beings are foils to the only perfect human being, Jesus Christ. As we shall see, however, God invites a fallen human response to his Logos. As implied by the self-revelation of God and in the person and work of Christ, mutual understanding comes through logos, which is to say, by means of dialogue.[30] We come to know not merely by listening, but also as we speak, are heard and known.

Beyond this, when considering the phenomenological and psy-chopathological consequences of interpersonal sin, modern psychology should be regarded as a rich discursive resource. Indeed, in fields where sacred texts are relatively silent, such as interpersonal neurobiology, de-velopmental psychology, and psychopathology, Christians can find much that is helpful. For this reason, I fully intend to gratefully appropriate findings which obtain as the fruit of what, in the Reformed tradition as it follows Augustine,[31] we call "common grace" (Van Til, 2015; cf. "creation grace" in Johnson, 2007).

---

30. The Greek, διά λόγος (*dia logos*), "through the word" (see John 1:3), supplies a handy christological mnemonic for this hermeneutical principle.

31. For Augustine, concurrences between secular thought and Christian doctrine were bound to occur and, as such, should not trouble believers. He (2008) argued, "Any statements by those who are called philosophers, . . . which happen to be true and consistent with our faith should not cause alarm, but be claimed for our own use, as it were from owners who have no right to them. . . . These treasures—like the silver and gold, which they did not create but dug, as it were, from the mines of providence, which is everywhere . . . must be removed by Christians . . . and applied to their true function, that of preaching the gospel" (II.xxxix-xl.144–145; pp. 64–65).

Reformed epistemologies have historically avoided any artificial bifurcation of "theology" and "science," so-called,[32] instead regarding all valid truth claims as a subset of God's-knowledge-of-things-as-they-truly-are.[33] That being said, I will also follow Reformed thinking in privileging Scripture as the only unassailable authority and final criterion of validity. In other words, the Logos of God provides us with the means of adjudicating truth. Divine discourse, as Van Til (1969) argues, possesses absolute hermeneutical sovereignty over all other "texts":

> [The Christian] should, to be sure, look sympathetically into the efforts of men in general when they seek to analyze themselves and their problems. There will be no doubt "elements of truth" in such an analysis; even so, ultimately, the idea of a standard of truth is involved in any "system of truth." The Bible is the only ultimate standard of truth. (p. 43)

32. Kuyper, for example, in his use of the term, "science," does not mean the study of exclusively natural phenomena within a positivistic epistemological system. He rejects modernism's attempt to claim "science" for a secular world (so, see Pearcey & Thaxton, 1994). Rather, Kuyper (1968) propounds a theological anthropology that allows interaction between theistic and non-theistic ideas and discoveries with Scripture as the final arbiter of any truth claim. He is quick to add, however, "As soon as the thinker of palingenesis [i.e., Christian] has come to that point in the road where the thinker of naturalism parts company with him, the latter's science is no longer anything to the former but 'science falsely so called'" (p. 176). Within this "system," valid insights that arise from secular inquiry might serve as building materials, so to speak, within the scientific enterprise so long as revelation provides its epistemological blueprint. He writes, "From our standpoint we do not assert that the subject of theology is those who have been enlightened, and that the subject of all other science is those of the natural mind (*psychikos*), but we claim that the only subject of *all* science is the consciousness of regenerated or re-created humanity; and that so large a part of scientific study can be furnished equally well by those who stand outside of this, is simply because this building also admits a vast amount of hod-carrier service [i.e., bricklaying] which is entirely different from the higher architecture" (pp. 602–603; emphasis original).

33. Along these lines, we may surmise that Adam and Eve, having eaten from "the tree of the knowledge of good and evil" (Gen 2:17), gained some knowledge in the process (see 3:22). And, in fact, they did come to a greater degree of self-awareness though one obviously tainted by their fallen state, as their subsequent actions indicate (3:7). Christian psychology and post/modern psychology share much in common when it comes to their respective understandings of, for instance, the phenomenology of shame and its negative impact on self and identity. Crucial differences exist, however, between the respective etiologies, psychopathologies, evaluations, and psychotherapies of shame in Christian and modern frameworks (see Johnson, 2017).

As Van Til suggests, the Christian should seek to balance an interpretative stance regarding secular truth claims somewhere between trust and suspicion. Yet, in this dialogical balance, Johnson (2007) affirms, the Scriptures hold "primacy" (p. 188).[34]

In considering the warrant for a Christian interpretative stance toward the Bible and other texts, Vanhoozer (1998) speaks of a "hermeneutics of humility and conviction" (p. 463). Accordingly, a humble hermeneutics acknowledges, "we will only gain understanding—of God, texts, others, and ourselves—if we are willing to put ourselves second and our interpretive theories to the test" (p. 465). Nevertheless, this humble willingness to question one's conclusions, whether exegetical or theological, must be balanced with the inferential certainty that God intends us to know some things truly on the basis of his self-revelation in the Bible and, supremely, in Jesus Christ (see p. 466). In light of these principles, I will employ a hermeneutics that privileges divine discourse over other "texts" while acknowledging the problematic dialectic of my own nature—*simul justus et peccator*. Accordingly, any faults herein implicate my own fallen hermeneutical judgment.

The path forward

Mirrors of Self is transdisciplinary work of applied Christology. Over the course of the ensuing chapters, I will apply the Christ event to a succession of related fields—epistemology, theology, anthropology, psychology, and psychotherapy—with the aim of offering a christological perspective on the nature and care of *individual* human persons. More than this, I intend to follow this line to its terminus: to veridical knowledge of *self*. Put another way, I invite the reader to study this route and take this path with me—to look into the mirror of who-Christ-is to see more clearly who-*you*-are.

Looking back at ground covered so far, I have reflected on two secular approaches to individual self-knowledge—one ancient and one modern. I contrasted these with Calvin's understanding of the means and

34. In outlining a biblical framework for Christian counseling, Johnson (2007) explains, "Primacy conveys that the first principles of Scripture—and not the first principles of alien worldviews (naturalism, humanism or postmodernism)—must contribute the infrastructure of the disciplinary matrix and edification framework of Christian psychology and soul care, orienting our research and theory-building, and setting the church's counseling agenda" (p. 189).

end of self-knowledge. Yet, as I noted, Calvin does not get us to our destination. For that, we must cross the epistemological bridge from theanthropology to psychology. In order to accomplish this, and at the risk of mixing metaphors, Christ is key. He alone explicates the nature of human personhood and of individual subjectivity; he reveals self as known by God. As God's ultimate self-revelation, Christ is the perfect mirror who shows us who we are.

Christ is also, I argue, the instrumental means of self-knowledge. This is not to say that no one knows anything about self without first knowing Christ. Rather, Christ is God's offer of the knowledge of the self-God-sees. Where barriers to this knowledge exist, Christ is there to remove them. He sees through our illusions and obfuscations. Self-knowledge that is christological in this sense undermines dissociation and self-deception by bringing human beings into a mutual, interpersonal knowledge of themselves before God through the person and work of Christ. Historical Christian thinking regarding self-knowledge maintained this dipolar mutuality; yet, the premodern emphasis on eudaimonist self-knowledge resulted in a truncated ethics. As it happens, Christ is also the key to all that may be coordinated with knowledge of self, among which, I include ethics and hermeneutics.

In Chapter 2, I will consider the biblical and historical foundations for this christological framework. As we will see, many of the ideals of eudaimonist thinking have been reconsidered since the Reformation. Relationality offers balance to individualism, a dialectic less evident in earlier thinking. With the historical groundwork completed, I will set to work in Chapter 3 on christological bridge-building. Tanner (2010) has called Christ the "key" to grasping the theanthropological construct we know as the imago dei. I will consider the imago in christological light before moving, in Chapter 4, toward applications of covenantal Christology. The relatedness of Christ to God and others through expressions constrained by his own human nature will be paradigmatic for the anthropological, psychological, and ethical considerations to follow.

Part III includes two chapters whose aim is to finally "locate" and identify the human self. Much ink has been spilt on this subject, most of it from a post/modernist perspective. Christian thinking, on the other hand, tends to either recapitulate Augustine's self-as-soul notion or follow secular cues. Misunderstandings abound. As it happens, where we finally locate the self suggests much about our theanthropological method. Orthodox Christology offers much-needed correctives for historical and modern perspectives alike. As to the origin of "the self," often attributed in modern philosophy to Augustine, I will demonstrate that he developed ideas he found in Scripture.

Having traversed the bridge from Christ's person and work to the nature and form of the human self, I will turn in Part IV toward identifying impediments to self-knowledge. The fallen human self is prone to dissociation and self-deception, the relationship between which is considerably complicated. Human sin and psychopathology, the causes and consequences of estrangement, plague the life of the self. Wholeness eludes us. In order to grasp the cure for our divided, discontinuous internal lives, we must understand what went wrong from the beginning. In these chapters, I enter constructive dialogue with a number of secular authors writing in the field of psychodynamic psychology.

In the final section of this work, I will outline a number of pastoral and psychotherapeutic implications of dialogical self-knowledge. Agapic relationality, I will argue, must stand at the ethical heart of all ostensibly Christian caregiving interventions. The primary task of caregivers is to embody Christ's ministry to sinful and broken human beings, offering reconciliation and healing in his name and by his Spirit. Crucial to the repair of the estranged self is the remediation of brokenness that accumulates in the context of fallen interpersonal relationality. Love, embodied in the person and work of Christ and enacted through caregivers, is the key to overcoming barriers to self-knowledge and healing the broken self.

God's work of reconciliation affects the believer at multiple levels. The highest level, that of the believer and God, is a necessary prerequisite for subsequent healing. In the context of agapic relationality, rhetorically encapsulated by the Pauline soteriological formula of *faith working through love*, an individual's formerly dissociated awareness of sin and shame may, over time, come to be resolved. Damage comes to healed as self comes to self-perceive in a caregiving context that fosters deep fellowship with God and others in his body. Self-deception, the ethical corollary of dissociation, can also be overcome as the dynamic of grace informs and directs the healing work. Finally, as the New Testament makes clear, the ecclesial context is vital to the task of working out Christ's purposes for his redeemed, reconciled people.

2

Biblical and historical Christian antecedents

CONTEMPORARY SECULAR ACCOUNTS OF the history of self-knowledge convey the distinct impression that Christianity has had little to offer to the discussion (see, e.g., Gertler, 2011, Chapter 2). Over the last five hundred years Western philosophy has become increasingly disinterested in theistic frameworks and disenchanted with its own Judeo-Christian heritage. The epistemological quantum leap history terms "Enlightenment" effected a parting of the ways between theology and anthropology. What God brought together in the God-man, Jesus Christ, modernity separated. Secular philosophy has yet to look back. A more sanguine reading of Western history, on the other hand, reveals a wealth of Christian perspectives on the subject of self-knowledge.

The secular rejection of theistic understandings about human beings should come as little shock to sharp-eyed students of history. Less familiar, perhaps, has been the resultant suspicion among theists regarding the human side of the epistemological divide. The ancient Greeks and the psychoanalysts sought after knowledge of self. We seek to know God. If the secular world wants the lesser fields of anthropology and psychology, they can have it. We will stand on the holy ground of theology. All of this is modernism run amok in the church. The Post-Enlightenment divorce in *Christian* epistemological thinking has resulted in a latter-day Gnostic dichotomy. Like good post/modernists, we have segmented and sequestered our knowledge of God and of human beings into silos. Worse still, we have denigrated self-knowledge as a strictly secular pursuit.

33

To read Calvin, then, is to catch a whiff of ammonium carbonate. Like smelling salts to the faint, his perspective shocks us out of our post/ modern stupor. Self-knowledge, as Calvin argues, stands as a fundamental and indispensable requisite for the knowledge of God. Neither can be securely held without the other. Those who suggest otherwise have fallen under the sway of modernism's siren song. As I have already shown, we must distinguish between *secular* self-knowledge on the one hand and *Christian* self-knowledge on the other due to the fundamental incompatibility of their epistemological and theanthropological frameworks. Once accounted for, this caveat ought not discourage us from moving ahead.

The point of departure between secular and Christian frameworks is the question of whether divine self-disclosure is the only final means of coming to a true knowledge of ourselves. When this key distinction is considered, the studied silence of modern philosophy on the Christian self-knowledge tradition becomes less surprising.[1] Christian perspectives, as we might expect, begin with God's self-revelation in his Logos, that is, in the Scriptures and, ultimately, in the person and work of Christ. The first step in laying our foundation for distinguishing secular and Christian self-knowledge is Christ. He is, as we shall see, the key to reconciling what modernism tore asunder.

The material in this chapter is organized into three main sections. In the first section, I will consider a number of biblical passages that illuminate the dynamic of dipolarity. These passages illustrate what Calvin said about how human beings come to know self through divine self-disclosure. In the second and third sections, I will consider two groups of historical Christian writers distinguishing between them on the basis of their anthropological ethics and hermeneutics. The first group includes those whose anthropology inclines toward an individualist understanding of human persons and an eudaimonist ethics. Within the second group, human persons are regarded more through a lens of sociality. I describe the ethics of this group as agapist.

Grenz's (2001) masterful survey of the imago dei supplies the impetus for this historical and ethical distinction. As he notes, every theological and anthropological text is contextually situated. According to Clark & Gaede (1987), all human knowledge is socially construed, which is to

---

1. Post/modernist philosophy's struggle to explain whether and how the self has privileged access to its own mental states and whether, indeed, the self exists at all are also, ultimately, traceable to its rejection of Christ as the means of defining and comprehending what it means to be truly human.

say, human beings know discursively and dialogically. What this means for our survey is that every perspective, whether secular or Christian, historical or contemporary, reflects some degree of influence from others. This is no less the case with say, Augustine or Barth.

Theistic writers consistently interact contextually with, and are influenced by, secular thinking. The perspectives of Augustine and Barth, influenced as they were by their respective historical contexts, developed along distinct lines. Both share a common theistic basis and a commitment to the epistemological and hermeneutical sovereignty of divine revelation. Yet, their considerable differences illustrate the degree to which all human discourse is contextual and dialogical.

Christian Scripture and the knowledge of self

It goes without saying, God has not disclosed himself to us in tidy categories. His Logos, as considered in the written text of Scripture and in the incarnate Son, defies facile systematization. Yet, the following brief survey of relevant biblical texts demonstrates a remarkable consistency. Calvin's theanthropological premise—that the knowledge of God and the knowledge of self relate mutually and reciprocally—finds ample warrant in Scripture.

Isaiah's dipolar self-discovery

The prophet Isaiah, for example, illustrates the dipolarity of self-knowledge as he relates the visionary experience accompanying his prophetic call. In chapter 6, he begins with what first caught his eye, namely, "the LORD," whom he beheld, "sitting upon a throne, high and lifted up" (v. 1).[2] In quick succession Isaiah fills in details: a majestic, otherworldly train filling the temple, angelic beings with covered faces and feet, words spoken loudly proclaiming God's holiness and splendor, and an earthquake that shakes the temple like an echo of approval. Senses overloaded, the prophet cries out in dismay, "Woe is me! For I am lost; for I am a man of unclean lips, and I dwell in the midst of a people of unclean lips; for my eyes have seen the King, the LORD of hosts!" (v. 5).

2. Unless otherwise noted, biblical citations are taken from the English Standard Version (ESV).

Isaiah responds to what he sees of God by disclosing what he sees in himself. His experience of divine self-disclosure awakens subjective self-discovery (Oswalt, 1986). As he beholds God-as-he-is, there arises within the prophet a dipolar awareness of his identity and position respective to God: he is "a man of unclean lips." Isaiah's standing before God—he is sinful, unworthy—is mirrored by its inverse in God's holiness and worth. He is *not* like God; he is like every other human being, all those among whom he dwells. Furthermore, he observes a separation between himself and God: "I am lost." On account of his status and standing, he is estranged—cut off—from God.[3] His fate is sealed until, that is, an intermediary touches Isaiah's lips with a burning coal and declares his guilt "taken away," his sin "atoned for" (v. 7).

Isaiah perceives himself, not as he gazes inward, but outward, illustrating dipolar or reciprocal self-discovery. This is undoubtedly what Calvin had in mind. To look into the face of God is to see oneself reflected more clearly. Whatever we may have "known" of self is irrevocably altered in the light of divine radiance. Isaiah was granted direct access to an experience of God's splendor; barring a similar beatific vision, we must content ourselves to look into the mirror of the Logos.

Paralleling Isaiah's adverse reaction to divine self-disclosure, we may expect a similar response to seeing ourselves as depicted in Scripture. God's word, after all, serves as a mirror (Jas 1:23) revealing the truth of who we are and how far we, as sinners, have fallen short of the glory of God (Rom 3:23). It should not surprise us, then, when we find ourselves resistant to its searching gaze. Human aversion to self-discovery is nearlyas old as humanity.

To this point, it was our first parents who first looked away from the mirror, defying God's Logos, and seeking to know themselves autonomously (Gen 3; see Wenham, 2014). The tree of the knowledge of

3. Isaiah's exclamation, נִדְמֵיתִי (*nidmēti*), "I am lost" (ESV), is somewhat ambiguous in Hebrew due to the contextually determined meaning of its verbal root, דמה (*dmh*) (see Koehler & Baumgartner, 2002). In its niphal (passive) form it can signify being silenced, a rendering which would yield no small amount of irony considering Isaiah's verbal response. It could also be translated anticipatorily, "I am destroyed, ruined" (most English translations). In numerous other occurrences in prophetic contexts, the verb is employed with this sense in anticipation of God's impending judgment on unrepentant cities or nations (Isa 15:1; Jer 47:5; Hos 4:6; 10:7; Obad 5; Zeph 1:11). Isaiah may, in fact, be anticipating that such judgment will fall upon him due to his sin and, should they remain "a people of unclean lips," upon Israel as well. This certainly seems to be God's intention respective to Israel in the oracle to follow (vv. 9–13) (see Oswalt, 1986).

good and evil offered something they thought they needed: a "wisdom" they were told would level the playing field. Having eaten of the fruit they believed would make them like God, their first impulse was to conceal themselves—from him and from each other. Tellingly, their attempted coverup reflected a desire to hide what they saw in themselves—nakedness before God, shame, guilt. In order to evade and obfuscate these unpleasant realities, they turned on each other and shifted the blame.

Even secular eyes can discern this hereditary proclivity in human behavior. Aristotle and Freud alike would observe this universal inclination toward dissociation and self-deception. As Johnson & Burroughs (2000) have observed, we have all inherited our first parents' archetypal exhibition of defensive evasiveness. Moreover, what Isaiah concluded—that he was "lost," estranged from God—has passed to us also as the interpersonal sequela of the fall (see Gen 1:23). We are cut off from him, from each other, and, when we consider the intrapersonal estrangement reflected in our dissociative and self-deceptive inclinations, from ourselves as well (see Rom 1:28–32). The Scriptures, then, disclose what we need to know of what we have become. Furthermore, through the Scriptures we encounter the one through whom we may come to know God and self. Through Christ, God reconciles us to himself, to each other, and to the truth of who we are (John 10:40; 14:9; Rom 5:10; 2 Cor 5:18; Col 1:22).

Jesus and the hypocrites

In Matthew's Gospel, Jesus is often overheard condemning religious hypocrisy among the socioreligious elite. In strong language he decries the Pharisees' attempts to fulfill the commands of God in service of self (see Matt 23). These hypocrites, he determines, honor God with their lips but not with their hearts (Matt 15:8). In his so-called Sermon on the Mount, Jesus warns his followers against a mere façade of righteousness. "You must be perfect," he admonishes them, not like the scribes and Pharisees, but "as your heavenly Father is perfect" (Matt 5:48; cf. Lev 19:2; Deut 18:3). This perfection, moreover, would need to be more than skin-deep.[4]

4. Reflecting on the Sermon on the Mount, Charry (1997) summarizes the "foundation" of Jesus' moral ethic for his followers as "imitation of the perfection of their heavenly Father" (p. 76). Hagner (1993) argues that the kind of perfection (τέλειος, teleios) in view here is "ethical perfection" (p. 135). Pennington (2017) rejects this gloss as "problematic" preferring instead to borrow from the Greco-Roman virtue tradition with his gloss, "'whole,' 'complete,' or even 'virtuous,'" reflecting his prioritization of

A survey of his moral teaching within the Sermon on the Mount reveals the depth to which moral perfection must penetrate in order to qualify as such. He cautions that the supposed perfection of the ostensibly righteous does not qualify as such before God (Matt 5:20). So, for example, in his application of the law against murder (Exod 20:13), Jesus condemns all forms of unresolved interpersonal conflict between believers (Matt 5:21–26). Likewise, lustful intent qualifies as adulterous act according to his moral metric (Matt 5:28; see Willard, 1998). Moreover, perfection, according to Jesus, demands a compassionate and generous disposition even toward one's enemies. As God demonstrates love in causing the sun to rise and rain to fall on all people without distinction, so too should Christians show love to even "those who persecute you, so that you may be sons of your Father who is in heaven" (Matt 5:44–45; see Stott, 1978).

According to Jesus, the telos of Torah is τέλειος (teleios), perfection—a moral, ethicospiritual conformity to the revealed will of God (see Matt 19:21; cf. Rom 10:4[5]). Yet, as Jesus taught, perfection must equally apply to our actions as well as our intentions toward others. The clear implication of his teaching is that outward behavior might serve as did the fig leaves of Adam and Eve, concealing who we really are and what we have done. Perfection for the believer requires the full participation of "the heart,"[6] our perception of which demands "aggressive self-scrutiny" (Charry, 1997, p. 76). The function of divine revelation is to foster this type of ethicospiritual self-examination among believers—a fact that becomes increasingly clear in Jesus' repeated remonstrances of religious and moral hypocrisy that follow.

In laying out the dangers of hypocrisy, Jesus highlights the fact that even when done in supposed service to God, religious acts may conceal sinful motives. He warns believers to give, fast, and pray in ways that preclude honor and recognition for self. A crucial test for false motives

---

the eudaimonist theme of human flourishing or "wholeness" throughout the Sermon (p. 70).

5. Christ is the perfection that the law demands and which, by faith, we grasp only through our union with him: "For Christ is the end [τέλος, telos] of the law for righteousness to everyone who believes" (Rom 10:4).

6. In modern English usage, the heart has come to stand metonymically for an individual's emotions or affections (see Elliott, 2006). However, in Scripture "heart" (typically, Heb. לֵב, lēb, Gr. καρδία, kardia), refers more comprehensively to "the center of a person" (Pierre, 2016, p. 241). Sorg (1979) identifies the heart as the psychospiritual organ responsible for human "feeling, thinking, and willing" (p. 181).

is, then, whether one is willing to practice "righteousness" where others cannot see (see Via, 2005). As Carson (1999) notes, public prayer and other apparent acts of devotion to God may tempt believers into sinfully drawing approving attention to themselves (p. 58).[7] Sincere Christian spirituality, on the other hand, is humble and quiet—done, as it were, "in secret" (Matt 6:4, 6, 18).

The hypocrite bears only the appearance of righteousness. Without the full and genuine participation of the heart her faith is a sham. For Jesus, hypocrisy is the ethical fruit of moral self-deception—a not so subtle willingness to believe the best about one's motives despite clear evidence to the contrary (see Spiegel, 1999). "Why do you see the speck that is in your brother's eye," he inquires, "but do not notice the log that is in your own eye?" (Matt 7:3). Jesus knew, as did Aristotle, that awareness of another's transgression may be accompanied by a simultaneous blindness to one's own transgression of the same standard—and to a greater degree, for a plank is surely worse than a speck. Jesus implies that the hypocrite has distanced herself from some pertinent aspect of self-knowledge and, in doing so, become self-deceived (1 John 1:8).

Dissociation serves self-deception in that it defends against a present awareness of an unpleasant moral truth about self. Our hearts may be wicked even as our deeds draw the praise of others (see Ps 12:2; Isa 29:13; Matt 15:8). When we couple resistance to veridical self-evaluation with harsh judgments toward others' failings, we add moral injury to insult. Jesus condemns the hypocrite for her self-deception as well as her concomitant condemnation of others. Since the fall, human beings have labored to conceal the painful reality about ourselves. That we are just as capable of hiding from dipolar self-awareness as our first parents Jesus acknowledged without question. Even among those ostensibly reconciled to God in Christ this tendency persists. If believers hope to overcome their psychopathological inclination toward dissociation and self-deception, it will be necessary for God to reveal the content of our hearts.

7. Truly, the hypocrite desires to "please man" (Yuille, 2012, p. 75; cf. Gal 1:10); but in another sense the "reward" (Matt 6:2, 5, 16) derived from acts of man-pleasing religiosity amounts to an ungrounded bolstering of self and a reinforcing of the false front behind which the hypocrite hides.

Davidic dissociation and self-deception

The biblical *locus classicus* illustrating the phenomenology of moral self-deception is undoubtedly the climax of the narrative in 2 Sam 12:1–15. There, Nathan the prophet confronts King David over his adulterous affair with Bathsheba and subsequent murder of her husband. By way of a clever parable the prophet provokes the king's indignation toward a greedy landowner who callously deprives a fictitious pauper of his precious ewe lamb. David's response to the prophet's parable graphically illustrates the inevitable ethical fruit of epistemic unipolarity,[8] which is to say, hypocrisy. So long as David has the mirror covered, in other words, he can see another's wrongdoing while remaining blind to his own.

Though himself guilty of adultery and murder, David rages against an invented injustice. "As the LORD lives," he decrees, "surely the man who has done this deserves to die. He must make restitution for the lamb fourfold, because he did this thing and had no compassion" (vv. 5b–6). But by now the prophet's rhetorical trap has been set. "You are the man!," he cries (v. 7). You are the man you have condemned. What you have seen and hated in another, David, you have until this moment concealed in and from yourself. The prophet then issues his just decree on God's behalf: for all that David had done against another's household "secretly," God would bring about his judgment upon David and his household, publically and in kind (v. 12).[9]

It is important to note that David's faculties of moral discernment remained intact before and after his wrongful acts. What failed him, then, was not his conscience, but his awareness of himself. Until the prophet sprung his trap, the king had dissociated himself from the present knowledge of an unpleasant reality. He had committed adultery and murder and had covered them both up—even from himself. He did not experience feelings of guilt or shame until confronted by the reality of his actions. Moreover, his moral revulsion at the unjust deeds of another revealed no hint of embarrassment or contrition. He "anger was greatly kindled" (v. 5), though he needed help to recognize himself in the

---

8. Cf. Van Til's (1969) "monistic" thinking describing what I have here referred to as unipolar self-knowledge (p. 52).

9. David's prophesied comeuppance is found in 2 Sam 15–18 (esp. 16:20–22). Of note, however, is God's gracious commutation of the legal judgment mandated by the law in cases of adultery (see Lev 20:10) in response to David's contrition and humble confession (2 Sam 12:13).

prophet's story. Nathan's prophetic peroration triggered a much-needed awareness of himself and his actions. Seeing clearly for the first time, David acknowledged, "I have sinned against the LORD" (v. 13; cf. Ps 51:3).

Dissociation served David's resistance to self-knowledge by fostering self-deception. If the offending truth about himself could be hidden *from* himself, deleted from the record, as it were, he was then free to believe about himself what, all things being considered, was patently false. In this detached state, he knew himself to be "perfect." At some level just below the horizon of his present awareness, he knew better. Some noetic stimulus, after all, served to trigger David's dissociation. Yet, so long as no one else was writing the story David told himself, he was free to make up, and believe, a lie.

As the story of David demonstrates, the means of dipolar self-knowledge is more complex than not. Nathan was God's instrument of David's self-discovery. David recognized himself as "the man" through the prophet's logos. The "mirror" David beheld was not Scriptures; nor did he experience a vision of God like Isaiah's. In this case, a prophetic emissary acted on God's behalf. We learn in the first verse that "the LORD sent Nathan to David" to awaken him from his stupor. God acted through a mediator.

Along these lines, Jesus encouraged his followers that they would be able to assist in speck removal once they have dealt with their own planks (Matt 7:5). In David's case, God used another as mirror to bring the king to a place of self-awareness. He did this, we may presume, not because the king was unable to discern the wrong he had done, but because he had dissociated from the knowledge of his wrongdoing. Nathan presented David with an opportunity to see himself and his sin more clearly. In doing so, the prophet illustrates a reality that we will unpack over the course of this work: human beings, as divine image bearers, bear the ability and the responsibility to faithfully embody the mirror of the Logos. As we shall see, we need others to serve as mirrors of self to help us overcome our tendency toward sinful dissociation and self-deception (cf. Gal 6:1–10).

Self-knowledge in Christian eudaimonist contexts

Historical Christian pastoral theology did not suffer, as modern expressions do, from an artificial bifurcation between theology and anthropology (Purves, 2001). As Charry (1997) observes, prior to the advent of modernism, the theology of the church related inseparably, albeit propaedeutically, to the psychosocial and ethicospiritual concerns of believers.[10] According to Wolterstorff (2010), Hellenist philosophy held "that the ultimate and comprehensive goal of each of us is that we live our lives as well as possible, the well-lived life being, by definition, the happy life, the *eudaimōn* life" (p. 150). So, the ancient Greeks held the pursuit of wisdom to be instrumental to human flourishing as they defined it. Premodern Christian theanthropology, on the other hand, sought after *true* wisdom—the knowledge of God and of self—as prerequisite for the "blessed life."[11]

An eudaimonist ethics of self-knowledge, whether secular or Christian, is characterized by its relative emphasis on individual gain. Those who gain true wisdom, as circumscribed by each respective system, will be truly happy. The two differ, then, not so much in outcome but in means. Christian eudaimonism maintains, in contrast to its secular counterpart, that blessedness comes not through autonomous human means but as individuals come to know God.[12] The eudaimonist pursuit of Christian

---

10. The dichotomy between theological and anthropological discourse now extant in modern Christianity was influenced by Cartesian dualism. Kant reified Descartes and then proceeded to widen this epistemological and discursive gulf between the theology of the church and the realm of human existence and experience (Grenz, 2001; see Shults, 2003). Prior to the modern shift toward epistemological compartmentalization and atomization, Christian anthropology shared a close relationship with the theological concerns of the church. With the advent of the modern age, "science" so-called, came to occupy the place of primacy formerly afforded to theology (C. Taylor, 1989). Charry (1997) is undoubtedly correct that premodern Christianity's "theological realism" (p. 6) offers a more integrated approach to the Christian life than modernity's segmented, rationalistic, system(s) of truth. To be sure, it is decidedly *un*-modern to propound the mutual, reciprocal relationship between the knowledge of God and the knowledge of self.

11. Wolterstorff (2015) further observes a problematic aspect, from a New Testament perspective, of eudaimonist ethical frameworks. He considers eudaimonism to be "similar to egoism in that it is too agent-oriented" (p. 5). This is not to say, however, that eudaimonism will necessarily lead to an axiological rat race with every human competing for an individual share of wellbeing at the expense of others. The ancients held, as Annas (1993) reminds us, that "virtue" would provide a healthy check on an excessive, self-serving pursuit of happiness. Still, it must be observed that the New Testament often inverts classical eudaimonism by propounding a "blessedness" that, counterintuitively, comes through suffering and self-sacrifice (see Acts 5:14; Rom 5:3; 8:17; 1 Cor 6:7; 2 Cor 1:6; Eph 3:13; Phil 3:10; 2 Tim 2:3; 4:5; Jas 1:2; 5:10; 1 Pet 3:14; 4:13). Jesus' "beatitudes" (Matt 5:3–11) are notable in this regard.

12. Those who receive God's final verdict of "blessed" (see Matt 25:34; cf. v. 41) we

self-knowledge, then, relates to its ancient antecedents in stressing the individual gains of a well-examined, well-lived life as its fruit. Happiness comes through knowing God and self.

Christian eudaimonism, as will be shown, stresses the capacity of individuals to pursue self-knowledge along a vertical axis. The influence of Socratic thinking should, therefore, be clear. Through self-knowledge, for the Christian eudaimonist, happiness obtains in right relationship with God. Whether that relationship depends to any degree on others remains less clear. This perspective would dominate Christian ethics for much of its long history. As will be shown in the two sections that follow, adjustments to the ethics of Christian self-knowledge would await at least two significant shifts, the first being a shift away from Platonic conceptions of human nature. The second occurred as a result of a subsequent "turn to relationality" in secular and Christian anthropology.

Augustine, 354–430

After coming to Christ, Augustine, who prior to his conversion to Christianity had gleaned heavily in the fields of Platonic idealism, endeavored to establish and defend the faith from its more cultured intellectual despisers. Augustine's pre-conversion training in secular philosophy and rhetoric served him well in this effort (P. Brown, 2000). His writings would greatly benefit patristic and medieval churches as they contended for apologetic and pedagogic clarity and consistency (see González, 2015). Without question, Augustine believed the godless pursuit of self-knowledge was misguided and ill-fated. He did not suggest abandoning the quest altogether, however; rather, he reformulated it in expressly Christian terms (Rist, 1996). He kept the baby, in other words, and tossed the bathwater.

While Augustine ruled out a strictly anthropocentric self-knowledge, he still considered that Socrates was on to something. In Book Ten

---

should expect will be truly happy! As previously stated, eudaimonism is not wholly incompatible with Christianity. The distinctions being drawn here are subtle and should not be construed as suggestive of a dichotomy between either (1) eudaimonist and agapist systems of ethics, (2) individual or social anthropologies and psychologies, or (3) the ontological categories of substance and relation. Rather, as I hope to convey in the course of this work, the Bible generally and the Christ event in particular convey a hierarchical prioritization of the latter side of each of these dialectics.

of his monumental treatise, *On the Trinity* (2002), the church father proposes a Christian reinterpretation of the ancient Delphic maxim:

> Why, then, was it [the mind; Lat. *mens*] commanded to know
> itself? I believe it was so commanded that it might consider it-
> self and live according to its nature, that is, that it might desire
> to be ruled according to its nature, namely, under Him to whom
> it ought to be subject, and above all those things to which it is to
> be preferred. (X.v.7; p. 49)

An asterisk hovers above Augustine's embrace of Socratic self-knowledge.
God himself holds the pursuit of human self-knowledge, Christianly defined and pursued, to be virtuous.[13] What Plato had wrong, then, was the
means. For Augustine, humans beings may pursue their happiness apart
from God, but this quest is doomed to failure (see Luke 11:28; cf. Matt
7:23).

To remain ignorant of God, Augustine suggests, is to remain ignorant of self and amounts to living contrary to one's nature. There is an inherent contradiction, then, in any pursuit of autonomous self-knowledge.
The entire enterprise, when accompanied by the simultaneous rejection
of the means of veridical self-knowledge, is self-defeating. Augustine
(2002) clarifies how sin has made it possible for human beings to distance
themselves from knowledge of their contingency: "For [the mind] does
many things through evil desires, as though it had forgotten itself" (X.v.7;
p. 49). We forget ourselves at precisely the moment we fail to recall what
we know of God.

Augustine well-recognized the need for a master key for his theanthropological system. In seeking to decrypt human nature generally and
individual persons specifically, Augustine looked to the person and nature
of God. So, in Books Nine through Fourteen of the same text, Augustine
contends that human beings are psychological analogues of the Trinity.[14]

13. Wolterstorff (2010) interprets Augustine with considerable nuance on this
point. On the one hand, he argues that Augustinian anthropology depends to a great
extent on a Platonist or Neoplatonist framework (p. 191). Yet, he also perceives a shift
from Platonic "ascent" in Augustine's earlier works to Christian (eschatological) "anticipation" in his later writings (see pp. 200–201). I would simply argue that Augustine
reinterprets Hellenistic eudaimonism in light of the love-imperative in Scripture. He
does not, as Wolterstorff suggests, reject a Platonist ethics, but rather, as Rist (1996)
argues, he "baptizes" it.

14. Rist (1996) explains, "Augustine's minimal meaning is that our minds are
constituted by three activities, only formally distinct, which he eventually prefers to
identify as 'self-memory, self-understanding and self-willing.' . . . These activities in

Among other things, he viewed the threefold constitutional capacity of the mind for self-awareness (ontology), self-knowledge (epistemology), and self-love (axiology) as an image of the triunity of the divine nature (IX.v.8; p. 30).[15] Human beings, according to Augustine, image the divine nature incompletely, imperfectly, and inconsistently, yet, as they seek to know—and love—self as created in the image of God they may grow in knowledge and love of the One from whom this image derives.

Human love for God *and self*, then, mirrors God's own love for God's triune self. By contrast, Augustine held that human beings consummate an idolatrous self-love when we seek to know and love self autonomously: "[N]ot that the creature ought not to be loved," he clarifies, "but if that love for him is referred to the Creator, it will no longer be desire [*cupiditas*] but love [*caritas*]. For desire is present when the creature is loved on account of himself" (IX.viii.34; p. 34). Due to the fall, our human capacity for self-knowledge is damaged and curtailed by the corrupting influence of sin. Instead of seeking to know—and love—oneself as a bearer of God's image, we craft, like idols, images of self that we may "know" and love.

For Augustine, the fundamental anthropological sin of the Greeks was their desire to know and love self autonomously (see Brown, 2000, p. 170). Their ignorance of God led to their incapacity to know self truly. This self-blindness came as the fruit of sin and congenital self-deception. Paradoxically, true wisdom comes through acknowledging one's self-ignorance. Noetic "strength," to nuance Jesus, comes to those who first confess their weakness (cf. Luke 18:13–14). If the Greeks had truly sought after wisdom, "They should cry with the very bone and marrow of their inmost experience: 'I have said, O Lord, have mercy on me: heal my soul; for I have sinned before thee.' In this way, by the sure routes of divine mercy, they would be led into wisdom" (Augustine, 2010 III.ii.5).

God are obviously perfect, for he knows who he is, and knows it all the 'time,' but they are imperfect in us, though we can become more and more godlike" (pp. 145–146). Houston (2000) dismisses Augustine's analogy as a "fancied correspondence between us and God" not supported by Scripture (p. 323).

15. Charles Taylor (1989) notes the lengths to which Augustine went to link the mind/soul as the center of human subjectivity with the tri-Personhood of God. The latter (Augustine, 2002) employs Trinitarian language to describe the mind's relationship to self-knowledge and self-love: "And so there is a certain image of the Trinity: the mind itself, its knowledge, which is its offspring, and love as a third; these three are one and one substance. The offspring is not less, while the mind knows itself as much as it is; nor is the love less, while the mind loves itself as much as it knows and as much as it is" (IX.xii.18; p. 40).

The sin-estranged self, blind, weakened by self-ignorance can be healed and strengthened by acknowledging weakness and incapacity in light of God's perfect wisdom and strength.

Augustine's (2009) recollection of his own conversion to Christianity serves as a helpful exemplar. The story he tells is no rarified discourse on theological truths; it is personal and all the more profound. He begins with the visit of an acquaintance, one Ponticianus. Eventually, the conversation would turn to a surprising tale. Ponticianus shared about a friend who, much to everyone's chagrin and bemusement, had embraced the Christian faith, having "experienced a conversion inwardly" (VIII.vii.16; pp. 144). Yet, as the others laughed and carried on, a strange disquiet was steadily growing within Augustine. Though he tried to maintain his focus on the storyteller, his attention was drawn inward instead.

In the midst of Ponticianus's narration, Augustine recalls,

> This was the story Ponticianus told. But while he was speaking, Lord, you turned my attention back to myself. You took me up from behind my own back where I had placed myself because I did not wish to observe myself, and you set me before my face so that I should see how vile I was, how twisted and filthy, covered in sores and ulcers. And I looked and was appalled, but there was no way of escaping from myself. If I tried to avert my gaze from myself, his story continued relentlessly, and you once again placed me in front of myself; you thrust me before my own eyes so that I should discover my iniquity and hate it. I had known it, but deceived myself, refused to admit it, and pushed it out of my mind. (VIII.vii.16; pp. 144–145)

His inner turmoil would only intensify as he sat alone afterwards. He describes the experience as a "grand struggle in my inner house" (VIII.viii.19; p. 146). Eventually he would pick up a copy of the Bible, prompted by some voice he heard in the distance, and would, as he later recounts, be awakened to an awareness of himself as estranged from God, helpless, fallen, sinful. His Platonist piety shattered beyond remedy, he would confess the limits of his self-reliance and surrender to the same faith he had once mocked.

Augustine's *Confessions* depart significantly from the typical autobiographies of his day. For Brown (2000), the work reads more like the "self-portrait of a convalescent" than the "affirmation of a cured man" (p. 171).[16] Indeed, the latter reflects in startling and intimate detail on the

16. Warfield (1956) also endeavors to show that the *Confessions* of Augustine

state of his "morbid condition of . . . mind." "I was in conflict with myself," he concludes, "and was dissociated from myself [*dissipabar a me ipso*; lit., rent asunder by myself]" (VIII.x.22; p. 148). This internal struggle he characterizes as a battle enjoined by "two wills." The stakes of this battle amounted to whether he would look without flinching on himself as he truly was—as he was known by God to be.

Augustine's conversion story illustrates, in autobiographical terms, a Christian psychology of self-knowledge. In his own words, he keenly describes the experience of coming to greater self-awareness. Internal conflict raged between "self which willed to serve" and "self which was unwilling" (VIII.x.22; p. 148). A split in his mind prevented him from seeing what he did not wish to see.[17] Dissociation and self-deception persisted as psychogenic bulwarks against the unwelcome shock of self-discovery: "[T]he human mind, so blind and languid, shamefully and dishonorably wishes to hide, and yet does not wish anything to be concealed from itself" (X.xxiii.34; p. 200). His self-blindness, Augustine would come to believe, stemmed from his fallen desire for autonomy from the God in whose image he was made.

Augustine's narration exemplifies "conversion" from unipolar to dipolar self-knowledge. What we can see of self depends in no small measure on whether we perceive self in light of divine truth. So long as self remains separated and estranged from God, self cannot perceive or know itself truly. Like David and Isaiah experienced long before him, the initial experience of coming to know self-as-self-is-known carries considerable

---

differs in substance and intent from those "simple autobiographies" that concern themselves with "unveiling, uncovering to the sight of the world what were better perhaps hidden from all eyes but God's" (p. 338). Warfield's concern to distinguish the *Confessions* from its secular, humanist parallels, however, leads him at times into false dichotomy. So, for example, in spite of its title and Augustine's innumerable self-references throughout, Warfield concludes, "His actual subject is not himself, but the goodness of God" (p. 338). But surely Augustine's subject is not *either* himself or God; rather, it is both. Warfield, in electing to focus exclusively on the divine pole, departs rhetorically and conceptually from Augustine's own understanding of self-knowledge, specifically, that it relates mutually and reciprocally to the knowledge of God.

17. Endeavoring to defend against a spirituality of "interiority," Houston (2000) offers the following formula based on his understanding of "Augustinian self-knowledge": "True self-knowledge comes only through knowledge of God; knowledge both of self and of God comes only through the Bible" (p. 313). What is less clear in his explication of Augustine is the role human relationality plays in mediating the knowledge of God and of self.

psychological pain. Yet, as the Greeks remind us, human desire for self-knowledge remains.

God, so Augustine believed, overcame his congenital self-deception.[18] He did so by drawing back the dissociative fig leaf covering Augustine's sinful, shameful state. Through the latter's embrace of Christ as God's offer of reconciliation, he entered into a state of grace. As his experience demonstrates, the Scriptures are indispensable to dipolar self-discovery. Yet, it is worth noting the instrumental role Ponticianus's tale played in Augustine's conversion experience. For the church father, then, the secular pursuit of self-knowledge represents a failure to grapple with our fear of genuine self-discovery. Only in the light of God's perception of himself could his subjective, psychogenic barriers against veridical self-awareness be removed.

Gregory, c. 540–604

Christian eudaimonism after Augustine would be amplified by a diversity of historical developments. Clebsch and Jaekle (1994) argue that two crucial factors influenced the pastoral aims of the medieval church in particular. These influences include the Romanization of the Germanic tribes and the growth of the monastic orders.[19] With respect to the latter, pagan and Christian belief systems came to be syncretized within the culture. So, church leaders reacted out of necessity by stressing practical ethics over theology. Many of the pastoral writers of the day emphasized virtuous behavior as the measure of one's devotion to Christ. They offered inductive guidance for faithful Christian living and casuistic case studies for a variety of pastoral caregiving scenarios.

The church's emphasis on right living and virtue, biblically defined, resulted in an increasingly one-dimensional ethics. The continuing

---

18. Augustine (2012b) defends the orthodoxy of a doctrine of "original" sin against the claims of Pelagianism, a heterodox perspective on human goodness and ability (see Sanlon, 2014). One might argue that Pelagianism, which holds that the fallen human noetic capacity has *not* been fatally compromised, confirms the tendency, even among ostensible believers, to dissociate from veridical knowledge of ourselves. Scripture, on the other hand, holds the autonomous human will to be impotent apart from God's grace (see Ps 51:5; Rom 5:12; Eph 2:8).

19. The latter, they suggest, may well have been a reaction against the former (see pp. 21–23). As the prevailing culture came to be increasingly characterized by values and practices alien to Christianity, the monastery served as a refuge and retreat from the world, thus carrying considerable appeal.

influence of Socratic self-knowledge on Christian thinking remained strong. Self-examination for the medieval Christian mind targeted behavior, both mental and embodied acts, for signs of impiety. The assumption behind this approach entailed the possibility one could, without knowing it, commit a sinful act, shelter a sinful motive, or fail to perform some ethical duty (see Ps 139:23–24). Eudaimonia, the happy life, would be the subjective benefit of virtuous living. For those who sought refuge from a dark world in monastic communities, "virtue" would be strictly monitored and enforced. For some, "happiness" might have to wait on the life to come, assuming a sufficient degree of self-renunciation in this life.

Largely unknown to modern readers, Gregory the Great's (1978) manual for pastors has been called "the most influential book in the history of the pastoral tradition" (Purves, 2001, p. 56). The success of Gregory's *Pastoral Care* was undoubtedly due to a number of factors (see Oden, 1984), though the nature of its appeal for the present study is the degree to which Gregory's approach assumes the reality of the telic dynamic of self-knowledge, as also with its inimical inverse, self-deception. He offers extensive advice to pastors on assisting individual believers in the task of self-examination. In many ways Gregory's approach represents a more practical, pastoral outworking of an Augustinian theanthropology (see G. R. Evans, 1986; Houston, 2000).

For Gregory, the ethical aim of Christian spirituality and pastoral care was virtue. Whereas pagan philosophy defined virtue in secular terms, Gregory employed the Scriptures as his standard. Right living, for Gregory, was the result of dipolar reflection and evaluation. The believer who looks inward—at self—and upward—to God—would grow in wisdom and virtue. By his term for introspection, *consideratio* (consideration), Gregory signified that virtuous behavior demanded subjective examination of one's thoughts and motives (2 Cor 13:5; cf. Heb 14:2). Evans (1986) explains *consideratio* as "the exercise of an introspection which examines not only the inner man, but also his outward actions," and further, as "a way of self-knowledge" (pp. 19–20). In order to determine whether any mental or behavioral act be virtuous or, alternatively, vice masquerading as virtue, Gregory encouraged careful, humble self-reflection. The deed itself as well as any motives lying beneath it would require close scrutiny.

As a complement to the work of *consideratio*, Gregory also encouraged believers to spend time in *contemplatio*. Only through contemplation—that is, of God—does knowledge and love for God grow, thus curbing autonomous self-love and -reliance. According to Purves (2001), Gregory held that *contemplatio* trained believers to "balance" between the two centers of human existence, "the spiritual and the carnal" (p. 61). In this conception of human life, Gregory's dependence on Platonist ontology is clear. Yet, his notion of "balance" reflects his concern for fostering a healthy approach to Christian spirituality and pastoral care.

Individuals who focus only on outward appearances, as the Pharisees exemplify, are more susceptible to self-deception. Taking up Gregory's theme of "balance," Oden (1984) observes the former's pastoral concern that his parishioners not shelter hidden motives under a veneer of virtue. Rather, he sought "to nurture in the parishioner an appropriate balance of excellent behaviors without the self-deception that invites vice to parade as virtue" (p. 56). By way of practical advice, Gregory (1978) encourages pastors to recognize that

> vices commonly masquerade as virtues. Often, for instance, a niggard passes himself off as frugal, while one who is prodigal conceals his character when he calls himself open-handed. Often inordinate laxity is believed to be kindness, and unbridled anger passes as the virtue of spiritual zeal. . . . Wherefore, it is necessary that the ruler of souls [i.e., pastor] discern with care and vigilance virtues from vices. (p. 78)

The duty of pastors, then, includes serving as spiritual director to those under their care.

Growth in godliness and virtue demands a balanced approach to self-examination. Due to our resistance to self-discovery, Gregory considers the pastor's role to be crucial in promoting positive change. Indeed, he regards self-deception to be "a constant tendency of the fallen will." The answer to our struggle, then, is pastorally guided "[r]eality based self-knowledge [as] one of the central aims of a healing process" (Oden, 1984, p. 58).

For this task, Gregory enumerates an extensive list of approaches to dealing with vice. Nearly half of his treatise is taken up with specific cases, each section falling under the heading "How to admonish . . ." this or that moral failing. In the end, Gregory's approach does not advance far beyond an early Christian cognitive-behavioral framework. Yet, his pastoral concern for individual growth in dipolar self-knowledge, through *consideratio* and *contemplatio*, represents a practical outworking of Augustinian theanthropology.

John Calvin, 1509–1564

Constructive revisions to premodern conceptions of self-knowledge, as we will see, share the historical stage with other less favorable developments. Modernist epistemology, with its insistence on the bifurcation of human knowing, stands among the least profitable ancillaries to Christian self-knowledge. John Calvin, whose theanthropology precedes the rupture that was to come, effectively summarizes premodern Christian thought. In many ways he relies on Augustine and Gregory in his recapitulation of Hellenist eudaimonism. In other words, Calvin, like his forebears regards human persons, as well as the means and ends of human self-knowledge, through a dipolar rather than tripolar lens. Nevertheless, Calvin as a "systems" thinker would bequeath to us an epistemological *method* that serves well to this day.

Calvin's approach to human self-knowledge entails a basic outline of three key points. Understood as parameters of eudaimonist or dipolar self-knowledge, these three serve to summarize a millennium of Christian thinking. For the first, according to Calvin, knowledge of God and knowledge of self are related reciprocally, each assuming the other in mutual entailment.[20] For human beings, as has been said, knowledge of God and knowledge of self are inseparably conjoined.

Warfield (1956) summarizes Calvin's thinking on this first point in terms of contingency:

> The knowledge of God is given in the very same act by which we know self. For when we know self, we must know it as it is: and that means we must know it as dependent, derived, imperfect, and responsible [i.e., respond-able] being. To know self implies, therefore, the co-knowledge with self of that on which it is dependent, from which it derives, by the standard of which its imperfection is revealed, to which it is responsible. Of course, such a knowledge of self postulates a knowledge of God, in contrast with whom alone do we ever truly know self. (p. 31)

20. Barth (1995) characterizes Calvin's first parameter as the "synthetic" knowledge of God and self (p. 163). Dowey (1994) terms it the "correlative" aspect, "by which we learn the intimate connection that exists between the knowledge of God and of ourselves" (p. 18).

No human person can veridically self-perceive by purely autonomous means. In order to rightly apprehend self—which is to say, the form and quality of one's own nature, capacities, and particularities—the right apprehension of God must also obtain.

Following Aristotle, who observed that human persons tend toward self-obfuscation, self-knowledge as Calvin saw it is contingent on a reflective other—or Other, to be precise.[21] In contrast to Aristotle, then, Calvin held that the proper "mirror" for self-perception is God. This metaphor of the "mirror," according to Torrance (1957), was a favorite of the Swiss Reformer. The vantage point, moreover, from which human persons may behold God is through the word of God and in the face of Jesus Christ. So, Calvin concludes,

> [I]t is evident that man never attains to a true self-knowledge until he have [sic] previously contemplated the face of God, and come down after such contemplation to look into himself. For (such is our innate pride) we always seem to ourselves just, and upright, and wise, and holy, until we are convinced, by clear evidence, of our injustice, vileness, folly, and impurity. Convinced, however, we are not, if we look to ourselves only, and not to the Lord also—he being the only standard by the application of which this conviction can be produced (p. 5).

Calvin's second parameter of dipolar self-knowledge concerns the nature of human knowing. As Torrance (1957) argues, knowledge of God and self bears an interpersonal or experiential, rather than propositional, quality. Calvin's theological system entails a diversity of objective content, so to speak, but the knowledge to which he aspired was inter-subjective—a coming to know God and self in close relational proximity. Grasping the distinction between objective and inter-subjective knowledge is critical for understanding Calvin's theanthropology. Dowey (1994) explains that such "knowledge . . . determines the existence of the knower" (p. 26).

---

21. Though Calvin's argument follows that of Augustine, whose own formulation amounts to a Christian reinterpretation of Platonist thought, it was Aristotle, Plato's chief interlocutor, who proposed the necessity of a mutual, intersubjective self-perception for growth in self-knowledge (Shields, 2016). In his *Magna Moralia* he argues that the bond of friendship provides the suitable preconditions within which we may perceive self: "[A]s we are, we are not able to see what we are from ourselves. . . . As, then, when we wish to see our own face, we do so by looking into a mirror, in the same way, when we wish to know ourselves, we can obtain that knowledge by looking at our friend. For the friend is, as we assert, another I" (2.15).

Whereas, a simple, objective knowledge of God may stimulate the intellect, but, as such, need not bring constructive light to self.

For Calvin, knowledge of God is subjective and interpersonal—a knowledge that arises, in other words, in the context of relationship. This higher order knowledge of God arouses a personal, existential self-knowledge—a *knowing as I am known* (see 1 Cor 13:12)—that transcends a simple, objective—i.e., propositional—knowledge of self. In view of this existential perspective of knowledge, Torrance (1957) concludes, "[Humanity] was created an intelligent being capable of response to and communication with God, and created such that his *true life* depends on the maintenance of that communication" (p. 45, my emphasis). Torrance further argues, following Calvin, that the knowledge of God is "not real" until and unless it stimulates a reciprocal knowledge of self (p. 13).

So, Calvin held that God, by means of God's self-disclosure—through his Logos—brings human beings to knowledge of himself and of themselves, modernist objections notwithstanding. As suggested by the nature of this knowledge, the end of such knowing is the transformation of self. This, then, is Calvin's third key parameter: coming to know God and self entails, for Calvin, the reformation of self into the likeness of God (see Champion, 1988; Charry, 1997).

The notion of self-knowledge as an end in itself, a gain that solely benefits the knower, is foreign to Calvin. Rather, as God intends, human persons are renewed and transformed by means of this inter-subjective knowing. On the other hand, for those who never know self-as-self-is-known, the renewal of existence (i.e., "eternal life") God offers will remain unclaimed. The "damage" done to self by sin cannot otherwise be healed. In this Calvin offers a proleptic admonition to a strictly humanist, self-serving pursuit of "wellbeing" through self-knowledge such as that implicit in modern depth psychologies (see Johnson, 2007).

According to Calvin's framework for dipolar self-knowledge, through God's Logos we may grow in awareness of our faults and failings before a holy God. Moreover, as self is known in divine relief, it is revealed to be constitutionally and functionally deficient by contrast (see Rom 3:23). The knowledge that self is less-than incites a dynamic of self-displeasure, which impels us toward the renewal, the life, we now know we need.

Calvin (2008) held the proper aim of self-knowledge to be eudaimonia, not through self-knowledge alone but through transformation. Along these lines, he concludes,

> When viewing our miserable condition since Adam's fall, all
> confidence and boasting are overthrown, we blush for shame,
> and feel truly humble. . . . In this way, we feel dissatisfied with
> ourselves, and become truly humble, while we are inflamed with
> new desires to seek after God, in whom each may regain those
> good qualities of which all are found to be utterly destitute. (p.
> 147)

In coming to know self-as-self-is-known, we find ourselves to be "utterly destitute." But the quest for transformation drives us back to our
Maker who alone is able to redeem and reinstate those "good qualities"
Calvin considered humanity had lost at the fall. The end of dipolar self-
knowledge, then, is a renewed existence, a transformed life given by God.

Calvin's theanthropology reifies the ancient eudaimonist framework, while maintaining Augustine's Christian innovations. He faithfully
retreads the ancient pathway of self-improvement through self-knowledge. Notable distinctions include the sophistication of Calvin's "system"
as compared with Aristotle's basic conception of dipolar self-knowledge
and also the identity of other/Other. In addition, whereas, the two poles
of Aristotelian self-knowledge fall along a horizontal axis, Augustine and
Calvin rotate this dyad by ninety degrees. Dipolar Christian frameworks
hold God to be the reflective Other.

In eudaimonist conceptions of human personhood, the emphasis
falls on individual self-improvement through dipolar, reflective self-
knowledge. Human beings do not know themselves as God knows them.
As we come to know God in relationship with him, a dissatisfaction with
self arises for which Christ offers relief. Humanity's fall from God resulted in a disconformity to our divine design. The healing needed for
our dis-ease with self, then, is relationship with God. By means of God's
self-disclosure, we are drawn into an inter-subjective dynamic by which
self is transformed. Charry's (1997) term for this process, "theo-therapy,"
involves a two-fold "destruction of the self in preparation for the recon-
struction of a new self" (p. 215; cf. Gal 2:20). This principle, according to
Charry, lies at the heart of Calvin's anthropology and psychology.

Calvin believed, following the Scriptures, that fallen human beings
are born estranged from our Maker. So long as this state of affairs persists, we remain similarly cut off from veridical knowledge of self. Yet, as
we come to see God in the mirror of his Logos, we enter a renewed state
of existence wherein we experience a mutual knowing and being known

by God. In this way self comes to be transformed from broken and estranged to renewed in the image and likeness of God (see Eph 4:24).

Richard Baxter, 1615–1691

Following their break from the Roman church, the dissenting voices of English Puritanism applied their Reformational approach to theology with particular emphasis on pietistic spirituality and a renewed commitment to principled pastoral care (Deckard, 2010; Kapic & Gleason, 2004; Lewis, 1997; Packer, 2010; Yuille, 2013). Along these lines, Johnson (2007) regards the Puritans as "basically pastoral theologians" noting the emphasis within their writings "to comfort and encourage believers in their soul struggles" (p. 61). On the question of whether human beings might come to veridical self-knowledge apart from the knowledge of God, the Puritans were, with Calvin, decidedly skeptical.[22]

Perhaps more than any other expression of Christian spirituality, English Puritanism endeavored especially to root out and undermine barriers to self-knowledge (Badgett, 2018b). Motivated by concern for sincerity in the Christian life and growth in personal holiness, the Puritans assiduously—at times, ruthlessly—scoured their hearts for signs of hidden sin and self-deceit. Packer (2010) observes, "The Puritans ripped up consciences in the pulpit and urged self-trial in the [prayer] closet," in service to the twin tasks of "self-suspicion" and "self-examination" (p. 117).[23] They held as their charter for this practice of self-scrutiny the

22. In language perhaps shocking and foreign in the context of postmodern Western Christendom's regnant therapeutic deism, the Puritans excoriated the fallen human heart as hopelessly wicked and deceitful—full of "unsavory nastiness, odious ugliness" (Dyke, 2013, p. 14). Indeed, it is nothing less than "the fountain from whence all the streams of corruption flow," "the womb in which all these monsters are conceived," and "the shell in which these cockatrices are hatched" (p. 235; see Isa 59:5). The heart is not to be trusted, as it is "the greatest supplanter, the most crafty and subtle cheat of all . . . than which nothing is more treacherous and false" (Flavel, 2012, pp. 30–31; see Gen 6:5). The Puritans, moreover, sought to undermine confidence in individual self-perception: "There is almost nothing *but* deceit in our hearts; and therefore a godly man is watchful over his own heart" (Greenhill, 2010, p. 9; emphasis original; see Prov 4:23; 7:25). Veridical self-knowledge they considered to be among "the first and highest rank of difficulties" for practitioners of "true religion" (Flavel, 2012, p. 4; see Jer 17:9).

23. Packer (2010) further notes, "[I]t seems undeniable that the Puritans' passion for spiritual integrity and moral honesty before God, their fear of hypocrisy in themselves as well as in others, and the humble self-distrust that led them constantly to

Bible's teaching on the fallen human self and its tendency toward self-blindness and self-deception.

In 1656, Richard Baxter published an importunate call to biblical and holistic pastoral care known today by its abbreviated title, *The Reformed Pastor* (1974). For 350 years it has remained in print and today stands as one of the classics of the Puritan age (Lim, 2004). Baxter's principal agenda within the treatise, Purves (2001) notes, is to call Puritan ministers to a rigorous and disciplined pastoral ministry that advanced Reformational piety within the church as well as the home.[24] Like Gregory before him, Baxter sought to offer inductive guidance to pastors for the sake of their parishioners. Baxter's admonition, as with Gregory's instruction to his own peers, encouraged his fellow ministers not to neglect their own work of self-examination.

Along these lines, Baxter (1974) laments, "Too many [ministers] do somewhat for other men's souls, while they seem to forget that they have souls of their own to regard" (p. 134). It is all too easy, he notes, to preach on the dangers of self-ignorance and self-deception while remaining personally self-deceived:

> That those ordinances of God should be the occasion of our delusion, which are instituted to be the means of our conviction and salvation! and that while we hold the looking-glass of the gospel to others, to show them the face and aspect of their souls, we should either look on the back part of it ourselves, where we can see nothing, or turn it aside, that it may misrepresent us to ourselves! (p. 55)

The preacher of righteousness, Baxter laments, runs the risk of neglecting to apply the Scriptures as intended—personnally.

Like Calvin, Baxter considered the Logos to be God's mirror ("looking-glass") revealing self as it truly is. When improperly displayed, the mirror could serve as a pious-seeming fig leaf behind which self could hide. Such practices Baxter decried as hypocrisy. To preach but not to

---

check whether they had not lapsed into religious play-acting before men with hearts that had gone cold towards God, *has no counterpart in the modern-day evangelical ethos*" (p. 217; emphasis original).

24. Baxter specifically emphasized the need for catechism and church discipline as means of engendering proper Christian piety within the church. Moreover, he challenged pastors to imitate his example of visiting the homes of his parishioners on a regular basis to inquire into their spiritual state and encourage their growth in holiness by various practical means (Packer, 2012).

practice he held to be tantamount to what Jesus condemned among the religious class in his day (see Matt 23). Baxter sought to influence this tendency by exhorting ministers to "be humble self-accusers" (p. 135). For the sake of avoiding hypocritical self-righteousness, he appealed to "every man to exercise a strict jealousy and search of his own heart" (p. 142).

The relationship of self-knowledge and self-ignorance figures even more prominently in Baxter's (2010) memorably entitled treatise on 2 Cor 13:5,[25] *On the Mischiefs of Self-Ignorance and the Benefits of Self-Acquaintance.* The familiar formula of eudaimonist self-knowledge he articulates with pith: "He that is a stranger to himself . . . is a stranger to God, and to all that might denominate him wise or happy" (p. 41). For Baxter, then, eudaimonia—the state of being "wise" and "happy"—comes through acquaintance with God and self.

As Gregory sought to apply Augustinian theanthropology in practical, pastoral terms, so also Baxter carried Calvin's thinking toward praxis (see Houston, 2000). In language similar to the Swiss Reformer, Baxter likewise considered self-knowledge to be mutual and reciprocal, the key to which is the Logos of God:

> The knowledge of ourselves as men, doth greatly conduce to our knowledge of God. Here God is known but darkly, and as in a glass, and by his image, and not as face to face. And, except his incarnate and his written Word, what glass revealeth him so clearly as the soul of man? We bear a double image of our Maker: his natural image in the nature of our faculties; and his moral image in their holy qualifications, in the nature of grace, and grace of the new man. By knowing ourselves, it is easy to know that there is a God; and it much assisteth us to know what he is, not only in his attributes and relations, but even in the Trinity itself. (p. 64)

Among the chief "hindrances" to true self-knowledge Baxter includes two vices. The first he holds to be the sin of pride,[26] "which strongly inclineth men to think well of themselves, and to desire that all others

---

25. "Know ye not yourselves" (ASV).

26. Baxter (1974) considered that the sin of pride all too often leads otherwise godly individuals to think more highly of themselves than they ought (p. 137; see Rom 12:3); but with deep psychological insight he notes, "So far indeed doth pride contradict itself, that, conscious of its own deformity, it often borrows the homely dress of humility" (146).

do so too" (p. 362). In concert with the second—an idolatrous, countertherapeutic "self-love"—Baxter observes that pride "so blindeth men that
they can see no great evil in themselves" (p. 369). The twin epistemic
defeaters of pride and self-love, for Baxter, derail any hope of genuine
self-knowledge. One's pursuit, when obstructed by these barriers, can
make little progress toward veridical self-knowledge. Self-improvement,
the eudaimonist endgame, will remain elusive. Nevertheless, Baxter is
concerned to engender its humble pursuit out of love for Christ and a
desire to more closely resemble him.

Søren Kierkegaard, 1813–1855

Kierkegaard[27] (1967) held the "absolute need for God" to be foundational
to grasping human personhood and the quest of self-knowledge (p. 53).
Our existence remains incomplete, unfulfilled without him. Following Calvin's three parameters, Kierkegaard propounds a framework for
knowledge of self that is dipolar, intersubjective, and transformational.
Concerning the first point, Kierkegaard considers divine self-disclosure
to be the sole means of veridical knowledge of self. In regard to human
potential for autonomous self-apprehension, he concludes,

> Paganism required: Know yourself. Christianity declares: No,
> that is provisional—know yourself—and then look at yourself
> in the Mirror of the Word in order to know yourself properly.
> No true self-knowledge without God-knowledge or [without
> standing] before God. To stand before the Mirror means to
> stand before God. (Kierkegaard, 1975, p. 3902)

---

27. The philosophical writings of Søren Kierkegaard pose numerous exegetical
challenges. His meaning in any given context is so often obscured by the complexity
and subtlety of his thought, to say nothing of his syntax, and the difficulty of tracing
threads of argument woven throughout an extensive oeuvre. Regrettably, Kierkegaard
is sometimes mistaken for a secular humanist because of the radical subjectivity of
his anthropological framework. A fair reading of his less rigorously philosophical
writings, on the other hand, paints a clearer picture (Lippett, 2016). Johnson (2007)
situates Kierkegaard alongside "Augustine and Calvin" arguing that he "recognized
further that the construction of the Christian's self was a reflexive *project*, an interac-
tive, developmental process involving both forms of knowledge [of God and of self]"
(p. 430; emphasis original). Johnson further identifies Kierkegaard's defense of the
pursuit of Christian self-knowledge—what the latter terms "inwardness"—as "one of
the greatest legacies in the Christian tradition" (p. 430).

Human beings suffer from a noetic impotence that calls our epistemic judgment into question. Simply put, we are unable to see clearly enough to know self without divine aid.

On the other hand, the "mirror" of divine perfection—God's Logos—enlightens an otherwise darkened self-perception (Eph 1:8). For this reason, Kierkegaard (1991) exhorts those who gaze into the "mirror" of the Scriptures to affirm, "It is I to whom it [the text] is speaking, it is I about whom it is speaking" (p. 40).[28] A Kierkegaardian hermeneutics avoids the objectivist error of reading with "impersonality and objectivity." This amounts to looking at self with closed eyes. Whereas, to approach the mirror with "devoutness and fear of God," no longer distanced from "personality, the subjective," allows the Logos to speak inter-subjectively (p. 39).

Having become estranged from God by the fall, human beings tend toward self-blindness. When considering the Logos of God, we eschew accurate self-perception by means of our "impersonality" and "objectivity." On the other hand, "Truth," Kierkegaard (1992) concludes, "is subjectivity" (p. 189).[29] With respect to King David's case of epistemic blindness, Kierkegaard (1991) reflects,

> [O]therwise so devout and God-fearing, . . . [he] can maintain so much impersonality (objectivity) that he can go on living and pretend as if nothing has happened, that he can listen to the prophet's tale and pretend as if nothing has happened—until the prophet, weary of this impersonality and objectivity, . . . uses his authority and says: Thou art the man. (p. 39)

28. Kierkegaard's radically subjective hermeneutic should be distinguished from that of modern existentialism and secular postmodernism (contra Schaeffer, 1998) since it arises within an otherwise thoroughly Christian epistemology wherein the knowledge of God relates reciprocally with self-knowledge (see Tietjen, 2016, esp. Chapter 1). Kierkegaard rejects a false, objectivist dichotomy that would set the Bible up as either "about" God or us. Rather, he is following the implications of his theological anthropology: what the Scriptures teach us about God must surely bear on those created in his image. To be sure, if Scripture does not speak to us and reveal us as we are, then it can hardly make demands of us!

29. He should not be understood to suggest, as does postmodern subjectivism, that truth is relative. Rather, he is arguing for the need for a subjective—i.e., personal and affective—openness to God. It is one thing, in other words, for David to objectively condemn the guilty man for his sin; it is quite another for him to recognize that he *is* the guilty man and repent. This is Kierkegaard's "reveille" (Barth, 2011, p. 98), by which he sought to awaken Christendom from its modernist, objectivist somnolence.

Nathan, Kierkegaard observes, serves as the necessary impetus David needed to overcome his dissociation and self-deception. He needed to see himself as he truly was to be delivered from who he had become. Nathan held up a mirror.

Christ, according to Kierkegaard, is the ultimate epistemic key. As the incarnate Logos, he reveals God to us. As the only sinless human being—the quintessential image bearer—he discloses a perfectible humanity. Through him, then, we come to know both God-as-he-is and self-as-self-is. Along these lines, Kierkegaard (1997) reflects,

> Alas, who does know himself? Is it not exactly this to which the earnest and honest self-examination finally leads as its last and truest, this humble confession: "Who knows his errors? From my hidden faults cleanse thou me" (Psalm 19:12). And when a person examines his relation to Christ, who then is the human being who completely knows his faithlessness, who the human being who would dare to think that in his very self-examination there could not be faithlessness? Therefore you do not find rest this way. So, then, rest; then seek rest for your soul in the blessed comfort that, even if we are faithless, he still is faithful. (p. 287)

So, Christ is the means of self-knowledge for Kierkegaard (see Evans, 1990). Moreover, "rest . . . comfort," both entailments of eudaimonia, grow from "relation to Christ." Autonomous self-examination can only counterfeit these benefits.

To a greater degree than Calvin, to be sure, Kierkegaard develops the implications of interpersonal subjectivity viz., the believer's knowledge of self-before-God. True self-knowledge, he maintains, demands the individual "come to oneself in self-knowledge and before God as nothing before him, yet infinitely, unconditionally engaged" (Kierkegaard, 1991, p. 104). Furthermore, Kierkegaard (1980) argues that self-knowledge is a vital aspect of *becoming* a self:

> The law for the development of the self with respect to knowing, insofar as it is the case that the self becomes itself, is that the increase of knowledge corresponds to the increase of self-knowledge, that the more the self knows, the more it knows itself. If this does not happen, the more knowledge increases, the more it becomes a kind of inhuman knowledge, in the obtaining of which a person's self is squandered, much the way men were squandered on building pyramids. (p. 31; see Mark 8:36)

Human persons without knowledge of self-before-God can never, then, be truly human.[30]

Self-knowledge without a divine frame of reference amounts to little more than speculative philosophy (see Lippett, 2016). Never to have known self-before-God is the "greatest hazard of all" and tantamount to "losing the self" (Kierkegaard, 1980, p. 32). Those who have "no self before God" can be only merely "self-seeking" (p. 35). Without God, they find neither God nor the self they autonomously seek to become.

Kierkegaard's (1980) conception of personhood and more specifically his notion of an incipient human self correlates closely with his psychology of sin. A "sickness unto death" lies upon the estranged self, one that arouses a "despair" within (p. 22; see Marsh, 1987). This sickness is the weight of unrequited longing to become a self. The despair of impotent self-seeking rests upon all who know not self-before-God. This universal psychopathology has affected the whole human race. Its cure, "faith," flows from mutual, dipolar intersubjectivity: "in relating itself to itself and in willing to be itself, the self rests transparently in the power that established it" (p. 14). So then, "despair" may have the salutary effect of driving the individual to seek its cure in Christ. He alone, Kierkegaard maintains, can bring human persons to wholeness of self.[31]

In conceiving of the human self as primarily a "reflexive" relation (see Hannay, 1987), Kierkegaard further develops Calvin's notion of existential self-knowledge. Self relates reflexively to self only in right relation to God. Further, this relation is both static and dynamic, present and incipient. Moreover, in self's active, reflexive relating of self to self-before-God, self is becoming *itself*. He explains,

> The self is a relation that relates itself to itself or is the relation's
> relating itself to itself in the relation; the self is not the relation
> but is the relation's relating itself to itself. A human being is a
> synthesis of the infinite and the finite, of the temporal and the
> eternal, of freedom and necessity, in short, a synthesis. A syn-
> thesis is a relation between two. . . . The human self is such a

30. Kierkegaard would likely have found supremely ironic the degree to which modern philosophy and psychology have esteemed his writings, while simultaneously evincing a profound blindness to the strident polemic he levels against them (see, e.g., Kilborne, 1999; Mullen, 1988). Regrettably, modern willingness to "hear" him on the matter of his radical subjectivity does not likewise extend to his equally radical Christian theism.

31. For Kierkegaard, this amounts to "the deepest form of self-knowledge and the most valuable gift of grace" (Lippett, 2016, p. 222).

> derived, established relation, a relation that relates itself to itself
> and in relating itself to itself relates itself to another. (Kierkeg-
> aard, 1980, pp. 13–14)

This admittedly obtuse passage encapsulates the dialectical tension of dipolar self-knowledge. To put it another way: only in relating to itself does self come into relationship with God.

Hannay (1987) further explains "reflexive relation" as self's "conforming itself to . . . [Kierkegaard's] standing assumption—that there is a God and a need to stand before that God" (p. 31). Despair, the existential psychopathology of the estranged self, grows out of human alienation from God *and* self. Kierkegaard's paradoxical "God-man," on the other hand, offers the restoration of human persons to God *and to themselves*. Christ is, in himself, the means of self's relation to both. As such, the incarnation, not the crucifixion, instantiates God's agapic disposition toward fallen humanity: "No teaching on earth," Kierkegaard argues, "has ever really brought God and man so close together" (1980, p. 117).

Kierkegaard's emphasis on individual subjectivity, especially in his headier philosophical oeuvre, bears a strong eudaimonist aroma. Evans (2002) argues, however, that Kierkegaard is hardly the "arch-individualist" he has been portrayed to be. Although he is the most significant relation viz., self, "God is not the only 'other' to which selves can relate to and thereby become selves, though God remains the crucial 'other' for selfhood in the highest sense" (p. 79). Kierkegaard's (1998) discourses on Christian love, as Evans also notes, set out a more "social" understanding of human relations. Christian philosopher and ethicist, Wolterstorff (2015), regards Kierkegaard's ethics as agapist rather than eudaimonist (see pp. 111–12). For this reason, perhaps the Danish thinker serves best as a transitional figure between this section and the next.

Social personhood and the knowledge of self

The connection between Hellenist anthropology and ethics has been well-documented in contemporary literature (Annas, 1993; Cooper, 1986; Wolterstorff, 2010). Whether specific links can be drawn between ancient metaphysics and morality will be subject to a more substantial burden of proof. In what follows, I rely on the work of paleohistorical specialists. While care must be taken in every generation to carefully balance revelation and contextualization, it has been reliably proposed that Christian theanthropology—in both ontological and ethical implications—rested too heavily on Greek categories. What follows in this section, then, is a basic overview of particular critiques modern scholars have raised in regard to Hellenist anthropology.

Following Plato, classical Greek anthropology viewed human beings as a duality of "substance" and "particulars" (Silverman, 2002). Moreover, Plato considered that the substance of the immaterial human soul held ontological priority over the material body. Growth in self-knowledge, according to Plato, amounted to one's increasing awareness and appreciation of this grand metaphysical reality, and one that, with the proper application of virtuous wisdom would redound in individual and social benefit.[32]

Aristotle suggested that self-knowledge is a purely anthropocentric pursuit, yet one that depends on the mirroring assistance of an other. The beneficiary of this pursuit, in terms of its ethical outcomes, is the individual, though considering Plato's perspective on the *polis*, we may suppose that individual beneficiaries of eudaimonia would work toward a more just, more virtuous society. Nevertheless, according to the ancient schema, relationality is an accident of shared ontology. As Aristotle states, "[T]he great and the small, and the like, must be relative to something; but the relative is least of all things a real thing or substance, and is posterior to quality and quantity; and the relatives are accidents of quantity" (*Metaphysics*, 1088a21–25). Relationality is, therefore, *not* the primary, nor even central, determinant of human personhood. Nor does it necessarily offer sure means of self-knowing.

To varying degrees, as evidenced in the so-called philosophical "turn to relationality," modern thinking would question the fundamental premises of Hellenist ontology and ethics (Grenz, 2001). For Shults (2003), Aristotle's appropriation of a Platonist metaphysic ultimately led to an unwarranted "orthodoxy in Western philosophy" that considered "the relations of a thing to other things [as] not essential to defining or knowing what that thing is" (p. 15).[33] In other words, the Platonist priori-

---

32. As typified in Plato's cave allegory.

33. I will argue, with Shults, that self-knowledge, as with all other kinds of knowledge, requires relationality. But this is a far cry from dismissing the ontological particularity of things, as Shults appears intent on doing. Shults's relational anthropology, regrettably, tips too far in the opposite direction of substance dualism. In his historical outline of the "turn to relationality," drawing on the diverse findings of modern philosophy and psychology, he concludes, "we are 'made' for relational knowing and that the world is 'made' for being known relationally" (p. 58). In the final analysis, however,

tization of substance and particulars contributed to a subsequent emphasis in Christian thinking on the constitutive aspects of human being and doing. The result of this ontological bent is a privileging of the individual as sole agent and principal beneficiary of self-knowledge. Furthermore, as even secular ethicists have observed, it risks the instrumental coopting of others in the individual's pursuit of eudaimonia.

By contrast, the turn to relationality, as evidenced in the Christian theanthropologies of Barth and Bonhoeffer in particular, contributed to a shift in ethical thinking toward the *social* means and end(s) of self-knowledge (see Green, 1999). At the heart of biblical ethics, relationship—more specifically, love for God and others—provides an outline for rightly apprehending the telos of human existence (see, e.g., Mark 12:33; 1 John 4:20). As we might expect, the benefits of relationship to God are often articulated in expressly eschatological terms. Of note in this regard is Jesus' inverted axiology in the Beatitudes (Matt 5:3–12).

Jesus proclaims a happiness that is yet to come: "Happy are the mourners for they *shall* be comforted" (Matt 5:4). In other words, "you will finally be blessed by God," in a future God has prepared for you, "if, for the present, you 'hunger and thirst' after such blessings" (see Matt 5:6; cf. Matt 25:34). This promise is reserved for those who deny themselves and take up their cross in the here and now (Luke 9:23). We ought not conclude that God withholds all wellbeing for the duration of the present age (see Luke 18:30). Still, a biblical ethics decries the pursuit immediate gain, if to do so might compromise one's faithfulness to God. The pursuit of Christian self-knowledge *will* redound to the benefit of the individual; yet, for the present age, an agapist ethics more faithfully articulates the biblical—or better, Christiform—model.

I will repeatedly return to my proposal that Christian ethics, as with ontology, should be balanced and dialogical. Agapism and eudaimonism are no more opposed, I argue, than particularity and relationality. Rather, each balances and informs the other. Early Christian conceptions of human personhood, as we have already noted, rightly identified the reciprocal mutuality of the knowledge of God and self. At the same time, they evince an incommensurate appreciation of the role human persons play in affecting—and effecting—self-perception and self-evaluation (see McFadyen, 1990).[34] Modern philosophy's "turn to relationality" offers some

relationality depends on particularity. Otherwise, to what are relations related?

34. Modern secular psychology and psychotherapy have certainly contributed to this way of thinking as well (see Grenz, 2001).

needed correction for this imbalance. Yet, to dispense with the former will result in an equally unbalanced formulation.

Every historical perspective surveyed within the preceding section holds that veridical knowledge of self obtains in the context of individual relationship with God. Christian approaches over the last hundred years, by contrast, have sought to balance this individualistic formulation by entailing relationship between human beings as secondary, instrumental means of self-knowing. Human self-knowing is not, according to relational theanthropologies, a strictly dipolar affair. Only when balanced by both our individual *and* social aspects are human persons generally, and individual selves particularly, best known.

Christian theanthropologies since Kierkegaard have come, to varying degrees, to stress the covenantal and relational aspects of human being and knowing over and above the constitutive and substantial (Grenz, 2001). Often, relational ontologies and ethics find their basis in trinitarian theology (see, e.g., Zizioulas, 2007, 1991). Such approaches offer a constructive critique of individualist conceptions. Yet, what is finally needed is not to exchange one unhelpful dichotomy for another, but to foster a more balanced theanthropology. A balanced ontology will regard human beings in both their particular and relational aspects. A balanced ethics, moreover, will recognize that eudaimonia and agape—personal happiness and love for others—relate dialectically and hierarchically. This is to say that final, eschatological happiness comes to those who pursue love for God and for others as their greatest, highest aim.

Karl Barth, 1886–1968

By way of a conceptual bridge with the preceding section, I note that Price (2002) observes a close affinity on at least four key points in the theological anthropologies of Kierkegaard and Barth. First, like the Danish philosopher, Barth would adopt an epistemology that links the propositional with the personal. Knowledge of God, in other words, and knowledge of self are inseparable. For both men, "truth is subjectivity," would signify that truth "resides in an existing subject" (Price, 2002, p. 88; cf. Eph 4:21; 1 John 2:4). Second, Barth recapitulates Kierkegaard in appropriating a Calvinist-Augustinian epistemology of encounter. We come to know ourselves—as human beings generally, and especially, as individuals in need of redemption and reconciliation to God—through divine revelation.

The encounter made possible by God's self-disclosure—his Logos—bears immeasurable epistemic implication for our self-understanding.

Third, Price observes that, for both men, the cardinal means by which God effects human self-knowing is through his self-revelation in the person and work of Christ. On this point, Barth (1960) echoes Kierkegaard,

> Jesus Christ, as [the] Mediator and Reconciler between God and man, is also the *Revealer* of them both. We do not need to engage in a free-ranging investigation to seek out and construct who and what God truly is, and who and what man truly is, but only to read the truth about both where it resides, namely, in the fullness of their togetherness, their covenant which proclaims itself in Jesus Christ. (p. 47, emphasis original)

Fourth, Price considers that Kierkegaard and Barth both stress the priority of relationship in their conceptions of human rationality. However, whereas Kierkegaard situates his paradigm for this relationality within the intrapsychic "system" of the self as it relates to itself and to God, "Barth [interprets] human rationality . . . in terms of the capacity to form relations to God and others" (Price, 2002, p. 89). Where Barth's theanthropological system expands on Kierkegaard is precisely with respect to the priority of relationality between self and others—that is, with one's fellow human beings. His primary rationale for a social understanding of the self is humanity's status as image bearers of the triune God (see Grenz, 2001; Houston, 2000; Miell, 1989).

Discerning Kierkegaardian existentialist stubble in the brickwork of secular philosophers like Heidegger and Sartre, Barth would eventually come to identify what he perceived to be a blind spot in Kierkegaard's theanthropological system.[35] Though Barth (2011) did acknowledge the latter's influence on his early work,[36] he would in later life decry what he perceived to be a "pronounced holy individualism" (p. 99). In his

35. Barth's critique of Kierkegaardian theanthropology, as I suggest in the previous section, may be somewhat overdrawn.

36. Looking back on his earlier works, especially his *Epistle to the Romans*, Barth (2011) would acknowledge his own participation in the early twentieth-century "Kierkegaard Renaissance": "What attracted us particularly to [Kierkegaard], what we rejoiced in, and what we learned, was the criticism, so unrelenting in its incisiveness, with which he attacked so much: all the speculation that blurred the infinite qualitative difference between God and man, all the aesthetic playing down of the absolute claims of the Gospel and of the necessity to do it justice by personal decision; in short, all the attempts to make the scriptural message innocuous" (p. 98).

extension and development of Kierkegaardian self–God relationality, Barth (2010) would come to understand human nature through two relational dyads: (1) the paradigmatic I–Thou encounter of the individual and God effectuated in the person and work of Christ; and (2) the I–Thou encounter between human beings created in his image, the latter being both constitutive and regulative for human be-ing. Barth regarded the horizontal axis of relationality to be analogous with and contingent upon the first (see III/1, p. 185). "God exists in relationship and fellowship," he explains; "God created man in His own image, in correspondence with His own being and essence. . . . God is in relationship, and so too is the man created by Him" (III/2, p. 324). Barth's Christology, then, reinforced his trinitarian conception in that Christ's relatedness to God and to humanity serves as the image—"the sign given to humanity"—of what it means to be truly human (III/2, p. 222).

Barth (2010) considered that we human beings come to know ourselves by means of our relatedness to God through Spirit-mediated union with Christ and *also* as we reflectively self-perceive our shared image-bearing status with other human beings. Self-knowledge for Kierkegaard, by contrast, comes through the inward deepening, so-called, of the individual standing in faithful relationship to Christ. For Barth this essentially dipolar model needed balancing by the third epistemic pole of human-to-human relationality. On this point he concludes,

> Every supposed humanity which is not radically and from the very first fellow-humanity is inhumanity. At this point a distinction must be made *a limine*, and humanity must be protected against its decisive and definitive destruction. If we take away fellow-man from the picture of man, and describe the latter as a being which is alien, opposed or casual in relation to him, we have not merely given an inadequate or partially false representation of man, but described a different being altogether. (III/2, p. 228)

Barthian theanthropology regards self-knowledge as the epistemic fruit of two onto-relational axes—the vertical and the horizontal—the foundational axiom of which can be expressed in the statement, "I am in encounter" (III/2, p. 246). Growth in self-understanding obtains in the context of one's relatedness to God and also to other human beings. As we grow and learn who we are, our knowing and being known occurs socially. This reciprocal and dialogical relatedness, he avers, is initiated by "openness" to others:

> [W]here openness obtains, humanity begins to occur. To the ex-
> tent that we move out of ourselves, not refusing to know others
> or being afraid to be known by them, our existence is human.
> . . . The duality into which we enter when we encounter one
> another directly and not indirectly, revealed and not concealed
> as man with man; the participation which we grant one another
> by the very fact that we see and do not not see one another, and
> let ourselves be seen and not unseen by one another, these are
> the first and indispensable steps in humanity. (III/2, p. 251)

Reciprocal openness to others,[37] according to Barthian theanthropology, leads to a mutual self-knowing as self knows that other knows
self, and so on, in recursive regress (Miell, 1989). The coming to and
becoming of the self-in-relation occurs in the context of mutual awareness and agapic regard through reflection and exchange (see McFadyen,
1990). This does not mean that selfhood is ontologically identical to or
equivalent with relationship. Rather, relationality itself is possible precisely because of the idiosyncratic particularity conferred by God upon
self and other, I and Thou. Given "I am" and "you are," it follows that "I
am in encounter." As in Calvin's mirror of the word/Word, image bearers, though fallen and sinful, possess a contingent, correlative capacity to
reflect and, thereby, come to know one another. Our human capacity for
mutual reflectivity, I hasten to add, will likely be as finite and flawed as
human relationships tend to be (see Prov 27:19 NRSV).

Dietrich Bonhoeffer, 1906–1945

There is ample evidence that Barth's favorable reading of Dietrich Bonhoeffer would shape certain of his theanthropological innovations (see
Green, 2006, 1999; Greggs, 2016).[38] In particular, Bonhoeffer's christo-

---

37. Barth lists four criteria for human encounter, of which openness is the first.
The second consists of dialogue—that is, a reciprocal verbal exchange, a giving and
receiving of speech (III/2, p. 253). The third criterion requires a willingness to "render
mutual assistance in the act of being" (p. 260). In other words, speech should result
in action in aid of the other. Fourth and finally, to qualify as an act of basic humanity,
encounter between self and other must engage the heart: "We gladly see and are seen;
we gladly speak and listen; we gladly receive and offer assistance" (p. 265). This genuine concern for others, for Barth, does not amount to Christian love as specified in
the New Testament, but rather to our shared status as image-bearers (see pp. 274–75).

38. So, e.g., Bird (1981) cites Bonhoeffer as having first identified the connection
between male–female sexuality as a relational analogue of the imago dei. Grenz (2001)

logical approach to personhood may have made something of an impact on Barth (see esp. Green, 2006). More so than Barth, his younger counterpart concerned himself with the ethical implications of his theanthropology. Seeing a tendency among continental theologians, Barth among them, toward rarefied and abstract formulations, Bonhoeffer sought instead "to move theology to a world of persons, communities, historical decisions, and ethical relationships" (Green, 1999, p. 28). He labored, in other words, to dress his theanthropology in human flesh.

Bonhoeffer's practical and pastoral bent is evident in his earliest works where he defines "individual" personhood in terms of an ethical relatedness to "other." By doing so, Bonhoeffer (1998) rejected essentially post-Kantian metaphysical categories in favor of a socially construed onto-ethical personhood:

> [T]he metaphysical concept of the individual is defined without mediation, whereas the ethical concept of the person is a definition based on ethical-social interaction. From the ethical perspective, human beings do not exist "unmediated" qua spirit in and of themselves, but only in responsibility vis-à-vis an "other." (p. 50, emphasis original)

Bonhoeffer presumes that "social ontic-ethical basic-relations of persons" define human personhood (p. 50; emphasis original). Social basic-relations, for Bonhoeffer, finally determine the ontological and ethical bounds of I and You—self and other. As a consequence of his shift toward a social understanding of personhood, Bonhoeffer entails his ethics with his epistemology (Elliston, 2016). Human being and knowing, in other words, must inform and impel human doing.

In consideration of what Bonhoeffer regards as the pretense of secular self-knowledge, he regularly strikes a polemical tone. Human estrangement from God, induced and perpetuated by our sin, provokes in us an idolatrous quest for reflexive, autonomous self-understanding and self-actualization. "All knowledge," he concludes, "including particularly γνῶθι σεαυτόν, seeks to establish the ultimate self-justification of human beings" (Bonhoeffer, 1996, p. 138). In observing the modern self's fallen hubris, Bonhoeffer (2005) concludes, "Knowing good and evil in disunion with the origin, human beings become self-reflective. Their life now consists in understanding themselves, just as in the origin it was knowing God. Gaining self-knowledge is the essence and goal of life" (p.

---

notes that Barth cites Bonhoeffer favorably on this point (p. 294).

308). Zimmermann (2004), reflecting on Bonhoeffer's dim view of fallen humanity, considers the "human preoccupation with the idea of self-knowledge . . . [to be] a result of the Fall" indicative of "a deep disunity" within the human condition (p. 292).

As with every other historical figure surveyed here, Bonhoeffer holds autonomous self-knowledge to be a fatally misguided enterprise. In a clear indictment of secular depth psychologies, Bonhoeffer (2005) charges, "Seeking self-knowledge is the never-ending attempt of human beings to overcome their disunion with themselves through thought, and through unceasing self-differentiation, to find unity with themselves" (p. 308). True self-understanding, for Bonhoeffer, comes only in relation to God-in-Christ. Christianly understood, human personhood and the knowledge of self can only be had as benefits of our reconciliation to him:

> [O]nly those who have been placed into the truth can under-
> stand themselves in truth. Having been placed into the truth,
> they may now come to understand themselves in that fash-
> ion—precisely as a foreshadowing of their re-creation, of their
> "being known" by God. That is to say, they may now recognize
> themselves as having been created anew from untruth for truth.
> (Bonhoeffer, 1996, p. 181)

In clearer and more consistent terms than Barth, Bonhoeffer regards believers' faith-enacted, Spirit-mediated union with Christ as the means of tripolar self-knowing (Green, 1999). Coming to know self occurs, moreover, as we participate in a dynamic, voluntaristic imaging *of* Christ. Bonhoeffer's theological anthropology, then, more directly implicates ethical responsiveness to Christ's person and work as both the means and end of Christian self-knowledge. This crucial point is less evident in Barth (2010; though, cf. Webster, 1995).

The human capacity for image-bearing, according to Bonhoeffer, can never be abstracted from the call to follow Christ, to embody his cruciform love towards others, and to pursue deeper fellowship through the indwelling Spirit with God and within the body of Christ (see McFadyen, 1990). Through participation in Christ, we enact a christocentric ethical disposition characterized by loving self-sacrifice. This agapic ethical dialogue follows both a vertical and a horizontal relational axis.

Conclusion to Part I

As we shall see in the chapters to come, Christology informs and establishes every aspect of human being, knowing, and doing. Christ's person and work provides the surest means of apprehending God's design for human personhood as well as the ethical implications of self-knowledge. Indeed, Christ exists as the unique, yet archetypal, human instantiation of the knowing, loving relationality in which the Father makes much of the Son, the Son makes much of the Father, and the Spirit celebrates and effectuates their glorious relationship.

For human beings, the basis of veridical self-knowledge follows from Christology, in that Christ is the final means and end of genuine agapic relationality. He is the One who, through the Spirit, perichoretically effectuates interpersonal self-knowing in otherwise fallen, self-deceived individuals. Among other things, eternal life amounts to Christ's invitation to human beings to overcome barriers to the knowledge of God, self, and others that have accumulated due to our estrangement from God. More than this, he provides us with others to serve as mirrors—instrumental means—assisting in the removal of planks and specks alike. This he accomplishes as a dispensation of his own agapic relationality toward God and others through his Spirit-mediated union with us.

Part II

Christological Foundations
for Human Personhood

3

Christological anthropology
and human personhood

QUESTIONS REGARDING HUMAN PERSONHOOD cannot be abstracted from cosmological and ontological considerations. Before we posit a knowable self, we must first acknowledge that conceptions of *self*—and even, as it happens, *knowledge* (see Polanyi, 1974)—depend in no small degree on metaphysical pre-commitments and preunderstandings. Our thinking regarding the meaning and nature of human being and becoming are built on such foundations as these (see Stevenson & Haberman, 2004). As we might expect, ostensibly Christian epistemic frameworks—our systems for thinking about human self-knowledge—may vary markedly depending on the relative emphasis placed on any number of factors, whether exegetical, theological, ethical, etc. How much more so, then, should we expect a strictly theistic framework rooted in a conviction of the truthfulness of the Bible to diverge from those systems that altogether dismiss the authority and evidentiary import of divine revelation.[1]

As an aspect of God's Logos—his self-disclosure—the Bible speaks of human persons as created beings, contingent and dependent on a supremely sovereign, yet mercifully gracious Creator. His concern and disposition toward humanity, moreover, includes a number of divinely ordained ends, namely: the reconciliation of sinful humans to a holy God through the person and work of Christ, their participation in the doxo-logical agenda of trinitarian mutual self-regard and self-giving, and God's

1. Along these lines, Simone and Sugarman (1986) conclude, "[the] Bible is the text through which God reveals the knowledge of his creation to the creature that He makes receptive to such understanding" (p. 132).

telic determination regarding the divinely-mediated, human-enacted perpetuation of that agenda respective to one another. Relative to such a comprehensive schema, non-theistic frameworks seeking to grasp the meaning of human personhood, the ontoethical implications of the human self, to say nothing of the means and end of human self-knowing will surely lack more than a passing resemblance in all but the most basic questions.

What is a human being? What gives meaning and purpose to human existence? Do such things as a human mind, soul, or self, whatever these might be, exist? What constitutes optimal human psychosocial functioning? How ought persons live respective to the wider created order and to other human beings in particular? Frameworks situated in an essentially theistic worldview will necessarily differ, and to a considerable degree, from strictly secular schemata. In the final analysis, we may largely agree on taxonomy—what amounts to a human being and what does not[2]—yet, profound disagreement will necessarily characterize the respective ontologies and axiologies of theistic and nontheistic anthropological discourse (see Johnson, 2007; Moreland & Rae, 2000).

The imago dei in christological perspective

The theistic framework of the biblical writers at times led them to reflect on the ontological and cosmological implications of human existence and uniqueness.[3] In what is surely an instantiation of the dynamic of double knowledge of God and self, David, in Psalm 8, reflects on humanity's special place in God's design. God, he marvels, has established his

2. Increasingly, common ground on what qualifies as human is breaking down as the hegemony of cultural and political libertinism takes root in, especially, Western societies. The pursuit of reproductive "rights" as an aspect of a brand of radical feminism still on the rise in the United States has resulted in the blurring of taxonomic lines. An unborn fetus is, thus, only provisionally "human" in pregnancies where the child is wanted. In Europe where birth rates are much lower and mortality rates much higher, this taxonomic slippage reveals itself in societal conventions regarding assisted-suicide and the euthanasia of the terminally ill.

3. I presume that the biblical writers did not all share a single, monolithic perspective on any of these questions. At the same time, I regard their participation in writing the Scriptures, inspired as they were by the Spirit of God (2 Tim 3:6; 2 Pet 1:20–21), to have had a formative influence on their thinking. As God's Logos, the Scriptures grant us access to the mind of God and, as such, are foundational to any ostensibly theistic framework.

glorious name in all the earth; his worth far exceeds all he has made (v. 1). As Creator (v. 3), he stands as sovereign over all and, for this reason, has the only right to judge (v. 2). What amazes David, then, is God's determination that human beings should serve as his chosen stewards of creation. Despite our relatively diminutive stature, God has ordained that we should assume a place "a little lower than the heavenly beings" (v. 5 NET).[4] In light of God's exalted position, David marvels at humanity's high standing in relation to him: "Of what importance is mankind that you should pay attention to them?" (v. 4).[5] What indeed?

David's understanding of humanity, then, is conditioned by his knowledge of God. What he knows of those below, he grasps by looking above. Cortez (2008) regards the relational language of David's theanthropological reflection in explicitly covenantal terms:

> At each point, then, the very nature of the question ["What is man?"] points the reader toward humanity's covenantal relationship with its Creator. For [the] biblical authors, humanity is not an undefined term awaiting conceptual clarity. Instead, it refers to a creature clearly defined and delineated by its standing in relation to God. (p. 3)

David's explicit reference to the creation account viz., humanity's stewardship of the earth, commends Cortez's covenantal reading of the text (cf. Gen 1:26–28). As Barth (2010) notes, the writer of Hebrews, in consideration of the same Davidic text, draws a strong christological inference: the covenant partner of whom David speaks is, in an ultimate sense, Jesus Christ (Heb 2:5–9; see Barth, 2010, III/2, p. 20).

David, we should note, exemplifies humanity's distinctiveness, not merely by posing the anthropological question—"What is humanity . . . ?"—but specially by doing so within the context of relatedness to God—". . . that you regard us as you do?" (Horton, 2006). The ability to

---

4. The Hebrew word sometimes translated "God" (see ASV), אֱלֹהִים (*elohim*) is rendered "angels" in most modern English translations. It is best understood, however, in locative terms, i.e., those who dwell in the heavenly realms, above, in other words, the terrestrial plane. The heavenly beings, the *elohim*, would then include Yahweh, his divine council (see Job 1:6), the angelic host, etc. (see Heiser, 2015).

5. The Hebrew for "humanity," אֱנוֹשׁ (*enōsh*) employed here and elsewhere throughout the poetry of the Old Testament carries a strong theological connotation. According to Harris et al. (2003), "[T]he word frequently emphasizes man's frailty and humanness" in that it "reminds man of his transience and of his lowly position before the Almighty" (p. 59; see also Job 33:12; Ps 9:19–20; 90:3). This relational significance is, regrettably, lost in English translation.

explore and examine the nature of one's own existence is both essential to and distinctive of human beings.[6] Yet, David does not engage in isolated reflection on human nature "from below," formulating his anthropological ideas by reasoning "up" from the phenomena attendant to human existence.[7] Rather, he begins with what God has said concerning humanity.

To be sure, the capacity to ask the question, "Who or what am I?," whether or not we possess any ability to answer comprehensively or even satisfactorily, distinguishes us in fundamental ways from rocks and trees, stars and sloths. Furthermore, as our noetic and agentic capacities develop normally, over the course of time, we become increasingly capable of inquiring into the inner workings of our nature and existence. The impulse toward self-discovery and self-understanding appears to have been hard-wired into our nature. This tendency of human beings toward reflective introspection and metacognition—that is, thinking about one's thoughts—is undeniable.[8]

Nevertheless, what we make of our self-discoveries, how we frame and extrapolate from notions of self-understanding and how we conceive of what constitutes a healthy, "whole" self varies widely. Self-knowledge, then, that unique prerogative of humanity within the earthly realm of

6. I refrain from speculating here on any supposed similarities or distinctions between human nature and that of angels (or demons). The Scriptures offer scant insight into such matters (*pace* Delitzsch, 1885).

7. Barth (2010) remained famously committed to theanthropological methodology that begins with the revelatory "Word of God"—that is, from the personhood and nature of the divine Logos. "We have to think of man," he insists, "in the event of real faith as, so to speak, opened up from above. From above, not from below!" (I/1, p. 242). Yet Barth did open up to the possibility of a "from below" countermovement, which would necessarily follow the initial, "primordial movement from above to below" (cited in Rumscheidt, 1986, p. 84). Shults (2003) believes Barth's principal concern in arguing for an anthropology "from above" as opposed to "from below" is "to protect the sovereignty of God's revelation" with respect to anthropological method and "to deny any control over it by the human subject" (p. 120).

8. To say that these capacities exist within human persons is not to argue, at this early stage, for a particular model of the self. I will adumbrate a theological anthropology of the human self in Part III. For now, I note that the *nature* (and existence) of the self, particularly the immaterial mind/soul, is highly controversial and hotly debated, especially among secular scholars (see Gallagher, 2011; Siderits et al., 2013), while the noetic capacities of human beings are at least assumed. Moreover, any anthropological methodology "from below" is bound to remain unduly focused, as modern anthropology has become, on the structural and formal aspects of human beings *generally*. Biblical anthropology, on the other hand, should proceed, as Barth insisted, "from above"—the nature of humanity being inferred analogically and covenantally from the person and work of Christ.

God's creation, is highly perspectival and contingent. This is no less the case when undertaking a proposal for Christian self-knowledge. Yet, David's rhetorical exploration does not proceed, as nontheistic frameworks do by definition, from the bare facts of human existence and constitution.[9] On the contrary, the terminus a quo of his inquiry appears to be the assumption of God's unique concern and calling for humanity respective to the rest of creation. As Berkouwer (1962) observes, this perspectival approach to theanthropology is the rule rather than the exception in biblical contexts:

> Man is presented in many different ways in Scripture. He is shown in numerous contexts, with many facets; but in all this variation we meet again and again the one central and essential dimension of man, that in which he stands *not* as an isolated entity, but in the light and the presence of God. (p. 33; emphasis original)

Constitutive-covenantal theological anthropology

Christian theological anthropology has historically endeavored to explicate the essence of human being and becoming in terms of the imago dei. The biblical-theological formulation of "the" imago dei conceives of human nature principally in terms of our ontic and relational correspondence both to God and, on God's behalf, to creation (Berkouwer, 1962; Grenz, 2001; Pannenberg, 1985). Indeed, since the second-century teachings of Irenaeus, the imago dei has stood at "the heart of Christian anthropology" (Hoekema, 1994, p. 66).

From a biblical perspective human nature and personhood are expressly theological concepts. So, as Gunton (1991) writes, "To be made in the image of God is to be endowed with a particular kind of personal reality. To be a person is to be made in the image of God: that is the heart of the matter" (p. 58). Indeed, according to Bavinck (2004), no facet or nuance of human nature can be abstracted from this theological formulation:

> The whole human being is image and likeness of God, in soul and body, in all human faculties, powers, and gifts. Nothing in humanity is excluded from God's image; it stretches as far as

9. Indeed, as modern, secular anthropology has done since Descartes' infamous *cogito*.

> our humanity does and constitutes our humanness. The human
> is not the divine self but is nevertheless a finite creaturely im-
> pression of the divine. All that is in God—his spiritual essence,
> his virtues and perfections, his immanent self-distinctions, his
> self-communication and self-revelation in creation—finds its
> admittedly finite and limited analogy and likeness in humanity.
> (p. 561)

For Christian theanthropology, then, the imago demarcates a boundary line for subsequent discourse, providing epistemological and theological warrant (Grenz, 2001; Johnson, 2007). Yet, despite its historical and theological significance, direct allusions within the text of Scripture are notably few (see Gen 1:26; 9:6; cf. Gen 5:3; 1 Cor 11:7).[10]

As pertains to our present concern, the most significant reference can be found in the creation account of Genesis 1. In what amounts to the climax of the narrative, the entrance of humanity onto the scene assumes an undeniable place of prominence. Indeed, the writer conveys with startling language the impression that everything preceding has led to this crucial moment in the unfolding of God's creative agenda (Wenham, 1987). In contrast to the divine illocutions that brought forth every variety of plant and animal life—each "according to its kind" (לְמִינוֹ, lemini; vv. 11, 12, 21, 24, 25)—God creates human beings according to *his* own divine "image" (vv. 26, 27).[11] This "most striking statement" within the creation narrative serves to establish a firm and unyielding link between theology and anthropology for any ostensibly biblical framework (Westermann, 1992, p. 111).

On account of God's having created human beings in *his* image and likeness, Christian theological anthropology has proceeded with the presumption that humanity should function in some way within the created

10. Berkouwer (1962) argues that the concept, if not the express terminology, appears throughout the Old Testament. References to Christ as the consummate image bearer appear several times in the Pauline corpus (Rom 8:29; 1 Cor 15:49; 2 Cor 3:18; 4:4; Col 1:15; 3:10).

11. There are two terms, "image" (צֶלֶם, *tselem*) and "likeness" (דְּמוּת, *demūth*), employed by the writer to distinguish humanity's semiological relationship to God. Irenaeus (2012) famously differentiates between these two terms—the *imago dei* and *similitudo dei*—holding the latter to be textual and semantic support for what here and elsewhere has been termed the covenantal, dynamic, or relational image (V.xvi.2; p. 544). Despite widespread agreement that the text does not support such an exegetical distinction (see Hoekema, pp. 33–34), his larger point—that some aspect of human nature was lost at the Fall *and* something retained—is significant (see Grenz, pp. 146–47).

order as a representation of God (Hoekema, 1994; McMartin, 2013). This conclusion is borne out by the divinely appointed mandate that humanity fill the earth and subdue it (v. 28).[12] From the outset of God's covenantal dealings with creation, he establishes as the "sign" of his divine presence and rule human beings whom he has made according to his image (see Johnson, 2007, p. 13).[13] Moreover, the constitutional capacities with which we have been divinely endowed enable the proper functioning of our image-bearing role respective to God and creation.

Despite widespread agreement on the fact of humanity's essential nature as image-bearers, historical Christian writers have differed at times in their understanding of the imago dei. Respective emphases on human constitution and human function, what I term the constitutive and covenantal aspects of the imago, follow from these understandings.[14] Among the earliest formulations, Irenaeus (2012), in his defense of Christian orthodoxy against the encroachment of Gnosticism, bracketed his understanding of the imago in both constitutive and covenantal terms. Human beings, according to the bishop of Lyons, bear certain constituent faculties, to be sure. Yet, the existence of these faculties with which we encounter, chiefly, God direct us toward the fulfillment of God's purposeful design:

> Now God shall be glorified in His handiwork, fitting it so as to be conformable to, and modelled after, His own Son. For by the hands of the Father, that is, by the Son and the Holy Spirit, man, and not [merely] a part of man, was made in the likeness of God. Now the soul and the spirit are certainly a *part* of the man, but certainly not *the* man; for the perfect man consists

12. Humanity's *dominium*, or lordship over creation, has at times been directly identified with the image of God, rather than as a consequence of, or inference from, the imago; contra this perspective, see Berkouwer, 1962, pp. 70–71; Pannenberg, 1985, pp. 74–75.

13. In similar fashion the tabernacle and its contrivances can be said to represent on earth—and point to—their heavenly counterparts and archetypes. Of particular note is God's insistence to Moses (and, later, David with the temple) that each be built "according to the plan" God revealed to him on the mountain (Exod 26:30; 1 Chr 28:19; cf. Heb 9:23–24). Taken together these passages may indicate the divine will to apply celestial "templates" to certain terrestrial entities, including humans whose nature is imprinted in some way with God's own. It is thus that creation serves as the "glorious theater" within which the divinely ordained drama unfolds (Calvin, 2008, p. 21; cf. Frame, 2002; Vanhoozer, 2005).

14. Lewis & Demarest (1990) interact substantially with the major historical and theological perspectives on the nature of the imago dei (see esp., pp. 160–70).

in the commingling and union of the soul receiving the spirit of the Father, and the admixture of that fleshly nature which was moulded after the image of God. (V.vi.1.; p. 531; emphasis original)

Human composition by itself is not "the" image; rather, human beings are created according to the image in order that we might become conformed to that image, that is, Jesus Christ.[15]

With his already/not-yet formulation in regard to the image of God in human beings, Irenaeus generates a dialectical tension between its creational and eschatological aspects. We have it, but we seek it. Human beings bear an incipient or germinal imaging capacity by reason of our constitution. Yet, the fulfillment of our telic design comes only through active participation in God's agenda for those who bear his image. The divine Son, for Irenaeus, provides the model or the exemplar from which God conceived of human constitution—its formal/constitutive and functional/covenantal capacities. Just as clearly, Irenaeus holds that human beings can be conformed to that image only by means of union with God through the Spirit.

As God's "handiwork," humanity possesses the capacity to image God perfectly, though Christ alone accomplishes this. This potential exists precisely because human beings bear certain imaging capacities, as designed by God.[16] At creation, then, human nature was complete, yet perfectible—"modelled after" the true image of God the Son, while nonetheless "conformable to" that image.[17] So, according to Tanner (2010), Irenaeus's "prospective interpretation" of the imago supports a christological understanding "in which eventual growth into a better image takes center stage" only with the coming of Christ (p. 20).[18]

---

15. This is Irenaeus's *similitudo dei*. I have not maintained his distinction between image and likeness, but rather have folded his two terms into one term with two senses—what I call the constitutional and covenantal imago, respectively. The notion that Irenaeus promulgated an incipient version of an exclusively constitutional or "structural" imago (see Brunner, 2014) disregards his insistence that the *imago* and *similitudo* be considered inseparably in the person of Christ.

16. As Hoekema (1994) notes, "image" is both noun and verb (p. 95).

17. Tanner (2010) explains the apparent contradiction in this formulation by distinguishing between the "weak" and "strong" imaging of God of which human beings are capable (see pp. 23–24). I prefer instead to speak of an incipient and perfected image. Like newborn babes, we must grow into the fullness of our image-bearing design over time and in relationship to God.

18. Irenaeus holds that, prior to the incarnation, it was impossible for human

Limitations of the constitutive imago

Medieval Christian thinkers, in conceiving of the imago dei in human persons, tended to emphasize humanity's constitutional capacities over and against the proper functioning of those capacities in covenantal relationship with God and creation (Grenz, 2001). From the time of Augustine until the Reformation, the imago dei was chiefly held to be something human beings *possess* more so than something we *are* or, on account of our union with Christ, we *become* (Lewis & Demarest, 1990). Augustine (2012d), in representative fashion, writes "God, then, made man in His own image. For He created for him a soul endowed with reason and intelligence, so that he might excel all the creatures of earth, air, and sea, which were not so gifted" (XII.xxiii.23; p. 241).[19]

In contrast to Irenaeus, Augustine (2009) largely jettisons the prospective, telic aspect of the imago. The image of God is a capacity with which we are born and by which we are distinguished from the rest of creation: "We see the face of the earth adorned with earthly creatures," he declares redolent of Psalm 8, "and humanity, in your image and likeness, put in authority over all irrational animals by your image and likeness, that is by the power of reason and intelligence" (XIII.xxxii; p. 302). Yet, as is clear from his description of the *imago et similitudo* in terms of human "reason and intelligence," Augustine assumes a narrower denotive frame than does Irenaeus. For Augustine, the image amounts to those intellectual powers of persons human and divine.[20]

---

beings to image God perfectly, for as yet the true image of God-in-Christ had not been revealed: "For in times long past, it was *said* that man was created after the image of God, but it was not [actually] *shown*; for the Word was as yet invisible, after whose image man was created. Wherefore, also he did easily lose the similitude [likeness]. When, however, the Word of God became flesh, he confirmed both these: for He both showed forth the image truly, since He became himself what was His image; and He re-established the similitude after a sure manner, by assimilating man to the invisible Father through means of the visible Word" (Irenaus, 2012, V.xvi.2; p. 544; emphasis original).

19. Irenaeus may, in fact, be responsible for a dichotomy in thinking regarding "image" and "likeness." After all he distinguishes between them when a careful exegesis of Gen 1 suggests such distinctions carry no warrant. Augustine and subsequent medieval writers, however, conflated Irenaeus' unwarranted dichotomy of "image" and "likeness" into a simple strictly constitutive "image." Having dispensed with Irenaeus' prospective "likeness," "image" lost its incipient, telic (i.e., covenantal) sense. These many years later theologians are still probing the question, "What is the image of God?"

20. Augustine likely held a more nuanced view of imago than did the medieval

Augustine, according to TeSelle (1970), held to an intellectualized ideal respective to the flourishing of God's image in humanity. Grenz (2001) also observes, "For Augustine . . . the seat of the divine image in the human person is the soul in its intellectual dimension, insofar as the goal of the image is knowledge of God" (p. 155). It is likely that Augustine's situating of the image in the mind stems from his trinitarian conception of human personhood. Like the triune God in whose image we are made, Augustine held that individual human persons exist as an essentially internal "relation" of self, self-understanding, and self-love. From this, he (2002) concludes, "Behold! the mind, therefore, remembers itself, understands itself, and loves itself; if we perceive this, we perceive a trinity, not yet God indeed, but now finally an image of God" (XIV.viii.11; pp. 148–149).

Augustine's stress on the constituting role of the mind/soul is clear. Later medieval writers largely lost Irenaeus's broader conception of the image and embraced the more limited Augustinian formulation.[21] This is not to say that Augustine never considered the covenantal, telic aspects of human nature. Yet, as Gunton (1991) notes, a historical truncation regarding human relationality ensued from Augustine's having positioned the image *inside* individual human persons:

> Since [for Augustine] relations are qualifications of the inner Trinity, and not relations between persons, it becomes difficult to see how the triune relatedness can be brought to bear on the central question of human relatedness. God's relatedness is construed in terms of self-relatedness, with the result that it is as an individual that the human being is in the image of God, and

writers who followed him. Indeed, numerous modern scholars have observed the vestiges of a relational perspective in the church father that largely appears to have fallen by the wayside for the scholastics until the early reformers "rediscovered" it (see Grenz, 2001; Hefner, 1984; McMartin, 2013).

21. Grenz (2001) regards Thomas Aquinas as having provided the "final flowering" in the development of an Augustinian constitutive anthropology (p. 161). Moreover, he perceives in Aquinas's *Summa Theologica* an essentially Aristotelian metaphysic filtered through the theological framework of Augustine (see Merriell, 1990; Sullivan, 1963). As noted in Chapter 1, the Hellenistic legacy operating within the anthropologies of Augustine and Aquinas emphasizes the inner life, one's intellectual apprehension of reality, including self and "God," and an individualist, eudaimonist ethical framework. These have all been cited as the metaphysical foundations upon which modern, Western notions of personhood and wellbeing are constructed (C. Taylor, 1989), and against which the Reformers to some extent, and Barth more emphatically, would eventually push back.

therefore truly human. The outcome is another, theologically legitimated, version of the tendency to individualism. (p. 49)[22]

Calvin and the early Reformers operated within an essentially Augustinian theanthropological framework (Grenz, 2001). In regard to the imago, however, Calvin and Luther would both came to recognize limitations in a strictly constitutive formula. The image of God in humanity, both would observe, necessarily entails the willing "dynamic" response of human beings to their Maker. This response-ability, made possible by obedient submission to God, comes as a gift of God's grace. Remarking on the shift, Pannenberg (1985) observes,

> The medieval Catholic and the Reformed conceptions of the image of God differ . . . in that for the Reformers the image of God consists in the *actual relation* to God, while for medieval Latin Scholasticism it is, rather, a presupposition for this actual relation to God and is a formal structural property of human nature. (p. 50; emphasis original)

In his departure from the constitutive theanthropology of Augustine, Calvin employed his metaphor of the mirror by way of emphasizing a functional, covenantal imago (Torrance, 1957). In his commentary on Ephesians, Calvin (1965) describes humanity prior to the fall as being "created in the image of God, so that [we] might reflect, as in a mirror, the righteousness of God"; but that "image, having been wiped out by sin, must now be restored in Christ" (p. 191). Like a mirror, Calvin held the image of God in humanity to be the active reflection, albeit in limited fashion, of the goodness and uprightness of the divine nature (see Gerrish, 1981). This would mean that, subsequent to the Fall, humanity's capacity to image God, if "not utterly effaced and destroyed," was nonetheless wholly "corrupted," so that we exist now in a state of "fearful deformity" (Calvin, 2008, I.xv. 4; p. 107; see Torrance, 1957).

According to Niesel (1956), Calvin perceived "[t]he divine similitude . . . not in the fact that man is endowed with reason and will but in the fact that these faculties in original man were directed wholly towards

---

22. Gunton (1991) offers the following additional critique: "From the outset, there is in Augustine a tendency to develop anthropology in terms of neoplatonic categories. For him the human likeness to God must be in the mind or soul, so that other possibilities are excluded from the outset. One implication is that our embodiedness cannot be the place where the image, and hence our true humanity, is found" (p. 49).

knowledge of and obedience to God" (p. 68).[23] By the fact of our sinful disobedience as covenant members of the race of Adam (see Rom 5:12–19), the Reformers following Calvin held that human beings have become estranged from the God in whose image we were made. By reason of our sin-ruptured connection to God, we lost our likeness to God.[24] The image, having depended not as much on creaturely constitution but on covenantal communion with God, faded from view. Calvin (2008), in summary, avers,

> Therefore, as the image of God constitutes the entire excellence of human nature, as it shone in Adam before his fall, but was afterward vitiated and almost destroyed, nothing remaining but a ruin, confused, mutilated, and tainted with impurity, so it is now partly seen in the elect, insofar as they are regenerated by the Spirit. (I.xv.4.; p. 108)

What was lost in the fall—the image of God—could only be restored through the Spirit's redemptive work in regenerate human beings.

According to covenantal formulations, the image of God in human beings relies for its continued existence on the mutual self-perception of God and humanity in reflective communion. Whereas, to depart from that relationship is akin to moving away from a mirror: nothing of one's personal likeness may be perceived by looking strictly inward. Self-perception is not a matter of reflecting in Aristotelian fashion on humanity's common constitutive traits or capacities. A merely formal perspective contributes to a truncated anthropology—a two-dimensional image, as it

23. Following Barth, Niesel (1956) adds that, for Calvin and contra Augustine and Aquinas, "There is no neutral psycho-physical constitution of man. The fact that man was originally created in the image of God means rather that his whole psycho-physical existence was thereby moulded. . . . In using traditional [i.e., Augustinian] theological concepts in this connexion [sic] Calvin wishes to express clearly that man owed the right orientation of his being wholly to the goodness of his Creator. . . . This special distinction which exalts him above all creatures is thus not to be understood in the sense that man in creation was given something divine as his permanent possession. . . . The divine similitude depends rather on man's relation to his Lord" (pp. 68–69). A more nuanced, less Barthian reading of Calvin has been suggested in Engel (2002, see pp. 37–38).

24. Calvin denies "Augustine's speculation" that the human mind/soul is a psychological analogue—"mirror"—of the Trinity, "inasmuch as it comprehends within itself, intellect, will, and memory" (Calvin, 2008, I.xv.4; p. 108). Bavinck (2004), on the other hand, commends Augustine's trinitarian theanthropology yet suggests the exercise of "greatest caution in the psychological exploration of the trinitarian components of man's being" (p. 555).

were. Only by gazing at ourselves in the "looking glass" can we see all the ways we resemble and dissemble God.

Considerable complications arise respective to humanity's relation to God under a strictly constitutive rubric for the imago. Following on from Reformed thinking from Calvin to Barth, Brunner (2014) observes,

> If . . . the *Imago Dei* is conceived in the formal structural sense as the endowment with reason, as creative freedom, then Man possesses the Image of God *in himself*. *This* view of the *Imago Dei* is the gate by which a pantheistic or an idealistic deification of man can enter. . . . The result of this erroneous conception of the *Imago Dei*—as substance and not as relation—is a mistakenly "spiritualized" view of man and his destiny. (pp. 59–60; emphasis original)

A constitutive theanthropology, when dissociated from a covenantal perspective, cannot evade charges of rationalism, humanism, and, ultimately, of idolatry.[25] In the same way, human persons, so long as we remain estranged from God, can never fully image God. Moreover, the knowledge of self, when dissociated from the knowledge of God, remains incomplete, skewed, and faulty. The inevitable fruit of such self-blindness is sinful, pathological self-deception.

Toward christocentric covenantalism

Historical Christian theanthropology, as outlined in Part I, propounds a warrant for self-knowledge only in the light of God's knowledge of self. This correlative or mutual self-knowledge is reciprocal precisely because creaturely knowledge is contingent. We can only veridically know what God knows to be true. All other knowledge, falsely so-called, is finally without basis or merit. We may be right about any number of aspects of reality! Yet, what-I-am-before-God and what-I-believe-myself-to-be amount to mutually exclusive epistemic domains so long as my

---

25. Nor, to be clear, should the constitutive imago be severed from its covenantal outworking. Either way we are left with the "false dilemma" of dichotomy (Berkouwer, 1962, p. 101). As Anderson (1982) rightly observes, "To abandon any ontological basis for the imago in favor of an existentialist or sociological function is not only unbiblical but ethically impotent" (p. 76). The aim of Calvin (2008) and, later, Barth (2010) was to prioritize the covenantal over the constitutive image, though this is not always recognized.

self-perception remains autonomous. This conclusion follows from a covenantal understanding of the imago.

To be an image is to be a copy—a representative likeness. "Image" implies the existence of an "original" or antecedent unto which the former serves as a referent or "sign." Since the Reformation, conceptions of the imago dei in human beings have shifted away from the constitutive emphasis of the Middle Ages toward what I have here termed the covenantal imago. The culmination of this shift in the modern age can be located in the theological anthropology of Karl Barth (Shults, 2003).

In addition to his notable excesses and idiosyncrasies,[26] Barth offers two insights which together fill out our covenantal framework for human personhood. The first of these constructive elements of Barthian theanthropology is his relational conception of personal ontology. For Barth, the formula, "I am in encounter," is paradigmatic for personhood (Barth, 2010, III/2, p. 246). With this rubric Barth establishes that, apart from the existence and imposition of an "other," "self" loses its ontological significance.[27] "I" am not, until "I am in encounter." To ask the question, "Who am I?," then, must entail that preliminary consideration be given to our creaturely status: I did not make me; my origin comes from outside myself. Given the fact of our creaturely contingency, an avenue is opened by which we may now properly seek out both our Creator and others in his creation.

Barth finally rejects the possibility that self can be defined apart from its relations. He avers, "I am as I am in a relation. . . . I cannot posit myself without coming up against the self-positing of the other" (p. 246). Thus, Barthian theanthropology extends the logic of the double-knowledge of self offered up by Augustine and Calvin. With respect to the human self, Barth regards selfhood, as an aspect of human personhood, to be both epistemologically and *ontologically* dependent on encounter. Self, itself an aspect of personhood, exists only in relationship. Accordingly, "I" is meaningless apart from "Thou."[28] Along these lines, Torrance (1998)

26. Along these lines, Barth's early wholesale rejection of Aquinas' *analogia entis*—the "analogy of being" between God and humanity (see Barth, 2010, I/i, p. xiii)—resulted in an unbalanced theanthropology (see Von Balthasar, 1992a). He would eventually come to a more nuanced, balanced perspective later in his career (Barth, 1960, see pp. 44–45; cf. Oh, 2006).

27. Barth's trinitarian theology provides the ground for his ontology of personal encounter, the *analogia relationis* (Oh, 2006).

28 It should be noted here that Barth's insistence on a relational basis for personal ontology applies to the existence of self and not to one's substance. This is the language

follows Barth, "Relations between persons have ontological force and are part of what persons are as persons—they are real, person-constituting relations" (p. 230). Persons, then, are not so much the sum of their parts but the connection of those parts with others, so to speak.

Thus, while a phenomenological analysis of human nature may justly arrive at the conclusion that human individuals are constituted by a union of material and immaterial "substances"—a body and a soul, for instance—the emphasis of Barthian anthropology falls instead on the ontology of human personhood—personeity. According to this analysis, relationality stands not at the perimeter of human being and becoming, but at its very heart. The "nature" of human beings created in the image of God entails God's expectation that we become discrete instantiations of personhood, whose relatedness to God and others informs our existence. Understood in these terms, no truly autonomous, self-contained "self" can, in fact, be said to exist (see Zizioulas, 1985).[29]

Respective to Aristotelian metaphysics, relationality is a mere "accident" of one's phenomenologically conceived "substance." Following Calvin's lead, Barth, on the other hand, recognized that any anthropology for which relationality is accidental has the unintended (and unbiblical) consequence of positing the possibility of the knowledge of self *a se*—in itself (see Barth, 1995, pp. 162–63).[30] Accordingly, Barthian self-knowledge is

---

of personeity rather than corporeity. Just as the "Father" is Father only in relation to the "Son" and the "Son" is Son only in relation to the "Father," "I" am who I am only in relation to "you/You." Barth writes of human personeity, "[A]s I and Thou are together, their being acquires the character, the human style, of always being I for the self and Thou for the other. As we are in this encounter we are thus distinguished. On both sides . . . the being has its own validity, dignity and self-certainty. Nor is this human being static, but dynamic and active. It is not an *esse* but an *existere*. To say man is to say history" (III/2, p. 248). In support of this premise, Gunton (1991) notes, "The image is not a static possession, but comes to be realised in the various relationships in which human life is set" (p. 60).

29. This conclusion would obviously hold true, supremely and archetypally, for the personhood of the triune God, whom Christian orthodoxy holds to be a community of three persons (*hypostases*), though perfectly unified in essence (*ousia*).

30. Barth rejects the Aristotelian dichotomy of "substance" and "accident" that characterizes Aquinas's—and to a lesser extent, Augustine's—metaphysic, writing, "[T]he encounter between I and Thou is not arbitrary or accidental, . . . it is not incidentally but essentially proper to the concept of man" (Barth, 2010, III/2, p. 248). As mentioned in Chapter 2, the theological "turn" to relationality involved a series of shifts away from Hellenistic categories following in the wake of nineteenth-century continental philosophy (see Shults, 2003, pp. 22–23). Yet, Barth's insistence that human being is indivisible from human relating was anticipated in some ways by Jonathan

best understood in terms of one's particularity—"I am"—within the context of relationality—"in encounter." By this, Barth signifies the degree to which the individual's standing before God and others informs and establishes personhood.

Selfhood, understood in covenantal terms, is an interpersonal project, and one into which we grow over time. Along these lines, McFadyen (1990) explains that "[T]he sense of oneself as a subject, a person, is not individually but socially acquired" (p. 70). Zizioulas (1991) concurs adding,

> Both in the case of God and of man the identity of a person is recognized and posited clearly and unequivocally, but this is so only in and through a *relationship*, and not through an objective ontology in which this identity would be *isolated*, pointed at and described in itself. Personal identity is totally lost if isolated, for its ontological condition is relationship. (p. 46; emphasis original)

To define human beings strictly in terms of metaphysical "substance" risks effacing the uniqueness of personal identity, replacing the particularity of personal ontology with a derivative, universal humanity, of which "I" am merely representative.

Self-knowledge, on the other hand, posits the existence of a unique person whose identity nevertheless is entailed in a dialogical unity of the essential and the contingent. Put another way, self's intrinsic and particular aspects are linked inseparably with its dynamic and relational aspects. Personhood, according to this framework, exists within a dynamic process of reciprocal personeity.[31] Humanity, for O'Collins (2009), is best understood in this light:

Edwards who developed his own relational ontology in a "radical departure" from "traditional" Aristotelian metaphysics (Lee, 2000, p. 77). Crisp (2012) rejects certain aspects of Lee's reading of Edwards, yet notes the latter's unique, even idiosyncratic, metaphysical paradigm.

31. I will have more to say in regard to this point below. However, in support of the idea of reciprocal personeity, or what Shults (2003) calls "constitutive relationality" (see pp. 117–18), the language of correspondence in Genesis 2 is, perhaps, instructive. In vv. 18 and 20, the Hebrew term, כְּנֶגְדּוֹ (*chenegdō*), expresses the divine intention to create a corresponding other for the first man—one who shares his nature (see v. 23). God's pronouncement of "not good" in reference to the fact that the man is "alone" (v. 18) seems odd since God is himself present with the man in the garden (see 3:8). The standard account of God's disapprobation of the man's solitude in the garden posits that it would have been impossible for humankind to fill the earth and rule over it (Gen 1:28) without the ability to reproduce sexually (see Westermann, 1984). The fact

> Human beings are open-ended projects, called to develop dynamically, discover meaning, follow up insights, actualize potentialities, deepen their self-understanding as well as their relationships with others, and through experience to grow continually from cradle to grave. In a very real sense, we are not yet human; we are always becoming human. (p. 235)

Rightly understood, the pursuit of self-knowledge is inescapably relational. In the first place, there is no finally veridical knowledge of self, according to the Scriptures and as maintained in historic pastoral tradition, apart from the knowledge of God. Barthian theanthropology, then, extends this conclusion regarding the indispensability of divine–human relationality to include human-to-human relations as well. As Grenz (2001) explains, "Humans . . . are created to be the counterpart of God—that is, to stand in an I–Thou relationship to God. But they are also to copy and imitate the divine original by standing in an I–Thou relationship to each other" (p. 297). Moreover, as self willingly participates in the mutual self-positing of self and other/Other, relational self-knowledge assumes an expressly covenantal complexion. This means that *self*-knowledge is not self-*centered*. The "center" of self-knowledge is, by reason of its inherent dynamic of mutuality and reciprocity, relationship.

Following Calvin, Barthian theanthropology is inherently covenantal (see Barth, 2010, III/2, pp. 203–4; see also Price, 2002).[32] Barth's covenantal formulation of the imago dei defines human personhood, as Calvin sought to do, *coram deo*. With the necessary Barthian inflection, we grasp the indispensability of relationship between human beings as well. According to Calvin, God intended that his image would serve as

---

is, however, God could have allowed for the possibility of asexual reproduction among humans. If it is "good" enough for certain non-human species—e.g., sponges, aphids, and even some vertebrates—to reproduce asexually, there must be some other factor at work in the divine plan for humanity than the propagation and *dominium* of humanity. It seems clear from this passage that mutual correspondence between persons is a fundamental aspect of God's design for human nature. This would imply, moreover, that human "wholeness" and personhood is somehow contingent on one's relations to both God *and* others. So, Westermann (1984): "God's creature is humankind only in community" (p. 192).

32. Regarding the asymmetry of covenant, Barth (1979) concludes, "Through His Word God discloses His work in His *covenant* with man. . . . He discloses Himself as the *primary* partner of the covenant—Himself as *man's* God. But He also discloses *man* to be His creature. . . . He discloses man as God's man, as God's son and servant who is loved by Him. Man is thus the other, the secondary, partner of the covenant" (pp. 19–20; emphasis original).

a mirror within which the divine likeness might be perceived both in relation to himself and to all creation. The imago, then, provides a thean-thropological foundation for tripolar self-knowledge. What we can know of ourselves grows as the epistemic fruit of relationship with God *and*, as God's image bearers, with each other.[33]

Barth's second critical theanthropological contribution is his Christology. The psalmist's question, "What is humanity?" (Ps 8:4), for Barth, finds its ultimate answer only in the person and work of Christ (III/2, p. 218; see Grenz, 2004; Tanner, 2010). Indeed, he held Christology to be "the assumption behind all our other assumptions," rejecting any isolated conception of human nature generally, or the imago dei in particular, apart from the consideration of the God-man (III/2, p. 571).[34]

Cortez (2008) summarizes Barth's theanthropological methodology in terms of the personhood of Christ: "not something that can be known as 'a neutral point' but rather must be 'explained' by Jesus as it is manifested in his concrete existence" (p. 22).[35] McCormack (1997) defines Barth's methodological trajectory as one that initiates "from a centre in God's Self-revelation in Jesus Christ" (p. 454). Accordingly, Barth's anthropological method begins with Christology and then proceeds to

33. An additional dimension of covenantal self-knowledge is also suggested by the relationship between the imago and creation.

34. This trajectory inverts the secular paradigm which moves from the phenomena of human existence and particularity toward general, "scientific" conclusions about the nature of human persons. While medical and psychological science has yielded invaluable insight on any number of aspects of the human condition, its conclusions can never extend to questions of ultimate significance. Why are we here? Where are we headed? What must we become? Empirical science, limited by its own self-imposed disciplinary constraints to a phenomenology of (principally, material) human "substance," can offer no meaningful response to such questions. Yet, answers we must seek if, as the Bible teaches, we have a Creator in whose image we are made. Christ, then, is God's reply to humanity's quest for meaning. As Barth explains, "In our exposition of the doctrine of man we must always look in the first instance at the nature of man as it confronts us in the person of Jesus, and only secondarily—asking and answering from this place of light—at the nature of man as that of every man and all other men" (III/2, p. 46).

35. Cortez (2008) succinctly enumerates the three elements of Barth's Christology in terms of the election of Christ, his vicarious submission to the Father, and his mediatorial work on the behalf of humanity: "Not only is [Christ] the 'primarily and originally' elected human being, and the one human being who maintained the covenantal faithfulness of his relationship to God and thus secured human nature against the threat of non-being, but he is also the summons by which God encounters human beings and constitutes them as his covenantal co-partners" (p. 28).

draw anthropological inference (Barth, 2010, III/2, p. 54).[36] Following from this approach, Christ alone perfectly answers David's query concerning humanity. Jesus is the one truly human being (Tanner, 2010; D. F. Wells, 1984).[37]

Yet, the telic aspect of covenant must not be diminished. As Spence (1991) rightly concludes, "We become fully human only as we are conformed to the one whom God put forward as the exemplar of true human existence" (p. 97). In other words, if humanity is, indeed, a "sign" fashioned in some way to image the invisible, ineffable God, Christ is the ultimate fulfilment of that destiny (McMartin, 2013; see Rom 8:29). As such, only by focusing on his person and work can we unlock the "mystery" of humanity and so realize our destiny as God's image bearers in the world (Zizioulas, 1975, p. 433). Further still, in addition to being the one from whom we apprehend our vocation as image bearers, he is also the one through whom God restores his image in us to its fullness, and in whom we are coming to be truly and finally conformed to that image.

Within this framework, Christ in his humanity provides the key to understanding human nature, as expressed in its individual and corporate dimensions, as designed and determined by God, and as lived out *coram deo*. Moreover, he also serves as the relational "locus" between God and humanity wherein he effects our mutual reconciliation (Rom 5:11; 2 Cor 5:19; Eph 2:16), as well as the progressive renewal of the image in

36. Brunner (2014) concurs that any Christian anthropology must "start from the centre, from the revelation of God in Jesus Christ," yet he offers a subtle variance from Barth's approach: "Our Christo-centric method would be misunderstood, however, if we were to deduce from it that the first thing we have to do is to establish a doctrine of the Humanity of Christ. To look at man *in the light* of Jesus Christ is not the same thing as knowing Jesus Christ" (p. 53). The two approaches are, arguably, two sides of a single coin. Whereas, Barth's approach bears on anthropology generally; Brunner's perspective may, in fact, offer a more direct avenue to arriving at idiosyncratic self-knowledge—not through one's apprehension of the person of Christ so much as through direct, personal encounter with Christ himself.

37. Christ is the archetypal human being, but this is not the same as saying humanity is created in the image of Christ (Bavinck, 2004; contra Delitzsch, 2015; Crisp, 2016). My preference is that we consider humanity to be created *for* the image of Christ in order to emphasize its telic, eschatological bearing. Christ alone fulfills humanity's vocation in his perfect relating to the Father and to the world (McMartin, 2013). In his saving work he has accomplished—as in his person he *is*—the renewal and reorientation of the imago in humanity. Through our union with Christ and reconciliation in him to the Father, we, "having been conformed to the image of Christ, are now again becoming like God" (Bavinck, 2004, pp. 554–555; see Rom 8:29; 1 Cor 15:49; Phil 3:21; Eph 4:24; Col 3:10; 1 John 3:2).

us that had been corrupted at the fall (1 Cor 15:49; 2 Cor 3:18; Col 3:10). In support of a christo-anthropological perspective on the imago, Crisp (2016) avers,

> Christ is the archetypal human being, who represents God to humanity and humanity to God in his incarnation. He is also the prototypical human being, after whose image all other human beings are fashioned. Humans are able to represent God in the world in virtue of being made in the image of the God-man, the archetypal image-bearer. (p. 65)

Christ-imaging relationship to God and to others, the covenantal aspect of the imago, is formative for human personhood. We come around to becoming fully human as we image Jesus to God and others. McFadyen (1990) writes, "As our relationship with God is reconstituted through Christ, so are our relations with one another" (p. 114). As this dynamic is strengthened through the increasing appropriation of our Spirit-mediated union with Christ, we come to image the perfect human nature he embodies—in all its various capacities and degrees. Along these lines, Tanner (2010) concludes, "In sum, there is only one perfect or express image of God—the second person of the trinity—and that perfect image becomes the creature's own by way of a close relationship with it, the closer the better, a closeness consummated in Christ" (p. 14). So then, Christ is key to understanding the covenantal imago. God's final aim for our existence is that we should become as fully human as Jesus in relation to God and to others.

4

The outlines of christological personhood

IN THIS CHAPTER I will delve a number of christological implications for human personhood. The discussion, which spans two thousand years of inquiry into the person and work of Christ, is somewhat technical and strays a bit afield at times from the final aim of the present work. In defense of the study that follows, I note that bridge building is a delicate, painstaking enterprise. To argue that Jesus is the epistemic key to covenantal human personhood, as I do in the previous chapter, is all well and good. If I do not also demonstrate that Jesus was and is a person bearing God's image, I have only done half the job. What follows in this chapter amounts to laying down crucial epistemic support structures—the rebar, concrete, and trusswork, so to speak, without which the entire design would collapse. At the same time, Christ is already, by God's foreknowledge and design, the bridge between Creator and creature. The task I undertake, then, is not to invent some cleverly imagined blueprint. Rather, we need only examine the edifice God has made.

To be sure, a truly thorough investigation into the person of Christ is beyond the scope of the present work. The historical and modern literature on the subject is vast and varied. Still, in defense of the central thesis of this work—namely, that Christology supplies us with the epistemic keys to human personhood and, more particularly, the knowledge of self—it is necessary to articulate the several ways in which we may rightly and meaningfully regard Jesus Christ as a human being. The ink spilled over the past two millennia makes such an articulation no simple task. Yet, as Grenz (2004) concludes, "Christology informs the doctrine of humankind, for we cannot know what it means to be human without looking to Jesus, who as the *imago dei* embodying the divine purpose for humankind is the true human" (p. 627). So, simple or not, we must proceed.

Rightly understood, Christ's person cannot be abstracted from his salvific work—accomplished in the main at the cross—without seriously undermining its soteriological significance and, by extension, its theanthropological import (O'Collins, 2009). In the light of Christ's cross humanity's fallen yet redeemable state is clearly revealed and its gospel call distinctly heard. As the Scriptures instruct us, only through our union with the crucified Christ can we access the benefits of his atoning work done for us and for our salvation. Whereas, to apprehend his person without participating vicariously in his death, through active repentance and faith in him, is to yet remain outside the grace of God and cut off from the life he offers. No approach to human personhood can be truly christological where Christ's work is sequestered from his person.

Christ's humanity and ours

Christian orthodoxy maintains that Jesus Christ is a fully human being. On account of his status as a human being, he is able to perfectly fulfill humanity's creation mandate to image God in and for the world. Questions remain, however, regarding the means by which Christ *in his humanity* images God. Historical Christology, after all, posits the presence of *two* natures—one human and another divine—subsisting in the one divine "person" of the Son.[1] Attempts to parse the "human" from the "divine" in

1. The object to which the term "person" is understood to refer has, with the advent of modernity, shifted away from a classical ontological referent (in patristic and medieval usage) toward a more psychological sense. This shift has greatly problematized the task of relating Christology in its classical formulations to modernist anthropological conceptions (Runia, 1984; Schwöbel & Gunton, 1991). In the interests of maintaining continuity with the orthodoxy of the ancient christological confessions, I have employed the term "person" throughout this subsection in its classical sense. Understood this way, every human being-in-relation is a person (self) from the moment of conception. At the same time, in another real sense we are becoming persons through a dynamic process of reciprocal personeity (Zizioulas, 1991). For the sake of clarity, I will refer to the personhood of Jesus Christ, the eternal, divine Word of God, according to the classical usage throughout this section. As such, any sense in which he is "becoming" in his Person as the divine Son will be fundamentally distinct from the sense in which we are becoming persons, since his personhood is eternally and immutably "constituted" in timeless relation with the Father (Wellum, 2016). On the other hand, as will be shown, Christ's human personality (*personalitas*)

the life and work of Christ result in considerable difficulties. When, we may wonder, do we encounter Jesus operating according to—or in order to disclose—his divinity? In what instances, moreover, do we find Jesus' humanity presenting, if that is the right word, itself?

From our limited vantage point, we face an epistemic gap—a problem of knowability. The boundaries of Christ's two natures, difficult as they are to discern, imperil any categorical assurance we might enjoy when stating of Jesus, "See? This is what it means to be a truly human being."[2] Perennially frustrating inquiry, this epistemic gap problematizes the link between Christology and anthropology. Any potential anthropological inference from christological warrant becomes suspect when appeal can be made to Christ's divinity: "No, that's not Jesus acting as human, but divine." As Cortez (2016) notes, historic theological anthropology has more often intuited rather than defended the existence of sufficient warrant for christoanthropological inference (cf. Davidson, 2001). When we come to specifics, shoulders shrug. The gap endures.

The problem of Christ's personhood, so to speak, can be formulated from one of two angles, yet for the present discussion it may be best stated in this way: How can we posit Christ's true and epistemically meaningful humanity *without compromising his divine status*?[3] If the history and diversity of christological heresies offers any gauge on the matter, the solution is anything but simple (see Brown, 1988; Runia, 1984). The Scriptures declare that the divine Son has "become like his brothers and sisters in every respect" (Heb 2:17 NRSV), yet, as historical Christian orthodoxy has maintained, without any consequent diminution or degradation of his divinity (Galot, 1981; Macleod, 1998; Wellum, 2016). According to the New Testament, "The Word became flesh" (John 1:14), yet

and self-consciousness are fundamental aspects of his human nature (Galot, 1981). In his humanity, Christ "became" (ἐγένετο, *egeneto*) in the same ways all other human beings become: in relation to God and others.

2. Modern Christology typically follows Barth in holding that the miracles of Jesus attest to the divinity of Christ (see Wellum, 2016). Yet, within the synoptic Gospels Christ is portrayed equally as a human being chosen by God to fulfill the purposes of God the Father on humanity's behalf (i.e., "Son of man"). So, for instance, in the Matthean account of Jesus' healing of the paralytic, his forgiveness of the man's sins triggers not wonderment that God himself had stepped into human history, rather, the crowds "glorified God, who had given such authority *to men* [τοῖς ἀνθρώποις, *tois anthrōpois*]" (Matt 9:8; cf. Mark 2:1–12) (see Davis, 2006).

3. Brunner (2014) remarks that this is "the real intellectual problem of the doctrine of the Two Natures" (p. 360). This is an understatement, to say the least. Errors of judgment, in this arena at least, are fodder for heresy!

in so doing he did not at any moment cease to be the one by whose divine power creation coheres and is upheld (Col 1:17; Heb 1:3; see Bauckham, 2008; Harris, 1992).

Christ is and remains, therefore, the eternally begotten Son, the second Person of the Trinity, who, according to the Chalcedonian Definition of 451, shares "the same essence with the Father." Nevertheless, Chalcedon also affirms that this divine Son has become in the person of Jesus of Nazareth—mysteriously, paradoxically, irreversibly—human.[4] Thus did the early church fathers seek to establish Jesus of Nazareth as the same "person" as the divine Son, yet possessed of *both* a divine *and* a human nature from the moment of his incarnation.

At least since the fourth century, Christian philosophical theology has undertaken to explicate in metaphysical terms how the person of Christ can be both irreducibly human and divine. As recently as the high Middle Ages, it was a topic of especially seminal importance to theologians intent on deciphering the mystery of the incarnation (see Cross, 2005). Employing metaphysical categories inherited from the philosophical discourse of ancient Hellenism, the medieval scholastics, building on an essentially Chalcedonian foundation, reified the orthodox formula for Christ's personhood. They held that the "person"—*hypostasis*—of the divine Word became a human being like every other when, at the moment of conception within the womb of Mary, he assumed or took on a human "nature"—*physis*—such as all human beings possess. He accomplished

---

4. Care must be taken here to avoid suggesting either (1) the mutability of God the Son in using the language of "becoming," or (2) the existence of two "persons"—one human and one divine—by speaking as I have here of the second "Person" of the Trinity and the "person" of Jesus of Nazareth. The former (1) would represent a departure from the orthodoxy of divine immutability; the latter (2) amounts to Nestorianism, a heterodox Christology roundly condemned as tantamount to adoptionism by the ecumenical councils of Ephesus and Chalcedon in 431 and 451, respectively (Wellum, 2016). Yet, the fact that such views gained support in the early church may indicate the sincere desire to rightly interpret and "translate" the non-technical language of the New Testament into terms readily compatible with the regnant metaphysical paradigms of the day (DeWeese, 2007). So, though the Gospel writer declares that the Word "became [ἐγένετο, egeneto]" flesh (John 1:14), the early church held that the divine Word nevertheless remained unchanged by this union (see Barth, 2010, I/2, pp. 149–50). Furthermore, a Nestorian duality in the person of Christ may, perhaps, shield the divine Word from the scandalous suggestion that God "became" human, while, allegedly, preserving to the fullest degree the humanity of Christ. Yet, how then could Nestorianism not fail to fundamentally undermine the biblical dogma that the Word "became man, true and real man, participating in the same human essence and existence, the same human nature and form, the same historicity that we have" (p. 147)?

this without putting off or compromising his divine nature (or person-hood) in any way.

Later Christian thinkers noted, however, that Chalcedon's "Defini-tion" left *physis* (nature) and *hypostasis* (person) essentially undefined (Galot, 1981; Macquarrie, 2003a; Norris, 1996).[5] Among these later thinkers, Boethius, in his subsequent defense of Chalcedonian ortho-doxy, proffered definitions of "nature" and "person." As it happened, Boethius became largely responsible for grounding subsequent christo-logical discourse in an explicitly Aristotelian metaphysic (Grenz, 2001).[6] "Nature," he would write, "is the specific property of any substance, and Person is the individual substance of a rational nature" (Boethius, 1978, p. 93). Imagining Aristotle nodding approvingly is no exaggeration as he too held that a nature is not a substance—an object that exists in reality—but rather the constitutive set of properties *possessed by* a substance. By contrast, a person—whether that person be human or divine—possesses discrete properties in accordance with his or her nature.[7]

From these definitions, scholastic philosophical theology, over the next seven hundred years or so, would continue to develop what has in

5. Coakley (2002) determines that "the major achievement" of Chalcedon was in establishing a "'regulatory' vocabulary, on which semantic grid the events of salvation are now plotted" (p. 148). DeWeese (2007) surmises, "While some of the ambiguity resulting from the lack of clear definitions of the terms *physis* and *hypostasis* may have been intentional, some also resulted from the shifting metaphysical background in the Eastern portion of the church. There Neoplatonism, which would remain dominant in the West for several centuries longer, was being supplanted by a renewed form of Aristotelianism" (p. 121). DeWeese further notes the role political considerations appear to have played in alternately fomenting and resolving many of the christological controversies throughout the church's adolescence (pp. 121–22).

6. Boethius sought to curtail two nascent perspectives that appear to have arisen as a consequence of the ambiguity of Chalcedon (Grenz, 2001). His definitions of "per-son" and "nature" defended against the Nestorian notion that the person of the divine Word had assumed or "possessed" a separate and distinct human person resulting in the union of two persons into one body–soul composite. It also ruled out of bounds the Eutychian assertion that the divine and human natures had somehow blended or commingled into a single semi-human, semi-divine amalgam or *tertium quid*. Grenz (2001) observes the particular Aristotelian nuance of Boethius' definitions, remarking that they made possible "the claim that personhood belongs to the realm of unchang-ing essence rather than changeable characteristics" (p. 66).

7. By the late Middle Ages, Aquinas, Scotus, and Ockham would contribute a further nuance by distinguishing substance from *suppositum*—"an independently ex-isting ultimate subject of characteristics" (Freddoso, 1986, p. 28)—further grounding the personhood of Christ in the identity of the Word (see also Cross, 2005; DeWeese, 2007; Stump, 2002).

modern times come to be known as the "classical" metaphysical model of the hypostatic union—the coming together in one person—of Christ's two natures (Wellum, 2016; see Cross, 2005).[8] In so doing, the medieval model reified Boethius' strictly metaphysical definition of "person" and "nature." Modern anthropology has moved considerably far afield from such metaphysical categories. Yet, as noted in the previous chapter, the covenantal imago—being in encounter—has its basis in the constitutive reality of human particularity. The boundary of my personhood is defined by the range of my constituent parts (i.e., my body–soul composite).[9]

According to the classical definitions of "person" and "nature," in order for Christ to be regarded as fully human he must be a person who instantiates the "concrete particulars" common to all human beings— which would necessarily include a human body and a "rational human soul" (Crisp, 2007; Wellum, 2016).[10] So, as the classical formulation

8. The christological "formula" derived from Chalcedon, as summarized by Crisp (2016), contains four key metaphysical propositions: "1. Christ is one person. 2. Christ has two natures, one divine and one human. 3. The two natures of Christ retain their integrity and are distinct; they are not mixed together or confused, nor are they amalgamated into a hybrid of divine and human attributes (like a demigod). 4. The natures of Christ are really united in the person of Christ—that is, they are two natures possessed by one person" (p. 82). These pillars of Chalcedonian orthodoxy provide the discursive bounds of the incarnation, ostensibly preserving perspectives on Christ's human nature from in any way denigrating his divinity, or vice versa. Wellum (2016) articulates his own "classical" formulation of the hypostatic union in terms of the Chalcedonian–Boethian distinction between person and nature thus: "[T]he *divine person* of the Son, subsisting in the *divine nature*, did not become a human person but assumed a *human nature*, such that the same *I* is the *person of Christ* that now subsists in the *divine nature as God* and in a *human nature as man*" (p. 429; emphasis original).

9. Freddoso (1986) makes a crucial observation regarding the resistance in modern ethics to maintaining a metaphysical sense of personhood. If, as contemporary philosophers would have us believe, personhood is merely "evaluative" rather than intrinsic, then, "an entity *x* is a person only if the rest of us (or, perhaps, those in charge or those in the know) consent to treat *x* in the special way associated with personhood" (p. 50n5). Along these lines, Evans' (2002) "non-metaphysical" definition—"being a self is not being a special type of entity, but rather it is a matter of having a special status, a status that is linked to social relationships"—leads him to acknowledge an evaluative consequence for personhood: "On such a view, a human being may become a self, or might cease to be a self" (p. 73). Clearly, this perspective opens the door to potentially grave ethical consequences—a point that Moreland & Rae (2000) urge us to bear in mind.

10. Medieval scholars intent on maintaining the linguistic and conceptual boundaries of Chalcedon were confronted with the challenge of articulating their models of the incarnation within this discursive framework (M. M. Adams, 1999; DeWeese, 2007). At times, this resulted in conceptual and rhetorical figurations some modern

holds, the presence in the person of Christ of a human body–mind–soul means that he possesses a comprehensive array of human cognitive and psychosocial capacities distinct from, and supplementary to, the divine capacities he possessed prior to his incarnation. He is a divine person with a divine nature, his humanity, metaphysically speaking, having been added onto what he already possessed by reason of his divinity (Warfield, 2015). So, Runia (1984) explains, "[Christ] had a truly human mind, will, consciousness and personality" (p. 107).[11]

Again, orthodox Christology maintains that Jesus' human ratio-emotive faculties did not in any way supplant or diminish the divine mind, will, or consciousness of God the Son. Christ has both a divine and human mind and self-consciousness. On the other hand, this does

---

readers have regarded as problematic. By way of example, Swinburne (1994) remarks with no small irony on Aquinas's use of *hypostasis*, "For all humans other than Christ Aquinas held . . . the human person is the same thing as his or her individual human nature. . . . What, according to Aquinas, distinguishes Christ from other humans is that while Christ is a person who is a human being, he is not a human person" (p. 214). Crisp (2007) in his own articulation appears to equivocate on this point. Maintaining a medieval exegesis of Chalcedon, he avers, "The human nature of Christ is not a person independent of the Word. Nor is the human nature of Christ a person in itself, as it were, once the Word has assumed it" (p. 82); yet, "[the human nature of Christ] *becomes a human person* on its assumption by the Word" (p. 80, emphasis mine). As Freddoso (1986) rightly observes, the "medieval tradition" creates a distinction between "human person" and "person who is a human being" (30). Although metaphysically significant, this rhetorical concession does not in any way undermine our ability to posit Christ's full likeness to the rest of humanity. In other words, metaphysical considerations notwithstanding, the New Testament witness as well as the confessions of Christian orthodoxy prevent us from diminishing the significance—whether ontological or epistemological—of Christ's human nature.

11. Freddoso (1986) cautions against concluding from the medieval location of the "person" of Christ in the person of the divine Word that "Christ's human nature lacks its own *personalitas* (personhood)." The scholastics, he notes, explicitly denounced "the psychological claim that Christ lacks a human personality, where the English word 'personality' is taken in the usual way to connote a configuration of character traits and temperament" (p. 50n7). While the presence of two minds in Christ—one human and one divine—might suggest the existence of two relational centers, this would open the door to a Nestorian duality in which Christ-as-human relates *inter*subjectively (rather than *intra*subjectively) to Christ-as-divine. Morris (2001) develops an analogy with human psychology by adducing the interaction between a normal human being's conscious and unconscious "minds." This is probably wrong, however. Jesus, like all other human beings, possesses a conscious and unconscious mind *qua* human. What he possesses *qua* divine, we can only speculate at, but his fulfillment of his mission required that he function at all times under the strict rubric of his human nature. Otherwise, he would have violated the "in every respect" necessary to be "like his brothers and sisters."

not suggest, and we must avoid the Nestorian conclusion, that Christ is *two* persons granted his ownership, so to speak, of two distinct centers of cognition and volition. Rather, the conclusion of orthodoxy is that God the Son committed himself to thinking and willing *as a human being*. Only by his ownership of a human mind–soul and the requisite accompanying neurobiological structures could he accomplish this agenda. As Galot (1981) helpfully clarifies,

> Jesus' human nature is fully endowed with human reality and human existence . . . with a human consciousness and a human will, a soul that acts according to the laws of human psychology and remains distinct from his divine spirit, "without any commingling." Without losing any of its own qualities, this human nature is personalized by the relational being of the Word. (p. 306)

As should be clear by now, the manner in which the early church delineated the particulars of Christ's humanity fell under the same metaphysical rubric as the constitutive imago. They sought, in other words, to posit his ontic status *qua* human in strictly static, formal terms. Their model emphasized the "parts" and capacities of human nature—both Christ's and ours—and so, neglected what is, arguably, most fundamental to personhood, whether human or divine, namely, relationality (Zizioulas, 1985).

As Reformed anthropology from Calvin to Barth would later insist, the image of God entails more than a set of formal functions or structural capacities. The constitutive imago certainly provides a metaphysical basis for positing the covenantal imago—we *have* the image of God so that we might *be* imagers of God. Yet, to bear the capacity of an imager is meaningless without the (human) freedom to exercise it. From this, I conclude that Jesus fulfills the distinctives of the covenantal imago in his perfected relatedness to God and others, having done so as a truly—though not merely—human being.

So, while a metaphysical account may supply a discursive framework for the formal mechanics of the incarnation, it does not clarify the nature of Christ's relationship to the Father and to his fellow human beings as one who is "like his brothers and sisters in every respect." As Bavinck (2006) suggests, metaphysical models of the incarnation establish the parameters according to which Christ fulfills—or, perhaps, fills up—the constitutive imago dei with which humanity has uniquely been endowed (p. 259). On the other hand, from the moment of the incarnation, the person of the Son by reason of his human nature possessed the immanently human capacity to image God in the active, dynamic sense of the covenantal imago (see McMartin, 2013).[12] From this vantage point, then, Christology most meaningfully informs and interacts with anthropological discourse. As Barth (2010) pointedly remarked, Christology is "more than an obscure metaphysics" (IV/3, p. 136).

Christological reflection on Christ's humanity must inevitably transcend metaphysical considerations to be truly fruitful for Christian anthropology. As Brunner (2014) rightly observes, "[O]nce we begin to think in abstract terms of the *schema* of the Two Natures, then we cannot hold the unity of the divine-human Person save through the denial of [Nestorian] duality" (p. 362).[13] Even so, the unity of Christ's personhood must be preserved even at the risk of resorting to the category of mystery on the one hand (see Pannenberg, 1977) and error on the other.

Affirmations regarding the various parameters of Christ's humanity, once firmly buttressed by Chalcedonian orthodoxy, should necessarily proceed beyond the bounds of metaphysical discourse. Whatever parallels we may adduce between Jesus and us demand that we move past rarified abstraction. On this point, Davidson (2001) is clear:

> Christology is not about [metaphysics], but the dramatic exposition of the encounter between God and humanity. . . . The humanity which the Son of God assumes is not an 'impersonal'

12. This point should not be construed to suggest that the preincarnate Son did not image the Father actively and covenantally. It is crucial, nevertheless, to affirm that Christ *in his humanity* provides the ultimate key to understanding our human capacity to image God (so, Tanner, 2010). As McMartin (2013) rightly concludes, "[I]f we only have reason to think that Christ bears the image in virtue of his divine nature, then a major motivation for connecting anthropology and Christology will be lost" (p. 143).

13. Brunner (2014) goes so far as to conclude, "[T]he whole complex of problems raised by the doctrine of the Two Natures is the result of a question which is wrongly posed, of a question which wants to know something which we simply cannot know, namely, how divinity and humanity are united in the Person Jesus Christ" (p. 362). Barth would certainly proceed further than Brunner's apophatic avowal in his retrieval of Leontius' sixth-century *anhypostasia–enhypostasia* distinction (Barth, 1991, p. 157–58; see Crisp, 2007, Chapter 3; Davidson, 2001). Stated succinctly, the human nature of Christ is said to subsist only in the hypostasis of the divine Word. Apart from this proviso Christ's human nature is to be regarded as anhypostatic or impersonal, having "no reality in isolation from the subjecthood" of the second person of the Trinity (Davidson, 2001, p. 135). Yet, at the moment of Christ's incarnation the Word hypostasized his human nature rendering it enhypostasized by means of his divine personhood.

> substance somehow taken up. . . . God does not become incarnate *simpliciter*: God particularizes the history of Jesus as God's own. Jesus' fleshly existence, the life of this real man, is . . . as a genuinely human being . . . subject to all the normal conditions of creaturely finitude and even fallenness. Jesus is no demigod or angel, but one with us in the frustrations, struggles, drives and needs of human life. There is a radical and comprehensive solidarity with humankind. . . . Without this, talk of . . . 'solidarity' in any ultimately transformative or redemptive sense, would be meaningless, for Jesus would not truly represent God to humankind or humankind to God. It is by his obedience within the terms of this humanity, not as an ideal, that the incarnate Word deals with sin and reconciles to God. (p. 144)

Metaphysics, then, is purely preliminary to the deeper significance of the incarnation. In the previous chapter, I noted the distinction between the constitutive and covenantal imago and the import each brings to theological anthropology. To reiterate, the imago is the semiodiscursive "sign" of God, alternately reflecting and representing God along two axes—one vertical and one horizontal. As the Son, Jesus both perfectly reflects to God the image of the Father and "projects" that same image to—and onto—fallen humanity. In his assumption of human "flesh," the Logos does not merely impersonate, but rather en-personates, so to speak, a human being fully conformed—and, at least for the period of his terrestrial life, conforming—to the image of God. For this reason the writer of Hebrews, though operating with the highest of Christologies, speaks of Jesus having "learned" (ἔμαθεν, *emathen*) obedience and his "being made perfect" (τελειωθεὶς, *teleiōtheis*) with the result that he "became" (ἐγένετο, *egeneto*) for us the means of our redemption (Heb 5:8–9). Like every other human being, Jesus had to grow into the image. Unlike the rest of us, he actually got there.

The crucial distinction of a covenantal Christology, over and against a constitutive, metaphysical model, is its emphasis on the unity between Jesus and his Father, rather than on the union of his human and divine natures, which the former nonetheless presumes. While the latter provides epistemological warrant and conceptual clarity to the formal mechanics of incarnation, it offers no anthropological significance viz. Jesus' humanity. If we are to understand better who we are, what we are becoming, we must move beyond the facts and formulas of the incarnation. Having established the necessary groundwork, we may proceed to the next stage of our bridgework.

Jesus Christ the human being

The covenantal Christology I propose here presupposes, with classical orthodoxy, the metaphysical reality of Christ's two natures. With this ontological base properly established, we may justly speak of the two relational operations or schemata by which the person who is Jesus Christ relates to the Father as image bearer. According to the first, the divine Son, second Person of the Trinity, who eternally shares in the glory of the Father, images God *as God* (see John 1:1-5; cf. 17:5). Secondly, though fully divine, Christ the incarnate Logos became a fully human being, who, having acceded to the divine plan for the redemption of humanity, willingly set aside certain prerogatives of his divine nature that he might image God to God *as one of us* (Phil 2:6–8). To be clear, in taking on a human nature, the Son's divine nature suffered no loss or degradation; he did not, in other words, become less than fully God. Rather, he accepted limitations on the *expression* of his divine nature in order that he might "become like his brothers and sisters in every respect."

It is crucial for us to grasp the implications of Christ's full humanity. Respective to the *missio dei*—the redemptive purposes for which God the Son became human—only insofar as Christ images God *as a human being* could he accomplish this purpose. More will be said on this point in short order. At this juncture, however, this critical point should be made clear: human beings, on account of our rebellion, broke covenant with God and so became estranged from God. What Jesus accomplished at the cross (see John 19:30) was both to redeem humanity from its fallen, sinful state *and to reconcile us to God*. A ransomed humanity is only halfway there, so to speak. By means of his full humanity, Christ also mediates humanity's reconciliation to the Father by drawing us, by means of the Spirit, into covenantal union with God. Christ mends the union, which we broke, by becoming sin for sinful humanity and suffering humanity's estrangement from God in our stead (Rom 5:10; 2 Cor 5:21; Eph 2:13; Col 1:20, 22; 1 Pet 1:17–20; cf. Ps 58:3; Isa 1:4; Ezek 14:5). Christ accomplishes this by renewing in us the covenantal imago that had been lost at humanity's fall.

As God, the Son perfectly reveals the Father to us; as a human being, Jesus not only makes visible the invisible God but he also reveals in himself the perfection and perfectibility of the imago dei to which we have been called. In the latter sense, Christ's revelatory role assumes its greatest anthropological significance. Fittingly then, Athanasius (2012) concludes, "[T]he most holy Son of the Father, being the Image of the

Father, came to our region to renew man once made in His likeness, and find him, as one lost, by the remission of sins" (p. 43). Likewise, Spence (1991) assigns Christ's primary revelatory role to his human, rather than divine, nature and cautions, "[W]henever the divine nature is considered as directly determining the humanity of Christ, some aspect of his human nature is either neglected or denied" (p. 92). From the vantage point of the covenantal imago Christ reveals the Father inasmuch as he is the true image of God, not merely or even primarily due to the fact of his divinity.

God's will from the beginning, after all, was that humanity would serve as the visible sign of his glory and goodness in the world (Gen 1:26–27). Christ accomplishes this expressly human vocation in and through his human relatedness to God as the fulfillment of the covenantal imago. This crucial distinction could potentially be lost or effaced by placing undue emphasis on a constitutive Christology. As Pannenberg (1977) explains,

> The actual event of the unification of God and man in the temporal execution of the course of Jesus' existence is obscured by the perception—in itself correct—that Jesus' human existence in the whole of its historical course has the ground of its unity and meaning (and thus also of its facticity) in the fact that Jesus is the eternal Son of God. (p. 338)

If, on the other hand, the deeper significance of Jesus' historical existence is to be found not in his "ontological dependence" on the Word but in his eminently human "dependence on the Father," then Christ may also be shown to be the perfect image of God who reveals what it means to be fully human (p. 339).[14]

For all its merit and validity, on its own terms Chalcedonian Christology establishes the conditions but not the means by which Christ is the fulfillment of the covenantal imago dei. The key to understanding human nature *coram deo*, on the other hand, is Christ in his humanity.[15] As a

14. Had God the Son never assumed a human nature he would still perfectly reveal the Father (as "the Son"), yet we could not affirm his full humanity, and thus any direct christological link with the imago dei would be lost. Due to the fact of his subsistence as the divine Word, Christ reveals true God; but only in his Spirit-mediated dependence on the Father does Christ reveal true humanity—making the image visible, as it were (John 1:18; Col 1:15; 1 John 4:12[!])—and inform a Christian understanding of human self-knowledge.

15. Pannenberg (1977) has termed this christological dilemma, "the impasse of the

human being Christ images God, as one of us, along two relational axes—to/with God and to/with his fellow human beings. While God the Son may well be the Person upon which the image of God in human beings finds its conceptual (i.e., theological) basis, only in examining Jesus Christ the human being do we encounter sufficient ontological and epistemological basis for drawing anthropological inference regarding human personhood.

The human self-consciousness of Jesus

From the fifth century, the orthodoxy of Chalcedon—one person, two natures—has withstood the weight of intense philosophical and theological pressure, proving resilient in the face of its erstwhile theological and cultural despisers.[16] Yet, in emphasizing the dogma of the metaphysical unity of Christ's personhood, a commensurate emphasis on Christ's fulfillment of the covenantal imago has, arguably, been lost. Noting this deficit, Spence (1991) writes,

> [A] survey of the history of doctrine suggests that the Church has by and large failed to bring its perception of Christ as the incarnation of the eternal Son of God into a coherent relation to the Gospel portrayal of Jesus as a man of the same nature as ourselves who is inspired by the Holy Spirit. Such a failure . . . has resulted in the widespread neglect in practice of a foundation of Christian anthropology, that is, the doctrine that in the life of the incarnate Christ there has indeed been an historical exemplification of "true man." (p. 75)

The resulting imbalance has had the unintended consequence of problematizing discussions regarding Christ's humanity (see Ware, 2012).

As previously stated, to aver that Jesus is God does not imply that he is less than fully human, only that he is not *merely* human. Some seem to

two-natures doctrine" (p. 323). He further explains that "the concept of the incarnation, inescapable though it is, cannot explain the unity of God and man in Jesus Christ because it is itself an expression of this unity, which must be explained and established on other grounds. The impasse reached by every [historical] attempt to construct Christology by beginning with the incarnational concept demonstrates that all such attempts are doomed to failure" (p. 322).

16. According to Runia (1984), since its inception, this "old Christological dogma" has remained, "the shibboleth that distinguished orthodoxy from liberalism," for Eastern and Western churches, for Catholic and Protestant believers, and among all major branches of reformational piety (p. 13).

fear that positing certain human limitations in Jesus runs the risk of compromising his full deity. Among the thorniest of questions, the problem of Jesus' human self-consciousness ranks higher than most.[17] The problem can be stated in different ways; for example: Was Jesus, in his humanity, undiminished in knowledge from the moment of his conception? If not, was he nonetheless conscious of himself as the eternal Son throughout his earthly tenure? Did he possess the capacity for direct, unlimited cognitive access to the mind of God at any given moment? Finally, even if we answer in the affirmative to these questions, by which operation or schema did he possess his awareness, whether by means of his divine nature or through his Spirit-enacted relatedness to God?

Asked another way: Was Jesus' consciousness of his identity something he came to akin to the ways in which every other human being grows in self-awareness? Did Jesus' human mind–soul possess a full, divinely "infused" knowledge[18] of his identity and vocation as the divine

17. In his now-dated christological study, R. E. Brown (1967) argues that one reason for the hesitancy among Catholic scholars in pursuing this line of inquiry had been the fear of "repercussions" for the "charge of denying the divinity of Jesus" (p. 41). This hesitancy ensued, he observes, in spite of the biblical affirmations of Christ's full humanity and the Chalcedonian asseveration that the eternal Son became in the incarnation "consubstantial with us according to his humanity; in all things like unto us, without sin." Brown goes on to remark pointedly that "only when one has a strong faith in the divinity of Jesus is there a real problem about admitting that his knowledge might have been limited" (p. 42). Surely this is the case.

18. The suggestion that Jesus "knew" his identity as the divine Word requires that further qualification be made between knowledge and consciousness. Along these lines, Rahner (1966) helpfully distinguishes between the knowledge of particular objects and what he terms "nonobjective consciousness." The latter he defines as an "*a priori*, nonobjective knowledge about oneself [or God] as a fundamental given of the spiritual subject in which it is by itself and simultaneously aware of its transcendental reference to the totality of possible objects of knowledge and freedom" (p. 200). McDermott (1993) clarifies Rahner's distinction in what amounts to very Kierkegaardian language: "Immediate self-presence and presence to God as the ultimate goal of all our knowing and loving are forms of nonobjective consciousness, not knowledge of objects. Consciousness of self and of God as the goal of our spiritual dynamism are concomitant with our knowledge of objects, and compared with the latter can seem dark and fragile. Self and God as goal of our self-transcendence are indirectly given in consciousness through our implicit awareness of self as origin and God as ultimate 'whither' of all our knowing and loving" (p. 204). In other words, consciousness of self is subjective (and consciousness of other/Other intersubjective) rather than objective, though it necessarily entails at least some objective knowledge (see Burke, 2002, pp. 152–53; Moloney, 1999). Thus, for Rahner, Jesus could have come to consciousness of himself and of God *qua* human in a manner analogous to our own acquisition of subjective knowledge of God and self apart from a direct perception of God and self as "objects" of knowledge (cf. Pannenberg, 1977, pp. 330–31).

Word sent from the Father to redeem humanity during every moment of his incarnation; or did he come to this awareness by means of human experience analogous to normative human development?[19] If the former, then we would surely have reason to question the existence of any christological basis for relational self-knowledge rooted in reciprocal personeity. If, on the other hand, Christ the human being grew in his consciousness of himself as Israel's Messiah, and further as the divine Logos from all eternity by means of his Spirit-empowered yet immanently human relationship to God, then this would potentially provide sufficient warrant for the development of a christological account of relational self-knowledge in human image bearers.

With due deference to Chalcedonian orthodoxy, O'Collins (2009) concludes, "With respect to his divinity Christ is omniscient, but with respect to his humanity he is limited in knowledge" (p. 240). One challenge confronting orthodox Christology, then, is to explain in non-contradictory terms how both an unlimited and a limited knowledge can be apposite with respect to a single person.[20] Traditionally, *qua*—meaning, with respect to or in the capacity of—has provided the rhetorical means

19. Vos (1953) determines that such a "purely speculative" question can have no bearing on Christology due to the lack of "biographical data for the pre-baptismal period of Jesus' life" (pp. 88–89). Vos does not appear to regard Luke 2:41–49 as carrying sufficient exegetical weight to merit inquiry into Christ's pre-baptismal self-consciousness, though, conversely, he cites 2:49 as evidence that Jesus considered himself to be the Son of God (see pp. 143, 170). Surely, despite the paucity of such texts, there is sufficient *theological* warrant, derived from the biblical affirmation of Christ's humanity (Heb 2:17), to justify explorations of Jesus' development of a fully human self-consciousness.

20. Together with the Trinity, the doctrine of the incarnation has historically elicited more accusations of paradox or even blatant contradiction than any other. By way of example, there is Feuerbach's (1989) classic denunciation of Christianity as "*a contradiction . . . personified in the God-man*" (p. 332; emphasis original). He further concludes, "The divine nature, notwithstanding the position that Christ was at once God and man, is just as much dissevered from the human nature *in* the incarnation as *before* it, since each nature excludes the conditions of the other, although both are united in one personality, in an incomprehensible, miraculous, i.e., untrue manner, in contradiction with the relation in which, according to their definition, they stand to each other" (pp. 333–334; emphasis original). This is not to say, however, that every assault on the facticity of the incarnation has come from outside of Christianity (see Hick, 1977). Despite such accusations of contradictoriness, O'Collins (2009) issues the orthodox defense of coherence: "The incarnation is a paradox (an apparent contradiction that on closer inspection proves not to be incoherent) but not a blatant, logical contradiction. This belief has not been shown to be metaphysically impossible or logically incoherent like talk of a 'married bachelor' or a 'square circle'" (p. 240).

of distinguishing metaphysically between the divine Word's existence and functioning in and through his two natures (O'Collins, 2011). Axiomatically, God the Son is, *qua* divine, omniscient (Harris, 1992; Wellum, 2016). As an immanent aspect of his divinity, God possesses an eternally present awareness of all that is knowable (Helm, 2011; Ware, 2000).

Jesus is a divine person with two natures: one divine, one human. What we conclude about Christ's "person" and "natures," however, carries us only so far.[21] What is needed is a more penetrative analysis of Christ's humanity in light of the covenantal imago. Accordingly, Jesus *qua* human emptied himself of his infinite, divine self-awareness of his unique identity as the divine Word, the second Person of the Trinity, at the moment of his incarnation. More significant still, the basis of his human self-knowledge was not ontological but relational—not, in other words, on account of his being God, but by means of his human relatedness to God and others.[22] Jesus, *qua* human, grew in self-knowledge.

The most natural objection raised to the proposition Jesus' knowledge was limited by reason of his humanity is that ignorance suggests an imperfection.[23] Contra this objection, Moloney (1999) concludes, "It is

21. Wright (2011) shares his own concern that constitutive Christologies shed insufficient light on the matter: "Unless we can give some sort of account of Jesus' own self-understanding, I simply don't think it's good enough to talk about two minds (or one), two natures (or one), or about the various combinations and permutations of persons and substances" (p. 53).

22. Wellum (2016) suggests his tacit rejection of this distinction. Drawing heavily on the Johannine attestations of the Word's divine union with the Father, he concludes, "*The incarnate Son relates to the Father in divine-filial dependence as he has from eternity*" (p. 431; emphasis original). Thus, Wellum shifts the locus of Christ's relatedness to the Father away from his humanity toward his divinity, essentially conflating the economic relationships within the Trinity and Jesus' human relatedness to God (p. 430; cf. John 6:38). As of the incarnation, the divine Son relates to the Father, according to Wellum, as he has from all eternity, yet, from the moment of the incarnation, he may now do so within the context of his human nature (i.e., his body–soul composite). Wellum's approach shares much in common with the trinitarian Christology of Catholic theologian Hans Urs von Balthasar who viewed the vocation (*missio*) of Christ as a modal extension of the intratrinitarian procession (*processio*) of the eternal Son from the Father (Balthasar, 1992b; see Swain & Allen, 2013). Respecting Balthasar's approach, Moloney (1999) notes, "Sonship . . . and the obedience which is its primal expression, are the fundamental themes of Christ's consciousness and knowledge. Through the notion of sonship, that which the Word is at the heart of the Trinity can be transposed into the language of this world" (p. 91).

23. This seems to have been a concern Aquinas endeavored to obviate in positing that Christ possessed the "beatific vision" of God "from the first moment of his conception" (*Summa Theologica*, III, q. 34, a. 4; see Moloney, 1999, pp. 57–58).

far from clear how one can vindicate any reality in Christ's humanity if one denies him a human consciousness and freedom" (p. 108). Indeed, to grant Christ unlimited access to divine "consciousness and freedom" problematizes any meaningful sense by which he can be said to be human. Along these lines, Pannenberg (1977) warns,

> [T]o attribute to the [human] soul of Jesus a knowledge of all things past, present, and future, and of everything that God knows from the very beginning, in the sense of a supernatural vision, makes the danger more than considerable that the genuine humanity of Jesus' experiential life would be lost. (p. 329)[24]

A limited Jesus, on the other hand, suggests ample anthropological inference. Do we risk heresy by positing a Jesus who comes, over time, to veridical knowledge of himself?

The New Testament witness to the life and ministry of Christ, to say nothing of the Chalcedonian formula, expressly grants license for positing limitations in the knowledge and self-consciousness of Jesus *qua* human. Jesus himself, after all, explicitly acknowledged his own "limited" knowledge respective to the date and time of his return (Matt 24:36; see parallels). This fact, Berkouwer (1972) confesses, presents us with "a great mystery about the person of Christ" (p. 258). Other passages strongly suggest that Jesus obtained experimental knowledge of himself,

---

24. Pannenberg, in his well-known adumbration of a Christology "from below," seeks to ground "the recognition of [Christ's] divinity" by "rising from the historical man Jesus," particularly from the historical fact of his resurrection in and by the power of God, rather than through the theological formulation of the incarnation established by Chalcedonian orthodoxy (Pannenberg, 1977, p. 33). Yet, despite his concerns regarding a *strictly* ontological Christology, he nonetheless affirms his commitment to "retain the truth included in that [traditional] formula" (p. 339). It is unclear on what basis, then, Gunton (1997) maintains with stark certainty: "Pannenberg rejects the Christology of Chalcedon" (p. 23). Runia (1984), for instance, deems as "evident" the fact that "Pannenberg's Christology, through starting 'from below' . . . ultimately comes very close to the classical Christology," though he acknowledges the latter's commitment to developing a "variant of the Chalcedonian tradition" (pp. 36–37), and further notes that Luther himself insisted on a Christology "from below" on exegetical grounds (p. 97). Where Pannenberg certainly does fall short is in his twin denunciations of the historicity of the gospel accounts of Jesus and of his virgin conception. In spite of Gunton's critique of Pannenberg as "over-rationalist," he nonetheless sees "possibilities" toward what he calls "a purified Christology from below" suggested by Pannenberg's theology (Gunton, 1997, p. 30). Gunton hastens to add that such a Christology would need to begin with "the New Testament Jesus" rather than proceed through any "Hegelian framework of meaning" and unity (p. 31).

of others, and of the world like any other human being (Luke 2:52; Mark 5:30-33; John 11:34).[25]

In light of this data Bray (2012) concludes regarding Jesus, "[A]lthough he was a divine person, he was functioning within the parameters of his human nature and could not exceed them without compromising the integrity of his humanity" (p. 570). Wellum (2016) further insists, "[Jesus] knows as a man, which entails that he knows subject to the same laws of perception, memory, logic, and development as we do" (p. 455). Yet, what can we make of Jesus' knowledge of himself? Who did he believe himself to be at any given moment?[26]

The preincarnate Word is a divine person who *qua* divine knows himself exhaustively and eternally. Yet, in taking on a human nature the divine Son willingly subjected himself to the covenantal dynamic by which all human beings come to know themselves, namely, through his agapic relationality to the Father and to others. Therefore, in all things divine or mundane Christ grew in knowledge—of God, himself, and others—as all human beings do. So, Macleod (1998) avers, "in all these respects" Christ's knowledge "was parallel to our own" (p. 167).

Furthermore, at every occasion when Jesus appeared to possess knowledge that he could not have come to possess through natural human means (see Matt 17:27; Mark 14:13; Luke 2:47; 5:4-6; John 1:47;

---

25. Alongside these passages, others can be cited to demonstrate Jesus' possession of extraordinary, even supernatural, knowledge (see John 1:48-49; Mark 11:2, and parallels; Matt 17:24-27).

26. From the moment of Jesus' emergence from Galilean obscurity, the Synoptic accounts depict him as a man preternaturally aware of his unique identity as well as his divinely appointed vocation. As events unfold, at every turn he seems to know more about himself and where he is headed than his closest followers manage to grasp (Mark 8:33; Luke 24:25; John 12:16; et al.). Yet, interestingly, what the disciples come in fits and starts to acknowledge—and what he expressly forbids them to disclose—is not his deity, but rather his status as Israel's Messiah (Matt 16:16; John 11:27; cf. Matt 26:63; John 10:24). On the other hand, ignorance of Jesus' *messianic* identity is something the Gospel writers take pains to preemptively and assiduously undermine in their readers. Indeed, the mention of John the Baptist's conferral of messianic distinction on Jesus as well as the evangelists' editorial connection of the former's prophetic ministry with Isaiah 40:3-11(see Matt 3:3; Mark 1:2-3; Luke 3:4-6; John 1:23) seems intended to forestall any potential ambiguity in this regard. Arguably, only in the Gospel of John does it become explicit that Jesus is not "merely" the Messiah—i.e., the "son of God" through whom God intends to fulfill the promises he made to (and through) David for his people Israel—but God himself come among us to fulfill what only a divine Son could accomplish, namely, the redemption of the world (Köstenberger & Swain, 2008; Wright, 1996).

4:18; 11:14), he received such knowledge as a "gift" mediated to his human mind by the Spirit from the Father. So, Wellum (2016) again, "In his humanity, the Son knew as we know and received supernatural knowledge in relation to the Father and by the Spirit, as other prophets in Scripture received revelation" (p. 457). As with his knowledge of the events and affairs of all things external to himself, Christ's knowledge of himself was constituted throughout the course of his life into a fully mature, well-developed self-consciousness by means of his relationships with God and with others. Jesus knew, in other words, like we know—in relationship.

As an object of his human self-knowledge, Jesus' understanding of himself as the divine Word would have been entailed within the rubric, "things that he had to learn as he grew" (Ware, 2012, p. 126). In other words, Jesus' human development would have been—and not merely seemed—perfectly normal.[27] Regarding the means by which Jesus came to awareness of himself, O'Collins (2009) concludes,

> [Jesus'] personal identity (as Son of God) did/does not depend upon his human awareness of himself—that is to say, upon the self-consciousness mediated through his human mind. Yet, his (human) sense of his own identity did depend upon his awareness of himself and his experience of the world. . . . His self-identification depended upon a self-consciousness of the world 'out there.' Through his (human) awareness of his own personal identity, Christ knew not only his distinct identity in himself but also his identity-in-relationship (his 'social' self) as subject-in-relation to the God whom he called 'Abba.' (p. 244)

As Jesus grew in his consciousness of God and of himself, he would, over time, come to grasp the astounding reality of his unique identity and relationship with the Father.

---

27. Crowe (2006) writes, "The ordinary child does not know the word 'I' but has to learn to use it . . . I see no reason for asserting anything different about Jesus" (p. 210). It is difficult to imagine the reason for the dismay of Jesus' family and neighbors at his sudden, apparent pretensions—to their thinking—concerning his identity and mission had they witnessed anything other than a normal, mundane upbringing in which he evinced the limitations, both cognitive and behavioral, common to every stage of human development (see Matt 13:55–56; Mark 3:21; John 7:5). On the other hand, had Jesus only *seemed* to develop the ability to think and act as, say, a normal human toddler forming words and phrases out of gibberish, or a ten-year-old learning to parse the logic of a given proposition, etc., would we not be right to reckon him a merely docetic Christ?

Spence (1991), in defending the preservation of a distinctly human self-consciousness in Christ, notes that only the conclusions and not the means of Jesus' introspection would have differed from ours:

> There seems no reason . . . to consider the functioning of Jesus' human self-consciousness as discontinuous with our own, forming and developing as he grew in his experience of himself, the world and of God. Rather, it was in the content of this perception of himself that the distinction lay. (p. 94)

As you and I come to veridical awareness of self, we (rightly) conclude that we are not divine persons. This knowledge is mediated to us through our relationship with God and others. Jesus' grew in self-knowledge by means of the same relational schemata, though he reached a very different conclusion!

To be clear, the center of subjectivity—the "self" or "I"—of which Jesus *qua* human became conscious was that of a divine Person, according to the classical, metaphysical understanding of person as *hypostasis*.[28] Yet, though "owned" and enervated by the Person of the divine Son, Jesus' human self-consciousness nevertheless grew in perception and awareness through the normal, human process of covenantal (i.e., relational, dialogical) self-knowledge. Jesus' knowledge of his identity, therefore,

---

28. This conclusion presses the distinction between Christ's (unitary) self and his (dual) self-consciousness to a greater degree than some have been willing to countenance. So, for example, Schoonenberg (1971) has argued, "If in Jesus Christ the human ego or act-centre stands psychologically outside his ontological person, it is then clearly not the ego or act-centre of Jesus" (p. 70). Along the same lines, Pittenger (1959) objects that a bifurcated consciousness expressive of the singular person of the Word, "makes Jesus nothing more than a body manipulated as an external instrument for deity" (p. 95). By way of answer to these critiques, Moloney (1999) cites Bernard Lonergan's work clarifying in metaphysical terms how "two distinct levels of consciousness, the human and divine" can be "grounded in an 'ego' which is ultimately one" (p. 112). He writes, "[T]he principal interest in [Lonergan's] approach lies in the possibility it gives us of appreciating the unity of Christ's conscious activity without trespassing on the question of his personhood. Problems of the development of Christ's consciousness and knowledge are questions about his human subjectivity. Subjectivity is an area of diversity and development. All the richness of human psychology can be found there. Even the sense in which the human ego is said to develop is to be accounted for on this level. But clearly this subjectivity must have some principle of unity proper to itself. The diversity of acts in our conscious activity are not total confusion" (p. 113). Indeed, I argue that that only by grounding *human* personhood in this christological dialectic—Christ's unitary essence within a dual existence—will the otherwise illusory human self finally be rescued from the radical contingency being thrust upon it by postmodern deconstructionism and ontological anti-realism.

included the facts of his divine personhood, his status as a fully human being, "like his brothers and sisters in every respect," and his divine mission to restore humanity to covenantal union with God.

In light of this proposition concerning the contingency of Jesus' self-knowledge, his temptation in the wilderness assumes a deeper significance. Situated as it is so soon after God's public declaration, "This is my beloved Son" (Matt 3:7), the wilderness temptation will serve to "put to the test . . . precisely Jesus' *sonship*" (Gerhardsson, 2009, p. 20; emphasis original). The devil's attack appears, it would seem, to target Jesus' inter-subjectively construed perception of his unique identity: "If you are the Son of God . . ." (Matt 4:3; 6; see parallel in Luke 4:3; 9; see Wright, 1996). It begs questioning what possible purpose the devil's suggestive query might serve if Christ was divinely—which is to say, omnisciently, beatifically—immune to the possibility of self-doubt? If, on the other hand, the certainty of his identity and vocation was mediated to him not by his divine nature but by his perfect *human* reliance on the Father—specifically, God's declamatory approbation at the Jordan—Jesus' limited self-awareness would have allowed for the possibility that Satan's attacks really tested him.[29] "You believe that God has declared you to be the Son of God?," a bemused devil smirks, "How can you be so sure you have not become self-deceived? You should prove it!"

Jesus' confidence in his identity as the Son of God and in the uniqueness of his relationship to the Father was the primary target of the tempter's testing. As France (2007) concludes, "The devil is trying to drive a wedge between the newly declared Son and his Father" (p. 127). Although the divine Word could have opened his own human mind to the reality of all the awareness and knowledge he possesses *qua* divine,

29. The point that Jesus was tempted in this way should not be construed to suggest the peccability of the Son (see McKinley, 2009). McDermott (1993) offers two crucial senses in which it was impossible for Jesus to sin: "Jesus' earthly life was that of the Son of God incarnate, the definitive self-communication of God to the world. As such, he could not have sinned; he could not have chosen contrary to his deepest character as the authentically human and the incarnate self-expression of God. But, given the supreme importance of his freedom for our salvation, when we consider Jesus as a *viator* on the way before his resurrection, then we do better to say that as he continued to choose the Father's will through the various states of his life, it became increasingly impossible *morally* for Jesus to sin; his human will became developmentally more and more confirmed in grace . . . so that his death was not only the darkest and most 'testing' period of his life but also the time when his freedom acquired definitive shape as fully belonging to God his Father and fully in solidarity with those for whom he lived and died" (p. 207; emphasis original).

this would surely have been tantamount to turning stones into bread—accommodating his human weakness by recourse to the prerogatives of his divine nature. Such a decision would have amounted to a "sin" against his human nature. As a human being, he relied instead, as all human beings must, on "every word that comes from the mouth of God" (Matt 4:4). God had declared him to be the "beloved Son"; his word would suffice.

Moreover, given the limitations of his humanity, Jesus' human mind could not probe in the opposite direction, so to speak, to gain direct awareness of his identity apart from the mediating influence of the Holy Spirit.[30] As Spence (1991) concludes, "His human self-consciousness knew and experienced God always indirectly and by means of the Holy Spirit, for only in this way could it remain truly human" (p. 94). In solidarity with the rest of us, Jesus trusted and obeyed the God whose Son he (rightly) believed himself to be. For those of us struggling to believe God's word regarding our identities, the writer of Hebrews offers, "because he himself has suffered when tempted, he is able to help those who are being tempted" (Heb 2:18).

Jesus' knowledge of himself grew as the Holy Spirit confirmed his identity and vocation throughout his career, whether at his baptism, in his miracles, and through his understanding of the Scriptures.[31] From

30. The asymmetry of the two minds of Christ is vital to maintaining a dyothelite (two-willed) Christology as well as an orthodox perspective on his human and divine natures. Regarding the link between Christ's two natures and his bifurcated consciousness, Moloney (1999) concludes, "If there are two levels of nature in Christ, then there are two levels of consciousness as well" (p. 109). Likewise, O'Collins (2011) observes, "The relationship between these two minds was and is radically unsymmetrical. During the earthly life of Jesus, the person of the Word (through his divine mind) knew the human mind (of Jesus) as his own human mind, but not vice versa" (p. 14). Moreover, if Christ possesses two minds with two wills, then it might also be proper to say he possesses two agentic loci, one divine and one human (though the latter, in some sense, is a subset of the former).

31. This seems to be Wright's (1996) main thesis regarding Jesus' self-understanding. He does not claim that Jesus was unconscious of his identity as the divine Son (contra Wellum, 2016; see p. 169n51); rather, Jesus' self-knowledge was indirect and inferential, along the lines of Rahner's nonobjective consciousness. Wright concludes, "As a part of his human vocation, grasped in faith, sustained in prayer, tested in confrontation, agonized over in further prayer and doubt, and implemented in action, he believed he had to do and be, for Israel and the world, that which according to scripture only YHWH himself could do and be. He was Israel's Messiah; but there would, in the end, be 'no king but God'" (p. 653). To afford Jesus (*qua* human) direct access to an awareness of his divinity, as I have already demonstrated, would transgress the asymmetrical relationship and "unidirectionality" of his divine and human minds, thus effacing the significance of his humanity.

this, we may provisionally draw the inference that Christ's knowledge of himself as the eternally preexistent Word—"before Abraham was, I am" (John 8:58)—resulted from his increasing, developmentally appropriate relatedness to the Father through the Spirit. The conclusions he drew about himself came from a supernaturally endowed—yet eminently human—grasp of the Scriptures, rather than through any direct, unmediated deposit of his own divine nature.

Agapic reconciliation as the work of Christ

The covenantal image of God finds its ultimate fulfillment in the agapic relationality Christ evinced in his dedication to the Father and in his devotion to his fellow human beings. By way of contrast, in the garden humanity failed in its calling to maintain relational unity with God. In contrast to Christ, we abrogated our vocation, abandoned our place of correspondence to God and, on God's behalf, to each other. As a result of humanity's sin, we lost our likeness to God and fell from our former state and status as covenantal image bearers.[32] The devastating effects of this fall now pervade the fallen self-consciousness of human beings as evidenced in our pathological inclination toward sinful self-blindness and self-deception. Our ability to know ourselves has been fatally curtailed by this estrangement—from God, from others, and from self—brought about by sin.

We lost our knowledge of God and self because we did not love. In our present predicament, we cannot love because we do not know. Christology provides a theanthropological framework for genuine knowledge of God and self in that Christ in his person embodies, even as in his "work" he enacts, the covenantal link between agapic relationality on the one hand and the mutual, perichoretic[33] knowledge of God, self, and others on the other. Put another way, on account of his perfect, loving

32. This is Calvin's point of emphasis regarding humanity's "loss" of the image. If the image is merely constitutive, then the repercussions of the fall appear to be mainly limited to individuals, their minds, bodies, and other formal attributes.

33. Again, "perichoretic" refers to the kind of interpersonal, dialogical knowing that comes only through the penetrating presence of the Spirit of God. It is not, therefore, a "person-*perichoresis*" like that within which the triune Persons of God eternally subsist, but a "nature-*perichoresis*" in which human beings participate in the divine life that Christ experienced *qua* human with the Father through the Spirit.

"attachment" to the Father, the man Jesus could not become sinfully self-ignorant or self-deceived.

Moreover, Christ embodies agapic relationality with other human beings not merely, as an eudaimonist ethics might suggest, by the pursuit of personal wellbeing in and through wise and virtuous communion with God and others. To the contrary, he is "for us" (Eph 5:2): he submits his own life and wellbeing to the will of the Father (Matt 26:39); he serves others at great personal cost (Mark 10:45); he forgives his enemies (Luke 23:34); he lays down his life for his friends (John 15:13). Indeed, the life of Christ is characterized by the fierce pursuit of agapic "attachment" to the very ones whose sin robbed them of their likeness to him and whose rebellion drove them to crush and despise in him the true and perfect image he sought to restore in them (Isa 53:3).

By shifting away from a constitutive Christology to a covenantal framework, the significance of the ethical "work" of Christ comes into sharper focus. Indeed, Christ is "for us" in the sense that he completes his work on our behalf. He is also "for us" in the sense that he offers to us what only God could grant. As such, Christ's role as mediator and reconciler between God and humanity is crucial for grasping the meaning of his person. "Reconciliation," says Barth (2010), "is the fulfillment of the covenant between God and man" (IV/1, p. 22). Whereas a constitutive Christology stresses the "parts" of Christ's person, a covenantal Christology, as Calvin, Luther and other early Reformers would underscore, points to the significance of Christ's work on humanity's behalf.

Melanchthon, for one, staked a firmly polemical emphasis on Christ's covenantal work (see Berkouwer, 1954; Gerrish, 2015). Frustrated with what he called the "sophistry" of medieval scholasticism, he (2007) decried its metaphysical emphasis, believing it to have beclouded the essence of the gospel:

> [T]o know Christ [is] to know his benefits and not as [the scholastics] teach, to perceive his natures and the mode of his incarnation. . . . [I]t behooves us to become acquainted with Christ who has been given as a remedy for us, or to use the language of the Scripture, "for our salvation." (pp. 68–69)[34]

34. In similar terms Luther would rail against a speculative metaphysics of the incarnation: "Christ is not called Christ because he has two natures; what is that to me? But he bears this glorious and comforting name from the office and work which he took upon himself. That he is by nature both God and man belongs to himself, but my comfort and benefit is that he used his office on my behalf, and poured out his

Melanchthon's stress on the redemptive work of Christ, along with Calvin and Luther, offered a corrective for, rather than a break with, scholasticism. According to Berkouwer (1954), the Reformers' chief concern was to understand "*why* Christ has put on human flesh" in order that we might "learn to know Christ as medicine, as our complete salvation" (p. 102; emphasis original).

Echoing their conclusions, Barth's (2010) critique of medieval scholasticism grew out of a similar "theological mood" to that of Melanchthon, Luther, and Calvin. As pertains to the former inquiry into matters of "untheological metaphysical speculation," Barth determined that "[t]he Scholastics had become fools in investigating these things and the *beneficia Christi* had been obscured thereby" (I/1, p. 416).[35] The task of dogmatic Christology, Barth maintains, is to stress "what [Christ] is as the One who makes reconciliation, as the One who fulfills the covenant, as the One in whom the world and man have been and are converted to God" (IV/1, p. 126). For the early Reformers and those, like Barth, retracing their footsteps, the person of Christ is best perceived in his covenant-fulfilling work on our behalf.[36]

---

love and became my Savior and Redeemer" (Luther, *Werke: Kritische Gesamptausgabe*, 17/1:255; as cited in Berkouwer, 1954, p. 103).

35. Barth was equally, if not more, concerned to defend the early Reformers' lack of nuance from its misappropriation at the hands of Bultmannian (i.e., Ritschlian) liberalism (I/i, pp. 416–17; see Barclay, 2015, pp. 135–36).

36. Brunner (2014) inverts the standard christological methodology by beginning with the work of Christ before moving on to his person. The basis for his decision can be found in the "substantive" character of Christ's titles, which, he argues, "all describe an event, a work of God, which He does through Jesus in or for humanity" (p. 272). Distinguishing between the "person" and "work" of Christ, certainly to the degree the early Reformers did, may in the end be unhelpful. For, indeed, the constitutive person of Christ dialogically mirrors his covenantal work, and vice versa. So, as Barth (1960) writes, "Jesus Christ is in His one Person, as true *God*, *man's* loyal partner, and as true *man*, *God's*. He is the Lord humbled for communion with man and likewise the Servant exalted to communion with God. . . . He is both, without their being confused but also without their being divided; He is wholly the one and wholly the other. Thus in this oneness Jesus Christ is the Mediator, the Reconciler, between God and man. Thus He comes forward to *man* on behalf of *God* calling for and awakening faith, love, and hope, and to *God* on behalf of *man*, representing man, making satisfaction and interceding" (pp. 46–47; emphasis original). Christ is *in se* an ontological "work" of reconciliation between God and humanity. His atoning death, then, is the means by which he *effects* reconciliation for God's people (Eph 2:16).

Christ the Mediator and Reconciler of God and humanity

The work of Christ is to bring us to the Father, to renew the covenantal relationship between God and humanity by restoring us to his image. The instrument of Christ's atoning work—the means by which he effected this work of reconciliation and restoration—is the cross (Rom 5:10; Eph 2:16; Col 1:20, 22). If the gospel of God *is* Christ—the one sent from God in order to restore humanity to God—the cross is the "heart" of that gospel (Packer, 2007). Indeed, the cross is, as Warfield (2015) has demonstrated, the very "essence of Christianity" (pp. 479–80). The vital link between Christology and soteriology becomes most evident therein.

"With his wounds," the prophet declares of the Messiah, "we are healed" (Isa 53:5; cf. 1 Pet 2:24). Moreover, the New Testament makes clear that this healing amounts to more than a merely subjective renewal of individual human beings. Christ died to restore fallen humanity to its former status as covenantal image bearers through their union with him. Having become estranged from God due to our sin, we needed God to act on our behalf if there was to be any hope of reconciliation (Rom 5:6–8; 8:3). This fact alone supplies Calvin (2008) with sufficient cause to postulate the necessity of the incarnation:

> What was best for us, our most merciful Father determined. Our iniquities, like a cloud intervening between him and us, having utterly alienated us from the kingdom of heaven, none but a person reaching to him could be the medium of restoring peace. But who could thus reach to him? . . . Thus the Son of God behooved to become our Immanuel, i.e. God with us; and in such a way, that by mutual union his divinity and our nature might be combined; otherwise, neither was the proximity near enough, nor the affinity strong enough, to give us hope that God would dwell with us. (pp. 297–298)

Christ's death, archetypally representative of humanity's estrangement from God, is thus, simultaneously, paradoxically, the means of its reversal. The "remedy" for our alienation from God, brought about as it had been by humanity's breech of covenant faithfulness, is Christ's atoning death *in our place* (p. 298).[37] In the end, Christ's cross is "the ultimate

---

37. Barth (2010) echoes Calvin on precisely this point: "What took place [at the cross] is that the Son of God fulfilled the righteous judgment on us men by Himself taking our place as man and in our place undergoing the judgment under which we had passed. . . . *Cur Deus homo?* In order that God as man might do and accomplish and achieve and complete all this for us wrong-doers, in order that in this way there

expression of God's loving choice to be with sinners" (Tanner, 2010, p. 248). With this "gift" of "God's *love*," Christ actualizes his "movement of personal and individualized commitment—toward the unworthy" (Barclay, 2015, p. 479; emphasis original; cf. Barrett, 2013). This reconciliation is the healing of which the prophet speaks.

Atonement and the gospel of peace

At the cross the triune God accomplished infinitely more than a bare demonstration of love—an exemplar of reconciliation. By means of Christ's atoning death, supremely, God has *effected* believers' salvation, unilaterally granting them the full measure of his gracious love in and through Christ (Rom 1:16; Eph 1:3; 2:8–9; see Harris, 2005, pp. 436–37). As a result of his initiatory movement toward sinners, there need be no fear of future judgment or alienation (Rom 8:1). In Christ, his people are "at-one" with—i.e., reconciled to—God (Rom 5:10). This is the essence of atonement. In fact, little of what is typically entailed in "salvation" can be excluded from its broad compass. As Yarbrough (2000) determines,

> 'Atonement' may be defined as God's work on sinners' behalf to reconcile them to himself. It is the divine activity that confronts and resolves the problem of human sin so that people may enjoy full fellowship with God both now and in the age to come. While in one sense the meaning of atonement is as broad and diverse as all of God's saving work throughout time and eternity, in another it is as particular and restricted as the crucifixion of Jesus. (p. 388)

Whereas numerous accounts of "the" atonement[38] have arisen from within Christian history, when taken as a whole, these accounts illustrate the richness with which the New Testament writers depict its significance

---

might be brought about by Him our reconciliation with Him and conversion to Him" (IV/1, pp. 222–23).

38. Demarest (2006) traces the meaning of the English "atonement" from its early provenance in the Authorized Version (AV) where it was first used to translate καταλλαγή (*katallagē*) in Rom 5:11. It is employed there, he argues, to signify "the restoration of harmony between estranged parties (suggesting 'reconciliation')"; yet, as he notes, it would become "gradually broadened to include notions of propitiating God and expiating sins." Only over time, he observes, would "atonement" come to its modern denotation as "the *means* whereby reconciliation, propitiation, and expiation are achieved" (p. 167; emphasis original).

for fallen humanity (Blocher, 2005; Franks, 1962; Stott, 2006). No single theory of the atonement elicits universal approval, but broad agreement surrounds the premise that, with Christ's death on the cross, God has reversed the estrangement brought on by human sin granting us access to a renewed agapic fellowship with him and with one another.[39]

Reconciliation, as a central aspect of Christ's atoning work, is not strictly bipolar, but tripolar. The cross makes us one, with God, and with all those formerly estranged from God. Addressing the first of these twin aspects of reconciliation, the apostle Paul supplies a basic outline of renewed relationality between God and humanity. With Adam's sin (v. 12, 18), he writes, human beings became irretrievably estranged from God—enemies of righteousness (v. 10, 19; cf. Rom 1:18; Eph 5:6; Col 3:6). As of Christ's death on the cross, we gain access to reprieve from this enmity by means of faith in Christ (vv. 9, 11; cf. Eph 2:16; Col 1:20).

Christ has opened the way for us to return to the Father (cf. John 14:6; Heb 10:19–20). Moreover, although Paul's use of "justification" language (δικαιο-, dikaio-) is regarded by many scholars as the exegetical focus of the passage,[40] as Gerrish (2015) notes, reconciliation is its result (see pp. 164–65). Paul links justification—God's declaration of forgiveness—with reconciliation—the resumption of covenant relationality. So, for Murray (1968), "Peace with God is a blessing coordinate with justification," since it "denotes relationship to God" and a "status . . . flowing from . . . reconciliation" (pp. 158–159). In Pauline theology, the two terms are "alternate ways of describing God's work in Christ," though,

39. A succinct summary of historical atonement theories can be found in Blocher (2005).

40. For numerous scholars of whom Wright (2009) is representative, "the whole passage is 'about' justification" (p. 238). Eschewing this tendency, Martin (1989) concludes that the theme of reconciliation stands at the center of Pauline theology and that Paul's discussion of justification is "preparatory" and "indispensable as a basis" for the unfolding of his central theme: the "new relationship with God" that informs the believer's life (p. 139). At the opposite extreme, Moo (1996) ranks "reconciliation" behind the themes of "justification," "hope," and "glory" (v. 10) since these three appear to frame Paul's argument in Rom 5:1–11 (i.e., justification leads to peace/reconciliation leads to hope leads to glory). In surveying the entire Pauline corpus he concurs with Käsemann (1971) that the terminology of reconciliation is "too infrequent," the ideas "too undeveloped," and that it is "better" to regard reconciliation as "one image . . . among many others" employed by the apostle to illustrate God's saving work in Christ (Moo, 1996, p. 297n20). Contra this conclusion, however, is Paul's own summary of his entire ministry—and, indeed, of gospel ministry generally—as being one of "reconciliation" (2 Cor 5:18), though clearly justification occupies a place of prominence in his polemic and apologetic agendas.

rightly construed, justification should be seen as the objective "basis" of reconciliation (Schreiner, 2008, p. 364).

For Paul, humanity's intersubjective gain—reconciliation—obtains as the result of God's objective declaration: "*since* we have been justified by faith," he writes, "we have peace with God" (v. 1). Justification, then, amounts to a remedial prerequisite to God's conciliatory aim, that is, the cessation of hostilities between formerly estranged parties and the resumption of amicable relations (see Porter, 1993). Moreover, it is by reason of our Spirit-effected union with Christ that believers "enjoy" this renewed fellowship with God (Campbell, 2012, p. 259; cf. Rev 3:20).

As regards the second aspect of reconciliation, Paul in two of his letters, elevates the theme of reconciliation between believers as a function or extension of Christ's atoning work. In Ephesians 2:1–22, the apostle reminds his Gentile readers of their former state of alienation from God (v. 12). Under the terms of God's covenant with Israel, non-Jews stood outside the bounds of the titular and covenantal people of God. Yet, as Paul reminds these Gentile believers, those "who were once far off have been brought near by the blood of Christ" (v. 13; cf. Gal 2:11–16). Further, Paul expressly affirms the link between Christ's person and work: believing Jews and Gentiles have been made "one" in Christ (v. 14) because Christ himself is "one" (see Eph 4:5–6; Col 3:11; cf. 1 Cor 1:10–13; 8:6). On the basis of this "gospel of peace" (Eph 6:15), Paul declares an end to the "hostility" that formerly characterized relations between the two: "[Christ] himself is our peace" (2:14). With his death he has brought about the death of estrangement (v. 16).

According to Thielman (2010), the peace Paul has in view in these contexts is a peace *with* God rather than a peace *from* God, though the former precipitates the latter (p. 364; cf. Gorman, 2015).[41] In Colossians 3:15, the "peace of Christ" to which Paul refers is not primarily personal but interpersonal (cf. 1:20). Bruce (1984), in noting the vertical and horizontal aspects of Christ's peacemaking work at the cross, concludes, "Christians, having been reconciled to God, enjoying peace with him through Christ, should naturally live at peace with one another" (p. 157).

---

41. Porter (1993) remarks that, according to ancient Greek thought, relational "peace" was predicated on "a state of objective wellbeing" in the individual (p. 696; cf. Martin, 1989). This paradigm would certainly make sense within an eudaimonist ethics; however, it inverts the New Testament framework wherein God authors peace between himself and us resulting in the happy consequence that peace is now possible both *for* individuals (intrasubjectively) and *between* individuals (intersubjectively).

To which Martin (1989) adds, "[T]he Pauline teaching on reconciliation gains a fresh dimension by being applied to persons-in-community" (p. 198). To this I would add, only by enacting our role in peacemaking's horizontal dimension can we appropriate our "blessed" designation as images of the Son (Matt 5:9).[42]

Perichoretic self-knowledge through agapic relationality

Agapic relationality with God and between human beings finds its clearest basis in the person and work of Christ.[43] Moreover, only by means of our Spirit-mediated union with the person and work of Christ—through our dying to self and living unto God as Father and for the good of others—can human beings access and appropriate the covenantal dynamic that Christ embodies and effectuates. Only by "abiding" in him and in his perfect love can humanity escape the infecundity of autonomy (John 15:4–11). The aridity and barrenness of life "outside the garden," moreover, not only severs the vitality of our relationships with God and others but in our relating to self as well. Sin—that which sunders self from God—likewise leads to estrangement from self, inducing an inevitable dissociation of self from self-consciousness.

Having lost sight of God, we became blind to self. Yet, in spite of our blindness to self, we insist that we can see and know ourselves truly, though what we "perceive" is none other than the intrasubjective parallel of idolatry: a self-image crafted to serve our interests. And so, we become self-deceived. Christ has come to restore our vision, yet our pathological inclination is to maintain that we have no need of his healing (see John 9:39–41). To acknowledge our need means we must cast down the graven images we most cherish.

So, Brunner (2014) rightly concludes:

---

42. Drawing on Paul's doctrine of reconciliation through union with Christ, Williams (2010) addresses the gospel sins of racial hostility and discrimination among believers.

43. Why would the Trinity not be the clearest basis? For one, believers are not commanded to imitate Triune relatedness as we are called to imitate Christ (John 15:12), though the latter can be said to relate analogically to the former. Secondly, we can only infer the nature of immanent relations between divine Persons. But we are able to "see" and know Christ in his relatedness to the Father. As I have argued, the image to which we are called to conform is that of Christ (Rom 8:29). He is our archetype and the "key" to understanding human nature and relationality.

> [N]owhere so much as in the sphere of self-knowledge does sin
> blind men to the truth, and cause so many hindrances; further,
> that before he is stripped bare in the light of revelation man does
> not want to be exposed to the light, but either he thinks of him-
> self in naturalistic terms, which provide him with convenient
> excuses, or he sees himself in a romantic idealistic light. Hence
> it is part of the genuine Christian experience that only the man
> who has been influenced by the truth of Christ is honest with
> himself, because he alone dares to look the naked truth in the
> face. (Brunner, 2014, p. 47)

To consider self in the light of Christ is to risk beholding self as it truly is—sinful, defective, unclean. In rejecting and running from the light, we are rejecting and running from ourselves (John 3:19–20).

On the other hand, love for God in Christ deactivates this intra-subjective hostility and estrangement—the internalized, reflexive self-loathing that arises from shame and its concomitant fear of exposure (Kierkegaard, 1980). Through the believer's willingness to "abide" in his love, God-in-Christ brings about the reconciliation of self and self-consciousness, inaugurating a peaceful "relation" that, through his Spirit's working, may issue forth into intrasubjective healing and wholeness.

As suggested in the previous section, constitutive and covenantal Christologies (and, therefore, christological anthropology as well) are best appropriated and adumbrated dialectically. Christ *acts* from who he *is* (Bonhoeffer, 1996). What he achieves in effecting our salvation is the exposition of his Person. As the divine Word, his identity and his instrumentality are inextricably linked (Barth, 2010; see John 4:34; cf. Isa 55:11). So, in the incarnation he brings together divine and human existence with a singular essence. Whereas, at the cross he reconciles God and humanity as he suffers and dies "for" both. To divest ontology from its soteriological significance runs the risk of fatally undermining the christological warrant for anthropology. What we say about the person of Christ bears directly on the work of Christ, and vice versa. Put another way, his cradle and his cross are inseparable.

Moreover, the same is also true, as we might expect, with respect to our human being and becoming. Human beings' *possession* of the imago is conditional upon their *participation* in our image-bearing vocation. The direct implication of the believer's renewed amity with God-in-Christ, following the reversal of our vertical estrangement brought on by the fall, is the New Testament's call for agapic relationality between believers. "Just as I have loved you," Jesus commanded his disciples, "you also are to love one another" (John 13:34). Understood christologically, the imago is instantiated in and through the believer's relation to Christ and, on Christ's behalf, to others. On the other hand,

> Self-interested and self-seeking individuals who, in relation, are only there in, for and with themselves are destructive of the possibilities of genuine relation and identity. For true persons are centres directed beyond themselves in a process of self-transcendence and return. (McFadyen, 1990, p. 151)

In light of this perspective, Christian baptism is best understood as an expression of the believer's union with both Christ's person and work. "In baptism," Beasley-Murray (1973) writes, "we *put on* Christ; the baptismal life *is* Christ"; yet, equally, "in so far as it is truly lived it will be Christ-like" (pp. 286–287; emphasis original; see Rom 6:4; Col 2:12). Along these same lines, Christ's call to take up one's cross and follow him is also instructive (Matt 16:24; see parallels; cf. Gorman, 2009). The notion of the inseparability of life *in* and *for* Christ becomes most evident, however, in Paul's illustrative designation of the church as "the body of Christ" (Rom 12:4–8; 1 Cor 10:16–17; 12:12–31; Eph 3:6; 4:4–16; 5:30; Col 1:18; 24; 2:19; 3:15). Ridderbos (1975) provides the basis of Paul's use of "body" language by linking believers ontologically with the crucified Christ: "[A]lready in his suffering and death he represented [the church] in all its parts and united it in himself into a new unity" (p. 377). Now, through the Holy Spirit, Christ is truly present in and among believers effecting their conformity to his image (see Bonhoeffer, 1998).[44]

Thus, union with Christ speaks to both an ontic and ethical renewal that takes place within believers. And this union of Christ's body, as Douty (1973) explains, has sufficient potency to bring about its reflection among every member: "as each person is joined to Christ by the incoming of the Holy Spirit, it necessarily follows that all those who are thus united to Him, are also united to one another" (p. 238). In sum, as Christ is, so we are called to be, both individually and corporately. Moreover, as Christ has done, so we are called to do. Only this way will Christ, in Bonhoeffer's words, *"take form among us today and here"* (Bonhoeffer, 2005, p. 99; emphasis original). Finally, as Gunton (1997) concludes,

---

44. While "body of Christ" language in Paul should be understood metaphorically, there is ample reason to assume an underlying ontological reality to which the apostle is referring (Campbell, 2012; Pelser, 1998).

> [T]he Church is the place where the logic of the divine love that
> is Jesus takes form in the present, and in so far as it does, it
> becomes real also for the rest of humanity. It is when the com-
> munity is taken up into the love of God that it becomes that love
> for and on behalf of mankind. (p. 177)

All of which, as God would have it, redounds unto the glory of God in
Christ.

Implications of union with Christ

Due to the pervasive and devastating effects on humanity effected by the
fall, the Christian life is, perhaps, best characterized as the long-term
remediation of the broken, self-deceived self through believers' ever-
increasing appropriation of the benefits of our union with Christ (see
Johnson, 2017).[45] Agapic reconciliation to God-in-Christ grants human
beings the means by which self may overcome its pathological inclination
toward dissociation and self-deception. Dissociation—the psychological
means by which we hide ourselves from ourselves (see Matt 7:3–5)—en-
ables the individual to ignore unpleasant realities pertaining to self. It is
a form of noetic or cognitive detachment from self. Self-deception, on
the other hand, is a higher order, ethicospiritual maneuver by which we
believe what we could not were we to acknowledge the painful truth.

Through believers' real (i.e., nonfigurative) union with God-in-
Christ, mediated by the Spirit, and instantiated in relationship with
others, however, they may gradually come to see themselves through
the eyes of the loving Other. Where formerly the motivation to remain
willfully ignorant and self-deceived regarding personal weaknesses, sin,
etc.[46] only perpetuated these dissociative tendencies, in time, the self can
become increasingly capable of bearing the weight of self-awareness.
What self could never handle alone is made less unmanageable in loving
relationship (Gal 6:2; see Stratton, 2006). Christ, abiding perichoretically
in self and others, brings about a reconciliation of sorts between self and
self-consciousness.

---

45. The role other human beings, and especially those within the body of Christ,
play in this process will become increasingly clear in later chapters.

46. In later chapters, I will enumerate some of the ways in which brokenness and
sin perpetuate dissociative and self-deceptive tendencies.

Healthy, loving "attachment" of self to Christ and others helps disarm internal defenses and resolve intrasubjective hostility.[47] As a result, the disordered, dissociated, and self-deceived self, now reconciled to Christ, may come to assume "its own perfect shape through attachment to the divine image" in Christ (Tanner, 2010, p. 16):

> By way of this attachment, its very human character becomes an image of God in a stronger fashion than before. . . . By having the one whom they are not, the Word, for their own in Christ, [believers] should one day be able to lead human lives that imitate God in the most perfect way possible for mere humans. (pp. 16–17)

Moreover, as our unconscious motivations to dissociate unpleasant truths about self decrease, the likelihood of self-deception becomes increasingly remote.

God has made possible our secure attachment to Christ through the incarnation and the atonement.[48] Taken together they actualize the ontological and covenantal aspects of the union of God and man, and the reconstitution of the covenantal imago dei in human beings. Christology instructs us, according to Galot (1981), to define person as "a relation that possesses a reality of its own" (p. 299). Only through relationship— to God, self, and others—do human persons come to be conscious of self as self. "Consciousness of I comes only in relation to a you," offers Wellum (2016), such that, "As different I's interact, each discovers the incommunicable character that makes it an I in relation to you's" (p. 428; emphasis original).

Our contingent, relationally constituted self-consciousness takes shape in predictable ways. What we can know of self, which is to say self-consciousness, must be distinguished from the static, non-directional mode by which we acquire objective knowledge:

---

47. "Attachment" is an important term in modern psychology that I will explore further later on. At this stage, I use the term primarily theologically as a psychologically-informed expression of union with Christ (see Tanner, 2010).

48. And also Christ's resurrection and exaltation, without which the Spirit would not have been given (John 16:7). In the present context, however, the emphasis is on Christ's person and work: incarnation most directly relates to Christ's person, and atonement to Christ's work. The work of the Spirit, by contrast, is in effecting the union of Christ with his people, which should not be separated from the person and work of Christ.

> Knowledge simply discovers reality, and by definition leaves its object unchanged. Consciousness is constitutive of reality: it moves the subject from being unconscious to conscious, and so leads it into a new level of activity and attainment. Consciousness is that element in our conscious activity by which we are aware that it is *we* who are carrying out this activity. (Moloney, 1999, p. 109; emphasis original)

Consciousness of self as self is a formative process. On the other hand, consciousness of self-in-Christ, mediated through our Spirit-actualized attachment to an agapic other, is a *trans*formative process. By means of our union with Christ, we are made new. Over time then, our newness in Christ leads to intrasubjective wholeness as we appropriate the intersubjective benefits of our union with Christ.

Perichoresis—entis et analogia

"Attachment" is illustrative of relationship and, particularly, dependence. It speaks to the asymmetry of the believer's union with Christ. A similar Johannine term, found in Jesus' teaching on the vine and the branches, is "abiding," from the Greek μέν- (*men-*) for remain or reside (Danker, 2001; see John 15; cf. Isa 5:1–7). Paul in his letter to the Romans employs similar imagery in describing Gentile believers as having been "grafted in" to the one people of God (Rom 11:17–21). In both biblical usages, the link between metaphor and objective reality can be discerned in the need for believers to remain vitally "attached" to Christ, drawing on the life-sustaining power of his own divine existence as mediated by the Spirit. To be attached to Christ is to become dependent upon him for life and growth into his image (see Tanner, 2010).

With a similar semantic range to "attachment," though arguably richer in meaning, *perichoresis* is an ancient—and expressly—theological term. Popularized in the eighth century by John of Damascus, *perichoresis* refers to "the simultaneity of rest and movement, of coinherence and interpenetration" characteristic of God's triune Personhood (Harrison, 1991, p. 55). According to the earliest use of *perichoresis*, nearly four hundred years before John of Damascus, the term can be used in reference to "the intimate communion of the two natures of Christ" (Otto, 2001).[49]

49. Harrison (1991) traces the term's provenance to Gregory Nazianzen's famous, fourth-century epistle (no. 101), wherein the father suggests in passing a mutual reciprocity in the relationship between Christ's divine and human "names," describing it

Over time the original christological conception of *perichoresis* shifted away from the Son's divine activity in and through his human nature. Eventually, formulations of intratrinitarian communion came to dominate its usage.[50] As Macleod (1998) observes, "*perichoresis* . . . became a trinitarian rather than a Christological term, and the concept of a *perichoresis* between the two natures in the incarnate Mediator was never developed" (p. 194). More recently, Crisp has addressed this christological lacuna. He (2007) clarifies that this "nature-perichoresis"—the interaction of Christ's two natures as instantiated in the incarnation—should be conceived as "an asymmetrical relation between the two natures of Christ" (p. 19).[51] As such, the relationship between Christ's divine and human natures is unidirectional, unlike the mutual, symmetrical, perichoretic communion of trinitarian persons.

---

thus: "being mingled like the natures, and flowing into [περιχωρουσῶν, *perichōrousōn*] one another" (Nazianzen, 2012, p. 440). Pannenberg (1977) notes that Gregory failed, at this early stage, to adequately circumscribe his meaning; as a result, he regrettably implied a Eutychian commingling of the natures in Christ (p. 297). The Chalcedonian Definition would provide the clarity needed on this point.

50. The life and being of the triune God has historically been characterized as a dialectic of "union and distinction" (Barth, 2010, p. 369): three persons (*hypostases*) sharing a single, divine essence (*ousia*). Thus, "[God's] life is a life of free distinction and communion in the *perichoresis* of the Father, the Son, and the Holy Spirit" (Hunsinger, 2004, p. 172). From the eighth century, the doctrine of trinitarian *perichoresis* has "expressed the truth that the Father, the Son and the Holy Spirit are distinctive Persons each with his own incommunicable properties, but that they dwell *in* one another, not only *with* one another, in such an intimate way . . . that their individual characteristics instead of dividing them from one another unite them indivisibly together" (Torrance, 1996, p. 172). Augustine (2002) connected the three-in-one personhood of God directly with the imago dei in individual human beings; several limitations of his characterization of the human mind as a triunity have already been noted. Since Barth (2010), the doctrine of divine *perichoresis* has led to the flowering of trinitarian anthropology (see Oh, 2006). Grenz (2001) is representative: "The ingenious use of perichoresis to describe the manner in which the trinitarian persons are constituted by the mutuality of relationships within the life of the triune God opened the way for the development of a dynamic ontology of persons-in-relationship or persons-in-communion. This ontology characterizes the essential nature of personhood as consisting of mutuality and interdependence" (p. 317). While there is certainly reason enough to affirm this *analogia*, a better, i.e., more direct, route to a perichoretic conception of self-knowledge is through the "nature–perichoresis" instantiated in the person of Christ.

51. Crisp (2007) goes on to characterize this "nature-perichoretic relation" between Christ's divine and human natures as a "penetration" rather than "interpenetration" (p. 22). In this he differs from John Damascene who held that the human nature of Christ was divinized upon its appropriation by the indwelling Son (*De fide orthodoxa* 3.7).

While the divine person of the Word "owns" and enervates the human body–soul composite of Christ, the reverse is not the case. Furthermore, on the basis of this christological formulation of *perichoresis*, Crisp (2007) concludes,

> God *could* act upon other human beings in the way in which he acts upon Christ. All that distinguishes the perichoretic relation that Christ's human nature experiences with his divine nature, and that my human nature experiences with God, is the degree to which the divine nature of Christ penetrates his human nature. (pp. 25–26; emphasis original)[52]

Understood in this light, this "nature-perichoresis"—the "penetration" of Christ's human nature, i.e., his body–soul composite, by the divine Word—may be understood as an alternate, christologically derived analogue of the believer's "attachment" to Christ mediated through the indwelling Holy Spirit.[53]

To be clear, it is not in any shared being (*entis*) through which God and the believer mutually coinhere at a metaphysical level.[54] This kind of "person-perichoresis" can only be posited, with qualifications,[55] of the divine persons of the Trinity (Kilby, 2000; contra Moltmann, 1993). *Perichoresis* is an onto-relational concept, the most perspicuous spatiotemporal

---

52. So long as Crisp distinguishes between person-*perichoresis* and nature-*perichoresis*, his analogy between how God's Spirit acts upon Christ's human nature and other human beings holds. At the level of application, we may consider Paul's discussion of fruit of the Spirit in Gal 5:22–26. One's ethicospiritual dependency on Christ depends wholly on the reality of perichoretic union with Christ (cf. John 15:5). Surely, a merely metaphorical union—one that is not real, but only to be imagined or considered as real—is not what Jesus means with his parable of the vine and the branches. And yet, it is his nature rather than his Person, classically understood, in which believers share.

53. Put another way, the Person of the Son assumes dual natures, one human and one divine, in becoming Jesus of Nazareth. By way of analogy, believers may be understood to be individual loci of two persons, one human and the other, the indwelling Spirit of God.

54. Rightly, Otto (2001): "Seeing the image of God as mirroring the perichoretic 'tri-personal being-in-communion' of God . . . is useful as an analogy, provided it maintains the ontological basis and necessary distinctions of the persons involved" (p. 379).

55. The caveat in this case is the necessity of preserving the relational distinctions that characterize Father, Son, and Spirit; so, Crisp (2007): "The persons of the Trinity share all their properties in a common divine essence apart from those properties that serve to individuate each person of the Trinity, or express a relation between only two persons of the Trinity" (p. 31).

instantiation of which is the incarnation. There, as we have seen, God and humanity have come together at the level of *entis*, albeit "inconfusedly, unchangeably, indivisibly, inseparably,"[56] into "a perfect unity which does not destroy but affirms otherness" (Zizioulas, 2007, p. 307). This union, moreover, is unique and, as such, unrepeatable. However, on the basis of the metaphysical "penetration" of Christ's human body–soul composite by the person of the divine Word, we may postulate the possibility of an analogous onto-relational union between God and human beings (other than Jesus of Nazareth) that takes place in our Spirit-mediated union with the person of Christ.[57]

The nature of our union with Christ is, finally, ineffable. As Paul remarks, the real presence of Christ in and among believers is a "mystery," though it remains our "hope of glory" (Col 1:27; see Fee, 2009; Mersch, 2011). In spite of its mysterious character, the genuine, perichoretic union of Christ with his people demonstrates God's commitment to be not only God-*for*-us, but God-*with*-us.[58] Mersch (2011), in eloquent summary, writes of this mystery,

56. The Chalcedonian fathers opposed the principal christological heresies of their day with two terms apiece: ἀσυγχύτως (*asynchytōs*, without confusion) and ἀτρέπτως (*atreptōs*, without mixture, change) in opposition to Eutychianism; ἀδιαιρέτως (*adiaipetōs*, without division) and ἀχωρίστως (*achōristōs*, without separation) against Nestorianism.

57. Macleod (1998), in considering the "special kind and intensity of inter-personal unity" of being to which the doctrine of *perichoresis* refers, concludes, "there is no analogy in human experience" (p. 141). Yet, he then proceeds to cite numerous New Testament provisions for positing an analogous—i.e., non-identical, referential—relationship between divine intrasubjectivity and human intersubjectivity. Among these, Macleod includes the one-flesh union of husband and wife (Eph 5:23), and the union of Christ and the church which, he notes, Jesus expressly links to his own divine communion with the Father (John 17:21–23). Clearly, these serve as biblically construed analogues. For this reason, it is better to aver that, due to the "infinite qualitative distinction" between God and humanity, there can be no human *equivalent* to intratrinitarian *perichoresis*. The "mutual indwelling" and "interpenetration" of human beings both with the person of Christ and, metaphorically, with each other due to their shared union with the Savior is, however, closely related to the perichoretic relationship of the person of Christ respective to his human body–soul composite, i.e., the incarnation (Crisp, 2007; Otto, 2001). In other words, Jesus Christ *is* the *analogia perichoresis*.

58. The corporate dimension of this commitment is a vital aspect of Paul's body of Christ metaphor. McFadyen (1990) carefully defines the metaphorical sense in which believers are united "perichoretically" with one another in Christ: "The interpenetration of the partners, mediated by the presence of Christ both within and between them, may be neither literal nor complete; but is, rather, metaphorical and limited. Furthermore, the understanding so reached will be neither complete nor direct, but

As His excellences pass into men and transfigure them, so do
their miseries pass into Him and are there consumed. In Him,
by His Blood and His Cross, sin has been destroyed; and the
consequences of sin—[Christ's] sufferings, humiliations, and
death—become a means of expiation, a source of life and joy.
Briefly, in Him and in Him alone is the restoration and the en-
nobling of man. Freed from his hideousness, transformed into
the likeness of Christ, man can draw near to God. (p. 4)

By contrast, to be "alone"—left to ourselves, to be only who we are in and
of ourselves—is truly "not good" (see Gen 2:18).

The life inaugurated by the Spirit in believers—as members of a renewed humanity capable of imaging God in and through their relation to
Christ and each other—should, therefore, be seen as a perfectly "natural"
extension of the enlivening and sanctifying work of God. Here Moltmann (1997) gets it right: Christ works through his Spirit to bring about
"the healing of life that is sick, and the becoming-whole of a life that has
become divided and split" (p. 52; cf. Payne, 1995). The dissociated and
self-deceived consciousness of the believer, moreover, is but one sphere
of his ongoing palingenetic work. So, this intrasubjective remediation is
best conceived within the framework of "a perichoretic understanding
of the construction of the self in relationship"—relationship, that is, to
God-in-Christ lived out in agapic communion within the body of Christ
(Grenz, 2001, p. 312).

The "ecclesial self"

The divine design for human existence, as informed within this christological framework for personhood, entails three aspects best conceived
dialogically. The first is its ontological condition of unity in differentiation: individual human persons "come to be" only in communion with
others. The second dialogical aspect of human existence is its ethical
import respective to identity and instrumentality: we come to be known,
as Christ also did, by our "work" in relation to others. Who-we-are and
what-we-do reciprocally establish and inform the other. Finally, human
knowledge of self obtains perichoretically along both axes of human relationality: we come to a mutual, interpersonal self- and other-awareness

---

inferential and intimated. The ethical distance between the partners therefore remains,
and their presence in each other does not imply a unification, but a community between them" (p. 136).

by means of the mysterious working of the penetrative presence of God's Spirit. This operation is not strictly dipolar, whether vertical or horizontal, but tripolar.

To these first three, a fourth temporal or telic aspect must also be considered. According to Grenz (2001), God's design for human existence may be understood corporately and eschatologically, in terms of our relation to Christ's body, as a "person-in-bonded community." His so-called "ecclesial self," the corporatized entity comprising "the new humanity in communion with the triune God" (p. 305), is made up of all those presently indwelt by the Spirit of God. Grenz further explains,

> The relational life of the God who is triune comes to representation in the communal fellowship of the participants in the new humanity. This assertion calls for a relational ontology that can bring the divine prototype and the human antitype together. The conceptual context for such an engagement is the philosophical idea of the social self, which, in turn, can be understood theologically as the ecclesial self. (p. 305)

Grenz's ecclesial self is an expressly eschatological reality, which is to say, it is defined by the dialectic of "now" and "not yet."

In Christ we who have been made new are being made new in anticipation of the day when Christ is revealed and we shall be made new (Col 3:4; 1 Pet 5:4; 1 John 3:2). As Grenz relates, "[T]he inbreaking of eschatological power into the present constitutes a corporate people who are all in Christ and consequently who are being transformed into the image of God in Christ" (p. 250). The image of God, then, is not so much an endowment, but a destiny: "At the heart of a Christian conception of the soul is a theological anthropology that speaks about humankind in toto and the human person in particular as a creation of God destined to be the *imago dei*" (p. 3; see Almon, 2017). For this reason, human personhood is an eschatological program—ontologically constituted, ethically orientated, epistemically informed—to the end that we should finally image God as one body of Christ in the world (see Rom 8:29).

Conclusion to Part II

Christology, we are told, is in crisis (see, e.g., Ramm, 1985). Not since the early church Fathers grappled with the heterodoxies of antiquity, so the story now goes, has the biblical (i.e., classical, orthodox) understanding of the person and work of Christ been so beleaguered. The reasons for this loss of confidence in the ancient christological formulas are clear:

> Our age is in many ways like that of the Fathers of Christian theology. They lived at a time when old orders were crumbling, and found themselves not only thinking the foundations of the Christian tradition but also rethinking the nature and reality of human knowledge. Now that we face the apparent collapse of so much of the culture that the Western Fathers, and Augustine in particular, helped to construct, we find that our situation is remarkably similar. (Gunton, 1997, p. 1)

This historical perspective ought to ease any anxiety that our foundation might finally give way.

Gunton's observation notwithstanding, I note a crucial distinction between ancient and modern resistance to orthodox Christology. Reflective of the respective spirits of each age, I observe an apparent inversion of oppositions—or "dualisms"[59] (p. 86). For the early church, the incarnation was no less scandalous a doctrine than it is today. God had become human? How and why it should be so incited no small degree of controversy. Under the influence of Neoplatonic ideals, orthodoxy's early despisers opposed the apparently absurd notion of Christ's full-bodied humanity, so to speak, on the grounds that it irrevocably demeans the dignity—to say nothing of the divinity—of God.[60]

Viewed from this perspective, early Christian heterodoxies bore an immanently theocentric shape. They represented that age's resistance to God coming down to earth. Neoplatonic epistemology and axiology

---

59. Gunton explains, "In this context dualism does not refer to a metaphysic in which two different kinds of reality are supposed, but one which conceives two realities as either opposites or contradictions of each other. Mainstream Christianity has always held that God is other than the world but, because he is its Creator, has denied that the two are related in a negative way. Because the created order is dependent upon God, he can be conceived to interact with it. Dualism denies such an interaction, either explicitly or by conceiving the two in such a way that it becomes impossible consistently to relate them. In this sense, both adoptionism and docetism, the earliest and most logically primitive Christian heresies, arise from the same root. Because their assumptions are dualistic they are compelled to deny either that Jesus was fully God or that he was fully man. It is not difficult to understand, also, how [modern] attempts to abstract a merely historical Jesus from the New Testament material about him operate with similar presuppositions" (pp. 86–87).

60. The identification of Mary as θεοτόκος (theotokos) "mother of God" (lit. God-bearer), initially triggered concern not that Mary had been inordinately and unjustifiably elevated, but that God had somehow been demeaned (Percival, 1991, pp. 206–7).

emphasized humanity's need (and ability) to ascend to higher orders of being, philosophy being understood as the chief means for making this ascent. The incarnation had upended this expectation: God had descended to earth, had taken on flesh in order to redeem, of all things, *human* flesh. Christological dogma, then, overturned both human wisdom and boasting in a single act of divine humility (1 Cor 1:20). How could such a ridiculous notion survive under the weight of Platonist critique? Yet survive it has.

Early Christian opposition to classical orthodoxy mainly consisted of objections to its perceived denigration of God.[61] The christological formulae adumbrated over the course of several centuries in the creeds would come to serve as an increasingly complex system of theological levies preventing the erosion of Christ's deity while positing with increasing specificity the distinctives and parameters of his humanity. This early opposition has been essentially inverted in modern christological debate (see Gunton, 1997; O'Collins, 2009; Runia, 1984).

The stress of ancient Christology, conditioned as it was in conversation with Neoplatonism, fell on the theological side of the christological coin.[62] Of less concern was what Christology made of humanity. Modern christological dogma, situated as it is in the age of totalitarian humanism, finds itself wrestling with the anthropocentric priorities of our post/modern age (Macquarrie, 2003b).[63] Our age has witnessed an inversion of epistemic and axiological priorities: whereas the ancients felt it was beneath God to become human, arguably, modern objections to the incarnation are often reducible to the notion that it somehow denigrates humanity.

In either age, the argument goes, Christ cannot be truly one if he is the other, whether divine or human. What is at stake today, what the ancients never conceived, is what humanity has come to believe about humanity. We have told ourselves a story about who *we* are. Orthodox

61. Macquarrie (2003b) questions whether an "unconscious docetism" may not be at work in modern calls for a return to pre-Enlightenment Christologies (p. 343).

62. Thinkers like Plotinus and Porphyry sought their answers in a realm beyond and above the feeble, mundane concerns of human beings. Modernity has inverted their quest: ultimate meaning is not to be found "out there," but "in here"—that is, within the seemingly fathomless depths of, alternatively, the human mind, human self-consciousness, or even, *reductio ad absurdam*, within the human brain (see Cozolino, 2017).

63. Schleiermacher is often cited as the father of modern anthropocentric Christologies (Macquarrie, 2003b; O'Collins, 2009).

Christology threatens our preferred narrative. Of particular significance in this theanthropological clash is our apparent concern to preserve an elevated status for the human self and its self-consciousness.[64] As O'Collins (2009) observes, "The consciousness of individual subjects and their experience of themselves and the world have at times become the sole focus of attention and have been turned into the major and even exclusive criterion for christological argument" (p. 217). God is dead, in other words; long live human beings.

In order to regard Jesus as fully human, some deem it necessary to jettison any meaningful sense of his deity (see Hick, 1977). In pursuit of a Christ "for us" and "with us," this humanizing trajectory in Christology marginalizes as increasingly superfluous and old-fashioned any insistence on his deity. "If Jesus as the Christ is to be our man," determines Robinson (1973), "he must be one of us: *totus in nostris*, completely part of our world . . . ; in other words, a man in every sense of the word" (p. xi). Christology of this sort has clearly been dislodged from its ancient ontological/constitutive foundations in favor of a strictly functional/covenantal model. In light of this, we would do well to heed Macquarrie's (2003b) admonition that modern Christologies preserve a link with patristic and medieval models: "Metaphysics or ontology in some form or another is not finally dispensable in any adequate christology" (p. 344).

The line of argument taken throughout these two chapters has followed from the premise that human nature is explained only in relation to Christ. Our knowledge of ourselves as human beings is finally explicable only by Christ's humanity and, in particular, his relatedness to God through the Spirit. Furthermore, in regard to the individual pursuit of self-knowledge, self and its self-consciousness come into clearest focus only when perceived through the person of Christ. He is the lens through which we see ourselves as we are and as God calls us to be. His is the

64. As Macquarrie (2003b) observes, modern anthropology since the Enlightenment, having become dissociated from any theological entailments, actually diminishes humanity's status within the cosmos even as it pursues its deification. On the one hand, "[H]umanity . . . has been encouraged to think of itself as the highest being of which we have any knowledge and to be moving into an unlimited future in which the earth will be brought ever nearer to the heart's desire"; even so, any supposed status humanity may arrogate to itself is effaced by our vainglorious renunciation of the God in whose image we are made: "[M]odern thought has downgraded the human race. It has stripped humanity of its claim to be a special creation of God and his special concern. It has exiled him from the centre of the universe to an obscure planet in an obscure corner" (pp. 360–361). From our obsolescence, then, we need a Savior who is Christ the Lord!

image to which we become conformed through active participation in his nature through perichoretic union with him. Through covenantal relatedness to God-in-Christ, to each other, to self, and to the world we are transformed into true human beings. In submission to Jesus as Lord, out of love for his person and gratitude for his atoning work, we come to image Christ and fulfill our divine design.

As ensuing chapters will make increasingly clear, God's Christiform calling to believers entails their contingent, analogous correspondence to each other such that they too become mirrors for others. More than this, human correspondence that fulfills its covenantal bearing seeks to fulfill a supreme ethical calling. As self and others relate to one another agapically in Christ, his presence and grace provide the means by which we may become instruments of the dialogical transformation of others—in both themselves and their self-consciousnesses—who are made in the image of God.

Part III

Self and Self-Knowledge
in Christological Perspective

5

Christ and the human self-in-relation

As NOTED IN REGARD to ancient and modern Christologies, Christian thought regarding the human self has likewise wrestled against oppositional—i.e., dualist—thinking. Considering the close kinship between Christology and anthropology disclosed in the doctrine of the imago dei, we should hardly expect the self—its nature and even its very existence—to avoid similar trouble.[1] As we shall see, the contribution of modern and postmodern perspectives, though ultimately lacking the explanatory power of a robustly Christian approach to human personhood, nevertheless offer some corrective to the shortcomings of ancient and medieval paradigms. Whereas, the latter, largely dependent on Augustinian anthropology, located the human self in the soul; the former came to view self less as a formal constituent than a functional or, more precisely, relational construct (see, e.g., Harter, 2015).[2] As it happens, neither perspective by itself is sufficient.

1. When discussions concerning the nature and existence of the soul (which I do not equate with self) are factored in, controversy only multiplies. I have intentionally avoided the use of "soul" except in reference, along with "mind," to the metaphysical (i.e., nonphysical) aspects of human nature. The question of whether the human mind/ soul is a metaphysical "substance" may bear significantly on ethical concerns (Moreland & Rae, 2000). However, I can see no compelling reason to equate self with soul for the sake of positing a constitutive (i.e., ontological) basis for the existence of self.

2. Defining "the" self is notoriously complex and contestable. The present discussion in no way attempts to comprehensively trace the history of post/modern debate on the subject, but rather to suggest a third way—one that is grounded in the person and work of Christ. But by way of illustration of the postmodern shift toward an understanding of "the" self as construct, theory, or psychological form, Goethals and

A similar shift in Christian thinking regarding the self has frequently been identified as a consequence (cause?) of the philosophical turn
to relationality (Grenz, 2001; cf. Shults, 2003). The evidence of a shift
toward relational theanthropology can be discerned to some degree in
Calvin and Kierkegaard, and more fully in Bonhoeffer and Barth. Their
questioning of constitutive frameworks for the imago dei correlates with
a contemporaneous shift that took place in philosophical discourse. As
I noted in Part II, covenantal theanthropology must remain grounded
in its constitutive foundation lest we undermine any christological significance and coherence with respect to the imago dei. Much contemporary thought regarding the image, I find, overcorrects for the excesses
premodern metaphysical formulations when it attempts to dispense with
them altogether. Christian theanthropology on the other hand, when sufficiently grounded in a christological framework, may more easily bear
the tension of dialectic.

Augustine (2012c) confessed that his highest aspiration was to
know God and himself.[3] That "double" knowledge is even possible
follows from Christology. Nevertheless, in advance of traversing the
conceptual and disciplinary gap between Christology and psychology—
broadly conceived as the study of human inter/subjectivity—an additional observation must be made concerning the challenges of disciplinary

---

Strauss (1991) cite the early philosophical psychologies of Wilhelm Wundt, William
James, and the sociological contribution of Horton Cooley. In particular, James (1961)
stressed the knowability of the empirical, phenomenal self—the *me* as I appear to myself—over and against the experientially transcendent self—the *I* who self-perceives.
According to Goethals and Strauss (1991), "James's discussion of the *me*, and its constituent parts, the material me, the social me, and the spiritual me, and in particular,
his treatment of self-esteem and the multiplicity of social selves, remain highly influential 100 years later" (p. 2). In postmodern psychology, James's I-self has largely
dropped out of view leading Vitz & Felch (2006) to sound an alarm. What is necessary,
they argue, is an understanding of selfhood that can withstand the impulses of postmodern deconstructionism.

3. More specifically, "God and the soul, that is what I desire to know [*Deum et
animam scire cupio*]" (Augustine, 2012c, I.vii; p. 539). Like Aristotle before him, Augustine regards relationship to be contingent upon knowledge, rather than the inverse.
When Reason, his intrasubjective dialogue partner, inquires about his regard for others, he replies, "[I desire] that together and concordantly we might inquire out God
and our souls. For so, whichever first discovers aught, easily introduces his compan-
ions into it" (I.xx; p. 544). Conscious of his former struggles with concupiscence, he
denounces any relationship that Reason suggests might potentially "impede" him in
his "inquiries." Augustine's approach to self-knowledge is often accused of being overly
rationalistic (Stock, 2010).

rapprochement.[4] That such a gap exists should not surprise us. In the first place, the Scriptures establish, and orthodox Christian belief maintains, that God is transcendent, standing far above the created order (1 Kgs 8:27). His glory reaches farther beyond the realm of human existence than human thinking could ever aspire (Isa 55:9). Having considered the Lord's majesty and glory, the Psalmist can only shake his head: "What is humanity?" (Ps 8:4) by comparison.

As Barth (2010) helpfully reminds us, the divine mind and nature can only be brought down to earth, so to speak, by the exercise of divine initiative—never by human ambition or effort. With the rise of Kantian epistemology, however, rational, systematic inquiry into the nature of the triune God and the incarnate Son who perfectly reveals him became unjustifiably and unbiblically sequestered from the human sciences to the detriment of both.[5] As a result of this historical dichotomization, two unfortunate inclinations have arisen in modern discourse: the objectification of theology, which increasingly speaks of God without reference to self, and the secularization of psychology, which now seeks sovereignty over, among other things, the knowledge of self (cf. Diller, 2014).

To no small degree, Christian thinking has followed this dualistic trajectory. It goes without saying that the theological and anthropological disciplines cannot be collapsed into a single theanthropological compendium without erasing vital distinctions necessary for maintaining Creator–creature distinctions. The two domains into which each speaks are irresolvably disjunct. Yet, in light of the biblical doctrines of the image of God, the incarnation of Christ, and the gospel of reconciliation, Christians can hardly dispense with the important work of transdisciplinary dialogue while claiming to uphold the revelation of God granted us in his Logos.

In Christ, God and humanity have become one, "indivisibly, inseparably," while still "inconfusedly, unchangeably." If the Incarnation is true, then both disciplinary distinction and transdisciplinary dialogue are possible. Christ *makes* them possible. In other words, God's self-disclosure

4. I refer here to attempts to delimit the Christian care of persons by excluding as either unbiblical or unscientific approaches which allow for transdisciplinary dialogue or which pit "theology" and "science" against each other. Although most perspectives allow for some discourse between theological and psychological domains, there are outliers on both sides of the spectrum that eschew efforts at disciplinary intersectionality and dialogue (see E. L. Johnson, 2010b; cf. Hunsinger, 1995).

5. Kuyper (1968) avers, "[I]t only weakens the position of theology to prosecute her studies as though she stood alone" (p. 619).

in the person and work of Jesus Christ, who is the image of God and of humanity, has granted us the very epistemological license to traverse the gulf. Christ reveals true God; and he discloses self truly. In Christ the mysteries of God and of self are disclosed to us (cf. Col 2:3). Any framework for relating the two must be rooted in the doctrine of the imago dei, christologically understood, preserving all necessary distinctions and caveats and resisting any impulse to either antithesize or conflate that which it endeavors to relate.[6]

Though perennially vulnerable to charges of—and lapses into—contradiction on the one hand, and overly facile, "weak" integration on the other, attempts to relate theology and psychology need not be subject to summary dismissal (see E. L. Johnson, 2011). With proper attention and care and in light of the person and work of Christ, these two disciplines may yield light and understanding. Calvin certainly believed so, and Augustine before him. What we must resist, then, is the impulse to separate what, in Christ, God has brought together.

Epistemologically grounded in the Scriptures and the historic teachings of Christianity, Christian psychology commends the study of the self as an aspect of human personhood, and growth in self-knowledge as a necessary element of psychotherapeutic remediation and psychospiritual edification (E. L. Johnson, 2007, 2017; see Maier & Monroe, 2001; Roberts & Watson, 2010).[7] Christian psychology rejects the notion that modernism somehow invented the care and cure of the human self, while acknowledging the reality that such has come to be dominated by post/modern thinking (Holifield, 1983; see Cushman, 1995). Though this is the current state of affairs, we need not be reluctant to proceed.

---

6. When lacking the proper christological balance, the Kierkegaardian/Barthian "infinite qualitative distinction" foments an un-Christlike dichotomization of theology and anthropology. So, on the one hand, Neoorthodox pastoral theologian Hunsinger (1995) rightly argues, "[T]heology and psychology represent material that cannot be integrated into a unified whole. They are logically diverse; they have different aims, subject matters, methods, and linguistic conventions. They do not exist on the same level." There is truth in what she says, yet she too hastily concludes, "as language and thought worlds, they are not to be integrated with one another *in any systematic way*" (p. 6, my emphasis). Another look at Chalcedonian Christology may be in order. Cannot the person of Christ be termed a "system" in which God has integrated—made whole—the two into one? Hunsinger seeks to avoid conflation but lapses into antithesis. Another way to avoid conflation is balance—dialogue.

7. Along these lines, Roberts and Watson (2010) argue for the need for a "psychology that accurately describes the psychological nature of human beings as understood according to historic Christianity" (p. 155).

Secular ideas about the self, whether Aristotle's, Freud's, or others', offer both a foil and an interlocutor for Christian thinking. On the one hand, we should anticipate regular disagreement between them in regard to the self and its proper care. On the other hand, as Reformed theology instructs us, God's common grace at work in the world should lead us to expect instances of concordance as well (Van Til, 1969, 2015).[8] In either case, the Christian psychologist will acknowledge—and rejoice in—the God who has authored the truth both perspectives seek. Neither Augustine nor Calvin found it necessary to dismiss secular truth claims for the mere cause of being secular!

Christian psychology is an exercise in theological anthropology that endeavors to perceive human nature and normativity through the lens of revelation, yet with a willingness to listen in on conversations taking place outside the church. As such, Christian psychology bridges the gap between the epistemological domains of God and the self, working by God's grace toward the reconciliation of the seemingly irreconcilable. We must condition our listening with God's self-disclosure, of course. Yet, with Christ as our key, the proper conditions are set. We may proceed.

Self-in-relation: The objective subject of self-knowledge

What is the human self? Is it real or rhetorical? If real, where can we locate it? Do we all have it? Can we lose it? Where do we begin to frame our search? By way of prolegomena to the next span of our bridge, let me first make clear: agnosticism regarding the existence, "form," and epistemic warrant for the human self should properly be regarded as tantamount questioning the same in relation to God. Moreover, if we, as Christians, console ourselves about the certainty of God's existence, we ought not equivocate about the self. It has become somewhat fashionable of late, at least among some in Christendom, to resist post/modernism's secularizing influence over the culture by dismissing the objects of post/modernist inquiry. Better to focus on knowing God than self. If the so-called self exists, the story goes, it is irrelevant to theological inquiry.

Again, Calvin (2008) instructs us on this point: the pursuit of the knowledge of God is misguided, objectivist, and ultimately futile when dissociated from knowledge of self. We can only know God as the mutual,

---

8. Christian approaches to knowledge must never aver the incapacity of the unredeemed for accurate observation and ratiocination (see Van Til, 1980).

reciprocal entailment of our knowledge of self.[9] The reverse is also true, we can only know self as we come to know God. If, on the other hand, the human self does not exist, the way to knowing God is necessarily shut. Ontology and epistemology are linked. Nothing finally unreal can be truly known, only imagined. All our vaulted imaginings regarding God are meaningless if he does not finally exist. Agnosticism regarding the human self implicates a stark epistemic reality: what we decide regarding the self, whatever it may be, cannot but impact our understandings of God.

Christology is our epistemic key to both God and self. In examining the person of Christ, we learn that self, as an aspect of human personhood, is the relational—i.e., covenantal—subject of self-knowledge. Apart from Christ, who in his humanity relates from the locus of his humanity to God and to the rest of humanity, the human self becomes subject to a radical contingency. Cut loose from its christological moorings, self comes under the influence of, alternatively, modernist naturalistic positivism and postmodern antirealism. According to the former, the human self does not exist and cannot be known. According to the latter, the self is a wholly contingent social construct. As such, the postmodern self is whatever the individual—or better, society—believes it to be.

Christology offers us epistemic access to the self and the relational means of self-knowing. In his person, Christ relates by means of the Spirit to God and to others. Through his work he delivers us from our estrangement from both, bringing us into perichoretic union with himself and with each other. As the Spirit does with the man Christ, so the Spirit brings us to God's own knowledge of himself and to God's knowledge of ourselves. In doing so, God-in-Christ supplies the means by which self-estrangement, the autocentric or intrasubjective basis for dissociation and self-deception, may be resolved.

Moreover, the benefits of Christ's work find application along the three axes of human relatedness—that of self to God, to others, and, reflexively, to itself. Herein lies Christology's most direct contact with human psychology. If dissociation and self-deception are understood in covenantal terms as ethicospiritual consequences of the fall, then reconciliation—that blessed christological theme—must surely supply their

---

9. If Calvin's truism holds, then to whatever degree one pole of human "double" knowledge may be impaired by mental deficiency or the noetic effects of the fall, the other will also be impaired. In other words, if I cannot know one, I cannot know the other.

cure. Finally, it may also be noted that the christological doctrine of reconciliation impels us to work at repairing the epistemological breach that has set contemporary theology and psychology at loggerheads.[10]

Diverse perspectives on the self

Recent Christian scholarship regarding the self demonstrates a surge of interest around transdisciplinary dialogue (see, e.g., McMinn & Phillips, 2001; Turner, 2008; van Huyssteen & Wiebe, 2011; Vitz & Felch, 2006). As an object of Christian theological, anthropological, and philosophical inquiry, the self is a hot topic. The impetus for all this interest has arisen in response to influences and oppositions with secular thinking. Nontheistic perspectives on the self are diverse and far from monolithic. Many counter and contradict each other. Sifting through the various secular paradigms can be a disorientating and dizzying affair.

So, for example, considerable pressure has mounted from *modern* philosophy and psychology to define the self strictly in evolutionary terms as a cultural, cognitive, or even cellular "achievement."[11] Christian responses to such perspectives tend to stress the degree to which developmental or achievement models account for certain biblical and psychological data, while maintaining the primacy of self's ontic reality (see Beck & Demarest, 2005; Delitzsch, 1885; E. L. Johnson, 2007; Roberts, 2001; Talbot, 1997). Kierkegaard (1980), for instance, viewed the self as an ethical achievement while eschewing any basis for its contingency other than that of the individual's standing before God (see Evans, 2002). Modernist perspectives necessarily degrade the ethical quality of human persons who lack the ability to "achieve" full selfhood. Eugenics, abortion, euthanasia are the predictable outcomes of such notions.

On the other hand, *postmodern* critiques of the self emphasize its contingency in other respects. They stress a phenomenological approach, which yields, as we might expect, a "self" characterized by multiplicity and fragmentation (see Vitz & Felch, 2006). Whatever remains of the self following its deconstruction by the ironically certain uncertainty of

10. Cf. Loder & Neidhardt, 1992; Shults, 2008.

11. Self- and other-recognition does indeed take place at the level of biomolecular and immunological interactions (López-Larrea, 2012). However, any supposed warrant for determining from this finding an evolutionary basis for human self-consciousness is clearly a function of worldview and plausibility structures, not of empirical science *per se* (see P. E. Johnson, 1993).

postmodernism can hardly be labeled unitary. While most Christian responses to the idea of a multiplicity of selves emphasize the normativity and eschatological bearing of a unitary self (McFadyen, 1990; Thiselton, 1995; White, 1996), others have suggested a reappraisal of this position (see Turner, 2008; Woodhead, 1999). In the face of such strong secular oppositions, Christian perspectives on the self and self-knowledge have struggled at times to find their footing.

Secular competitors of the Christian self

The ancient and venerable notion of a unitary, persistent self "located" in the metaphysical substance of the soul has been in decline in secular thought for some time (Martin & Barresi, 2008; Solomon, 1988; cf. Beck & Demarest, 2005; Cooper, 2000). Indeed, secular perspectives on human nature generally and the self in particular have largely shifted away from ontological narratives toward empirical and phenomenological models, the latter being largely dominated by naturalist and positivist priorities (see Goethals & Strauss, 1991). Among the many unforeseen consequences of the Copernican and Kantian revolutions, humanity seems to have experienced a series of identity crises, out of which grew compensatory compulsions to master both the cosmos without and the human psyche within.

As medieval cosmologies fell, so too their ancient theological foundations came to be discarded. Gradually, the self became decoupled from the soul; what could be known of the soul fell outside the bounds of empirical inquiry.[12] Theology, it was believed, was unable to provide sufficient certainty in the face of modern angst. Surely, science could be better trusted to bring our anxiety to heel. So it happened that out of the chaos of this epochal upheaval the modern "world-mastering rational

12. Modern Christian ethicists like Moreland & Rae (2000) often reify the premodern model of the soul-as-self in the interests of preserving a metaphysical basis for personhood. How can we defend the rights of the unborn, the mentally infirm or terminally ill, they ask, if personhood is not grounded in "substance"? Furthermore, if, as postmodern perspectives insist, self is a developmental construct, a cognitive achievement, or a neurobiological epiphenomenon, what becomes of the human person after the death of the body? Notably, Christian models of the self rooted in evolutionary frameworks often cavalierly dismiss or ignore such concerns (see, e.g., Shults, 2003). As demonstrated above, without some sort of ontological anchor, notions of person, self, and personal identity become vulnerable to a radical contingency, the ethical and theological consequences of which are immense (see Cooper, 2000).

self" would emerge (Grenz, 2001, p. 67). In this sense the Enlightenment should be viewed as a self-styled work of intellectual and psychological palingenesis—humanity's deliverance out of the primordial waters of premodern ignorance and fear from whence it had finally emerged (cf. Macquarrie, 2003).

Descartes and Locke had laid the philosophical groundwork for the modern self. In the writings of Kant, then, the subject of knowledge acquired near-divine status (Martin & Barresi, 2008; C. Taylor, 1989). In tracing the development of modernity's "transcendental pretence," Solomon (1988) acknowledges Kant's seminal role in establishing the supremacy and universality of individual human experience (p. 40). Expanding on this theme, Grenz (2001) argues,

> Kant's epistemology transformed the knowing process into a relationship between the autonomous self and the world waiting to be known through the creative power of the active mind. ... Rather than viewing the self as one of several entities in the world, Kant's thinking self in a sense "creates" the world—that is, the world of its own knowledge. (p. 76)

Michener (2007) identifies the "two major characteristics" of the Kantian self in terms of the "all-encompassing" purview of its knowledge and its "right to project from the subjective structures of one's mind to general truth claims on the nature of humanity" (p. 22). By such means, all of reality could be defined as a constellation of epistemic objects that should be placed under the hegemony of the knowing human subject.

Under Kant's influence, the human self came to be defined exclusively in terms of self-consciousness, "as a replacement for the notion of the soul, which had fallen on hard times" (Martin & Barresi, 2008, p. 297). Considering the dissatisfaction with medieval theological paradigms, the shift of self from metaphysical substance to strictly subjective reality was, perhaps, inevitable. Yet, the stark implications of this shift are difficult to justify. Regarding self-knowledge Kant would claim, "I have no *knowledge* of myself as I am, but merely as I appear to myself" (Kant, 2007, p. 169; emphasis original). To be clear, this is not any postmodern agnosticism regarding the existence of self; rather, Kantian epistemology places the object in itself, in this case the knowing self, outside the bounds of direct observation in order to prioritize the subjectivity of knowledge (Bird, 2006).

If self cannot know or experience itself (or God) directly, the episte-mological priority necessarily shifts toward the subjective end of knowing, essentially permitting the knower to define reality on strictly phenom-enological grounds. Perception or consciousness of self (and God) now encompasses the totality of our epistemic access. Moreover, any potential disparity between the "noumenal" self and its "phenomenal" appraisal is moot. The former—self-as-it-truly-is—cannot be known; now, self-as-it-appears-to-me is all in all. Under a phenomenological rubric, revelation is vanquished; observation is now king. And the knowing self becomes, for all intents and purposes, its own god.

Knowledge, according to modernist dogma, comes through rational, empirical scrutiny and analysis. Observations and conclusions regarding the self may now be systematized and universalized in the interests of "science," so-called. Thus, as Grenz (2001) explains, "Kant's self did not merely know itself. Rather, in knowing itself it supposed that it knew all selves, as well as the structure of any and every possible self" (p. 77). Kant's "radically anthropocentric" (C. Taylor, 1989, p. 366) conception of self and its knowledge can be summed up in his "motto of enlighten-ment:" "*Sapere aude* [Dare to be wise]! Have courage to use your *own* understanding!" (Kant, 1991, p. 54, emphasis original). In plain terms, following from Kant, I am who I believe myself to be.

By the grace of God, the Kantian self would eventually fall into dis-repute with the rise of postmodernism. In the twentieth century, psycho-logical theorists would follow William James in conceiving of the self as an aggregate of multiple empirical "selves" (Goethals & Strauss, 1991).[13] James differentiated the self along Kantian lines with the empirically transcendent I-self—or "pure ego"—on the one hand and numerous phe-nomenal me-selves—as discrete expressions of an "empirical ego"—on the other (James, 1961, p. 43). Recognizing the innumerable exocentric influences that contribute to the formation of these me-selves, he out-lined several ways in which they interact hierarchically and conflictually within various social contexts (pp. 53–54).

James's phenomenal me-self, unlike his I-self, was not a static real-ity, but a dynamic one influenced and shaped intersubjectively over the

13. Martin & Barrisi (2008) note that, as early as John Locke's *Essay Concerning Human Understanding*, "self" had been conceived of as a "momentary entity" rather than "a temporally extended one" (p. 144). James (1961) would argue something simi-lar in his discussion of the human subject's constantly changing "stream of conscious-ness" (p. 18).

course of one's life. Yet, as Harter (2015) explains, James' multiple self model took on a different cast as the underlying assumptions of modernism came increasingly under question:

> [James's] characterization of *multiple Me-selves* represented the reality of self development, including the challenges that such multiplicity provoked. The field began to shift toward an increasing zeal for models depicting how the self varied across situations and relational contexts. . . . Postmodernism had clear and definite implications for how the self would now be conceptualized. The self shifted to an arbitrarily or socially constructed identity (rather than a personally crafted self). (p. 5; emphasis original)

From James until the present, I am who *we* make me to be.

So, the Kantian thesis of reflexive self-knowledge and self-construction was abandoned. Self-mastery, postmodernism rightly argued, is a sham. Postmodernism had called into question humanity's ability to master anything, let alone the illusive and ineffable self. Interestingly, on James's own terms the empirical self is often a mess of conflicts and irrationality. From the vantage point of postmodernism, however, James's unitary I-self could likewise be sustained no longer. Having decoupled the self from the soul and discarded the link between the phenomenal and the experientially transcendent aspects of personhood, the human self would become wholly contingent (Vitz & Felch, 2006).

By the mid-nineteenth century philosophical doubts had arisen as to the ability of the modern self to truly know itself (see Ricoeur, 1977). The events of the first half of the twentieth century, especially the extent to which humanity had witnessed its own inhumanity in two world wars, appear to have further crystallized this skepticism regarding the rationality and knowability of the human self (Martin & Barresi, 2008; Solomon, 1988; cf. Ryle, 1949). Kant's belief that his noumenal self could not be truly known would eventually crest in a tsunami of postmodern suspicion that anything could be known in itself. The epistemic objects most vulnerable to this skepticism were those the Christian Scriptures are most concerned to disclose: God, self, and others. Our first-person perspective, flawed and fallible as it is, undermines our claims of epistemic access, hermeneutical veridicality, and ethical normativity. "Can the self ever encounter the other," postmodern philosophers would muse, "or do reason and interpretation alike ultimately result in self-absorption?" (Vanhoozer, 1998, p. 383).

Having perceived the overweening ambition of modernist conceptions of the self and intent on dethroning regnant hegemonies, postmodern thinkers eventually came to express deep reservations about a unitary self. To date, postmodern critics of the modern self, which grew out of the self-as-soul understanding, have opposed it on both philosophical (Metzinger, 2009; Siderits, 2016) and psychological (Cushman, 1995; Gergen, 1991) grounds, eventually leading Solomon (1988) to determine that the modern self "has now disintegrated into nothingness" (p. 126). Echoing this theme, Barresi & Martin (2011) conclude,

> [T]he unified self, if indeed there ever was such a thing, has receded from view. Those who seek it today in both the philosophical and scientific literatures soon discover that none but the carefully initiated can wade into the waters of theoretical accounts of the self without soon drowning in a sea of symbols, technical distinctions, and empirical results, the end result of which is that the notion of the unified self has faded from view. (p. 52)

Following Descartes and Kant, modernity had defined the self in terms of rationality, the essence of which is expressed, above all, in human reason (see Harter, 2015). Yet, the reality of our postmodern experience of self is that it is often anything but rational and reasonable. Beset on so many sides, the modern self, as Vitz & Felch (2006) have forcefully argued, is now in crisis.

Secular approaches seeking to define and delineate the self set out from a variety of starting points, whether phenomenological, narratival, semantic, or philosophical.[14] Having renounced any putative theological warrant, these contemporary understandings of the self suffer perennially from uneasy footing. Once anthropology is decoupled from theology, over time, the idea of a unitary, persistent self must give ground to a multiplicity of models reflective of the various cultural, developmental, evolutionary, and religious influences to which subjectivity itself may been subjected. In what may be regarded as a predictable result,

---

14. Neisser (1997) summarizes modern and postmodern vantage points in clear enough terms: "If we are in search of the self, we can look either inward or outward." A modern perspective on the self looks "inward," focusing on "private experience, on mental representations, on the self-concept." Postmodern perspectives, if they do not deconstruct the self altogether, look instead at "outward" influences: "to see the self as embedded in its environment, ecologically and socially situated in relation to other objects and persons" (p. 19).

The contemporary self has become destablised, both theoreti-
cally and experientially, as modernity's individualism continues
to retreat from the postmodern world. . . . Whereas the unity of
the experiencing subject has always been philosophically problematic, a broad consensus suggests that the self's existential
predicament became increasingly precarious as local communities and their idiosyncratic customs and traditions gave way to
the globalised society. . . . As the traditional sources of identity
crumbled away, a novel and distinctive kind of identity emerged
characterised by its multiplicity, mobility, ephemerality and su-
perficiality. (Turner, 2008, p. 2)

From the perspective of Christianity, it might be argued that modernity had set out to construct a self that amounted to an anthropological Tower of Babel by which humanity might finally attain to the status
of divinity. Seeing our hubris, God, in his infinite wisdom, has cast the
modern mind into a sea of confusion and a plurality of postmodern perspectives. Having rejected any theological basis in favor of philosophical,
psychological, or evolutionary frameworks, the secular self has foun-
dered for want of an epistemic anchor by which it might be rescued from
fatal contingency. In the final analysis, what we say about humanity must
follow from our conclusions about humanity's Creator: "If God is dead,"
political philosopher Stephen Clark (1989) rightly concludes, "so also is
the Self" (p. 37). This, too, is true.

A christological perspective on the human self

The two poles of secular thought on the self could not be further apart,
yet they should both be viewed as expressions of what Martin Kähler
has called the "confused self-understanding human beings have when
left to their own resources" (cited in Pannenberg, 1985, p. 92). The humanist assumptions of modernity had resulted in an unfounded optimism regarding the self and its knowledge. In its most egregious excess,
modernist anthropology failed to account for the sinful, fallen condition
of humanity cut off from life and fellowship with God. Postmodernist
observations that self is often unstable, multiplicitous, and contextually
contingent—valid inferences all—only confirms this.

As Christians, we should expect phenomenological approaches to
self to reveal deep and persistent divides in our sense and experiences
of self (McFadyen, 1990; Turner, 2008; Woodhead, 1999). On the other

hand, the postmodern rejection of a persistent, unitary self grounded in objective reality amounts to an overreaction in the extreme (cf. Megill, 1985). After all, as even the most ardent philosophical antirealist will acknowledge, "in an interesting sense" selves are "phenomenological 'everyday objects'" (Metzinger, 2011, p. 281).

In many ways, it seems that the failure of the promise of modernity triggered the wholesale collapse of any confidence in the foundations of Western civilization, the unitary self being no exception.[15] The resultant fear and confusion stirred up by the disintegration of modern notions of the self may also be seen as a fulfilment of Kierkegaard's prophetic insistence that attempts to ground the self in anything other than "the power that established it" would only lead to despair (Kierkegaard, 1980, p. 14). Numerous defenses of the self have, in fact, been mounted by Christian writers advocating expressly theological perspectives. Interacting with both modern and postmodern thinkers, Thiselton (1995), for one, argues for a philosophical reappraisal of postmodern eulogizing for the self on the basis of Christian truth claims. In his sweeping survey of the philosophical and psychological history of the self, Grenz (2001) offers a trinitarian basis for the self grounded in the imago dei. Jensen (2012) has demonstrated one among a myriad of ways that Christology may be fruitfully employed in support of a Christian view of the human self.

Deliverance from the infecundity of modern and postmodern perspectives on the self comes to us *from above*. As modern and postmodern perspectives grapple with each other for narratival primacy, Christology proffers a perspective on the human self that is grounded in the dogma of the imago dei, the divine design for which has been perfectly fulfilled in the person and work of Jesus Christ. As established in the previous two chapters, our basis for a Christian psychology of the self is none other than "the Son of man."[16] The approach taken throughout the rest of this chapter and the next presumes the epistemic primacy of the Christ event—that is, the sum of God's revelation in and through the incarnation

15. Some postmodern Christian approaches have rightly suggested that the "modern" self is itself a historical, narratival construct (see Turner, 2008; Woodhead, 1999). This is not the same as saying the self-that-is, my true self, is a construct, as we shall see.

16. Johnson (2007) notes that postmodern pluralism has, perhaps ironically, played a part in fomenting the development of a robustly Christian psychology. The fall of "the modern ideal of a generic, all-encompassing psychology to which all open-minded, rational parties can agree" may be perceived as a boon for Christian perspectives as it opens the door to a renewed dialogue (p. 255).

and the reconciling work of Jesus Christ. If indeed Christ is to be taken at his word, there can be no better place to search for such "treasure" than Christology (see Col 2:3; cf. Matt 13:44).

Toward a surer foundation

The provenance of the unitary self—the objective I who reflexively perceives self as a discernible object of personal reflection and contemplation—is often traced to Augustine (Cary, 2003; see also Grenz, 2001; LaCugna, 1991; C. Taylor, 1989). Turner (2008), suggesting the degree of contingency regarding the self with which he is comfortable, goes so far as to dub Augustine "the creator of the inner self" (p. 1). In noting the early Father's seminal influence on Western notions of the self, LaCugna (1991) avers,

> Largely due to the influence of the introspective psychology of
> Augustine and his heirs, we in the West today think of a person
> as a "self" who may be further defined as an individual center of
> consciousness, a free, intentional subject, one who knows and is
> known, loves and is loved, an individual identity, a unique per-
> sonality endowed with certain rights, a moral agent, someone
> who experiences, weighs, decides, and acts. (p. 250)

More likely, Augustine should be credited with synthesizing and crystallizing philosophical and psychological ideas about human subjectivity that he had received from biblical and Greek thinkers alike.[17] In fact, it was what Plotinus said about the "soul" that influenced Augustine's

---

17. Neoplatonists following Plotinus are sometimes credited with the idea of an "inner space" within which the "soul" or true seat of being ostensibly resides (Cary, 2003). According to such narratives, Augustine is primarily responsible for establishing the Western assumption that this inner space is "private" or personal (p. 5). Yet, as will be shown, the biblical writers had been operating with a well-developed sense of the inward aspect of human existence for some time (see Cooper, 2000). The psalmist declares in parallel construction, "Bless Yahweh, my soul, and all my inner parts [כָּל־קְרָבַי, cōl-qerabai] his holy name!" (Ps 103:1, my translation). Isaiah, in referencing his inner, emotional turmoil, employs a term, קְרָבִּי (qirbai, lit. "my entrails"; cf. "my inmost self," ESV), that the translators of the Septuagint rendered τὰ ἐντός μου (ta entos mou, lit. "that which is within me"). Paul refers a number of times to his own "inner man" (ἔσω ἄνθρωπον, esō anthrōpon; Rom 7:22; 2 Cor 4:16; Eph 3:16). Perhaps, in light of this, it would be more accurate to affirm Augustine's role in synthesizing biblical and Hellenist notions of human subjectivity for subsequent Christian thinkers (so, Rist, 1996).

understanding of the self (Rist, 1996).[18] In grounding self in a Christian metaphysics conditioned by Neoplatonism, Augustinian anthropology succeeded in substantializing the self, thus establishing it as an ontological—and epistemological—entity. For a millennium thereafter, theories of the self granted it cogency and rationality by linking it metaphysically and rhetorically to the human soul, which, understood Christianly, was entailed by the constitutive imago. Therein arose the confidence that *the self is the soul* or, allowing for the Cartesian nuance, *the self is the mind.*[19] The two became inseparable and interchangeable both ontologically and hermeneutically (cf. Zimmermann, 2004).[20]

This union of "self" and "soul" would go essentially unquestioned through the high Middle Ages. From Augustine to Aquinas, the uneasy union of Platonic and Aristotelian frameworks would be maintained. A final rupture would eventually come, however, in a series of tectonic

18. Plotinus sounds at times remarkably biblical in his description of the "soul" as the life-animating substance behind all material reality: "Let every soul [ψυχή, *psyche*] recall, then, at the outset the truth that [S]oul is the author of all living things, that it has breathed the life into them all, whatever is nourished by earth and sea, all the creatures of the air, the divine stars in the sky; it is the maker of the sun; itself formed and ordered this vast heaven and conducts all that rhythmic motion; and it is a principle [φύσις, *physis*] distinct from all these to which it gives law and movement and life, and it must of necessity be more honourable than they" (*Ennead* V.i.2). Yet, what places Plotinus wholly outside any biblical cosmology is his supposition that every "soul" shares a common, derivative existence with the "Soul" of divine being: "for they gather or dissolve as [S]oul brings them life or abandons them, but [S]oul, since it never can abandon itself, is of eternal being" (V.i.2; cf. IV.iii.9). According to Caluori (2015), Plotinus employs "soul" as a species of "hypostasis" allowing him to determine that the divine Soul "is his soul" (p. 4). Clearly, this is problematic from a Christian standpoint. Orthodox Christology would eventually offer much greater clarity of terms and referents, distinguishing soul/mind from person/self—a clarity that Christian anthropology would do well to imitate.

19. LaCugna (1991) further argues that "in many respects," Descartes was "a good Augustinian" (p. 250). His rationalistic approach to the self, capsulized in his *cogito ergo sum*, would become the bedrock of modern anthropology. Counter to Augustine, however, Descartes reverses the order of epistemological priority from one of (divine) objectivity to that of (human) subjectivity. Truth, even that which is ultimate and divine, must be searched out and discovered by and within the human subject—the ego or "I." In this way, as Charles Taylor (1989) notes, "Descartes gives Augustinian inwardness a radical twist and takes it in a quite new direction, which has also been epoch-making" (p. 143).

20. By grounding self in the "substance" of the mind/soul, it became possible to read "self" into biblical texts retrojectively. Contemporary English translations have nearly universally followed this trend, rendering Hebrew and Greek references to individual subjectivity with terms like "inner being" and "self."

clashes to which history would eventually refer in explicitly palingenetic terms—i.e., Renaissance (see Barresi & Martin, 2011). Descartes, some two centuries later, would maintain a dualistic understanding of human nature, yet, he baldly elevated "the reasoning subject as the beginning point for knowledge and reflection" (Grenz, 2001, p. 70).[21] In doing so, he reified Plato's notion of the autonomous, self-sufficient self.

With a certainty borne of humanistic zeal, Descartes would write to a friend, "[N]othing can be in me, that is to say, in my mind, of which I am not aware," a supposition which "follows from the fact that the soul is distinct from the body and its essence is to think" (cited in Hatfield, 2014, p. 336). In recapitulating Plato, Descartes had "freed . . . the soul from its Aristotelian accretions" (Martin & Barresi, p. 126). Yet, his attempt to reground the self/soul in Platonic metaphysics would eventually prove the undoing of this pairing. Indeed, Descartes's radically dichotomist anthropology would eventually play a seminal role in fomenting the split between soul and self:

> Descartes's main contributions to theorizing about the self and personal identity were, first, to lend the tremendous weight of his authority to a Platonic view of the self, which would eventually be recognized as scientifically useless, and, second, to introduce the idea of the reflexive nature of consciousness. . . . In a larger sense, however, he championed the new mechanistic view of nature that in the hands of others would eventually undo even his own theories of the self. (Martin & Barresi, 2008, p. 131)

Moreover, as a result of the rift between the natural and supernatural worlds, a great epistemological chasm would open up leading to the bifurcation of empirical and theological approaches to knowledge (see Diller, 2014). Over time, this divide would widen into a dichotomy of competing plausibility structures, "scientific" and "religious" frameworks eventually becoming irreconcilably estranged from each other. What became of Christian articulations of the self would depend on one's epistemological point of departure—whether *from above* (theological) or *from below* (anthropological).

If, on the other hand, as Calvin held, the knowledge of self is inextricably linked to the knowledge of God, then the human self can never be

---

21. In allowing rationality to serve as the supreme faculty of the mind/soul, Descartes followed Augustine. Nevertheless, in his modernist optimism, he elevated the potential of autonomous human achievement far beyond Augustine's estimation (C. Taylor, 1989).

finally established—whether ontologically, epistemologically, or axiologically—apart from its theological/christological basis. This would mean, then, that strictly philosophical approaches to the self cannot, whether as putative descendants of Plato or Descartes, supply their own warrant. As it happens, contemporary Christian philosopher Ricoeur has said as much.

Though Ricoeur's (1995) framework of the self bears a striking resemblance to a covenantal model, it nonetheless fails to establish its own basis, leading to yet another foundation-less—i.e., humanist—anthropology. He rightly emphasizes, for example, the hermeneutical import of a self constituted in interdependence with others. The ethical implications inherent in the formation of one's "narrative identity" exist for the French philosopher in a dialectical relation of "selfhood" and "sameness"—that is, in the self's being-in-relation-to-other—over time (see pp. 113–14). Yet, Ricoeur's ontology of selfhood arises *ex nihilo*, as it were. He eschews as "cryptophilosophical" any theological warrant for human personhood. As Ricoeur himself confesses, his "culturally contingent symbolic network" should be understood to stand as an "heir to the philosophies of the [Cartesian] cogito and as continuing their self-foundational claim" (p. 25; cf. O'Donovan, 1994; Topping, 2007). Reason—faulty, flawed, fallible human reason—supplies sufficient warrant.

Ricoeur's approach to the self and its knowledge suffers the same deficiencies and distortions as Descartes's—and, as it happens, Plato's.[22] His warrant for selfhood offers no final basis in the self-disclosing Logos. As such, philosophical perspectives like Ricoeur's fail to link the self to—and so ground it upon—any greater reality than a strictly human (inter)subjectivity. No such perspective, whether ostensibly Christian or not, can see past its own self-imposed epistemic unipolarity.[23] We cannot finally know self apart from God's knowledge of self.

Christology, on the other hand, offers a more secure epistemological base upon which we may build an understanding of self (see Bartholomew & Goheen, 2013; cf. Isa 28:16). As Dooyeweerd (1984) rightly concludes, "From a Christian point of view, the whole attitude of philosophical thought which proclaims the self-sufficiency of the latter, turns

22. My critique of Ricoeur should not be taken as a dismissal of the vital contribution he has made as a Christian philosophical ethicist.

23. The same is true when applied at the psychospiritual order of discourse: self can never finally displace its own barriers to self-knowledge apart from the knowledge of God-in-Christ. Autonomous human reason will always fail us.

out to be unacceptable, because it withdraws human thought from the divine revelation in Christ Jesus" (p. v). Indeed, "all attempts . . . to bring about an inner synthesis between the Christian faith and a philosophy which is rooted in the self-sufficiency of human reason" cannot but fail to supply their own warrant.

Strictly philosophical approaches, like Ricoeur's, will contribute salutary corollaries to a Christian psychology of the self and its self-knowledge. For epistemic warrant, on the other hand, we require an exocentric perspective on human personhood rooted in the self-revelation of the living God. As Zimmerman (2004) has said,

> Western philosophy has impeded the natural human desire for self-knowledge by getting wrong both the knowing subject and the quality of knowledge itself. Conceiving the knowing subject as isolated consciousness and knowledge as rational facts or eternal truths of universal reason has created an illusion of self-knowledge in which we invent ourselves by chasing after psychic fantasies. (Zimmermann, 2004, p. 297)

Thanks be to God, then, that he has granted us in the Word-made-flesh a surer foundation upon which to construct a Christian psychology of self. Along these lines, Barth, Pannenberg, and, especially, Bonhoeffer have laid much of the necessary christological and anthropological groundwork.

The christological contributions of Barth, Pannenberg, and Bonhoeffer

Although Barth was keen to move away from the rarified metaphysics of medieval scholasticism in favor of the relationality of covenantal personhood, he nevertheless insisted that anthropological inquiry must first be grounded upon its proper christological foundation. Indeed, every anthropological problem, Barth (2010) argued, should first be examined theanthropologically through the person and work of Christ:

> The nature of the man Jesus alone is the key to the problem of human nature. This man is man. As certainly as God's relation to sinful man is properly and primarily His relation to this man alone, and a relation to the rest of mankind only in Him and through Him, He alone is primarily and properly man. . . . If we rightly consider the special difficulty of a theological

anthropology, there can be no question of any other point of
departure. (III/2, pp. 43–44)

According to Barth, the human self should be conceived in Christo-
Trinitarian terms as the "I am" of dynamic relationality (see Oh, 2006;
Webster, 1995; cf. Horton, 2005). The "Thou art" of God inaugurates
and institutes personal identity. As of God's creation of the first couple,
this relationality is tripolar. "I am" followed from the divine "Thou art"
spoken by God to Adam. A secondary, subsequent "Thou art" between
Adam and Eve confirms the divine declaration. "I am," then is confirmed
in relationship between human beings whose identity is dialogically
grounded. For all other human beings since our first parents, the existence of self, God, and others serve as counterweights preserving the
believing self's being-in-relation. God's intention, "following the pattern
of" the *perichoresis* of Christ's own relatedness to God and other, is that
self be known covenantally (Oh, 2006, p. 104).[24]

Within this framework, self may be understood as the subjective
pole of a multipolar intersubjectivity that entails the individual's relatedness to God, to other human beings, and, reflexively, to self. The key to
self's proper covenantal function is balance. On the one hand, an over-
emphasis on the pole of self leads—as it did in the fall and as modernist thinking unwittingly perpetuates—to individualism, autonomy, and
estrangement from Other/others. On the other hand, balance can also
be lost in favor of a radically contingent, heteronomous self taken up in a
self-less existential limbo, ultimately estranged from itself. Taken to their
logical conclusion, postmodern and Buddhist conceptions lead in this
self-annihilating direction (see Biderman, 2008). In order to grasp at the
requisite balance, whether ontic, epistemic, or ethical, as Barth insists,
the basis of personhood must be located in the one who alone embodies
the covenantal imago and instantiates self along its two image-bearing
axes.

For Barth, Christ is indispensable to our understanding of human
persons. Berkouwer (1962) explains,

> It is clear that Barth's basing anthropology on Christology de-
> rives from the idea that we cannot understand "man" apart from

24. Bakhtin (1993) illustrates the proper ethicospiritual balance between self
and others in his description of the "architectonic" self (see Emerson, 2006). In later
chapters the ethical implications of the covenantal self will be applied to pastoral and
psychotherapeutic caregiving.

> his relation to God. In our opinion, this position is unassailable;
> man cannot be known with a true and reliable knowledge if he is
> abstracted from this relation to God. Man would then be, from a
> Scriptural viewpoint, nothing but an abstraction. (p. 93)

Furthermore, we know who we are as human beings as we come, with others, into right relationship to Christ. This is the case, in part, because Christ relates himself to God and to others, uniquely yet archetypally, within a perfect covenantal balance of particularity and relationality (cf. Ricoeur's "selfhood" and "sameness"), of freedom and responsiveness. As "the only son of God and man" (ὁ υἱός ὁ μονογενής τοῦ θεοῦ καὶ τοῦ ἀνθρώπου, *ho huios ho monogenēs tou theou kai tou anthrōpou*; see John 3:14–18), Christ alone discloses to us both God and ourselves.

Alternatively, self can also be understood, as Pannenberg (1985) suggests, as the reflexive center of a dialectical "exocentric" personhood. Self, for Pannenberg, is caught up in "a conflict between basic factors in the structure of human existence," namely, our "centralized organization" as discrete, embodied selves and our other-instantiated "exocentricity" (p. 84). The nature of selfhood, for Pannenberg, entails "being present to what is other than the self" (p. 85). Evidently, what he has in mind is the dynamic interplay by which selfhood is constituted in relationship to other (see McFadyen, 1990; see also Shults, 2003, pp. 132–33). Human beings come to selfhood through "the twofold reference of human self-consciousness that corresponds to the tension between centrality and exocentricity" (Pannenberg, 1985, p. 104).

Knowledge of self, then, arises within this dialectically individuated relationality—a knowing oneself in relation to other. Knowledge of self-in-relation simultaneously establishes and threatens self's equanimity—its centrality. We come to know self in relation to others who, distinct from self, function as discrete centers of gravity against which self must maintain itself. In language at times redolent of Freud, Pannenberg suggests that, in order to maintain its own equilibrium while simultaneously avoiding domination of other, self must embrace the "contradiction" of its own dialectical constitution (p. 86).

Pannenberg, like Barth, conceives of exocentric personhood in trinitarian terms. Yet, he also holds God's self-revelation in the person and work of the incarnate Christ to be the supreme historical marker of exocentric personeity (Pannenberg, 1994). Moreover, he finds that believers may proleptically appropriate this distinctly eschatological dynamic only in and through our Spirit-mediated participation with Christ.

Humanity's exocentric "final destiny" has been "manifested already in Jesus Christ and in which believers share already through the power of the Spirit, who is already effecting the eschatological reality of the new man in them" (p. 220).

Turner (2008), in summarizing Pannenberg's diachronic perspective, concludes, "[H]is eschatological grounding of the image means that personhood is conceived as perpetually in a process of becoming" (p. 132). We are granted personhood, and therefore selfhood, having been created as persons in the image of God; yet, selfhood, as an expression of personhood, bears an eschatological aspect. We are created as persons in order to become persons as our awareness of self deepens over time in relationship to God and others.

Bonhoeffer's contribution to a Christian understanding of self stands above Barth's and Pannenberg's in its dependence on an expressly christological anthropology. Indeed, Bonhoeffer's understanding of the person of Christ has been called the "conceptual center" of his entire theological program (DeJonge, 2012, p. 85). For Bonhoeffer, who preserves and recapitulates many of Luther's theological priorities, "Christology is not just one element of theology, but that which provides the content and distinctiveness of all theology" (Barker, 2015, p. 19). His Christology may be further distinguished from its Barthian counterpart, moreover, by reason of its Lutheran emphasis on the humiliation of Christ and his identification with sinful human beings (Bradbury, 2011). Godsey (1987), in reflecting on the differences between the two, concludes,

> Barth tended to emphasize the divinity of Jesus; Jesus Christ is the 'Royal Man' whose power is the decisive thing. . . . Bonhoeffer, on the other hand, stresses the hiddenness of divinity in the humiliated One; for him Jesus Christ is the man for others, the one whose power is shown forth in weakness. (p. 26)

Bonhoeffer holds that the glorified Christ must never be abstracted theologically or hermeneutically from the crucified Christ. In this way, he reiterates Luther's *theologia crucis* for a modern age (Barker, 2015). The crucified Christ, Bonhoeffer maintains, demonstrates God's gracious inclination toward sinful humanity: "[W]e can have the Exalted One only as the Crucified One. The resurrection of Christ does not get us around the stumbling block. Even the Risen One remains a stumbling block for us. If it were not so, he would not be for us" (Bonhoeffer, 2009, p. 359). Through his humility, suffering, and ignominious death, Christ demonstrates his solidarity with fallen humanity. His human weakness, not his divine splendor, reveals us for who we are.

Like Barth and Pannenberg, Bonhoeffer defines self as a species of relationality, its existence effected by what he terms "social basic-relations" (Bonhoeffer, 1998, pp. 34). Yet, not all selves are alike. Following Luther, the self of those who stand "in Adam" is *curvum in se*, curved in on itself. This fallen, "incurved self" is "cut off from self-understanding" and "opaque to itself" (Gregor, 2013, p. 63). Selfhood, for those who remain estranged from God, is locked in a kind of pathological reflexivity:

> [O]n its own, the I [self] cannot move beyond itself. It is imprisoned in itself, it sees only itself, even when it sees another, even when it wants to see God. It understands itself out of itself, which really means, however, that it basically does not understand itself. Indeed it does not understand itself until this I has been encountered and overwhelmed in its existence by an other. The I believes itself free and is captive; it has all power and has only itself as a vassal. (Bonhoeffer, 1996, pp. 45–46)

Whereas, the human self that comes to Christ for redemption is set free from this captivity and made whole in Christ.

Bonhoeffer distinguishes between two lines of humanity—two types of persons made in God's image. The crucial distinction between these two is their standing respective to Christ. The human self,[25] he insists, is either "in Adam" or "in Christ" (Bonhoeffer, 1996). Apart from Christ, "true selfhood and self-knowledge" are not possible; whereas, in Christ "the self's gaze [is] redirected" outward toward a "radical otherness" (Zimmermann, 2004, p. 300). The means by which those who stand outside of Christ come to be in Christ is grace.

Christ's person and work and the believing self's faith in Christ serve, respectively, as the fulcrum and lever by which God brings the incurved, fallen self into union with Christ thereby bringing self into proper standing before God. In coming to Christ, moreover, the believing self enters into Christ's own communion with God, or what Bonhoeffer referred to as the corporate, ecclesial "humanity of the new Adam" (Bonhoeffer, 1998, p. 142). From the vantage point of Christ's own relatedness to God and others, we may come to know self as we self-perceive from Christ's own self-perception. By grace, we become what he is.

---

25. Bonhoeffer's "Dasein" (see Green, 1999).

For the most part, Christian theological anthropology has maintained a distinction between the self and its self-consciousness—who-I-am and who-I-believe-myself-to-be (see McFadyen, 1990; Pannenberg, 1985; White, 1996). This distinction, now largely effaced by postmodernism, has historically facilitated a necessary hermeneutical inference: we are not always who and what we believe ourselves to be.[26] By way of illustration of the necessity for such distinctions, I note the basic theological proposition: God is who he is. Whereas, what we know of God is both truncated and subject to error, our limited consciousness of him being a reflection of our finiteness and fallenness. Following from this, then, we do well to infer that what we know of self should also be distinguished from self *in se*.[27]

The human self, for Bonhoeffer, is characterized by unity. On the other hand, human perception of the phenomenal self's disunity and fragmentation should weigh heavily in any Christian psychology, primarily as signs of human fallenness, brokenness, and finitude.[28] Neverthe-

26. Knowledge of the Jamesian me-self—the phenomenal self or the me-I-can-see—depends on an individual's ability to self-perceive. Observations concerning the phenomenal self may be mundane—I am tall, sitting, thinking—or weighty—I am good, ashamed, hopeful. It should be obvious, however, that my *self* is distinct from my self-*consciousness*. So, for example, "I am sitting," reflects one reality, while, "I am conscious that I am sitting," points to another. The two statements are not equivalent. Though one logically follows from the other, there are occasions where faults and/or limits in awareness may lead us astray. This is especially true when it comes to unseen psychological realities. My self-consciousness, self-theory, or self-schema—the metacognitive form(s) that represent me to myself—is *not* equivalent to my *self*. James (2012) reifies this distinction; yet it appears to have dropped out of many postmodern psychologies (see Cushman, 1995; Harter, 2015).

27. Similar to James's I-self, this self *in se* McFadyen (1990) terms the "transcendental" or "deep" self. "Deep 'self,'" he writes, "is . . . to be conceived of as a unity of or behind the unities represented by a plurality of local 'selves.' Personal identity in a particular relation is not a complete and exhaustive self-presence. Self-identity varies across a range of communication contexts ('I' as 'shifter') whilst maintaining itself in continuity at a level transcending any communication or relation in particular. Selfhood indicates personal organisation, a structured personal identity" (p. 103). McFadyen's "deep self" carries a lot of Kantian freight, however. In the final analysis, it may not be helpful to make such distinctions. Better to simply say, there are aspects of self that are opaque to human perception. McFadyen's principal argument—that human persons bear a selfhood that is unitary, singular—is crucial.

28. Turner (2011) argues that theological anthropology could permit accounts of a fragmentary self without resorting to the language of either sin or psychopathology. Regrettably, Turner's argument suffers from a dearth of biblical and theological support. Perhaps, a developmentally sensitive Christian psychology could permit the

less, with respect to distinguishing between self and self-consciousness, Bonhoeffer (1996) is unequivocal:

> [A] psychological concept is unable by nature to convey this unity; . . . human beings in their psychology elude self-comprehension. People do not know their motives; they do not know fully their sin; they are unable to understand themselves on the basis of their own psychic experiences, for they are amenable to any arbitrary interpretation. (p. 102)

Our phenomenological or psychological apperceptions of self should not be confused with what really is, "if," that is, "human beings are to be seen in light of the unity of God" (p. 102).

Psychological insight arising from observation will tell one story about who we are: fragmented, disorganized, multiple, subject from one moment to the nextto innumerable inputs and impulses. What we learn from Christ and come to be in him, however tells a far different story— one we do well to learn by heart:

> [U]nity must be sought where human beings have been created, or are created anew, and where this creation both happens to them and is something in which they participate. That oneness must be sought, furthermore, where human beings must know themselves, without interpretation, in clarity and reality. This means they must know that their unity and that of their existence is founded alone in God's Word [that is, the revelation of Christ]. (Bonhoeffer, 1996, p. 102)

Whatever experience and observation may tell us, we must search out the deeper truth to which the person and work of Christ testify.

What we can know of ourselves will resemble, due to our limitations and sinfulness, what we can know of the God in whose image we have been made. In other words, we should expect to find faults in our personal knowledge of God and of self. The fallen self *in se* enters the world estranged from God and, as a result, pathologically limited in its capacity to become whole and unified. Self–other attachments do foster the development of the maturing phenomenal self, yet can never displace the psychotherapeutic primacy of human–divine intersubjectivity uniquely obtained by means of reconciliation of the human person to

---

innovation he suggests, if his "ethical and ontological commitments to the singularity, continuity, and particularity of personhood" could be better clarified and defended (p. 134).

God-in-Christ. Only in Christ can the human self "achieve" wholeness. Even for believers, personal knowledge of self will often be fragmented and erroneous because we are finite and prone to sinful dissociation and self-deception.

Personhood, self, and self-consciousness

Personhood is an onto-relational status conferred upon individual human beings by God that is most properly understood as an ethicospiritual articulation of the imago dei (Barth, 2010; Berkouwer, 1962; McFadyen, 1990; Pannenberg, 1985). As such, personhood cannot be reduced to either a constitutive (metaphysical) or covenantal (relational) basis, though clearly ontology logically (and developmentally) comes first. Put plainly, we are persons whether or not we choose to be. Nevertheless, we are constituted by God as persons made in his image in order to fulfill our covenantal destiny of becoming genuine, God-imaging persons. Ontology may precede; but teleology supersedes (Bonhoeffer, 1996). Personhood is a calling.

To speak of self, on the other hand, is to posit the personal status and experience of *particular*—i.e., individual, personal—personhood (Evans, 2002; Kierkegaard, 1980; McFadyen, 1990; Vitz & Felch, 2006; see also Harré, 1998). In other words, all who bear the image of God are persons in at least a minimal sense. On the other hand, *I* alone embody, experience, and express personhood as my*self*, all other persons being subjectively defined in relation to me as *other(s)*. *I* alone actualize my selfhood.[29] Only *I* am *me*. This amounts to more than a rhetorical distinction due to the fact that, as a person covenantally constituted in the image of God, I bear an ontic and ethical reality. My "self" exists and acts because *I* exist and act.

Following from this ontoethical reality, human persons bear an intersubjective status—*I* am a *Thou* respective to *other(s)*—whether God, other humans, or objects in the world (Barth, 2010; Bonhoeffer, 1998; Ricoeur, 1995). As a matter of course, it is difficult to see how *self* makes any epistemic or ethical sense apart from *other*. Within a covenantal framework, epistemic and ethical considerations relate covenantally. To wit, the calling of selfhood is that I should image God in agapic relation to others made in his image. In relation to Christ, then, I come to know self

29. And thus, personhood as well (see McFadyen, 1990).

veridically as I act. This intersubjective perspective on self has alternately been articulated by Christian theologians as the "covenantal self" (see Horton, 2006, p. 201), the self as "relational substance" (Lowery, 2006, p. 278), and the "communing self" (Stratton, 2006, p. 247).

Selfhood, as an enactment and expression of covenantal person-hood, should be understood covenantally, which is to say, christologically (Horton, 2005). Therefore, the self should not be understood to be an exclusively subjective—whether phenomenological, psychological, or semantic—reality.[30] As such, self *in se* is not equivalent to "soul" (contra Moreland & Rae, 2000; cf. Cooper, 2000).[31] This thinking relies on an overly constitutive framework. Human beings *have* a soul; but they are much more than souls. Selfhood for human beings is constituted as an existential subset of human personhood in the relation of two irreduc-ible, dialogically related poles: the objectively (divinely) conferred "Thou art" actualized archetypally at creation and reiterated antitypally in hu-man procreation and relationality; and the subjectively appropriated "I am" that develops over time as an ethicospiritual expression of personal agency—a self-conscious being-in-relation to God and others in the world.

Crucially, I maintain, selfhood in the covenantal sense is not fully "achieved" apart from the individual's Spirit-mediated incorporation into Christ. Along these lines, Evans (2002), following Kierkegaard closely, employs the descriptor "minimal" to describe the basic selfhood possessed by every human being (p. 77). He proceeds to point out the telic aspects of selfhood, implicating its developmental and ethical considerations:

> [T]here is a tremendous difference between what we could call
> the minimal self, who is a "bit of a subject," and the respon-
> sible self who has a formed character. Nevertheless, even this

30. As predicted by Bonhoeffer, postmodern perspectives on the self, such as Har-ter's (2015), founder due to overreliance on phenomenology.

31. Although Horton (2005) helpfully outlines numerous distinctives of a cov-enantal Christology, he nevertheless concludes somewhat haphazardly, "The soul/spirit/intellect is the true self" (p. 91). Cooper (2000) employs the standard dualist vocabulary, yet with considerable nuance. To be clear, referring to the pastoral care of individuals as "soul care" should not, in the final analysis, be regarded as problematic. Clearly, the biblical writers' metonymic usage of "soul" (along with "heart," "mind," and other sundry terms) for the inner life and constitution of humans licenses such language. The concern in the present context is to more precisely identify the self as an onto-relational entity—a concern that the uncritical use of constitutive language, unavoidably, depreciates.

> minimal self must in some sense *be*; if it were nothing at all then
> there would be nothing to become—or fail to become. (p. 77)

An illustration is, perhaps, in order.

Self is like a seed planted by God in need of nourishment. By means of life-sustaining inputs and interactions within its environment, self grows and develops. In order to grow beyond its intrinsic limitations, self must be grafted onto the vine that is Christ (see John 15:16; cf. Rom 11:16). Only in so doing, will self bear "fruit that will last." Alternatively, self is the procreative union of God's creative design and projective purpose to raise up a son in his own image. On account of the fall and due to its estrangement from God brought on by sin, self must first be "born again"—"adopted" by the will of God into union with Christ (see John 3:3; 1 John 3:1; Rom 8:15; Gal 4:5).

The interactions most obviously and directly bearing implications for the development of the human self and its self-consciousness entail the nurturing environment of the child situated in the context of a loving family. Eventually, however, familial nurture and care must give way to the supremely consequential relationship of the believing self to God-in-Christ. Though we are conceived—both literally and metaphorically—as image-bearing selves capable of self-consciousness, our self-consciousness is truncated and skewed by pathological reflexivity. We become whole, mature selves once, having been granted the ability to self-perceive through eyes conditioned by divine revelation, we enter into covenantal relation to God and others. Moreover, the character of this covenantal relation is indispensably agapic.

By recapitulating the distinctives of Christ's person and nature, a christological distinction between self and soul becomes clear. In Jesus we encounter a divine person who *is* a self—a subject, an "I." To reiterate, the "person" (*hypostasis*) of the Word is eternally constituted as the divine Son in the context of his agapic commitment to be the image of the Father. Yet, as of the incarnation, he is simultaneously a human being who *has* a human mind/soul. If soul is equivalent to self, then the Word took on not only a human nature but a human self in Mary's womb. Clearly, to equate the self with the soul would imply the presence of a duality of selves in Christ—two centers of subjectivity, one divine and one human. This would result in a Nestorian Christ which, as such, is untenable under Chalcedonian orthodoxy.

Given Chalcedonian orthodoxy, self is not a formal constituent or capacity rooted in human nature, classically conceived, but of person-hood, the latter being established by God in human beings with his conferral upon them of the imago. According to covenantal Christol-ogy, human selfhood is evidently not contingent on the possession of any *particular* physical or metaphysical substance—i.e., soul—but on the onto-relational status of being made in the image of God for agapic communion with him. That being said, without the constituent parts of our shared human nature, we could hardly instantiate selfhood.[32] It is through and within the limitations of my body-soul composite that I act.

As human persons, we assume our proper telic trajectory as cov-enantal image bearers only through our entry into agapic communion by means of our reconciliation to God in Christ. Viewed from this angle, "the self-sufficient, self-constructing, therapeutic self authored by modern psychology" (Grenz, 2001, p. 86) can be seen for what it is: an idolatrous and ultimately doomed effort to frame human being and becoming as an exclusively human achievement. On the other hand, the divided, multiple "self" of postmodernism unconsciously implicates human fallenness in a way that self-as-soul understandings do not (cf. Rom 7:14–25).[33] Any suggestion of equivalency between self and soul is reductionistic at best.

On the other hand, we must understand the implications of the post-modern notion that one's subjective sense of self—i.e., self-consciousness, self-theory, or self-schema—is equivalent to the self *in se*.[34] Christology, again, offers helpful insight. Although the divine Son entered the world with a fully constituted *divine* self *in se*, Christ's *human* sense of him-self—his human self-consciousness—took shape over the course of his early life (see O'Collins, 2009; Rahner, 1966). Christ's self-consciousness

32. As stated in Chapter 3, human selfhood is inconceivable apart from metaphysi-cal considerations. How else could human beings "image" the invisible God, whether ontologically or ethically, without the formal constituents of a body-soul composite?

33. In other words, a phenomenally or experientially divided, discontinuous "self" does not imply any commensurate division in one's soul. That being said, our human self-consciousness, not self per se, can come to be divided and discontinuous, as I will demonstrate in later chapters.

34. Phenomenological presuppositions presently dominate most contemporary, including many Christian, understandings of the self. Harter (2015) summarizes the near-universal position of post/modern psychology that "the self [is] a cognitive con-struction" (p. 9). This is consistent with a Kantian epistemology which sequesters the "noumenal" self—i.e., actual self—beyond the bounds of human perception. James sought to maintain the knowability of his I-self. For postmodernists like Harter, the phenomenal self—James's me-self—*is* the self.

qua human functioned within the confines and limitations of his human body–soul composite. Clearly, the divine mind/soul of the eternal Son was never so constrained. Yet, as orthodox Christology has maintained since Chalcedon, Christ's humanity could never be subsumed by his divinity and remain humanity, as such. Within the constraints of his body/brain, Jesus' human mind/soul, including his developmentally appropriate capacity for self-awareness, functioned and grew as all human beings do.

Jesus' human psychology was thoroughly normal—even normative—in every way, sin excepted (Heb 2:17; cf. 4:15). Therefore, while Jesus' subjective center—his experientially transcendent self or "I"—persists as an expression of his divine Personhood rather than his human nature, his human experience of himself and his human self-consciousness do not.[35] Jesus' self *in se*, as an aspect of his divine Personhood, must remain immune to charges of mutability; yet aspects of his phenomenal, empirical self and his human self-consciousness nevertheless developed and grew over time beginning, presumably, in utero.

This is the case for all other human *beings*,[36] like Jesus, despite their being, unlike Jesus, merely human *persons*.[37] Barring any neurological damage or psychological deficit, human beings, like Jesus, universally

35. An additional problem with the contemporary psychological emphasis on the phenomenal self and postmodern adumbrations of self-as-self-consciousness can be discerned in the phenomena of self-deception. If self is identical with one's self-schema—a psychological construct intersubjectively arising from human self-consciousness—then self-deception becomes a logical contradiction. If I *am* who I believe myself to be then self is equivalent to self-consciousness. On the other hand, if what I believe or know about myself does not correspond to reality, then self *cannot* be equivalent to self-theory, self-schema, or self-concept. In fact, the discrepancy between one's phenomenal self and one's self-theory can sometimes be quite extreme. And this is the point: I am not always correct when I conceive of who I am. Especially when it comes to unpleasant realities about my veridical self, I need others' help to draw attention to the ways in which I have dissociated these aspects of myself from awareness and, with selective data, made avowals considering myself that are, unbeknownst to me, false (cf. Neisser, 1997, pp. 30–31).

36. The one exception to this seems to be humanity's first representatives. It is interesting to reflect on the implications of God's having introduced Adam and Eve into the world as mature agents, rather than as infants. They appear, at least in the creation narrative, to possess adult agency without having passed through earlier developmental stages.

37. This is clearly a fine distinction, but one that is necessary in order to maintain a conceptual link to Chalcedoninan orthodoxy. "Person" in contemporary parlance has lost its semantic connection to classical Christology.

experience the diachronic development of individual identity, agency, and, self-consciousness:

> Through our experience of other persons and the whole world, our self-consciousness and hence our self-identification develop and take a firm shape. Our experience of the world beyond the borders of our bodily self also mediates our conscious sense of our own self and its unity. Thus, we know our personal identities not only in ourselves but also in our relationships. It is especially through our experience of the world that our sense of ourselves grows and changes. (O'Collins, 2009, p. 244)

This is not to suggest that the human self *in se* does not, in fact, change in the course of time. Minimally, fallen human beings experience an onto-relational transformation at regeneration in their renewal by God's Spirit according to the covenantal imago (Bonhoeffer, 1998; see John 3:8; Rom 8:9).[38]

Palingenesis—our being-made-new in Christ—implicates every aspect of our being. Renewal amounts to much more than a mere modification of any formal constituent—i.e., soul—and it implicates much more than a shift in inter/subjective self-perception; it is rooted in the palingenetic work of God. The believing self is, in a comprehensive, eschatological sense, a "new creation" (2 Cor 5:17) having been objectively justified, subjectively sanctified, and intersubjectively reconciled to God-in-Christ. Yet, our experience of self-made-new develops and grows as an extension of this deep, divinely instituted reality. In relation to Christ and others, self is being progressively conformed to the image of the One who has once for all time reconciled self *in se* to God (see 2 Cor 4:16; Eph 3:16; Col 3:10).[39]

Three axioms of the covenantal self

By way of summary of the preceding discussion and introduction to the next chapter, three apothegmatic priorities may now be adduced regarding the nature of the self, the objective subject of Christian self-knowledge.

---

38. Additionally, the existence and immortality of the human self is contingent, whereas Christ's is not.

39. Paul stresses the reality of this regenerated mode of being with his language of the "old" and "new self [ἄνθρωπος, *anthrōpos*]" (Rom 6:6; Eph 4:22, 24; Col 3:9–10).

The onto-relational dialectic of self's being and becoming

The self or knowing subject, as an expression of the imago dei, is reducible neither to a constitutive or covenantal basis. Rather, it is a synthesis of these two bases most meaningfully articulated within a christological framework. While selfhood, as such, is not a possession but a status, it nevertheless bears a distinctly substantial character despite its being independent of metaphysical considerations.[40] As Evans (2002) concludes, "The self is an ethical task, not a fixed entity, but that task is itself part of the self's ontological givenness" (p. 81). Individual human beings bear their particular status as selves inherently due to their divinely endowed image-bearing capacity and calling. Yet, in its most comprehensive sense, selfhood can be "achieved" only through our active participation in covenantal communion with the triune God and with other human beings through union with Jesus Christ. Selfhood is both gift and invitation, at once conferral and calling, its ultimate contingency being located in the divine will to create and redeem human persons bearing his own covenantal character.

Since the fall, individual human beings instantiate selfhood in a truncated sense, having become fatally *curvum in se* due to the presence and influence of sin. Though all humans now possess a status and dignity as image bearers in a formal, constitutive sense, we are born estranged from God and cut off from the possibility of becoming fully human according to the covenantal telos of the imago. As such, the fallen human self is curved in upon itself, incomplete, and in need of repair. Due to its primal estrangement from God, the human self can become truly whole neither autonomously nor in the context of a merely horizontal relationality.

In spite of our limited capacity to image God, a covenantal disposition is nevertheless "hard-wired" into human nature motivating us to form attachments, whether "healthy" or pathological, in service to the development of the self-in-relation. Secondary instances of estrangement—i.e., relational trauma—may result in the malformation of self and further fragmentation of our human self-consciousness by obfuscating the nature and form of self. Only with the advent of the new birth do

40. I.e., the human self is existentially situated within creation as a psychosomatic unity; yet, according to historic Christian teaching on the afterlife, God preserves the existence of the self, by some mysterious means, following the death of the body (Cooper, 2000).

human beings assume their proper orientation as covenantal image bearers and obtain the promise of God's eschatological intention to utterly reverse and repair over time the damage done to self and its fragmentary self-awareness.

The perichoretic means of covenantal self-knowing

The covenantal self of the believer comes to accurately self-perceiveprimarily through perichoretic union with Christ and secondarily through the instrumental influence of others. The perichoretic—penetrative, indwelling—presence of the Holy Spirit is programmatic to this process. The Spirit reveals what cannot otherwise be seen and known, whether they be the deep things of God or of self. Self-knowledge, then, arises in relational contexts, never strictly reflexively. Like a dog chasing its tail, the autonomous self can never reach the object of its own self-reflection. On the other hand, in the context of agapic relationality, dialogical self-reflection may yield a perspective that the self is incapable of coming to autonomously.

The estranged self, cut off as it is from the life and knowledge of the one true God, is pathologically self-blind and self-deceived: "When it reflects upon itself, the human spirit stares into an abyss of potentiality without meaning" (Loder, 1998, p. 340). The fallen human self can never come to itself by direct approach as it is "ever seeing but never perceiving" (Luke 8:10). Only the intimate, perichoretic presence of Christ can provide the needed perspective. As Zimmermann (2004) rightly avers, "[W]e gain self-knowledge by losing all pretensions to self-understanding. Self-knowledge is not possessed but given as a gift" (p. 303). No "gain" of merely unipolar self-reflection can ever be trusted. But by gazing into Christ's many mirrors around us, given the mysterious but certain working of the Spirit, self can be perceived and known as it truly is.

The agapic ethic of covenantal self-knowledge

Third and finally, the ethical telos of covenantal self-knowledge is love. Christlike love, in contrast to other "loves" falsely so-called, entails a simultaneously self-denying yet self-regarding agapic concern for the good of others. Jesus himself epitomizes this love in both his person and work. Though Christ is a divine person, he became a human being and now perfectly fulfills humanity's covenantal commission to image God. As a human being, he came to know himself at every stage of his human development by means of his developmentally appropriate relatedness to God his Father. In addition, we may presume that Christ, in his identification with the humanity he came to save, came to know himself as all human beings do: in relation to others and to the world around him.

In coming to know himself, Christ simultaneously came to apprehend the proper sequence of his cruciform destiny: he would first be abased and abandoned at the cross, left to suffer and die on behalf of sinful humanity. He would entrust himself to his Father. He would be raised. He would be glorified. All this he would know and believe by faith. Christ's commitment to the cross fulfilled the telos of his having come to know his unique identity as the Word-made-flesh. Only as flesh could he die. Only as a human being could he come to a human knowledge of his destiny to die on behalf of his fellow humanity.

Jesus' human self-knowledge was never an end in itself, but rather the means by which he came to know and love both God and other. His covenantal knowledge of self, moreover, now redounds corporately within every member of his Christiform people. So, Bonhoeffer (2001) writes,

> We [Believers] are to be like Christ because we have already been shaped into the image of Christ. Only because we bear Christ's image already can Christ be the "example" whom we follow. Only because he himself already lives his true life in us can we "walk just as he walked" (1 John 2:6), "act as he acted" (John 13:15), "love as he loved" (Eph. 5:2; John 13:34; 15:12), "forgive as he forgave" (Col. 3:13), "have the same mind that was in Jesus Christ" (Phil. 2:5), follow the example he left for us (1 Peter 2:21), and lose our lives for the sake of our brothers and sisters, just as he lost his life for our sake (1 John 3:16). (p. 287)

Christ's human growth in self-knowledge parallels and paradigmatizes the covenantal dynamic whereby believers come to knowledge of self in relation to God and others. The eternal life Christ offers to the world grants fallen human beings what we lost at the fall—loving fellowship with God and others. Within this renewed covenantal dynamic, the human self *in se* is restored and (re)formed in union with Christ. We experience this eternal life, in part, as a perichoretic knowing and being known by God and, in the context of Spirit-enabled ecclesial life, by fellow believers.

Eternal life, for believers, is more than a state of mind—a status or mode of self-consciousness; it is fundamentally a rebirth or regeneration at an onto-relational level. Nevertheless, a vital transformation of believers' knowable selves takes place as believers appropriate, over time and at successively deeper levels, the psychological benefits of their union with Christ. The mental life of believers, which includes our thoughts and our self-consciousness, comes into conformity with that of Christ (Rom 12:2; E. L. Johnson, 2017). Increasingly, our self- and other-understandings come to image the very "mind of Christ" (1 Cor 2:16; cf. Phil 2:5). Furthermore, like Jesus, this self-consciousness-transforming interaction with God, others, and creation is mediated to us through the inescapable reality of our embodied existence to the end that we love God and love other mutually and perichoretically.

6

Toward a Christian psychology
of the covenantal self-in-relation

EPISTEMIC SYSTEMS, AS A general category, should not be denigrated as mere inventions of the modern mind. If anything, the impulse to organize knowledge into discrete domains—whether theological, anthropological, or otherwise—should more properly be viewed as the fruit of two cosmic realities: the orderly nature of the divine mind that has been imprinted by means of the imago upon human nature; and the corroboration of the divine mind discoverable by human beings within his self-revelation. In other words, by the grace of God we have been granted epistemic access to the mind of God—his perception and determinations regarding, primarily, himself, human beings, and the created order (Barth, 2010; Kuyper, 1968; Van Til, 1969). What we discover, though presently subject to the limitations of our noetic fallenness and finiteness, Reformational/ Augustinian epistemology has ever held to be sufficiently comprehensive for the formulation of human systems of knowledge regarding, mini-mally, that which is necessary for human redemption and for the living out of our faith in the present age (see 2 Tim 3:16).

Though asystematic in its presentation, God's written revelation speaks authoritatively to the nature and meaning of those realities most apposite to its fundamental telic orientation: directing human beings to the reconciliation God offers through Jesus Christ. In the Scriptures and through the person and work of Christ, believers come to know him and, mutatis mutandis, themselves as well. What we come to know, when con-ditioned by love, we know rightly. As demonstrated throughout Chris-tian history, divine revelation is not resistant to systematization; on the contrary, the knowledge of God revealed in his Logos is wholly compatible with our God-given impulse to organize and systematize. If it were not so, then all the efforts of everyone from Irenaeus to Augustine and Calvin to Barth have been hopelessly misguided and ill-fated.

The Bible and the knowable self

The task of Christian *theology* has ever been to "rightly divide"—i.e., systematize—what God's Logos discloses *about God* (cf. 2 Tim 2:15): who he is, what he is like, his aims and motives, his will and his ways. By contrast, what Christian *psychology* attempts is the epistemically contingent task of systematizing God's disclosures—discoverable in the Scriptures and the person and work of Christ—regarding human beings.[1] Christian psychology, then, takes seriously Calvin's supposition that the knowledge of God and self are reciprocal and mutually entailing. If neither task, according to Calvin, is possible for human beings without the other, though these two epistemic objects are of infinitely disparate grandeur and worth, then neither can they be exclusive of each other. Indeed, to sequester, marginalize, or disparage inquiry into the nature and worth of the human self is tantamount to its theological inverse since, as Augustine, Calvin, Bonhoeffer, *et alia*, have advised, self-blindness invariably blinds the self to God.

Moreover, these two domains of knowledge—of God and self—are implicated above all others in God's cardinal telos for his self-revelation: the reconciliation of God with his particular and corporate people, the fulfillment of which agenda will redound in his praise and glory for all eternity (see Phil 2:5–11; Rev 5:9–14). What Christian theology attempts must not, therefore, be dissociated from Christian psychology—and vice versa—lest the epistemic aims of both be fatally undermined. In the final analysis, we have ample warrant for reconciling Christian theology and Christian psychology from the epistemological implications of Christology, to say nothing of the doctrine of reconciliation at the very heart of the Scriptures. As with Christian theology, attempts to systematize biblical teaching on the self and self-knowledge should be regarded as

---

1. There is more to Christian theology and psychology than this, to be sure. There is much to be discovered concerning God and self in the natural world. But the Logos of God is the proper starting point and hermeneutical anchor, so to speak, for all subsequent *Christian* truth claims regarding God and self.

successful to the degree with which the product of such efforts comports and coheres with these doctrines of revelation and reconciliation.

Respective to human beings generally and particular human beings as well, the Bible has much to say. What the Bible reveals about us offers a kernel from which may grow a Christian system regarding self and its self-knowledge. Moreover, the self-knowledge to which biblical writers at times aspire suggests strong divine approval in such a quest. Nevertheless, an initial survey of certain relevant texts reveals a curious contradiction. On the one hand, Jeremiah suggests that "the heart"—that psychospiritual organ at the center of biblical anthropology—"is devious" and "perverse," and, as such, it cannot be known (Jer 17:9 NRSV; cf. 10:14; 14:18). Perhaps self-knowledge really is beyond our grasp. On the other hand, Jesus implies that some degree of self-knowledge is possible and necessary if we are to avoid the snare of hypocrisy. We must "take the log out of your own eye," he counsels, "and then you will see clearly to take the speck out of your brother's eye" (Matt 7:5).

What these two passages minimally demonstrate is the provisional nature of any human claim to self-knowledge. Jeremiah's likely intent is to call into question the self-perception of all whose hearts have turned away from God (cf. Jer 17:5). Whereas, Jesus also implies believers can become self-deceived (see Badgett, 2018b). Paul implicates all humanity in having sinned and fallen from God (Rom 3:10–18); none of us should presume to have overcome every inclination toward self-obfuscation. If I conclude, based on Jeremiah's own peroration, that my own heart is "devious and perverse," the prophet could hardly accuse me of self-deception. In the final analysis, whether self knows self veridically depends on the degree to which my self-knowledge accords with God's own knowledge of me (cf. Jer 3:15).

Determining God's knowledge of anything, let alone self, is clearly problematic. But this ought not utterly confound us since a similar epistemic quandary stands at the heart of all claims at theological knowledge (see Frame, 1987; Marshall, 1999). On the one hand, the Bible firmly situates the divine mind and nature beyond the reach of human reason and comprehension. God's ways and his thoughts are not like ours (Isa 55:8). The greatness of his splendor is indeed beyond our ability to fathom (Ps 145:3), moving the Apostle to confess, "Oh, the depth of the riches and wisdom and knowledge of God! How unsearchable are his judgments and how inscrutable his ways!" (Rom 11:33).[2] Yet, paradoxically, the

---

2. Cf. Job 42:1–6; Pss 139:6, 17–18; 147:5; Isa 57:15; 1 Cor 2:10–11; 1 Tim 6:13–16.

Bible also affirms the knowability of God *in part*.[3] Knowing God, Jesus affirms, is tantamount to "eternal life" (John 17:3).

Tellingly, God's eschatological agenda includes supplying human beings with "the knowledge of the LORD as the waters cover the sea" (Isa 11:9; cf. Hab 2:14). Some knowledge of God, however feeble and faint, is indispensable for salvation (see Luke 1:77; 2 Cor 2:14). Presently, we may, with Moses, see only the train of his glory (Exod 33:23). With Job we perceive only the "outskirts" of his ways (Job 26:14). With Paul we peer through the glass dimly (1 Cor 13:12). But, if the Scriptures are true, then human beings can reasonably claim some mediate knowledge of God through the working of his Spirit so long as it accords with the self-revelation of his Logos. Following from this inference, the same must also be true of the knowledge of self.

The knowable self in Scripture

The self may be defined as an individual's personal onto-relational identity or that which, in persons human and divine, is representative of idiosyncratic personhood.[4] Definitions of the human self, having been conditioned by modernist thinking, tend to emphasize only inner aspects of personal identity—the psychological self. Augustine is often credited as being the "creator" (Turner, 2008, p. 1) or "inventor" of this inner "self" (Cary, 2003; cf. Grenz, 2001; LaCugna, 1991; C. Taylor, 1989) Writing from a Christian perspective, Grenz (2001) recapitulates this historical trope with minimal nuance:

> The self as we know it today is characterized by interiority—that is, the distinction between 'inside' and 'outside'—together with a sense of personal identity as a unified being. Viewed from this perspective, the self is a modern invention. Yet the stage was set for the emergence of the self much earlier. More particularly, the genesis of the concept lies in the turn inward that began in earnest with Augustine and was augmented by Boethius. (p. 60)

So, the modern self, as a conceptual reality at least, has its "genesis" in the inwardness of Augustine. At least, this is the how the story goes.

---

3. See 2 Cor 2:14; Eph 1:17; 4:13; Phil 1:9; Col 1:9–10; 2:2–3; 3:10; 2 Pet 1:2–3, 8; 2:20; 3:18; 1 John 2:20.

4. Taylor (1989) all too often evinces an inclination to view the self as a mere conceptual or semantic reality to which language and cognition may point, but having no ontological basis.

So often has the story been told, in fact, that it begs questioning.[5] If an Augustinian genesis account is accurate, it becomes possible, if not necessary, to regard "self" and "self-consciousness" as mere intellectual or rhetorical constructs. A Christian orthodoxy concerned to maintain fidelity to Scripture could easily dismiss them as unnecessary accretions, modernist distractions invented by secular minds. "Modern self" becomes inescapably redundant. Christian orthopraxy respective to the care of human beings, moreover, might justifiably reject the pursuit of self-knowledge as unnecessary and even unbiblical. Best we return to searching out more theological knowledge and leave the scripturally unwarranted "self" to die a natural death.

On the other hand, the putative merit of the familiar thesis regarding the provenance of the self must be evaluated lest too hasty a judgment be made. Whether Augustine's appropriation of Neoplatonism led to the "creation" of an inner self, canonized and systematized by modernist dogma, *is false if the Bible itself provided his primary intellectual resources.*[6] If Augustine invented the notion of inwardness, out of which the so-called modern self grew, then we should expect not to encounter this tendency in biblical texts. Patently, the burden of proof cannot be satisfied simply by re-reading Augustine whose writings, without question, are steeped in biblical language and allusions. Instead, we must look for passages of Scripture containing references to and reflections upon the inner life of individual human beings. From such passages, we might conclude that something resembling a proto-self—an implicit psychology (or psychologies) of self—existed long before Augustine. We might further conjecture that divine revelation itself supplied Augustine—and supplies us—with a necessary conceptual foundation upon which to build.

---

5. Cary (2003) contends that Augustine's invention amounts to a Christian mingling of Plotinus and the Bible wherein he conceives of the self as "an inner space where God is present" (p. 31). Taylor (1989) avoids speaking in such stark terms: "It is probable that in every language there are resources for self-reference and descriptions of reflexive thought, action, attitude. . . . But this is not at all the same as making 'self' into a noun, preceded by a definite or indefinite article, speaking of 'the' self, or 'a' self. This reflects something important which is peculiar to our modern sense of agency" (p. 113).

6. The modern self is a creation of modern Western thinking. But the question posed here is whether its "genesis" is to be found in Augustine or whether Augustine got it from the Bible. I argue the latter, though plainly the "modern self" is, by definition, not to be found in the Scriptures.

Ample evidence in the Bible of an inner, knowable self as an everyday object of human awareness and reflection would supply a significant defeater for crediting Augustine with its "genesis." Therefore, we must return to the Bible with relevant queries ready at hand. Some of these are as follows: Do the biblical writers, for example, imply an awareness of the existence of an individualized interior life, even if they do not always pursue any deeper self-awareness than did Augustine? Do they engage at times in reflection upon and disclosure of certain psychic dynamics that suggest their identification of an "inner" center of inter/subjectivity? Does their pursuit of God lead them strictly outward, upward, so to speak, or do they pursue dipolar relationality with God inwardly in some psychologically significant, internally situated, locale? Furthermore, does the apparent presumptive normativity of a unified personal identity underlie biblical anthropological perspectives, however rudimentary or asystematic those perspectives may be?

If any or all of these questions may be answered, even provisionally, in the affirmative, then contemporary assertions that the self is an extra-canonical "creation" of Augustinian (or Cartesian, or Jamesian, etc.) origin should be reexamined.[7] Furthermore, if suggestions of a self-concept and its reflexive phenomenological counterpart, the empirical self, may be discerned within the Scriptures, it would be difficult to argue that Christians ought to avoid either the scientific systemization of knowledge regarding the human self, or the personal quest for dialogical self-knowledge in relation to God and others. The quest for knowledge of self, Christianly conceived, would have found its epistemological basis in divine self-revelation.

One further note before proceeding on our search for self in Scripture. It bears stating that contemporary English translations of the Bible reflect at least some minimal dependence on an Augustinian anthropology, evident in the frequent use of terms like "self" and "inmost being." In many instances, these usages occur in translations whose committees we might expect to be resistant to the influence of modernity or who are otherwise philosophically committed to formal equivalency. So, while

7. To be clear, Trinity is a post-canonical concept; but its epistemological basis is found in the Scriptures, not later writers. The same is true, I argue, with the self. Indeed, Baumeister (1999) argues from a secular perspective that human experience forms the basis of selfhood and observes, "The fact that everyone can use the term 'self' with such ease and familiarity suggests that the concept of selfhood is rooted in some simple universal human experience" (p. 1). Of course, post/modern Western conceptions of the inner, psychological self are a creation of modernity.

the presence of such language may indicate the pervasiveness with which modern terms and concepts have come to dominate Western thinking in ways incommensurate with authorial intent, it may also be that the use of "self" may follow from the plain meaning of the contexts, independent of any anachronistic imposition by modern translators upon the original writers' intended meaning(s). Significant Christian scholarship has contributed tremendous insight into the biblical writers' use of terms and concepts. Consideration of these contributions alongside a careful exegetical examination of relevant Old and New Testament contexts is, therefore, in order.

Dyadic constitution

The most faithful readings of Scripture have demonstrated that human beings are constituted as a dyadic unity of inner and outer aspects (Cooper, 2000; Hoekema, 1994; Wolff, 1974).[8] Despite the limitations of such terms, "body" and "soul" have typically been identified as the metaphysical domains that together compose the embodied and relational existence of human beings. Due to concerns that these terms might have come to reflect a Platonic dualism, significant exegetical, theological, and philosophical effort has been spent demonstrating the validity of a constitutional psychosomatic unity—that is, a unity of *psychē* and *sōma*. The two coinhere in one essential, phenomenological, and relational whole for the duration of our earthly lives. From this, Cooper (2000), concerned with the Bible's testimony regarding life after death, determines, "Human persons [are] psychophysical unities during life"; only "at death" are they "dichotomized" (p. 195; cf. Robinson, 1952, p. 14).

Similarly, Hoekema (1994) concludes that human beings ought not to be conceived of "as consisting of distinct and sometimes separable 'parts,' which are then abstracted from the whole"; rather, "man must be seen in his unity" (p. 203). Nevertheless, although there is a oneness to human being, we cannot fail to hold a clear picture of "duality" in humanity's inner and outer existence (see Berkouwer, 1962; Cortez, 2008; Hoekema, 1994).[9] Our embodied existence, in other words, can only be

8. Cf. the effort to engage philosophically, scientifically, and theologically with recent challenges to this thesis in, e.g., Crisp et al. (2016).

9. Reformed objections to the term "dualism" tend to automatically assume, and then reject, the Platonic/Cartesian sense of the word. Cooper (2000) has helpfully shown that this is unnecessary: "[T]he term does not automatically entail a Platonic

rightly conceived in dialectical terms: as Cooper (2000) avers, "Only . . . [a] 'holistic dualism' will tell the whole story" (p. 164).

Inner life in the Old Testament

While a philosophical or theological synthesis of the relevant biblical data reveals a dyadic constitution, clearly, the biblical writers themselves were less concerned with systematic anthropology; their focus was the phenomenological world of everyday life (Anderson, 1982; Hoekema, 1994). Anthropological terminology, for biblical writers, often functions synecdochically and transposably. In Hebrew, for example, words like *nephesh*, *rūach*, and *lēb*, though frequently translated, "soul," "spirit," "heart," respectively, often bear the same referent and imply *the whole person* rather than any discrete formal or psychological faculty (A. R. Johnson, 2006; Wolff, 1974).[10]

Indeed, even anatomical references may directly correlate with the inner life of human beings. In sum, as Robinson (1952) explains, "all words pertaining to the life and constitution" of human beings can function, at different times, interchangeably:

> The parts of the body are thought of, not primarily from the point of view of their difference from, and interrelation with, other parts, but as signifying or stressing different aspects of the whole man in relation to God. From the standpoint of analytic psychology and physiology the usage of the Old Testament is chaotic: it is the nightmare of the anatomist when any part can stand at any moment for the whole. (p. 16)

For this reason, word choice alone does not tell the whole story. In order to grasp at what the biblical writers might have understood about themselves, and their inner lives in particular, we must look more closely at what they say and imply. More to the point, we must inquire: to what degree does any pursuit of dipolar self-awareness—interpersonal self-reflection—direct them inward?

---

or Cartesian dualism of essentially different substances. It does not necessarily require adoption of Aristotelian form–matter or Kantian noumenal–phenomenal categories. . . . It does not require viewing body and soul as self-contained, independently functioning entities, at least not during earthly life. These are the sorts of unbiblical dualisms which theologians are rightly worried about" (p. 164).

10. Unlike Greek (σῶμα, *sōma*), ancient Hebrew has no term for the whole body (Robinson, 1952).

The psalmist's *nephesh*

References to psychospiritual dynamics abound throughout the Old Testament. The Psalms, in particular, contain numerous indications of the active reflection of their authors on personal mental and emotional states. In numerous passages we encounter suggestions of the author's awareness of an inwardly situated, psychogenic constitution. In Psalm 42, for example, the writer inquires, "Why are you cast down, O my *nephesh* [נַפְשִׁי, *naphshi*], and why are you in turmoil within me?" (vv. 5a, 11a). The Hebrew term employed here, commonly translated "my soul," is one of many anthropological terms employed as a referent for the whole person (Wolff, 1974; see Waltke, 1980).[11] Yet, the psalmist is not diagnosing any physiological state or medical condition; this is no sore throat. Rather, he, *himself*, is distressed. He refers to his "downcast" *nephesh*, in the same way we talk about a "heavy heart." It may seem that not the psalmist but his *nephesh* is "downcast"; but this is a poetic device employed by the writer for the important work of "soul"-searching.

Self-as-subject assumes the role of concerned bystander and counselor upon observing self-as-object's own emotional turmoil: "Are you okay? What has you down?" In order to accomplish this rhetorical maneuver, the psalmist synecdochizes and personifies a particular formal constituent, his *nephesh*, as a psychological "space" (see Ryken, 1993, p. 342). By means of a poetic apostrophe, and with dramatic flair, he inquires after his own depressed and disturbed condition. To be clear, however, he is reflecting on the psychospiritual roots of his *own* anguished emotional state. "What's wrong with you, self?," he seems to be saying. He appears to believe, moreover, that apostrophic self-talk could result in a favorable psychotherapeutic outcome. "Cheer up, trust God," he admonishes, "it won't be long before you are praising God again" (vv. 5b, 11b).

---

11. In his seminal study of Old Testament anthropology, Wolff (1974) concludes, "Today we are coming to the conclusion that it is only in a very few passages that the translation 'soul' corresponds to the meaning of *nepeš*" (p. 10). Schwarz (2013) identifies a significant reason "soul" can be a "misleading" gloss: "When the 'I' becomes synonymous with *nefesh*, it shows that humans do not have a *nefesh* but as living beings they are a *nefesh*" (pp. 6–7). The psalmist's *nephesh*, in other words, is him*self*. This accords with Waltke (1980) who holds that "in some contexts *nephesh* is best rendered by 'person,' 'self,' or more simply by the personal pronoun" (p. 590). Depending on the context, A. R. Johnson (2006), suggests that *nephesh* may be understood as "a *pathetic* [i.e., deeply emotional] periphrasis for . . . a pronoun" (p. 18; emphasis original).

If we dig deeper into the cause of the writer's emotional turmoil, we discover an important reality. For reasons he does not appear to fully understand, the psalmist is grieving over a subjective sense of distance from God. This distance may be geographical, metaphorical, or both (Goldingay, 2007; Schaefer, 2001). Whichever we conclude, the result is the same: his *nephesh* "pants" (v. 1) and "thirsts" to be near God again (v. 2). Along with his tears over this enduring separation, his *nephesh* is being "poured out" (vv. 3–4). Employing vivid poetic imagery, the psalmist has directly linked the activity of his *nephesh* with his emotional distress, which we do well to note has been triggered by a troubling interpersonal dynamic. He perceives a distance between himself and God whose presence he directly associates with "the house of God" in Jerusalem (v. 4). "God is in the temple," Goldingay (2007) concludes, "and the problem is that the suppliant cannot get there. There was no problem about God's location; the problem lay in the suppliant's location" (p. 24). "[A]lienated from God" due to an imposed separation, his grief is acute (Schaefer, 2001, p. 109).

In this context, *nephesh* is best understood as the psalmist's center of subjectivity—the seat and source of human emotional and spiritual life (Schaefer, 2001; see A. R. Johnson, 2006; Waltke, 1980). More specifically, as Wolff (1974) avers, in Psalm 42, *nephesh* denotes "the self of the needy life, thirsting with desire" (p. 25). The psalmist's *nephesh*, not entirely unlike Descartes's "soul" or James's "I-self," bears his unique personal identity.[12] Yet, with the added allusions to its somatic and relational aspects, *nephesh* in this case should be taken to refer to his whole person—that is, his embodied, covenantal self (Goldingay, 2007).[13] Moreover, what he discerns about his "self" is instructive: a reflexive analysis of his *nephesh* has revealed something of watery "abyss" (תְּהוֹם, *tehōm*; v. 7)—unfathomable and inscrutable as the deep waters, raging and threatening to overwhelm him (Schökel, 1976, p. 7).[14] Like God's ways, it would seem, the

12. Kaiser & Lohse (1981) observe that *nephesh* can also refer to that which remains of human persons after the death of the body (see, e.g., Ps 49:15).

13. In vv. 1, 2, Goldingay (2007) glosses נַפְשִׁי (*naphshi*) with "my whole person" before reverting to the standard translation, "my soul," in subsequent verses.

14. Water metaphors predominate in Psalms 42 and 43 (Schökel, 1976). Notably, the Hebrew for "cast down" (יחש, *yḥsh*; lit. "to dissolve") and "[to be] in turmoil" (המה, *hmh*; lit. "to be turbulent") can both bear metaphorical meanings having to do with water (Koehler & Baumgartner, 2002). Schökel (1976) rejects a strictly naturalistic interpretation of תְּהוֹם (*tehōm*) as "old-fashioned" (cf. NET), preferring instead to see the "two contrasting images of water" as central to a highly subjectivist interpretation of these psalms. The life-giving "streams of water" (v. 1) have become, for the psalmist, a torrential "roar of waterfalls" (v. 7) indicating "a dramatic tension in the soul" (p. 7).

psalmist's *nephesh* is to a certain degree opaque (cf. Ps 19:12; Jer 17:9). Yet, though he seems not to fully understand his distress, he does list a number of circumstantial triggers, all of which have served to compound his sense that God has "forgotten" him (vv. 9–10). The writer knows some things about himself; the rest is hidden from his self-reflection.

In his classic treatise on Psalm 42:11, Puritan pastoral theologian Richard Sibbes (1658) discerns an underlying psychopathology of sin in the writer's self-disclosure. He determines that the psalmist's disquiet is the result of some sin-borne interruption in his fellowship with God.[15] Though the writer discloses no such personal lapse in the present context, Sibbes links what he holds to be King David's "unruly passion" with either "the guilt of those two foul sins of murder and adultery" (cf. Ps 51:4), or else, if "not these actual sins," then "the sin of his nature, the root itself" (p. 124; cf. Ps 51:5). The psalmist, he concludes, carries "a nature . . . subject to break out continually upon any occasion," one that exists within every regenerate person "from the remainder of old Adam within" (pp. 124–125).

Working out from his exegetical prejudice, Sibbes offers a psychological model of the self in which psychospiritual distress is exclusively linked to sin:

> [W]e must conceive in a godly man, a double self, one which must be denied, the other which must deny. . . . It is a good trial of a man's condition to know what he esteems to be himself. A godly man counts the inner man, the sanctified part, to be himself, whereby he stands in relation to Christ. . . . That which most troubles a good man in all troubles is himself, so far as he is unsubdued. (pp. 102–103)

Sibbes, in other words, discerns a bifurcated inner self in the writer. His diagnosis for this "double self" is to bring that which is "unsubdued" into right "relation to Christ."

We may justifiably question whether sufficient textual warrant exists for the conclusion that the psalmist's distress stems from sin. Sibbes's conjecture lacks the necessary exegetical basis to conclude that some

---

15. In similar fashion to Sibbes, Augustine (2012a) correlates and applies the psalmist's emotional distress to his own experience of conviction: "Is it [Augustine's *nephesh*] disquieted on account of God? It is on my own account it is disquieted. By the Unchangeable it was revived; it is by the changeable it is disquieted. I know that the righteousness of God remaineth; whether my own will remain stedfast [*sic*], I know not" (p. 135).

specific sin or even a general sinful nature lie at the root of "all troubles" in human beings. Might we not just as easily conclude that the writer, in this case, is desperately homesick?[16] Having suffered the persecution of "adversaries" who, with their taunts, inflict "a deadly wound in my bones," he has clearly become discouraged (v. 10). Since the psalmist does not specify any sinful act or disposition, Sibbes's inclination (along with Augustine, 2012a) to credit him with such may, in fact, reveal more about the degree to which a Stoic regard for emotion had influenced his anthropology (cf. Elliott, 2006; Roberts, 2007). His suggestion that the human self must be "subdued" certainly comports with a non-cognitive theory of emotion (see Strongman, 2003).

Irrespective of its source, whether due to sin or some other, morally benign cause, the psalmist's lament reveals a profound acuity of self-perception. Though he recognizes various instrumental triggers—his enemies' persecution and the veiled presence of God—he nonetheless looks inward for the cause of his psychological unrest. He exhorts his *nephesh*, "Hope in God; for I shall again praise him" (vv. 5b, 11b), deploying an essentially dialogical means of buoying his flagging spirit. By looking ahead to the reunion with God and with the people of God that likely awaits him in Jerusalem, he encourages himself with confidence in God's coming deliverance to press on. His hope for psychospiritual rest and satisfaction arises from his baited anticipation of appearing before God (see v. 2; cf. Ps 4:8). Though he now suffers due to a relational breech—"the torment of isolation" (Wolff, 1974, p. 218)—he knows he will be healed. Whether his emotional wellbeing has been compromised due to sin or homesickness, the medicine his "self" needs is closer proximity to his God.

Lēb and *qereb* and the inner self

Nephesh is not the only poetic means of referencing one's inner life in the Old Testament. In Jeremiah 4:14 two other anatomical terms carry similarly clear psychospiritual connotations. In the midst of an extended pronunciation of pending judgment, the prophet utters the following

16. So, Wolff (1974): "In Pss. 42/43 the speaker is one who has been carried away into a foreign land. In his forsakenness he misses particularly the services of the congregation. When in his loneliness he 'thirsts' for God, this means in concrete terms that he longs to take part once more in the pilgrimages to the sanctuary, in order there to find the assurance of the God who is his joy" (p. 218).

plea, "Jerusalem, wash your heart [לִבֵּךְ, *libēch*] clean of wickedness so that you may be saved. How long shall your evil schemes lodge within you [בְּקִרְבֵּךְ, *beqirbēch*; lit. in your inner parts]?" (NRSV). While *lēb* has a clear anatomical referent, "heart," *qereb* is a more generic term signifying the internal organs, bowels, or, perhaps, "the cavity for the inner organs" (Wolff, 1974, p. 63). In the present passage, however, the two interchangeably refer to the seat of sinful motivations.

Evidently, Jeremiah does not believe the inhabitants of Jerusalem should interpret his plea concretely. Evil schemes do not become "lodged" within the viscera. The washing of the heart that he exhorts comes through repentance. The prophet is calling the people of God to turn from their sinful ways and to seek the Lord's salvation. Anderson (1982) calls *lēb*, "the center of the subjective self" (p. 211). As the present context demonstrates, *qereb* may serve interchangeably. Although they can also denote a concrete, anatomical referent, terms such as *nephesh*, *lēb* and *qereb* may often, justifiably, be interpreted as forerunners of the modern self. The latter, typically rendered "you" in English translations, demonstrates its clear connection with the whole person. In either case, the writer identifies an internal, anatomical locus and assigns it metonymic and psychological significance.

In other instances we find similar rhetorical connections between internal organs and psychospiritual states: Jeremiah's "liver" is "poured out" in grief (Lam 2:11); Asaph's "heart" becomes "embittered" (Ps 73:21); the king's "kidneys" rejoice over the wisdom of his son (Prov 23:17). For the ancient Hebrew poetic writers generally, "the inside of the body . . . is of less interest anatomically and physiologically than psychologically" (Wolff, 1974, p. 63).

Semitic anthropology may have been functionally holistic, but evidently Hebrew writers possessed the conceptual and linguistic means to refer to their inner aspects of personhood. Not only this, they spent time reflecting on and interacting with themselves at the psychospiritual level. All of this, they believed, grew out of their having been made in the image of God.

As Cooper (2000) points out, the first human being was composed of a dyadic combination of "dust" and "life-breath," the latter having come directly from the out-breathing of God (p. 48; see Gen 2:7; cf. Job 32:8; Isa 42:5). God's chief concern, then, is humanity's stewardship of the inner life, where his "breath" resides (Prov 20:27; Ps 139:23). On the other hand, that which is physical or substantial in human nature concerns

God significantly less (1 Sam 16:7), except as an extension of covenantal personhood—one's being-in-relation to God, to others, and to creation. Depending on the individual's orientation respective to God, we are repeatedly told that good or evil deeds arise *out of* an inner, psychological location, whether "heart," "soul," "gut," etc.[17] Fix the inward reality and the outward reality would follow. That being said, the ontological dualism of Platonism and the "functional holism" of Semitic anthropology are quite distinct (Cooper, 2000, p. 47; see also Robinson, 1952).

New Testament interiority and the indwelling Spirit of God

When Old Testament references to anthropological constitution suggest a distinction between human beings' inner and outer existence, it is frequently subtle. By using functional, anatomical metaphors for the immaterial aspect of human beings,[18] Semitic idiomatic reference to personal subjectivity tends to stress the holistic embodied nature of the self. The self entails the whole person, not merely an inner self encased in a bodily shell. Nevertheless, as the foregoing discussion of anthropological terms indicates, subjectivity is often depicted as an internal reality—an inward extension of the psychospiritual and relational aspects of personal being.

In the New Testament, by contrast, the distance, so to speak, between inner and outer existence is generally more pronounced.[19] This

17. See Job 1:5; Pss 10:13; 14:1; 28:3; 55:15; 78:18; 85:8; 125:4; Eccl 9:3; Jer 5:24; 32:40; Ezek 14:3; Zeph 1:12.

18. As in the Semitic usage of non-anatomical referents for the person such as *rūach* (spirit) or *neshama* (breath).

19. Calvin (2008) held that body and soul (or spirit) are distinct substances in the, mostly, Platonic sense. Some modern theologians maintain this position for various reasons (Beck & Demarest, 2005; Moreland & Rae, 2000). But, Ladd (1993) concludes that, from the perspective of New Testament anthropology, "body, soul, and spirit are not different, separable faculties of man but different ways of viewing the whole man" (p. 457). Cooper (2000) concurs adding, "Synecdoche is a common occurrence in the New Testament, as it is in the Old. Often anthropological part-terms are plausibly interpreted as referring to the person as a whole. They might even be translated properly as personal pronouns" (p. 97). So, for example, Jesus warns his disciples not to fear those who can "kill the body but not the soul; rather fear him who can destroy both soul and body in hell" (Matt 10:28). Jesus is not suggesting a dichotomy of substance but of orientation, which is to say, "an ethical-religious antithesis" (Cooper, 2000, p. 99). A faulty interpretation of this passage might conclude that

may, in fact, be due to the expanded anthropological vocabulary available in Koine Greek (see Robinson, 1952). It may also reflect the influence of Greek thought. Whatever the reason, we would be mistaken to perceive a discontinuity between Old and New Testament anthropology. Better to see the latter as a development from the former. In any event, in numerous passages throughout these first-century Christian texts, writers display an implicit awareness of and sensitivity to subjective interiority as a universal experience attendant to individual human existence. What we find in such passages is perfectly consistent with its ancient Semitic antecedents.

According to Grenz (2001), contemporary notions of self are distinguished by their emphasis on "interiority—that is, the distinction between 'inside' and 'outside'—together with a sense of personal identity as a unified being" (p. 60). What makes the modern self, "modern," is not so much its emphasis on individual identity, then, but on the location of that personal identity *within*. Modernist dogma identifies Augustine as the "inventor" of this conceptualization of personal identity as inward. Accordingly, to search in the teachings of Jesus for suggestions of a personal, interior "space" within which identity resides is to commit, we should presume, exegetical malfeasance.[20] Yet, this is exactly what we find in a few key texts.

Woven into his discourse to his disciples on the eve of his crucifixion, Jesus makes several telling remarks regarding God's plans for the future. Having affirmed in John 14 the perichoretic union of the Son with the Father (vv. 10–11), Jesus describes a similar union in which believers will also participate. This union will take place with the coming of the Holy Spirit (see Köstenberger & Swain, 2008, p. 146). The "Spirit of truth abides with you," Jesus clarifies, "and he will be in you" (v. 17). In typical Johannine fashion, the referent of divinity shifts with little to no warning: "I will not leave you orphaned; I am coming to you." Evidently, "the Spirit of truth" who will come will be identical to "the Spirit of Christ" (see Ferguson, 1997). "On that day," Jesus continues, "you will know that I am

---

God cares more about "soul" than "body." To the contrary, Jesus simply means that believers should be less concerned with pleasing their fellow human beings than God. Whereas the former can "kill the body but not the soul," the latter can condemn whole persons—"*both* soul and body"—eternally.

20. Grenz's limited qualification of the modern self may be the source of the confusion about whether Augustine can reasonably be credited with its genesis (cf. C. Taylor, 1989). Clearly, there are significant historical and sociological distinctions between biblical and post/modern notions of "self."

in my Father, and you in me, and I in you (ἐν ὑμῖν, *en hymin*; vv. 18, 20).[21] Jesus, through the Spirit, will return after his death to some place *inside* his followers. Can this be right?

Understandably perplexed, one of Jesus' disciples inquires as to the manner in which he will be present with his disciples yet unseen by the world (v. 22). Jesus responds, "If anyone [ἐάν τις, *ean tis*] loves me, he will keep my word; and my father will love him [αὐτὸν, *auton*], and we will come to him [αὐτὸν, *auton*] and make our abode with him [παρ᾽ αὐτῷ, *par' autō*]" (v. 23 NASB).[22] The world will not be able to see Jesus because he will only "manifest" himself within the internal "abode" of individual believers (Michaels, 2010).[23] We conclude from this that Jesus is not here referring to the parousia: he will only be "seen" by believers (Keener, 2010; Michaels, 2010; contra Carson, 1990; cf. 1 John 2:28; 3:2).[24] Moreover, the event Jesus indicates in this passage—the outpouring of the Spirit—will occur not long after his resurrection (cf. John 20:22).[25] What is significant

21. While the plural, ἐν ὑμῖν (*en hymin*), might plausibly be translated "among you" or "in your midst" (cf. ἐντὸς ὑμῶν, *entos hymōn*, in Luke 17:21), the whole thrust of the passage suggests that Jesus means "within each of you individually."

22. The NRSV corporatizes its rendering of the pronouns in this verse ("they/ them"), rather than accurately translating the singular pronouns found in the Greek text. Carson (1990) clarifies that the Spirit indwells "the person who so loves and obeys Jesus" (p. 504).

23. Should the verb for "manifest" (ESV, ASV, RSV), ἐμφανίζ- (*emphaniz-*), be alternately translated "disclose/reveal/show" (NIV, NET, NRSV, HCSB, NASB), thereby reducing any potential mystical overtones (cf. the various glosses offered in Danker [2001])? It would seem that Judas (not Iscariot) sought clarification on this very point (v. 22): How would Jesus limit his appearing to just his followers and not the whole world? In other words, what did Jesus mean when he said, ἐμφανίσω . . . ἐμαυτόν (*emphanisō . . . emauton*)? Jesus' answer to him is noteworthy: he promises to come, with the Father, to the individual believer and "we will make our abode with him" (v. 23). Jesus, exegeting his own use of ἐμφανίσω (*emphanisō*) with very concrete language, clarifies: believers will "know" him because he will be "in" them (v. 17). This certainly suggests much more than that he will grant insight as to his identity or, even, special epistemic access to saving faith. More than this, the triune God will "manifest" himself by taking up residence within human individuals in much the same way Israel's God dwelt formerly in the tabernacle/temple (cf. John 2:19, 21; 1 Cor 3:16; 6:19; 2 Cor 6:16). Any ostensibly mystical overtones, therefore, appear to be present in the original text (see Keener, 2010, p. 975; Michaels, 2010, p. 787).

24. Carson (1990) collapses the timeframe of the Son's appearing to the disciples into a single eschatological parousia that is nonetheless "inaugurated" with his postresurrection appearances (pp. 502–3). Unlike Carson, Keener (2010) does not dissociate Jesus' appearing from his "continuing presence among his community" (p. 975).

25. Evidently, Jesus' Spirit will dwell *within* believers in some way analogous to his

about this coming union of believers with Christ is the location of this union: by means of the Spirit, Jesus intends to dwell "*in* them, not merely *with* them" (Ferguson, 1997, p. 71; emphasis original).[26]

Jesus indicates that the indwelling Spirit, sent from the Father and breathed out by the Son, will dwell within believers. But where? In what manner of "space" does the Spirit take up residence? In a second illustrative passage recording the glorified Christ's missive to the church at Laodicea (Rev 3:14–22), we encounter similar language. Having become "lukewarm" (v. 16), the believers in Laodicea are instructed by the exalted Lord in the appropriate means of repentance: "Those whom I love, I reprove and discipline, so be zealous and repent. Behold, I stand at the door and knock. If anyone [ἐάν τις, *ean tis*] hears my voice and opens the door, I will come in to him [εἰσελεύσομαι πρὸς αὐτὸν, *eiseleusomai pros auton*] and eat with him, and he with me" (vv. 19–20).[27] Apparently, Jesus intends that their repentance should include allowing him back into their midst. Yet, as in John 14, he especially seeks entrance into *individual* believers, not merely the broader community.[28]

If an Augustinian "genesis" account of the inner self is to be believed, we may reasonably ask where Christ, by means of his Spirit, intends to dwell *within* individual believers. To be clear, such a location for Christ's presence does not need to be physical or even literal (i.e.,

---

having dwelt bodily *alongside* his disciples during his earthly ministry (v. 25; Michaels, 2010, pf. 790–91).

26. So, Keener (2010): "[H]ere Jesus may play . . . on the image of a new temple or the eschatological promise of God dwelling among his people. . . . But whereas most of the biblical promises and early Jewish images about the Shekinah applied to Israel as a whole, Jesus' promise applies to the experience of individual believers. Effectively, Jesus' hearers may have envisioned the Jerusalem temple . . . dwelling in the believer" (p. 976).

27. A common enough verb, εἰσέρχομαι (*eiserchomai*), can simply mean come in or go out—of a building (Luke 19:7), a crowd of people (Acts 19:30), or the kingdom of God (Mark 10:23). Notably, it is used to describe the action of Satan on Judas when the latter received bread handed to him by Jesus (John 13:27). According to Danker (2001), it can also refer to "transcendent and moral–spiritual phenomena," i.e., the "spiritual coming of God" (p. 394).

28. One can only imagine the perpetual frustration and discouragement individual Christians would suffer if Christ's presence could be excluded by, say, apathetic or unconverted church members. Any suggestion that Christ only dwells "among" and not "within" might imply this possibility. The NRSV's avoidance of singular pronouns in John 14:23 is, therefore, problematic. The "best" exegetical alterative, according to Mounce (1997), is to view such references as "personal and present rather than ecclesiastical and eschatological" (p. 114).

spiritual) to be part of the writers' anthropological understanding. Still, if there is no interior "space" assumed by these passages, whether literal or metaphorical,[29] then where has Christ taken up residence? Where do believers "eat" with him and he with them? How can such passages be understood without granting that their writers understood themselves individually and particularly to be vessels of God's presence? For that matter, if human beings are "vessels,"[30] as the apostle Paul maintains (see Rom 9:21–23; 1 Tim 1:20–21; cf. 2 Cor 6:16), does this not also suggest some sort of psychospiritual interstice wherein the presence of God may come to dwell within human beings?

Paul's use of "self" referents

In turning now to Paul, we encounter some of the most compelling evidence for a pre-Augustinian, canonical sensitivity to an "inner" self (see Chamblin, 1993). Indeed, of all the New Testament writers, Paul affords the greatest attention to psychological matters (Beck, 2002; Theissen, 1987). Before proceeding with observations on Paul's view of the self, however, a word of caution is in order. Modern theologians have wrestled mightily in determining what Paul knew or believed about the self (see Becker, 1993; Bultmann, 2007; Conzelmann, 1974; Gundry, 2005; Käsemann, 1971; Stendahl, 1963).[31] At the root of much of the debate

29. By *literal* space I do not mean *physical*. The question is whether Christ through the Spirit *actually* resides "within" believers or merely intends that they take comfort from his metaphorical (i.e., non-actual) "presence." In other words, should we only *imagine* him to be so near to us that there is in fact no separation between us? Of course, a metaphorical indwelling would bring small comfort, but it would still suggest that the New Testament writers were operating with a tacit understanding of an interiorized and unique personal identity. On the other hand, if the triune God has truly taken up residence within (and among) each and every believer through the perichoretic presence of the Spirit, then a unique, interior "space" is *real*—irrespective of our ignorance regarding its nature or composition.

30. In his rebuke of Pharisaical spirituality, Jesus explicitly references an inner/outer ethicospiritual distinction in human beings using the metaphors of a cup (i.e., vessel) and a tomb (Matt 23:25–28; Luke 11:39–41). For both of these, the metaphors involved imply an inward and outward reality respective to human function and identity.

31. Axton (2015) discerns three basic perspectives on the Pauline view of the self and its relation to itself (or reductively to the "body" [σῶμα, *sōma*]), to others, and to God. These three perspectives Axton associates, respectively, with Bultmann (2007), Käsemann (1971), and Becker (1993), each of whom emphasizes one of the three

stands the hermeneutical concern to read and apply Paul appropriately. So, Dunn (2006), for example, warns of the "danger" of bringing our "un-examined presuppositions about how the person is constituted and read them into what Paul says" (p. 53).

We must resist the temptation, therefore, to anachronistically proj-ect contemporary anthropological notions into Paul's first-century think-ing (see Stendahl, 1963). I would add that the Scriptures, moreover, are the word of God; they must be permitted to direct our thinking even as we faithfully seek understanding (see Vanhoozer, 1998). For this reason, I will take great care in drawing anthropological and psychological impli-cations from the apostle's writings.[32]

While disagreements abound regarding any putatively Pauline per-spective, notably, all modern writers agree that Paul *has* a perspective on the self, albeit one that is rudimentary and asystematic. The conclusion, it would seem, is inescapable. After all, "self" language abounds in Paul.[33] As Jewett (1971) notes, Paul's use of terminology is often polemical rather than systematic. When he appears to employ Hellenistic anthropological conceptions, he may in fact be working to reformulate and redefine them according to a Semitic framework. So, in Paul,

> [O]ne finds the reflections of a single gnostic conception of the "inner man" as the pneumatic core of a person, enabled by its di-vine nature to receive and comprehend the divine wisdom, but held in bondage by the material body. Since Paul must reshape this concept to meet the requirements of his argument, . . . he does not arrive at a single clear definition [of the self]. (p. 460)

relations over against the others. Axton rightly discerns that "the three positions are not so much opposed as different facets of a capacity that sets man simultaneously into communication and confrontation with himself (Bultmann), others (Käsemann) and God (Becker)" (p. 159n13). His conclusion is amenable with my own thesis regarding the onto-relational, embodied human self.

32. I am optimistic, along with Osborne (2006), at the "possibility of delineat-ing the author's intended meaning and then recontextualizing that meaning for the contemporary context" (p. 498). To this end, I will employ Chamblin's (1993) basic "two step" hermeneutic for reading Paul. The first step is "to make him and his writ-ings rather than ourselves the center of gravity. That is, . . . we must make an effort to enter into his world and discern his perspective on reality." The second, then, "is to share Paul's experience of reality" (p. 33). When it comes to the Scriptures, this deceptively complex hermeneutical maneuver can only be accomplished with divine aid and assistance.

33. I assume Pauline authorship for the thirteen epistles that bear his name and that have historically been attributed to him.

Nor do we expect such a definition from him. What Paul assumes, then, is the very Semitic idea that human beings are constituted as a dyadic synthesis of inner and outer aspects.

In speaking of human beings, Paul "always employs the grammar of persons: the 'I,' the self, the core person" (Cooper, 2000). Notably, he does so with minimally dualist overtones: "If Paul is a dualist," Cooper concludes, "he is strictly speaking a self–body, person–body, or ego–body dualist, not a soul–body dualist" (p. 156).[34] At the same time, Murray (1968) holds that Paul's inner self amounts to "that which is most determinative in his personality . . . what is central in will and affection" (p. 257). Gaffin (2013) concurs adding that Paul's "'inner self' or 'heart' has in view who I am at the core of my being, in my *pre-functional* disposition" (p. 63; emphasis original).

Yet, crucially, Paul holds that God's reconciliation of persons to himself, though limited for the present age to the inner aspects of the self, will be applied to whole persons in the age to come:

> [W]hat is now true of the Christian as inner self is not (yet) true *for* the outer self. However, for the present, that is, until Christ returns, that is true only *within* the outer self. It is true only in the outer self for which the inner self is inner. . . . [W]hat is true for believers is not yet true *for* their bodies, but for now, until death and looking toward the future resurrection of the body, it is true only *in* the body. (pp. 63–64; emphasis original)

Paul's inner self, in other words, amounts to the subjective center of human personhood—the locus of psychological function and ethicospiritual agency.

At no point does Paul suggest, as Augustine later would, that the inner self is equivalent to a metaphysical substance (i.e., soul). The self cannot be entailed within a strictly constitutive framework. Yet, neither is the self a construct or form of the mind; it exists independently of any consciousness or awareness we may possess. That Paul likely thought in such terms will, in short order, become clear.

---

34. Cooper (2000), in defending a minimalist dualist anthropology, charges Calvin with "philosophical prejudice" in his uncritical appropriation of Augustine's Platonist reading of Paul (p. 95; cf. Calvin, 2008, pp. 104–5).

The nature of the Pauline "inner self"

Although Paul employs the language of an "inner self" (ἔσω ἄνθρωπον, *esō anthrōpon*) in several places (2 Cor 4:16; Eph 3:16; Rom 7:22), one of them is particularly noteworthy. According to Romans 7:7–25, the apostle had discovered a confounding dichotomy in his own "inner self" (v. 22), his consternation having, at some point, reached a fevered pitch (see v. 24).[35] He explains this schism in terms of his subjective sense of himself: "I do not understand my own actions," he bleakly confesses (v. 15). Paul further reports his past renunciation of sinful concupiscence in the interests of desiring only that which God's law pronounces to be "holy and righteous and good" (v. 11). Nevertheless, he acknowledges that God's "command" forbidding covetousness[36] has, in fact, elicited within him "all kinds of covetousness" (v. 8).[37]

35. A historically and sociologically sensitive review of the various interpretations of Paul's "I" in this passage will, no doubt, reveal a correlation between interpreters' respective readings of this passage and their perspectives on human nature. To wit, Augustine and the early Reformers, with their dim view of human ability, held that Paul's "I" refers not merely to Jews under the law of Moses but to all people, himself before all others (cf. 1 Tim 1:15; see Packer, 1999). Modern exegetes, on the other hand, have increasingly tended toward a more optimistic reading of the passage, arguing the "I" in Paul's discussion is either retrospective—referring to his experience pre-conversion—or rhetorical—in reference to the condition of all "under the Law" or all "in Adam" (see, e.g., Bultmann, 2007; Fee, 2009; Witherington, 2005). Moo (1996) rightly concludes that exegesis alone cannot determine the referent of Paul's "I" with absolute certainty, though he nonetheless prefers the retrospective/rhetorical reading. Schreiner (1998), on the other hand, determines that "the arguments are so finely balanced" between the various perspectives that the best option is to conclude that "Paul does not intend to distinguish believers from unbelievers in this text" (p. 390; see also Seifrid, 1992, pp. 226–244). In other words, he holds that Paul intends in this passage to personalize the universal human experience of double-mindedness respective to the "good" commands of God, and then proceeds to direct believers to the freedom from condemnation under the law and enslavement to the flesh offered through perichoretic union with Christ (see Rom 8:1–17).

36. The verbal stem, חמד (*ḥmd*), employed in the Mosaic prohibition, "You shall not covet [לֹא תַחְמֹד], *lo tiḥmod*" (Exod 20:17) is also found in the description of the fruit of the tree in the middle of the garden as "desirable for making one wise [וְנֶחְמָד . . . לְהַשְׂכִּיל, *wenehmad . . . lehashbēl*]" (Gen 3:6). Since the concupiscence of humanity's first parents *preceded* their fall, it seems unlikely that Paul holds believers to be immune in the present age from this tendency (along these lines, note Paul's conditional statement in Rom 8:9). Witherington (2005) observes the double allusion in Romans 7, yet rejects any connection with Paul's ongoing experience of inner conflict following conversion, opting instead for a strictly rhetorical reading of the passage.

37. Moo (1996) notes a "qualitative nuance" in Paul's use of "all kinds of

The underlying cause of this internal contradiction cannot be found in Paul's thinking about the law—he holds it to be good—or his avowals and intentions concerning the law—he has determined to do what is good. He, therefore, deduces from the discrepancy between intent and outcome that some other "law" must be at work within his "members" (v. 23)—that is, his constituent parts. Some internal division prevents him from making a simple, conscious decision to do the good he desires to do. Curiously, he frames the dichotomy in himself as one of "mind" (νοῦς, *nous*) and "flesh" (σάρξ, *sarx*). Paul desires to subject himself to the "law of God" (νόμος θεοῦ, *nomos theou*), yet his "flesh" remains intractably bound to this second, persistent tendency he identifies as the "law of sin" (νόμος ἁμαρτίας, *nomos harmartias*).[38] This internal conflict, moreover, has resulted in tremendous psychological distress (see v. 24). In coming to terms with this nomic conflict within himself, Paul looks to Christ for help to manage and overcome his "flesh" by means of the "Spirit" (8:4).

Paul's ultimate paraenetic aim in Romans 7 is to point believers toward the reality of life lived in and through the power of God's Spirit (Fee, 2009). Apart from the supervening influence of the Spirit, Paul warns, individual human beings are incapable of accessing and exercising control over certain aspects of their thoughts and actions.[39] He concretizes "sin"—his incapacity respective to the righteous decrees of God (v. 17)— and locates it within himself. Something *inside* Paul, despite his having termed it "flesh," is what keeps him from desiring what he ought not.

---

covetousness [πᾶσαν ἐπιθυμίαν, *pasan epithymian*]" that likely includes the sinful desire of every manner of object upon which human beings might cast their gaze (p. 436). All such desire is the legacy of the first fall into illicit concupiscence in the garden (cf. Jas 1:14–15).

38. Cf. Col 3:18 where Paul refers to the "fleshly mind" (τοῦ νοὸς τῆς σαρκὸς, *tou noos tēs sarkos*) of the individual who boasts of visions or encounters with angels. As has already been mentioned, Paul employs anthropological referents asystematically.

39. Remarkably, Fee (2009) determines against all internal evidence that "within Paul's argumentation [in Rom 7–8] there is no hint of an internal struggle within the believer's heart" (p. 821). He comes to this conclusion by presuming that the Pauline dichotomy between σάρξ (*sarx*) and πνεῦμα (*pneuma*) can be imposed without qualification on the two basic human constituencies—the regenerate and the unregenerate—in spite of, and in apparent contradiction to, Paul's already/not yet vision of the believer's inaugurated but still to be consummated life in Christ. Fee presumes from this, "It is not possible, therefore, that from Paul's perspective such a Spirit person would be . . . unable to do the good she or he wants to do" (p. 822). The inescapable logical consequence of Fee's exegetical pre-commitment is his inference that Paul "may not have addressed the issue of [believers'] personal struggle with sin" (p. 822n41).

By referencing sinful desire—covetousness—Paul likely implicates humanity's pre-Fall lapse into autonomous ambition and self-sufficiency (Gen 3:6; cf. 1 Tim 2:14). It was sin arising from unauthorized desire—of the forbidden fruit—that resulted in estrangement from God in the first place. Paul observes that this inclination has not wholly disappeared from every aspect or facet of his inner self. In other words, there are times when *he*—that is the-self-he-wills-not-to-be (cf. Kierkegaard, 1980)—desires what he knows he must not.

The pervasive and consistent inability of Paul's "I" to fare better than his first parents suggests a universal human tendency toward autonomy, which, for unbelievers, only serves to compound the breach in the image bearer's relationship to God. With believers, on the other hand, sinful desire does not suggest any deficiency in the presence or potency of the Spirit; rather, its stubborn presence must stem from lingering divisions in the knowable self—or its psychological working out in the believer's self-consciousness—that must be repaired in and through the believer's active participation in the sanctifying work of Christ.

That redeemed individuals all too often observe contradictions in personal cognition, affection, and volition is, arguably, self-evident (Packer, 1999). Paul's personal reflections along these lines are instructive. In verse 17, for example, he differentiates his true "I"—the self who loves the law of God—from the one who sins against his express desires and commitments: "[I]f I do what I don't want, . . . it is no longer me doing it, but sin that lives in me" (vv. 16–17 NET). According to Murray (1968), here Paul "appears to dissociate his own self from the sin committed" (p. 263). In other words, it is not that Paul is unaware or unconscious of his sinful behavior (Schreiner, 1998), but rather of the source within himself from which it issues forth. In the apostle's own judgment, his inner self is "split" (Dunn, 1988, p. 388).[40]

Paul draws this psychological inference on the basis of an extant, observable dichotomy in his thinking and acting from moment to moment. Though he has resolved himself to live wholly unto God, there are times when errant thoughts, desires, and behaviors belie his commitment. Paul concludes that some aspect of himself which he cannot see, and of which he has no firsthand knowledge, is nevertheless active in him (cf. Ps 19:12). As the flickering of starlight suggests the gravitational

---

40. Dunn (1988) further determines that the reason for the split in Paul's "I" is that every redeemed self "belongs to [two] epochs at the same time," namely, "the era of the flesh and the era of the Spirit" (p. 388).

interference of unseen celestial bodies, so Paul's constancy and devotion to the good remain intractably curtailed by some internal dynamic— "sin"—the source of which he ascribes to his "flesh."

By referencing the split in his redeemed self, Paul affirms the diachronic, eschatological bearing of salvation. We are *becoming* what God has declared us to be in Christ. Along these lines, Packer (1999) confirms that all Christians, for the duration of the present age, will "have a two-sided experience" characterized by the influence of two internal powers, "the uplifting of the Spirit and the downdrag of sin" (p. 78; see Owen, 2006). This "unabolished antinomy" in the believer, Delitzsch (1885) claims, effects a "moral separation" (p. 418) between the eschatological wholeness of the self *in se* and the known self—i.e., self-schema, self-theory—that persists in a state of internal conflict and division.[41]

Again, there is no suggestion of any deficiency in God's holiness or his ability to strengthen the believer against the influence of sin. On the contrary, the notion of antinomy explicates the complex inner workings of the divided self—one that is eschatologically whole in Christ, yet presently conflicted and divided due to lack of self-knowledge. Believers are being made whole in their resemblance to Christ by the ongoing cooperative agency of self and Spirit. Moreover, by referring in this passage to his remaining sin as not-me, Paul can, in a sense, "dissociate himself from the disowned, but nonetheless overpowering, dynamics of lawlessness" stubbornly remaining in his inner being (Lake, 2005, p. 468). What remains of the "old" Paul is not really Paul at all.

Like a recalcitrant child, Paul's "flesh" simply will not submit to the rule of his "mind," though by this statement Paul does not seek to exonerate himself. In grasping at Paul's meaning, Calvin (1995) determines, "This is not the entreaty of a man who is excusing himself, as if he were blameless. . . . It is a declaration of the extent of the disagreement between

41. Sin "lives within [οἰκοῦσα, *oikousa*]" (7:17) the sin-estranged person and rules uncontested, as a "law" unto itself (v. 23). By way of contrast, Paul says that the Spirit of God "lives in [οἰκεῖ, *oikei*]" (8:9) the one who has been reconciled to Christ, thus abolishing the "law of sin" and ratifying the "law of the Spirit" (8:2). Nevertheless, although sin's authority has been overthrown in the eschatological sense, believers can still "quench" (1 Thess 5:19) and "grieve" (Eph 4:30) the Holy Spirit. When the Christian sins, he or she is "in the flesh [ἐν σαρκὶ, *en sarki*]"; only by operating "in the Spirit [ἐν πνεύματι, *en pneumati*]" can believers eschew the influence of "the flesh" and avoid falling back under a rule of law that no longer applies to them (Rom 8:9, 12–13). Either way, believers will continue to struggle, as Paul suggests, in their attempts to bring the *whole self* under the rule of the "law of the Spirit."

his spiritual affection and his flesh" (p. 151). In other words, Paul has identified a split in himself, some "part" of which has yet to be fully reconciled to Christ, despite his conscious and authentic commitment to the will of God. This part he designates with the polemical pejorative "flesh."[42] The solution to this impasse in his schizoid self, the apostle concludes, can never arise autocentrically; his self is, left to its own devices, "wretched"[43] and ethically impotent. Deliverance, Paul concludes, must come from relatedness to Christ through the Spirit.

Paul's depiction in Romans 7 of his "inner self" as an internal opposition of allegiances—"mind" and "flesh"—in need of a covenantal means of transformation and psychotherapeutic relief should in no way be seen as an attempt by the apostle to promulgate a formalized or systematized psychology (Chamblin, 1993; Roberts, 2001). Nevertheless, we should reject as unfounded any inference that the apostle held only inconsistent or ill-conceived views, whether theological or psychological.[44] As Roberts (2001) concludes,

> [The writings of Paul] are about God and they are about the human self, but they are not systematic in the ways that we expect modern theology and modern psychology to be. On the other hand, Paul's comments about God and about the human self can both be systematized: one can expound them as a complex and consistent view (p. 161).

42. In his letter to the Colossians, Paul even more graphically illustrates the putting off of the "flesh" with an allusion to circumcision (2:11–13). There he speaks of regeneration as the removal of "the foreskin of your flesh" ([ἡ] ἀκροβυστία τῆς σαρκὸς ὑμῶν, [he] akrobystia tēs sarkos hymōn, v. 13) suggesting the once-for-all redemptive act of Christ by which believers, through faith, have been made whole and clean by God (P. T. O'Brien, 2000). Yet, again, Paul's pastoral aim in this passage, indeed the whole epistle, is to call believers to continue to live in light of the salvific work of God by persevering in faith (v. 6; Moo, 2008). If the flesh were already wholly "put off," it is curious why Paul should exhort believers to "put to death what is earthly in you" (3:5; lit. your earthly parts; τὰ μέλη τὰ ἐπὶ τῆς γῆς, ta melē ta epi tēs gēs). Evidently, there are "parts" that, although eschatologically accounted for by God's grace, may yet need to be integrated into the believer's otherwise whole self.

43. The Greek word for "blessed" (μακάριος, makarios; cf. Pennington [2017], pp. 42–43), Danker (2001) cites as an antonym for "wretched" (ταλαίπωρος, talaipōros).

44. Jewett (1971) notes Paul's tendency to employ anthropological terminology inconsistently and unsystematically throughout his letters. Nevertheless, Harding (2016) helpfully reminds us regarding Paul's occasional lack of terminological consistency, "While recognizing that Paul's letters are not systematic theology, this does not entail that he did not possess consistent ideas" (p. 22; emphasis original).

Paul's psychology, in other words, is clear enough to Paul.

Minimally, what Paul observes in himself, and what he implicates in all of humanity, is an ongoing internal conflict brought about by the influence of sin to which we are pathologically and inescapably subject apart from our willing submission to the influence of Christ's Spirit (see Rom 8:10; cf. Jas 4:1). At any given moment, Paul's "I" may be operating either in an Adamic mode of autonomous self-sufficiency or in a Christic mode of perichoretic mutuality respective to the Spirit. Paul indicates, "I myself am [αὐτὸς ἐγὼ, *autos ego*]," which is to say, his inner self, is "enslaved [δουλεύω, *douleuō*] to the law of God *with the mind*," yet, simultaneously, paradoxically, "[enslaved] to the law of sin *with the flesh*" (7:25).[45] What determines the mode in which "I" operates is, for Paul, whether "I" permits "not I, but Christ" to enable and empower "my" choosing (8:2; cf. Gal 2:20).[46]

As the subsequent passage makes clear (Rom 8:1–13), Paul has found that a more salutary ethical outcome can be obtained—along with its concomitant psychotherapeutic benefit—by the believer's immediate and ongoing commitment to move in step, as it were, with the Spirit of Christ (v. 4; see Packer, 1999). This happy state of intersubjective mutuality has resulted for Paul in "life and peace" (v. 6). Clearly, though believers are continually at risk of operating "according to the flesh"—which is to say, autocentrically, *curvum in se*—our union with Christ has resulted in our eschatological deliverance from congenital autonomy and estrangement.

For the duration of the present age, we may operate in accordance with the mind and will of God's Spirit. All those who "live by the Spirit" may experience an anticipatory victory over "the flesh" as the outworking of their final eschatological reconciliation to God in Christ (v. 5). In

45. As Cooper (2000) explains, "When such terms are used in opposition, as flesh against spirit, they do not necessarily indicate different substances or structural constituents of humankind" (p. 103). Thus, to determine that the believers are literally two-selved—internally old *and* new—or two-natured—internally "flesh" *and* also "spirit"—carries Paul's rhetorical dichotomy too far (*pace* Roberts, 2001). Rather, for the duration of the present age believers have one metaphorically "split" inner self that, in contrast to the wholly estranged unbeliever, can operate within an Adamic or Christic mode at any given moment. (It is likely, in fact, that believers' every thought and action involves some mixture of both modes.) Following from Paul, the regenerate have a *single* nature which, having been renewed through union with Christ, remains in a state of conflict with the still-fallen outer self, yet is being renewed daily through active obedience to Christ (see Col 3:10).

46. Clearly, Paul considers that the unbeliever has no access to this second mode of being when it comes to obedience to and love for God's good law (Chamblin, 1993).

doing so, we exemplify a new Christic humanity defined and empowered by access to intimate interpersonal communion with God. Crucially, reconciliation does not mean that believers have somehow become autonomous selves now capable of standing on their own, as it were. Rather, as perichoretically indwelt selves, our newfound thinking, desiring, and choosing can occur only in active accession to the supervening presence of the divine Christ.

Furthermore, the ramifications of reconciliation to Christ include the repair, through the integration of self with the actively penetrating Spirit of God, of the intrapersonal fragmentation and dissociation Paul describes. In Christ, we become not only holy but whole, just as he is whole (cf. Heb 10:14). The human self that is truly united with Christ's self cannot remain forever schizoid, or else it would call into question the doctrine of reconciliation. And, evidently, Paul held that Christ is working to bring human persons into conformity with his own image (Rom 8:29; 12:2; cf. 1 Pet 1:14–16). Christiformity, the Spirit-enabled, diachronic work of Christ in the life of the believer, operates at both an ethical as well as a psychological level.[47] "Spiritual change," according to Roberts (2001), "is a *kind* of psychological change, namely psychological change brought about by . . . the work of the Holy Spirit in the life of the believer" (p. 163; emphasis original).

Regarding God's role in bringing about ethical and psychological change, Chamblin (1993) concludes, "For Paul . . . the Spirit's work is vital; persons cannot be made whole without it" (p. 98). In other words, the Pauline doctrine of union with Christ may not be reduced to a mere status or even an ethical determinant. Union with Christ signifies that, through the Spirit's working, Christ and the believing self now persist— mysteriously, ineffably—in a state of onto-relational unity, yet without destroying the personal idiosyncratic identities of either (see Col 1:27). What this demands of believers is nothing less than a full and mature agentic dedication to participation in and submission to the mind and will of the God–man (E. L. Johnson, 2017; see also, Fitzpatrick, 2013; Payne, 1995; cf. Campbell, 2012).

---

47. Due to the nature of our embodied existence, psychological transformation, over time, effects change at the neurobiological level as well (E. L. Johnson, 2017; see Siegel, 2012).

Conclusion to Part III

As early as the first century, Christian inquiry into the nature and form of the center of human subjectivity had, it would seem, already begun to take place. Though fairly rudimentary, psychological insights found in the Pauline oeuvre demonstrate the warrant for, and necessity of, a Christian understanding of the covenantal self and its limited, divided self-consciousness (see Chamblin, 1993; Roberts, 2001). Furthermore, what Paul observes in himself—his thoughts, his behavior—supplies ample justification for the development of a Christian psychology of self-knowledge.

Like Augustine, Paul engages in introspection and reflection on the nature of his inner self in relation to God (see Beck, 2002). Unlike Augustine, Paul does not identify his "inner man" with the soul, but with the covenantally embodied whole person who, having been united to Christ, now shares corporately in the life of the Spirit along with all other believers. Augustine's inward quest may have laid the historical groundwork for post/modern notions about the self. He can hardly be solely credited with its genesis, however.[48] Extant canonical reflections, perhaps best labeled as "seeds of the self" demonstrating understandings and experiences of individual human persons on their inner aspects, date from as early as the ancient poetry of Israel's chief lyricists.

In modern and postmodern expressions of Western Christianity, understandings of the self have taken an expressly non-Pauline turn toward autonomy on the one hand and heteronomy on the other (cf. Stendahl, 1963). As we should expect, neither modernist autocentricity nor postmodern exocentricity can offer the proper onto-relational balance for the Christian covenantal self. Christian psychology, assuming it begins with the biblical testimony regarding human persons, aims at the systematization of human knowledge regarding the subjective center of human personhood.

The ultimate aim of such systematization is not the system itself but the relationship to which covenantal Christian self-knowledge directs us. Covenant drives us to know self not merely with the mind/intellect or the soul/spirit, but as whole persons relationally conceived and agapically

---

48. Grenz (2001) rightly identifies the origins of modern philosophical notions concerning the self-as-soul/mind with Augustine's writings. The dichotomization of philosophical-psychological and biblical-theological frameworks for understanding the self, on the other hand, reflects a very modern and very un-Augustinian ideal.

oriented. As with Paul, so throughout Scripture, "Until the whole person is affected true knowledge has not occurred—whether one is speaking of knowing oneself, knowing other people, or knowing God" (Chamblin, 1993, p. 49). Genuine communion with God, with others, and, yes, *with self* remains beyond the grasp of the autonomous, schizoid self of fallen human beings. Whereas, by means of Christ's active mediatorial influence working along each relational axis, we come to know ourselves as God intends.

Part IV

Christian Self-Knowledge, Sin, & Psychopathology

Chapter 7

A Christian psychopathology
of self-knowledge

IN ARRIVING VIA CHRISTOLOGY at a definition of the self—one that is ontologically grounded yet relationally contingent—we essentially bypass a quarter-millennium of philosophical and psychological handwringing over the matter. As it turns out, modern philosophical inquiry has advanced very little since Hume's (1746) failed attempt to locate the self within any real or metaphorical internal "space." The reasons for this should, by now, be clear: human beings have an ineradicable sense of particular selfhood—a *me*-ness that is experientially linked to the knowable realities attendant to our embodied existence. These realities entail both our inner and outer essences—*psyche* and *soma*, mind/soul and body. Yet, the individual sense of selfhood is forever dependent on correspondence to others, not any formal possession or trait (McFadyen, 1990).

Augustine's inward quest centered on the soul as the seat of subjectivity leading to modernist perspectives on the self as a solely internal (i.e., psychospiritual) reality (Grenz, 2001; C. Taylor, 1989). Modernist anthropology, following Descartes, sought out the self in the mind. Postmodernist psychology, on the other hand, "locates" the self, not in any formal constituent, but in an individual's relationally conceived *sense* of self (see Harter, 2015). Yet, these understandings of self ineluctably truncate what it means to be a human person created in the image of God. My self is *all* of me, not any *part* of me. Nor should we collapse who-I-am and who-I-believe-myself-to-be into equivalence. If *me*-ness cannot be reduced to any formal constituent or attribute without effacing some aspect of its ethical bearing, neither can a psychological construct bear any ethical status. Self-concepts do not act!

As biblical anthropology demonstrates, it is whole persons, covenantally conceived, upon whom God has conferred his imago and with whom he seeks communion. The ethical bearing of human selfhood, and therefore self-knowledge, is not merely inward, or even inward and upward, but rather inward, upward, and outward. And the knowable aspects of self—who-I-am—including its developmentally construed sense of idiosyncrasy—who-I-believe-myself-to-be—all serve the ethical bearing of covenantal selfhood—an eschatological *becoming* implicated by the image of God and inaugurated through reconciliation to God-in-Christ.

By establishing the self *in se* in terms of its being-in-relation to God and to others, it becomes possible to escape the epistemological cul-de-sac of post/modernist philosophical anthropology (see Bonhoeffer, 1996, 1998).[1] As it happens, this appears to have been the primary concern of William James (1961, 2012) whose distinction of I-self and me-self, or self-as-subject and self-as-object, greatly contributed, along with others, to the birth of contemporary self and social psychologies (Goethals & Strauss, 1991; Harter, 2015). Only God's knowledge of human persons will ever be exhaustive, yet *some* aspects of ourselves are indeed knowable. Moreover, in consideration of Scripture, a Christian approach to self-knowledge will emphasize not merely knowing self-as-it-is, but self-as-it-ought-to-be in light of the person and work of Christ.

When considered christologically, the human self is both an ontological given and an ethical imperative. Selfhood, therefore, is an expression

1. Harré (1998), in reiterating Hume's paradox, argues, "[The self] is not visible to a phenomenological scrutinizing of one's own subjectivity. . . . It is not available to private introspection, . . . [nor to] public inspection. . . . The self I seek is the self that seeks, so it seems that it is impossible to make introspective contact with myself" (p. 81, cf. also Ryle, 1949). Nor, indeed, should we expect any better outcome from the absurdly reductive quest to locate the self within the brain—a fact atheist apologist Daniel Dennett (1991) only confirms: "Searching for the self can be somewhat like [this]. You enter the brain through the eye, march up the optic nerve, round and round in the cortex, looking behind every neuron, and then, before you know it, you emerge into daylight on the spike of a motor nerve impulse, scratching your head and wondering where the self is" (p. 355). Yet, unless one grants Dennett's physicalist cosmology, such a search can hardly be deemed rigorous (or scientifically sound). A non-existent self, in fact, becomes a tautology in such a truncated epistemological framework. As it happens, venerable philosophical arguments linking self and "soul" seem to have prefigured more recent—and similarly misguided—attempts to link self and brain (see Neisser, 1997). Nevertheless, as demonstrated in the previous chapter, the self will not be so easily dispatched.

or extension of covenantal personhood. Like Christ, all human beings possess both an image bearing status and, consequently, selfhood, yet we fulfill the ethical imperative of our status only in proper relation to God and to others. Unlike Christ, human beings enter the world estranged from God and congenitally *curvum in se*. We need a mediator to reconcile us to the Father—a reconciliation the Savior obtained for us once for all time at the cross (Heb 10:10).

Christ's invitation to true personhood assumes a requisite knowledge of God, self, and others. Agapic relationality with God and others makes such knowledge possible (cf. McFadyen, 1990). In the absence of such knowledge, humanity's ethical calling is doomed from the start. Herein, human autonomy is revealed for what it is: a curse. Without love, there can be no knowledge; but without knowledge, however shall we love? Paul's observations regarding the ethical impotence of his autonomous inner self—his divided, discontinuous ἔσω ἄνθρωπον (*esō anthrōpon*; Rom 7:22; cf. 2 Cor 4:16; Eph 3:16)—dramatically illustrate this point (cf. Theissen, 1987). We are in need of saving from the estrangement in which we are ensnared!

God, in granting his Son as our means of reconciliation, offers to humanity an escape from our hereditary self-blindness and pathological self-love. By means of our union with Christ through the Spirit we enter a renewed, redeemed relational dynamic with God and others (Rom 8:1–39). Christ now lives in us; we now live in him. The implications of this "Christiform personhood" are astounding. Formerly fallen—relationally broken, estranged, crippled in our autonomy—we may now embody and enact the same covenantal telos of personhood from which we fell. In perichoretic relation to Christ, empowered by Christ's Spirit, we come to know and love, love and know, *in* Christ. Given the proper conditions, human persons indwelt by Christ come to enact this dialogical dynamic in relation to others. In other words we may become mirrors for others—mirrors of self, as it were—albeit contingently, instrumentally.

The implications of God's agenda of reconciliation through the person and work of Christ entail the displacement of all relationally induced barriers to self-knowledge. As the next two chapters will demonstrate, however, these barriers to veridical self-knowledge may be considerable. Ethical and psychogenic in nature, obfuscations and obstructions often reinforce each other. This is to say that there are times when I'd rather not know who-I-am, while at other times I cannot know. *Something* is blocking my view. Seeing clearly, veridically can be a complex undertaking.

To be clear, self-knowledge, even among believers, will continue to remain limited by human finitude and prone to error due to remaining sin. Furthermore, barriers to self-knowledge may also arise from a host of psychopathologies to which the fallen human self is susceptible. Therefore, the two primary impediments to veridical knowledge of self—sin and psychopathology—are best understood when considered dialogically. Inasmuch as these barriers may be located in contraventions of the covenantal self-in-relation—which is to say, lapses in agapic inter/subjectivity—their remediation lies in repairing such breeches. In short order, I will turn to the task of identifying these ethical and psychogenic barriers to self-knowledge.

Christology and transdisciplinary discourse

The gospel of the incarnate Word demonstrates that God has not willed for humanity to stand silent before him for all time (see Rom 8:15). To the contrary, the Word was made flesh precisely in order to reverse the estrangement between God and humanity that our sin had created—to remove the infinite interstice our rebellion precipitated. Christ in his person and work reveals the divine initiative to bring about rapprochement between divinity and humanity, the resumption of agapic fellowship and discourse (Bonhoeffer, 2005). Though humanity's sin and rebellion will continue to threaten this fellowship until the end of the present age, the people of God are called to bear witness to his reconciling work in their own commitment to incarnational communion and dialogue (König, 1989).

Orthodox Christology discloses the mystery of God's eternal design—the joining of divinity and humanity in the person of Christ in order to bring about a universal reconciliation (Col 1:20; Barth, 2010). At a disciplinary level, this means Christian theology will contribute to other disciplines to the degree that it is intrinsically appropriate;[2] and conversely, Christian theology should also listen to and learn from the natural and, especially, human sciences, biblically conceived (Clark, 2010; Johnson, 2010; cf. Hunsinger, 1995). The implications of orthodox Christology should be clear: what God has joined together in the person

___

2. By this I mean, e.g., philosophy to a greater degree than the human sciences, and the human sciences more so than the natural sciences.

and work of Christ, neither Christian theology nor Christian anthropology proper should seek to separate (cf. Matt 19:6).[3]

Christian psychology as dialogue

In the context of any transdisciplinary dialogue, an exchange of roles must eventually take place wherein speaker becomes listener and teacher becomes learner (see Bakhtin, 1986; Williams, 2001). This is how dialogue works. Consequently, when considering the nature of the self and its knowledge, theology may be permitted to speak first. Our being made in the image of God surely suggests as much. Yet, the principal of dialogue demands that consideration also be given to psychology—the discipline concerned primarily with the creaturely existence of human beings and their empirically observable aspects (see D. F. Ford, 2007).

Although psychology, as with all the human disciplines, should yield the place of primacy to theology in a Christian scheme of things, it must still be given opportunity to reply constructively.[4] As Clark (2010) explains, "In such a dialogue, theology can, within certain parameters, properly speak to science, and science can, within proper limits, rightly address theology" (p. 284; cf. Hiebert, 2008).[5] To which we may add, by

3. Hunsinger (1995), in applying a Barthian theanthropology to the question of transdisciplinary dialogue, draws the opposite inference: "[T]heology and psychology represent material that cannot be integrated into a unified whole" (p. 6). And yet, seemingly she contradicts this premise immediately thereafter: "Both perspectives are fully a part of the pastoral counselor, that is, they are integrated into the *person*" (p. 6, emphasis original). It seems to me that Hunsinger has rightly objected the overly facile and ill-considered use to which "integration" language is too often applied. Yet, in observing that there are, in fact, justifiable uses of the term, Hunsinger undermines the strength of her argument. If material from two disciplines *can* be integrated in the person of the pastoral counselor, what then is the final reason for saying the two *cannot* be integrated? Perhaps better to say, as I have sought to argue, that, analogous with the natures of Christ, the two disciplines remain in some sense unmixed and unconfused, yet they nevertheless coinhere inseparably, indivisibly in one epistemic whole (as they certainly must in the mind of God). Consequently, the two disciplines may interact discursively through transdisciplinary dialogue, a fact Barthian scholar Daniel J. Price (2002) recognizes—and for which Hunsinger commends him (see pp. 45–46)!

4. Following Barth, Christology is properly foundational to anthropology. The dialectical relationship between theology and anthropology is hierarchical—the former being first, therefore, among equals.

5. It may be natural to question whether the principal of dialogue between theological and anthropological disciplines undermines the doctrines of Scripture's authority and sufficiency. Clark (2010) deftly answers this concern: "Suppose a scientific idea

looking to Christ—whose person and work bear both ontological and epistemological implications—we may better grasp the imprimatur for a Christian commitment to the principal of transdisciplinary discourse.

As a branch of Christian inquiry, Christian psychology distinguishes itself from modern psychology in its metadisciplinary commitments to the epistemological primacy of Scripture *and* the principal of dialogue between the divine and human sciences (E. L. Johnson, 2007; Roberts, 1993; cf. Kuyper, 1968). When properly executed, this dialogue allows "Christians [to] speak in their own voice from the strength of their own psychology, the psychology inherent in the Bible and Christian tradition, and thus as full participants converse with the reigning psychologies of our day" (Roberts, 1993, p. 13). Christian psychology is, therefore, committed to its core to the priorities of an expressly theological anthropology. In other words, although the object of all psychological inquiry is, by definition, the human person, Christian psychology denies any modernist attempt to sequester human beings from the appropriate questions and concerns of Christian faith and praxis.

Christian theology is right to question the findings of *modern* psychology due to the latter's disciplinary commitment to epistemological and disciplinary monologism; yet, it would surely be a gospel sin to renounce every Christian effort to engage dialogically with psychological perspectives that regard human beings as the Bible does—created in the image of God for communion with him and with one another in and through the person of Jesus Christ (cf. Wells, 2007).[6] Christian

gains so much warrant that as a community of theologians, we agree it is necessary to alter some theological belief. That does not necessarily mean that science has superseded Scripture. More precisely, we place a particular scientific idea or theory into conversation with a particular theological tradition, model, or doctrine. That is, we bring *interpretations of Scripture*—theology—into conversation with *interpretations of nature*—science. So, we do not allow science to supersede the Bible itself. We allow it to override *interpretations* of the Bible. . . . [T]heology is a human interpretation of the Bible. Science, therefore, can rightly speak to theology" (p. 286; emphasis original). In contemporary parlance, "science" has become synonymous with phenomenological observation, rational analysis of empirical data, and the systematization of findings. A Kuyperian definition of science, by way of contrast, does not dichotomize the "data" found in revelation from that observable in creation (Kuyper, 1968; cf. Bartholomew, 2017). Reformed epistemology, following Augustine, has traditionally regarded both as valid sources of knowledge (Van Til, 1969). Evidently, Clark (2010) has yielded to the modern idiomatic dichotomization of "theology" and "science." I avoid such usage, preferring instead to speak of theological and anthropological "sciences," respectively (see McGrath, 2006).

6. Along the same lines, historian E. Brooks Holifield (2005) argues that pastoral

psychology, then, extends the implications of reconciliation into the domain of epistemology. What we may know of human beings, we come to know *through* dialogue.

Modern psychology and monological discourse

Modern psychology and psychotherapy, by way of contrast, have increasingly operated with a fundamentally schizoid philosophical and disciplinary "self"-understanding. In light of the fall of the self of Platonic/ Cartesian dualism and the dearth of any philosophical warrant for its existence, modern psychology has been essentially stripped of both its epistemological basis and axiological aim: the care and cure of human beings. After all, if there is no substantial "I" to be found behind the visible, knowable "me," who or what then is the object of psychotherapeutic concern? If the self is *merely* an exocentric consequence of the various environmental and contextual dynamics in which human individuals are situated, then surely psychological cure can be reduced to the bare manipulation of those external forces and inputs.[7]

To the contrary, existential and self psychologies, depth psychologies, and other related systems, persist in their presumption of the existence of a subjective center of psychological activity operating within a dialectic of autocentric activity and exocentric responsivity. Human beings, according to much of modern psychology, are more than the sum of their material parts. Not just a collection of biological imperatives or libidinal drives, there is *someone* behind or within—an interpersonal subject who acts and reacts with meaning and purpose, though often at a deeper level than may be directly apperceived or reflexively intuited

---

theologians "are better served when they live in both [discursive realms], letting each check the imperialistic tendencies of the other, than when they smooth out the differences or assume that religious and psychological concepts merely designate the same reality with different words. Of course, the two realms of discourse are not absolutely distinct. If they were, one realm could not in any way illumine the other. But the best illumination often occurs through emphasis on their differences" (p. 355).

7. The rise of behaviorism and, to a lesser extent, cognitive psychology in the twentieth century are strong indicators that such a shift did, in fact, occur (see Jones & Butman, 2011; van Leeuwen, 1982). Behaviorists such as Skinner (1976) and Wolpe (1978) consistently rejected the notion of any subjective center of agency from which human behavior and cognition arise. Whether or not such views ring true with human experience, they nevertheless distinguish themselves by remaining consistent with a modernist epistemology driven exclusively by positivist priorities.

(see Goethals & Strauss, 1991; Harré, 1998; Neisser, 1997). Most secular psychologies assume as much, and rightly so. Yet, modern psychologies can never supply, at least on their own terms, a sufficient explanation for the existence of this deep-level subjectivity—the *why* and *how* of what we are (cf. Leary, 2004).

What is needed, and what Christian psychology supplies, is a perspective on human beings grounded in divine revelation and which finds its fulfilment and ideal expression in Jesus Christ. Created in the image of the triune God for fellowship with him, we are what we are unto God's glory alone (Johnson, 2017). Furthermore, we embody this image through covenantal union with and doxological response to the God who reveals himself in Christ. Christian psychology, with its rich understanding of persons as created in the image of God and accountable to him, seeks to apprehend the complexities of the human self in both theological and psychological terms.

Epistemologically situated at the intersection of divine revelation and human subjectivity, Christian psychology provides a much-needed transdisciplinary bridge between the two. Respective to the antinomy of the covenantal self-in-relation these two discrete yet related perspectives—theology and psychology—have much to offer each other. More than this, when properly related, the two demonstrate the proper epistemological application of the person and work of the God–man, Jesus Christ. Jesus reconciles God and human beings; in Christ, then, we discern our divine warrant for dialogue between theology and psychology.

Inaugurated eschatology and the covenantal self

United to Christ through faith, the covenantal human self assumes a diachronic, eschatological trajectory (Grenz, 2001; Horton, 2005). We *are*; yet, in Christ we are *becoming*. In order that we might better fulfill our image-bearing mandate, God has granted believers access in Christ to a "treasury" of wisdom and knowledge (Col 2:3), including among other things the perichoretic knowledge of God, self, and others (see Bonhoeffer, 1996, 2001). In other words, Christ grants us the ability to know even as we are known. To be sure, for the duration of the present age believers know only "in part"; whereas, in the age to come we will know more "fully" (1 Cor 13:12). Both now and in the age to come, we fulfill the agapic telos of our personhood when exercising the gifts of perichoretic knowledge. Furthermore, when we come mutually, reciprocally to a greater knowledge of God and self, we simultaneously share perichoretically in God's own life and joy (John 17:3).[8]

In contrast to ancient and modern paradigms, human wellbeing is not, strictly speaking, the primary aim of *Christian* self-knowledge. Eudaimonia or wellbeing arises eschatologically as a benefit of a genuinely agapic relationality.[9] Granted, humanity's first parents sought their wellbeing through knowledge. Yet, they sought it autonomously and so fell into sin and death. In seeking what only God can offer, they fell out of communion with the Source of all they sought! Pursued as an end in itself, human flourishing, like autonomous self-knowledge, is ultimately self-defeating. Yet, Christ offers his own perichoretic knowledge of the Father to fallen, sinful human beings by means of their Spirit-mediated, faith-enacted union with him.

The telos of Christian self-knowledge, on the other hand, is love— for God, for others, and for self. Only conditioned and innervated by love can human beings avoid the snare of autonomy into which Adam and Eve fell, and humanity along with them. Christians need not eschew the pursuit of eudaimonia in favor of an agapist ethics; yet, we are nonetheless called to model the eschatological conviction of Christ himself "who for the joy that was set before him endured the cross, despising the shame" (Heb 12:2). The joy and rest promised to believers comes not from its direct pursuit, but through our union and conformity to Christ (Luke 9:24).

Inaugurated eschatology suggests a persistent schism in believers' experience of redemption for the duration of the present age (Gaffin, 2013; Schreiner, 2008). What Christ's atoning death has finally purchased on our behalf—reconciliation between God and humanity—believers

---

8. Objective or propositional knowledge of God, by way of contrast, offers no such benefit, though it certainly obtains in the context of subjective knowledge (i.e., Rahner's nonobjective consciousness). In other words, in coming to know God better we will undoubtedly come to know more *about* God; the inverse, however, is not necessarily true.

9. New Testament ethics is not eudaimonist but agapic (see Wolterstorff, 2015). The telos of Christian ethics is love (Matt 22:37–40; John 15:12–15); whereas, eschatological wellbeing or "blessedness" arises as an inter/subjective benefit of Christian ethics, rightly applied. A hierarchical dialectic, therefore, best characterizes the relationship between agapist and eudaimonist perspectives. The former entails the latter, but not vice versa.

receive as a simultaneously present and future reality.[10] Whereas, "in Christ," we have been granted "every spiritual blessing in the heavenly places" (Eph 1:3); in another sense, Christians still await the eschatological deliverance of our final "inheritance" (v. 14). Therefore, though we "have died" to sin and our life is presently "hidden with Christ in God" (Col 3:3), believers must still "put to death what is earthly" in us (v. 5). In other words, until the final appearing of Christ, believers will continue to experience an internal opposition of contradictory dynamics (Johnson, 2017).

Even after conversion, Christians will struggle with a proneness toward autonomy; they will be inclined toward estrangement from God though they have, in Christ, been reconciled already and granted an everlasting communion with him through the Spirit. Packer (1999), in describing the "frame of 'inaugurated eschatology,'" concludes,

> [T]hrough the Spirit Christians enjoy the firstfruits, foretaste, initial installment, and dawning enjoyment of the life of the new aeon, the kingdom era of redeemed existence, while the old aeon, the era of existence spoiled by sin, continues, and the fullness of new aeon life remains future. The two ages overlap, and Christians are anchored in both, so that language proper to both is appropriate, indeed necessary, for describing their condition theologically. (p. 77)

Consequently, the self of the believing individual will bear characteristics of both the new and old ages. As of the moment of believers' reconciliation to God by faith in Christ, we possess a "'new self'" that "represents what [we] are in Christ instead of what [we] are in Adam"; just the same, this gift demands that we continually "put off the old person and put on the new" (Schreiner, 2008, pp. 31–32; see Eph 4:22–24).

---

10. So, Barth (2010), "The restoration, renewal and fulfilment of the covenant between God and man in the atonement made and revealed in Jesus Christ is complete as man's justification as a covenant-partner and his sanctification to be a covenant-partner, as the establishment and formation of the fellowship between himself and God, just as God's creation was perfect as the beginning of all His ways with the created order. But, like creation, it is not an end but a beginning—complete in itself and as such, but still a beginning" (IV/1, p. 109).

The relationship between sin and self-knowledge

When paired with a biblical understanding of the person and work of Christ, the doctrine of hereditary sin provides an illuminating and compelling hermeneutical framework with respect to the problem of human sin (see Goldsworthy, 2010). Generally, sin consists of opposition, rather than accession, to the innate God-oriented dynamic of the human self (Barth, 2010; Bavinck, 2006; Calvin, 2008; Edwards, 2009). Hereditary or "original" sin is nothing less than the universal tendency of all those descended from Adam to resist and oppose God (see Rom 5:12; Augustine, 2012b; Owen, 2006; Pascal, 1995; Sanlon, 2014). Notwithstanding the apparent anaphylaxis of modernism, the classical doctrine of original sin has nevertheless been reasonably defended against its detractors (Madueme & Reeves, 2014; McFadyen, 2000; cf. Barth, 2010, IV/1, pp. 478–79). Evidently, the doctrine strikes a dissonant chord with more favorable estimations of human nature (see, e.g., Williams, 2001). Nonetheless, it possesses tremendous explanatory power with respect to the so-called "problem of evil" (Blocher, 1999), and the inclination of all human beings toward interpersonal evil (see Doriani, 2014; cf. Herman, 2015).

The doctrine of original sin is indispensable, in fact, for apprehending the source of this pandemic in human ecology (cf. John 3:19; Rom 3:10–18). The permutations of human resistance to God are myriad—its devastating effects pervasive. Sin insults and effaces the divine image in humanity, deforms the self, disrupts its relations, and inhibits its God-oriented dynamic. Apart from God's work in Christ by which he resists our resistance to him—that is, his grace—human beings cannot overcome their sinful inclinations (see Rom 7:15–25).[11]

Thanks to our union with Christ as effected by the indwelling Spirit believers are redeemed from slavery to sin and reconciled to God (Rom 5:11). Though born estranged, we are adopted by God and granted the means to resist our own oppositional defiance (Rom 8:5–13). The happy result of this new state and status is that veridical self-knowledge is possible for the believer actively walking in step with the Spirit. Nevertheless,

11. The question of hereditary sin's "transmission" has occupied theologians since Augustine suggested a biological basis (i.e., traducianism; Augustine, 2012b; cf. Blocher, 1999). Under a covenantal anthropology no such theory of transmission is necessary. In other words, hereditary sin need not be "located" in any constitutive incapacity if its basis is covenantal. The reason all sin who are descended from Adam may be because, on Adam's account, all in Adam are born estranged from God (see Schreiner, 2008).

for the duration of the present age, believers' knowledge of self, as with the knowledge of God, will remain limited chiefly by two influences: remaining sin and psychopathology.[12]

Other factors may also impede growth in self-knowledge.[13] For example, brain trauma can severely limit one's capacity for knowledge of God and self. Evidently, damage that is rooted in somatic injury is far less responsive to the gospel than are sin and certain forms of psychopathology (Johnson, 2017; Stanford, 2017). Though God-in-Christ is "making all things new" (Rev 21:5), some varieties of biopsychosocial damage will be reversed only in the age to come. Barriers stemming from ethical and psychogenic sources may, in fact, prove as intransigent as brain trauma in certain cases. Given that Scripture focuses on these two, however, they will occupy the present discussion.

In otherwise mature, response-able agents, sin and psychopathology cultivate and perpetuate self-ignorance. As suggested already, self-blindness amounts to an estrangement from self that inheres in the autonomous self, its vertical and horizontal relational axes having been disrupted by the fall. In coming to Christ believers gain access, through Christ, to the gifts of self- and other/Other-knowledge to the extent that love conditions our pursuit. Sin—offense against the covenantal calling of image bearers—in addition to disrupting communion along these two axes, deprives self of self-knowledge as well. The ethical nature of certain barriers to self-knowledge stems from their source in sinful motives and actions.

---

12. Clearly, sin can be construed as a form, indeed the quintessential form, of psychopathology (Johnson, 2017). One reason for distinguishing between them, as I have done here, is the strong connection—both agentically and semantically—between sin and moral culpability. This connection is not necessarily entailed by other forms of psychopathology (see McRay et al., 2016). It may be that speaking of sin as psychopathology softens distinctions between the two that are best not softened. To avoid confusion on this point, and also so that I might describe the relationship between sin and other forms of psychopathology, I will distinguish between them. Finally, a distinction is also helpful in advance of enumerating in Part V discrete ethical imperatives and pastoral agendas respective to each.

13. In additional to these two, three further barriers to self-knowledge may be noted: neurological damage (i.e., brain trauma), cognitive or intellectual limitations (due to, say, genetic abnormalities), and, of course, human finiteness. These factors potentially mitigate growth in self-knowledge. Evidently, with our resurrected, glorified bodies we will be subject to far fewer limitations, both physically and cognitively. It is safe to assume, however, that we will never know everything there is to know about either God or ourselves (though cf. 1 Cor 13:12).

Psychogenic barriers, on the other hand, are often the result of others' sins *against* self. To be clear psychopathology, when understood within a christological anthropology, should be interpreted not simply as deprivations or deformations in an otherwise healthy, autonomous self. Rather, it follows as the sequela of estrangement—a consequence of humanity's relationally fallen state and status.[14] Interpersonal sin marks the self; wounds inflicted by others all too often leave scars. The self that is cut off from perichoretic communion along its horizontal axis will suffer the pain of disunion and isolation. Psychopathology, therefore, is often the result of the dislocation of the fallen inner self, not just from proper onto-relation to God, but also to others made in his image. God has created us in need of love from each other.

The tripersonal nature of the Godhead cannot be disrupted by discord or disunity: the three Persons of the Trinity are *one* (Rom 3:30; Gal 3:20; Jas 2:19; cf. Deut 6:4). To be otherwise would obviate God's nature. For human persons created in God's image, our sin-induced estrangement from God and other has resulted in the death of our ability to fully image, and thus benefit from, an analogous human being-in-relation. So long as we are not one with God, oneness with each other will likewise escape us. The result of our fractured oneness is that fallen human beings bear within themselves a corrupted and corrupting nature (Bavinck, 2006). True and lasting communion eludes us. Estrangement, on the other hand, is endemic.

This is not to say that human beings are all bad. The image of God in us prompts us to seek out genuine oneness—intimacy with some higher power and with other human beings. Like the Apostle Paul, we often want to do good. Yet, every transgression against our intended design—that by which we were to have reflected God's own nature within creation—further effaces the imaging capacity of all that it touches. The more we sin against each other, the more we damage what remains of God's image in us. We are broken and breaking each other.

This image-corroding dynamic is most directly observable in the degree to which developmental factors contribute etiologically to a wide diversity of psychopathological conditions (see Flanagan & Hall, 2014). In a real sense developmental disorders illustrate and give evidence to a myriad of ways "the sins of the fathers" are visited on successive

---

14. This is not to say that all psychopathology is related to one's own personal sinfulness (cf. John 9:1–7). For example, genetic abnormalities and noetic deficiencies, along with cancer and hurricanes, are best understood as consequences of the fall.

generations (see Lev 26:39). The bitter fruit of human interpersonal evil manifests in sin's destructive legacy. The predictable result of this stark reality can be observed in the remarkable depth and variety of psycho-pathological damage and disarray encountered in human beings.[15] Finally, in terms of the individual self, we may expect the severity of its extant pathologies to correlate closely with the degree of adversity and affliction suffered along its horizontal axis. The more damage done by others, the more damaged the self will be. Psychogenic barriers make growth in self-knowledge a challenging pursuit.

Perspectives on sin and the self

In referring to sin as "the ultimate relational disorder," Johnson (2017) suggests the extent to which it distorts and damages the self (p. 218). Yet, the connection between sin and the various psychopathologies of the covenantal self-in-relation is decidedly complex. Respective to the knowledge of self, sin and its psychopathological sequelae contribute significant barriers. With characteristic erudition Barth (2010) enumer-ates three ways in which sin disrupts the relational axes between self and Other/others. Drawing on Augustine and Calvin, he defines sin as "negation," which is to say humanity's "active opposition to the God who actively encounters [us]" (IV/1, p. 142). This negation takes three forms.

First, sin most obviously assumes the form of "pride" (p. 143)—a presumption of autonomous stature, a self-seeking that, if left unchecked, leads to rebellion against the divine command (see Isa 14:12–20). Sin arouses in humanity a fatal hubris that knows yet rejects the call to obe-dience. The second form taken by sin Barth labels "sloth"—the passive tendency toward moral and psychological "disorder" that inverts the call to be active, participatory image-bearers. Out of an internal resistance to the good, human beings come to repose in a willfulness that refuses

---

15. There are at least two senses in which psychopathology extends as a conse-quence of sin. In the first psychopathology arises as the direct result of personal sin, whether my own or as the sequelae left by those who sin against me (see Herman, 2015). In another sense, however, psychopathology arises in many cases not due to any moral fault or interpersonal transgression, but on account of humanity's fallen state. Like the blind man encountered by Jesus' disciples (John 9:1–7), such individuals suffer from a *dis-ease* of the self or illness of the mind that arises strictly organically. That this sort of suffering exists, like the man's blindness, points us all the way back to the fall as its root cause (Stump, 2012).

not to fall. We know the good we must do, yet do it not (Jas 4:17; cf. Rom 1:21; 7:16).

Third and finally, sin, according to Barth, takes the form of "falsehood." "[W]e are all incorrigible liars," he confesses. Telling ourselves that we know better than God, we deceive ourselves concerning our own judgments, our faculties of perception, and our personal moral caliber. So, Barth concludes, "Because man and the world live under the dominion of sin, lying to God and deceiving themselves, they live in self-destruction" (p. 144). Evidently, humanity's sin-induced estrangement from God is *not* simply doing the wrong thing. Rather, sin assumes at least three expressions. These three, I argue, correspond with three stages through which the human self is led to its eventual demise.

Rebellion leads to estrangement

According to Barth (2010), pride arouses, and arises from, an oppositional dynamic which, when consummated in a rebellious act, disrupts communion. Although created for agapic fellowship with the triune God and with each other, every human being has, with the sole exception of Jesus Christ, universally undermined and disrupted that fellowship through sin (see also Bavinck, 2006; Calvin, 2008; Kierkegaard, 1980). "All have sinned," the apostle avers, "and fall short of the glory of God" (Rom 3:9). What God intended as the pinnacle of his creative effort was that humanity should serve as his visible image—to bear in themselves some measure of his splendor and to reflect it outward (Gen 1:26; Ps 8; Edwards, 2006). Yet, our capacity to fulfill this vocation has ever been linked to obedience: "In the day you eat of it," God had warned the man, "you shall surely die" (Gen 2:17; cf. John 14:15; 1 John 3:4).

In spite of his warning, they ate. In their ultimate "act of defiance" (Barth, 2010, IV/1, p. 143) against the God in whose image they had been made, they overthrew any confidence in his trustworthiness. They sought autonomous rule over themselves as well as knowledge through autonomous means.[16] And so, they fell. Evidently, the "death" into which they fell amounted to a state of pathological estrangement—a relational rupture that has had devastating and pandemic repercussions for humanity

---

16. The tree they ate bore the fruit of "the knowledge of good and evil." Eve was tempted, in part, when she discerned "that the tree was to be desired to make one wise" (Gen 3:6).

(Rom 5:12; cf. Calvin, 2008). Since their fall, all who trace their descent from Adam live in a sort of half-life. Having only the appearance of life, they live in a perpetual state of spiritual death (see Eph 2:1; Col 2:13).[17]

In light of the biblical account of humanity's fall, it seems that the first man and his wife descended into a kind of sub-human existence resulting from their covenant-rupturing act of disobedience. If human persons fulfill their image-bearing vocation only in agapic relationality, then cut off as we are from fellowship with God and each other, we become somehow less than human. The self, rendered ethically impotent by sin, can never autonomously attain to full humanity due to its sin-induced estrangement. Furthermore, the breech affecting their communion with God has had equally dire consequences for human relationality.

Upon eating the fruit, Adam and Eve began immediately to exhibit signs of the corruption of their self- and other-understandings. Formerly, they felt no shame in spite of being naked (Gen 2:25). Having eaten the fruit, they desperately sought to hide their nakedness (3:7). As a consequence of human sin, any quest for authenticity and intimacy in human relationships is now more difficult. More than this, both the man and his wife attempted to shift blame for wrongdoing, each pointing the finger elsewhere in an effort to evade responsibility (3:12–13). Their ability to accurately assess blameworthiness had become compromised by defensiveness. Both preferred to search out the speck in another's eye than the plank in their own (cf. Matt 7:3).

Their latter state, along with all who are descended from Adam and Eve, came to be characterized by the "fundamental reversal of all

17. Exegetical attempts to set aside the veracity of the promised penalty—"on the day you eat . . . you will surely die" (Gen 2:17)—represent a misunderstanding of the kind of "death" to which God was referring (see Weeks, 2014; Wenham, 1987). If the imago is strictly constitutive, then death might be understood exclusively as the cessation of somatic vitality; whereas, the covenantal imago strongly suggests another sort of death, namely, a sin-wrought estrangement from God. Any argument that Adam and Eve would have interpreted God "literally" begs the question as to whether they could have understood death in *any* sense having never witnessed it. Although he interprets the death Adam and Eve suffered metaphorically, Wenham (1987) nevertheless asserts rightly, "[E]xpulsion from the garden was an even more drastic kind of death" (p. 74). To be sure, Paul is not speaking metaphorically when he declares to the Colossian believers, "And you, who were dead in your trespasses and the uncircumcision of your flesh, God made alive together with him, having forgiven us all our trespasses" (Col 2:13; see also Eph 2:1, 5). From this we may reasonably conclude that the expiration of the body is but a taste of the everlasting torment brought about by one's final estrangement from God (see Matt 10:28; Rev 20:14–15).

relationships" (Bavinck, 2006, p. 126). Sin's ultimate consequence is final, spiritual death, yet it also lies in the present age beneath all forms of human suffering and isolation, whether actual or perceived. As Stump (2012) observes, "The proclivity to moral wrongdoing is enough to guarantee that willed loneliness is common to human beings, affecting relations both among human persons and also between human persons and God" (p. 150). The damage wrought by the fall has broken us apart from God and from each other.

From estrangement to brokenness

Rebellion disrupts communion leading to a form of death that is not physical, yet inflicts upon the self-in-relation an even more profound and enduring injury.[18] The estrangement that follows from the loss of communion—with God and with others—inexorably leads to *internal* fragmentation and dis-integration. What interpersonal estrangement wreaks on relationships comes to be reflected *intra*personally as well. In other words, intrapersonal discontinuity and disarray—subjective brokenness—is the inevitable outworking of interpersonal sin. The covenantal basis for this supposition is clear: human beings can only be considered truly human within the context of our Spirit-mediated communion with God. We should expect, therefore, that the fallen, sub-human existence into which we are born will be attended by a diverse array of psychopathologies—malformations of the God-imaging capacities of persons.

Moreover, as a fallen humanity multiplies and fills the earth, so too should we expect to discern a parallel inflation in the inter- and intrapersonal infirmities characteristic of corruption (cf. Gen 6:1–5). Brokenness propagates brokenness. Beneath the reality of this tendency there lies a grim reality: psychospiritual damage often compounds the moral incapacity of the self leading to the increased likelihood of the perpetuation of damage (cf. Rom 1:18–32). The injuries of one generation upon the next, unless God intercedes, will be inflicted and amplified in generations to come. Rebellion begets estrangement begets brokenness begets rebellion, and so on *ad infinitum*. Humanity, if left to its own devices, will eventually self-annihilate.

---

18. God has promised to reverse physical death at the return of Christ. All who, due to their rebellion, are finally estranged from him will suffer eternal separation from God (Matt 25:46).

An important caveat regarding the relationship of sin and self-knowledge is needed here. The nature of interpersonal sin is suggestive an asymmetry wherein perpetrator and victim possess disparate levels of agency. The inability of perpetrator and victim to veridically self-perceive may look the same. Yet, crucially, the brokenness of the victim is very different than that of the perpetrator. In other words, two individuals with similar psychopathological sequelae may, in fact, have very different etiologies. While one person's struggle may stem from sinful choices, a second individual could potentially wrestle with similar brokenness that has been inflicted by someone else. Modern psychotherapy, by contrast, tends to ignore the relationship between sin and psychopathology, preferring instead to medicalize the latter and disqualify the former as "unscientific" (McRay et al., 2016, p. 95).[19]

In most cases we should expect human beings to bear damage inflicted upon them through the sins of others. Victims of interpersonal sin often bear similar scars to those whose intrapersonal damage might be described as self-inflicted. Further complicating matters, victims can become perpetrators, given sin's corrupting influence.[20] We may presume, therefore, that the relationship between sin and brokenness is not simple but complex. It might seem appealing to determine a flat cause and effect between individual sin and subjective brokenness, as some attempt to do. Yet, simplistic accounts of sin and damage run the risk of further compounding the harm victims of interpersonal evil have already endured. It is sinful to blame the victim!

A further pathogenic dynamic stems from an individual's personal sense of unworthiness or shame. The self that is cut off cannot finally escape the despair such isolation brings. This internal, reflexive dynamic is provoked by estrangement and compounded by feelings of guilt, shame, and self-loathing. Kierkegaard (1980) identifies this as a "sickness" of the

---

19. A relatively recent reversal of this tendency can be discerned in a number of secular engagements with developmental trauma, chronic childhood sexual abuse, and severe dissociative disorders (Herman, 2015; Howell, 2005; Miller, 2012). The notion of "evil," though defined in strictly humanistic terms, pops up occasionally in this literature.

20. This is particularly evident in developmental psychopathology. So, Johnson (2017), "[P]oor parental modeling, abuse, and neglect, particularly given how children are often blamed for their mistreatment in such contexts, shape the pre-agentic volitional capacities of childrenin ways that incline them toward patterns of personal sin and vice years before they will make adult decisions for which they will be held responsible as mature personal agents" (pp. 308–309).

estranged self: "A person in despair despairingly wills to be himself. . . . The self that he despairingly wants to be is a self that he is not, . . . that is, he wants to tear his self away from the power that established it. . . . But this is his way of willing to get rid of himself" (p. 20). Once consumed by this sickness, the despairing self will seek escape in death.

Sin is a cancer of the self for which there is no cure but Christ. Apart from him self remains trapped in its morally and relationally impotent estate. In helpful summary Stump (2012) concludes, "Some people are broken-hearted because of what has happened to them. . . . Some people are broken-hearted over what they have done to themselves or to others. . . . But it is also possible to be broken-hearted just over what one is" (p. 310). The broken self that refuses Christ's cure can never escape the despair such impotence brings. To purge that which plagues it, self must die. But the kind of death that is needed is not physical; rather, self must die *to self*. For Kierkegaard (1980), the self that is "healthy and free" is one that "only when, precisely having despaired, . . . rests transparently in God" (p. 30). Whatever the damage done to self, whether by self or others, it may be reversed, healed, in Christ.

From brokenness to self-deception

The final insult sin inflicts upon human beings is its obfuscation as the root of humanity's predicament. Through sin, we fell; in falling, we died. Along with the sting of estrangement so also came the onset of the torpor of dissociation and self-deceit. With the truth suppressed and forgotten, the lie, according to which we have not sinned nor is anything in us amiss, becomes plausible. As a result, we cannot recall how it all began. A computer virus has corrupted our networked database. Our ability to "make" meaning from our collectively stored memory has become compromised.[21] A crucial file has gone missing! Sin, it would seem, has deleted itself from the record.

---

21. Clearly, all truth and meaning is rooted in God; created beings do not "make" meaning in this sense. Yet, as of the fall, human beings are, in fact, meaning-makers in that we are perennially attempting to make sense of ourselves and the world around us. Due to our estrangement from God, however, we perpetually fall under the sway of autocentric and exocentric forces that impinge upon our thinking and reasoning. Theologians often refer to the "noetic effects of sin" in order to explain cognitive distortions respective to self, God, and others (see Moroney, 2000).

The meaning we now make of our predicament conforms to the lie our first parents believed and the choice that followed from it. "You will be like God," the serpent had promised, "knowing good and evil" (Gen 3:5). And, in a sense, we have become like God in that *we* now "create" what is good and true and separate it from all that is evil and false (Bonhoeffer, 2005). Like God, we do not question the uprightness of our judgments or discernment in distinguishing between them. Yet, in order that we might so believe, we must uphold the original lie, according to which we *are* like God. We certainly act the part. But the amount of self-deception required to maintain the delusion is diabolical.

As the serpent intended from the beginning, our refusal to trust God has led to a fatal error in our ability to know and be known (2 Cor 4:4). What we sought for the sake of "wisdom" only placed true understanding beyond our reach (cf. 1 Cor 1:20). In summarizing the human predicament, Johnson (2017) offers,

> Satan's allegation of God's untrustworthiness should be interpreted as the beginning of all human falsehood, including that which runs like a thread through so much human psychopathology, from conscious deception, to overgeneralizations, catastrophization, false core beliefs, false selves, body dysmorphia, gender dysphoria, same-sex attractions, false shame and guilt, defenses and defensiveness, dissociation, the misinterpretations and misrepresentations of others, and the hallucinations and delusions of psychosis. Satan has indeed blinded our minds. (p. 222)

The final stage of sin's progress is the corruption of human self-knowledge. The result of which is: all I believe I know of myself is suspect. Sin's influence has distorted humanity's noetic faculties. None of us is immune. Even otherwise "healthy" people are susceptible to critical and systemic misjudgments regarding themselves. Distortions in self-awareness now universally compromise all our truth-claims. All too often we epitomize the moral failings exhibited archetypally by our first parents. We demonstrate by our own dissociation, defensiveness, shame, and self-deception that we are their children. Getting at the truth of who we are demands more than perpetuating their same aspirations to autonomy.

Sin's defeat and eschatological wholeness

Christ gives us the cure we need (see Johnson, 2017). By means of the gifts he offers, he counters and overturns each of sin's three dynamic processes. In answer to our rebellion, Jesus offers his own active obedience to God. Countering our estrangement from God and each other, Christ's cruciform work reconciles us to both. Finally, for our sin-blinded eyes Jesus grants us veridical sight through his gift of the Spirit of truth.

In coming to Christ, all those formerly alienated from God find themselves perichoretically united to the second Person of the Trinity through the indwelling presence of the Spirit (Ferguson, 1997). Whereas in Adam we were reckoned by God as rebellious, suffering under the hereditary estrangement passed on to us, through union with Christ believers come to be reckoned as obedient and faithful children of God (Rom 5:12–21; 2 Cor 5:21; Eph 1:5; Heb 2:10; 1 John 3:1). In this way, we are made new.

Reconciliation reverses the self-annihilating trajectory initiated by sin's rebellion. Whereas disobedience led to estrangement, the righteous obedience of Christ, having been reckoned to the believer, brings the self into a state of communion and favor with God. Now "rooted and grounded in love" (Eph 3:17), the self possesses a covenantal security—a basal wholeness. Given time and proper care, security in Christ will work itself upward and outward, inhibiting sin's corrupting influence and healing the brokenness of interpersonal sin. Finally, the self that formerly hid from the truth of its corruption and embraced self-deception as a defense against guilt and shame now possesses the gift of the Spirit of truth. As Jesus promised, only by means of the truth—of who he is and who we are—will we be finally set free from sin's influence (John 8:32). Self-deception served the interests of the fallen self. Now reconciled and secure in Christ, the redeemed self has no need of such defensive strategies.

To be clear, the "location" of God's palingenetic work should not be circumscribed to any single constitutive coordinate (i.e., the believer's mind/soul). Jesus has not purchased redemption and reconciliation for minds or souls but for whole persons. Neither should we understand renewal as an exclusively psychological reality. The self is no mere cognitive construct. If it were, what then would be the ontological basis for palingenesis? The "location" of redemption, for the present age, would be purely metaphorical. No, believing selves really are made new (see

Campbell, 2012).[22] In its essence the covenantal self-in-relation is neither, strictly speaking, a formal constituent (i.e., mind/soul) or a psychological construct (i.e., self-consciousness).

The sphere of this renewal is limited to the inner aspects of the self for the present age. Paul suggests and biblical anthropology confirms as much. Crucially, these two aspects of human nature do not correspond with the dichotomy of Aristotelian "substance" and "accident," much less with physical "substance" and metaphysical "form."[23] Neither is the inner self merely a subjective reality. Rather, the bifurcation of the eschatological self of the believer by Paul into inner and outer aspects corresponds to the visible and invisible aspects of the human self-in-relation, aspects which Paul evidently holds to be objective existential realities (cf. Col 1:16).

On account of the eschatological bearing of redemption, the believing self is both objectively, ontologically new in Christ, and simultaneously being made new through active participation in the work of God's Spirit. The "inner self" of believers "is being renewed day by day," while the "outer self" awaits its full redemption in the coming age (2 Cor 4:16; see also Rom 8:23; 1 Cor 15:53). Although redemption is applied unevenly in the present age, both the inner and outer aspects of the believing self will be finally restored and renewed by the Spirit in the age to come. The present renewal of the inner self as well as the final eschatological renewal of the outer self—i.e., the resurrection of the body—are realities inaugurated by the indwelling presence of the Spirit of God (Ferguson,

22. I conclude from this that Johnson's (2017) identification of "[t]he self" as "the sum total of all the self-representations or self-schemata that a person possesses" is insufficient (p. 431). If self and self-schema are conflated, a logical problem ensues. By way of example: I may believe I am tall. Whether accurate or not, tallness is an attribute of my self-representation. My conception of myself as tall, however, depends on my accurate self-perception *in relation to others* (i.e., their height relative to mine). Whether I am truly tall cannot be determined by examining any self-representation or self-schemata; rather, I must examine what I can know of myself (in this case, my outer self) with others as "mirrors" of self. As stated in the previous chapter, the human self *in se* possesses an onto-relational status conferred by God having created human persons in his image. Following from this, I further suggest that Christiformity should not be delimited to the formation of believers' mental life (i.e., the formation of believers' inner self and/or self-concept). Nevertheless, I acknowledge the reality that, due to its eschatological frame, Christiformity remains for the present age essentially hidden (see 2 Cor 4:18; 1 John 3:2).

23. This is not to say that philosophical theology ought not to attempt, as Aquinas did, to dialogue with Aristotelian metaphysics. My point here is that the Bible may occupy a more prominent role in informing such conversations than it historically has.

1997; Schreiner, 2008; Wright, 2013). That is to say, God's salvation entails the onto-relational transformation through his own perichoretic presence of the inner, invisible aspects of the self.

For Paul, redemption has been objectively accomplished by God. Yet, it must be subjectively appropriated by the believer. The essence of Paul's indicative/imperative formulations implies that we must accept for ourselves God's *fait accompli* in Christ's atoning death at the cross. At the same time, he suggests that, "[a]t the point of conversion," the individual believer experiences regeneration as "an objective *positional* reality" (Fee, 2009, p. 854; emphasis original). There is no hint with Paul that this reality is merely metaphorical.

The ethical demands of the new self entail believers' active participation in God's salvific agenda—that is, the working out of our salvation "with fear and trembling" (Phil 2:12). That being said, God's renewal of the inner self, inasmuch as it stems from reconciliation to God through the believer's Spirit-mediated union with Christ, has already begun. In Christ, we are both new and being made new. God's desire for believers is that they grow in the knowledge of self as an aspect of the renewal of the inner self. His agapic agenda for his people, the church, demands no less. This means that, for the period of time between regeneration and either the death of the body or the return of Christ, we must participate in his work of mitigating and removing barriers to self-knowledge. Whether due to sin or psychopathology, such barriers impede the Christiform work of the believer made in God's image and for his glory.

The supervening presence of the Holy Spirit mitigates sin's corrupting influence thus reversing the trajectory of self-destruction outlined above. Perichoretic relationality—that is, intimate communion between self and God, as well as self and other—provides for the healing of the self and allows for growth in integrative self-knowledge. The "old" autonomous self, due to its sinful opposition to God, became isolated, broken, and self-deceived. Having been reconciled to God, the "new" self of the believer gains access to the implements of grace—psychospiritual healing and veridical self-perception—that Christ offers through the Spirit.

The believing self is made new, but intrasubjective barriers to accurate self-appraisal often persist. Whether the self-consciousness of the believer shifts commensurably from an "old" to "new" perspective depends largely on whether he or she comes to appropriate by faith the full truthfulness of the gospel and its attending promises. As Johnson (2017) confirms,

> [U]nion with Christ and all its spiritual blessings are given to all believers equally and immediately upon faith in him, providing essential resources for the building of their new self. The Lord Almighty says who they are now, so they now have the transcendent right—established outside themselves and their limitations—to appropriate their diving calling, including participation in the trinitarian communion and the construction of a new-self self-understanding, and make it the basis of their well-being and healing. (p. 431)

Believers must come to view the self as it now is—new in Christ—and subjectively grasp at a deep psychological level the ramifications of their objective renewal in Christ (2 Cor 5:17). In order for this to take place, barriers to veridical self-knowledge must be displaced.

Chapter 8

Christian psychology in dialogue

SELF-KNOWLEDGE MAY BE REGARDED as veridical only insofar as it corresponds to God's knowledge. Within a christological framework, the most direct route to veridical self-knowledge is the "mirror" of God's Logos— that is, the disclosure of God mediated to individual human beings by the perichoretic presence of the Spirit of truth informed by Scripture (Calvin, 2008). In other words, we can see ourselves truly through the eyes of Christ. Even so, as Paul's self-reflection in Romans 7 suggests, some aspects of self are elusive, hidden, or even resistant to direct observation. As I showed in the previous chapter, sin and psychopathology can obstruct and obfuscate even the believing self's inward gaze. These are the specks and planks which may, as Jesus suggests, problematize veridical self-perception (Matt 7:3–5).

Yet, in directing believers to remove such obstructions, Jesus affirms the plausibility of overcoming these barriers. Some ability, after all, for self-appraisal is prerequisite to fulfilling Jesus' command to "first take the log out of your own eye, and then you will see clearly to take the speck out of your brother's eye" (7:5).[1] The measure of our success in this endeavor often depends on our willingness to involve others. As Christ suggests and experience bears out, when the believer's ability to self-perceive has been obstructed by the barriers of sin and psychopathology, God may, and often does, employ others to serve as mirrors of self. On this point the account of King David and Nathan the prophet is illustrative (2 Sam

---

1. This may be the only occasion when Jesus directs his most severe pejorative, hypocrite, to believers (see Pennington, 2017, p. 260).

12; cf. Kierkegaard, 1991). God sent Nathan to reflect back to David just how plank-ridden his self-sight had become.

On knowing through dialogue

Covenantal anthropology commends dialogue as the cardinal principal of human self-knowledge. The triune God is a self-disclosing being of supreme worth and unwavering good. His knowledge of himself is exhaustive and inerrant; all that he reveals of himself is true. Human beings image God through discourse, in turn discovering, reflecting, and celebrating the truth of our being and nature insofar as it conforms to his own (Johnson, 2007). The realities of sin and psychopathology, however, frustrate this semiodiscursive agenda not only by corrupting our imaging capacities but also by warping and skewing the truth of who we are—who we believe ourselves to be. Although the Logos reveals us truly, we wrestle against the truth with an enduring intrapersonal resistance to veridical self-discovery. The lingering effects of past sins, the ongoing struggle to overcome remaining sin, and the challenges of dealing with brokenness make it likely—if not inescapable—that believers will continue to see through the glass more dimly than they might otherwise (see 1 Cor 13:12).

As God's people, believers possess the very oracles of God (cf. Rom 3:2); yet, in consideration of the sundry barriers to self-knowledge, we are more likely to employ those oracles in searching out the faults of others than in humbly yielding ourselves to them. This was the fatal flaw of the scribes and Pharisees in Jesus' day. We can hardly be less susceptible than they to such self-deception. If we hope to avoid their just condemnation, we do wellto heed his call to personally apply his self-disclosure to us, *about* us (see Heb 3:7–19). Moreover, by engaging in dialogical discourse—allowing for the possibility of a prophetic encounter with one another—we increase our chances of discovering and removing barriers to self-knowledge.[2] As it happens, the ethical imperative of agapic, covenantal self-knowledge demands no less.

2. The Reformed doctrine of Scripture's sufficiency is not overturned in the least by the principal of dialogue. No lacuna is here imputed to either the self-disclosure of God or to the hermeneutical enterprise, broadly conceived. To the contrary, the Scriptures are indeed "sufficient" to address every barrier to self-knowledge; yet, evidently *every* believer will continue to struggle with barriers to self-knowledge. The problem does not lie with the Scriptures, but in our ability to "hear" them. I argue that our

In dialogue with modern perspectives

The subsequent dialogue with modern perspectives on barriers to self-knowledge demands the prefatory caveat that "self," in post/modern psychological literature, is rarely distinguished from, alternatively, self-consciousness, self-concept, or mind.[3] A great deal of confusion on the part of the reader may be avoided by keeping this firmly in mind. Limited as it is by the constraints of a truncated epistemology, modern psychology can never, having divested any presumption of a divine Subject, arrive at the center of human subjectivity or, indeed, the ultimate aim of self-knowledge. This is not to say that modern psychology avoids referring to the self; but it does so without the benefit of a perspective anchored, so to speak, in divine self-revelation. So, while orthodox Christology informs a biblical anthropology by elucidating the distinction between self *in se* and its accompanying psychological form(s), post/modern psychology, by contrast, lacks the necessary epistemic resources to find the same.

Depending on the school of thought, post/modern perspectives tend to psychologize the human self. Alternately, self is conceived as a subset of the mind (Kohut, 1977), a construct of human cognition (Harter, 2015), a narrative fiction (Harré, 1998), and a "necessary illusion" (Bromberg, 1998, p. 7). "Self," in other words, is equivalent to self-concept—the discrete, personal mental construct we each imagine in answer to the question, "Who are you?" At the strictly theoretical level, differences between self *in se* and self-concept—what post/modern psychology insists *is* the self—are moot. If my self-concept is the self, I am free to craft its form and image as I like. The duty of post/modern psychotherapy is to remedy that which has come to pathologize this self-concept. Some aspect of the mind—a segment or bit of the construct, the narrative fiction, the "illusion"—has come to be broken. Healing is needed.

Herein lies the weakness of secular, unipolar epistemology, upon which post/modern psychology depends. With nothing real and substantial to point to, all that remains is what I imagine to be true. With

ability to rightly interpret and subjectively apply the revelation of God is adversely conditioned by two primary barriers to self-knowledge: sin and psychopathology. Modern psychology, as it happens, has spent considerable effort investigating the latter (i.e., the epiphenomena and remediation of various forms of psychopathology). Scripture's sufficiency is hardly impugned by the careful dialogical inspection of these findings.

3. Vitz (2006) rightly identifies self as "a subset of person" (p. xi), though his proposal for a "transmodern" conception of self seems overly accommodative.

respect to the self, post/modern psychology must maintain two apparently contradictory propositions: (1) the self does not exist except as a hermeneutical apparatus—a linguistic convenience or narratival expression of diachronic inter/subjectivity; and (2) every human person, though possessing a shared (human) nature, nonetheless bears a singular, idiosyncratic personal identity *that can be veridically known*. Indeed, the latter is a fundamental assumption of the psychotherapeutic process. Yet, if the former is true—if the self is a construct, a rhetorical convenience—to what entity does veridical self-knowledge correspond? Who, finally, is answering the question, "Who are you?" Surely, it is no self-concept giving reply, but *me, my*self.[4]

Among the numerous shortcomings of post/modern psychologies is the lack of a biblical perspective on human beings created by and accountable to God (see Vitz & Felch, 2006). This deficiency, due in large part to its presuppositional commitment to empiricism, positivism,[5] and methodological pragmatism, results in numerous theoretical and therapeutic shortcomings.[6] Nevertheless, despite its epistemological blindspots and general disciplinary antipathy toward a theistic worldview, modern psychology and psychotherapy provide an enormous wealth of observational insight into the pathologies of the knowable inner self. Faithful Christians may reasonably object to its philosophical

---

4. This problem is not solved by Harré's (1998) attempt to delimit the phenomenal self—his "Self 2"—to the personal attributes of individuals (p. 76). This maneuver irretrievably downgrades the individual human being to a constellation of Aristotelian "accidents" of particularity (see Silverman, 2002). Moreover, it fails the test of linguistic sensibility: *I* am *not* my attributes; rather, I *possess* and *evince* attributes. To posit that *I am* my attributes is tantamount to concluding that *self*-consciousness is an illusion. Atheist and Buddhist philosophers might affirm this concession, but a logical contradiction immediately ensues: if *self* does not exist, then *who* or *what* is experiencing the illusion of *self*-consciousness?

5. Tellingly, from the perspective of modernity the phrase, "scientific empiricism," is regarded as essentially redundant. However, this approach to the "scientific" study of the self is both epistemologically and therapeutically flawed. In contrast, a thoroughgoing Christian worldview rooted in the Scriptures and grounded in a christological paradigm provides the framework needed for any therapeutic model to possess genuine normativity.

6. For instance, modern psychology provides no clear, agreed-upon definition of a healthy human self, nor even agreement as to whether such a thing as a self exists. Rooted in a resistance to a covenantal (i.e., theological) perspective on human beings, this failure to adequately identify and define the self has led to innumerable second-tier misconstruals.

commitment to strict empiricism and monological discourse, and yet relish as a gift from God its genuinely helpful contributions (see Jas 1:17).

Within a Reformed epistemological framework, following Augustine and exemplified by Kuyper (1968) and Van Til (1961), the discoveries of secular science, if and when they correspond to how things truly are, may be seen as a gift of God's creation grace. So, Johnson (2007) rightly suggests, "[M]odern psychology's accomplishments constitute genuine scientific advances and deserve to be incorporated into a comprehensive Christian understanding of human beings" (p. 211). When grounded in the truth of God's Logos, the Christian pursuit of truth should be able to recognize genuine discoveries of secular science as gifts of grace, while simultaneously rejecting the flawed worldview within which such discoveries obtain. It is to a broad survey of the relevant discoveries that I will now turn.

The inner self and Freudian metapsychology

Phenomena suggestive of a conflictual inner self have been well-documented in modern psychology (Eagle, 2018; Lingiardi & McWilliams, 2017; McWilliams, 2011). The rise of Freudian psychoanalysis, in particular, popularized the notion of a conflicted inner self for the modern conceptual and rhetorical universe (Christian et al., 2017; Mitchell & Black, 2016). Perhaps ironically, the secular mainstreaming of "self" and "self-consciousness" appears to have righted a wrong nearly a quarter-millennium in the making. Kant, after all, had neatly tucked the self out of sight, defining self strictly in subjective terms: since, as the center of subjectivity the self *in se* cannot be directly observed, the knowable self, he reasoned, is all that may be known. According to this framework, discrepancies between self and self-consciousness become moot: effectively, we are who we believe ourselves to be.

In time, however, Freud would articulate and systematize a perspective that effectively (re)substantialized the self, if only conceptually and narratively, in order to explain the conflict evident in perennial human resistance to veridical self-knowledge.[7] As modern psychology would eventually come to recognize, Kantian anthropology left this resistance

7. Following Freud, psychoanalytic thought holds that the self *is* the mind or consciousness and, therefore, a construct (Bromberg, 1998; cf. Harter, 2015). Self- and other-understandings are also constructs. In spite of this conceptual flaw, confidence is maintained in the accessibility of veridical self-knowledge (cf. Neisser, 1997).

essentially unexplained. The phenomena of dissociation[8] and self-deception, after all, suggest the presence of divisions or barriers within one's
self-consciousness. By some unseen mechanism, the human mind "contains" more than it consciously knows. Though mysterious and ineffable,
that which lies below the surface of human consciousness nevertheless
affects how we think and act. For Freud and his disciples, a partial answer
to the mystery lay in an ostensibly bifurcated composition of the mind.
The conscious and unconscious mind(s) together, they reasoned, constitute the totality of human consciousness. Though ultimately theoretical,
the "unconscious" mind they inferred from a diversity of psychopathological signs and symptoms.

Fundamental to Freud's system is his metapsychological theory of
the structured psyche and its libidinal drives (S. Freud, 1905, 1923; see
Bucci, 1997).[9] In conceiving of the unconscious, Freud assumed that human beings were driven by repressed animalistic aggression and sexual
impulses (see Mitchell & Black, 2016).[10] What lies beneath the surface,
for Freud at least, resembled the vestigial psychogenic remains of our
evolutionary forebears.

Respective to the knowledge of self, Freud's primary contribution is
his putative discovery of unconscious mentation—that is, mental activity

---

8. Freud would eventually settle on *repression* rather than *dissociation* to describe
the distantiation of awareness from that which is unpleasant and anxiety inducing
(Howell, 2005). Freud regarded *repression* in mechanistic terms as an instinctual response to strictly intrapsychic conflict (S. Freud, 1915b); yet, paradoxically, he held
that the conscious mind—the ego—represses unconscious material at the behest of
the super-ego (S. Freud, 1923, p. 75). *Dissociation*, on the other hand, suggests an
interpersonal context for the structuring of awareness (Bromberg, 1998; Fairbairn,
1929; Whitmer, 2001); as such, it need not be entailed with Freud's highly problematic
metapsychology.

9. Freud's thinking shifted considerably over time. Interestingly, Freud came to
realize that his early topographical conception of the mind as conscious, unconscious,
and preconscious failed to adequately account for the phenomena he was investigating. As Christian (2017) explains, "A problem challenging this model was Freud's
growing recognition that not everything that is unconscious is instinctual in nature"
(p. 21). Specifically, Freud discovered that the desire to appear morally upright to self
and other (the putative function of the superego) suggests the presence of unconscious
motives and avowals (see Bachkirova, 2016). As will be shown, however, Freud's shift
to a structural account of the self as ego, id, and superego has its own considerable
weaknesses, especially as it relates to the phenomenon of self-deception.

10. Clearly, Freud's perspective on human nature diverges sharply from a christological anthropology, according to which humankind is created in the image of God
(cf. S. Freud, 1927).

occurring outside the individual's present awareness (S. Freud, 1915b; cf. Ellenberger, 1981).[11] It may be, however, that Freud was hardly the first to arrive at this observation. A closer examination of modern psychological history reveals that Freud likely gave currency to concepts previously employed by Pierre Janet, William James, and others (Ellenberger, 1981; Howell, 2005).[12] Whether any of these figures can be identified as the discoverer of the unconscious remains to be seen. As my earlier historical survey of Christian self-knowledge demonstrates, there have long been keen observers of discrepancies between self and self-consciousness.

The idea that human beings may possess knowledge of self of which they are unaware need not entail the problematic freight of its association with Freud. The apostle Paul, for example, not only condemned humanity for its suppression of the knowledge of God (Rom 1:18),[13] he also lamented the conflictual nature of his own inner self (Rom 7:22–23).

By way of modern contrast to Freud, the notion of unconscious mentation plays a significant role in a number of Kierkegaard's (1980, 1981) writings as well. Apart from the obvious presuppositional dissimilarities, what chiefly distinguishes Freud from Kierkegaard may have been the former's willingness to challenge one of the pillars of modernist orthodoxy from a strictly secular standpoint (see Evans, 1995).[14]

11. That Freud, along with his disciples, considered that he had discovered *the* unconscious is undeniable (Fromm, 1980; Mitchell & Black, 2016); cf. Erdelyi (1985) who notes that, "the problematical systemic Unconscious is abolished by Freud in 1923, becoming the id" (pp. 64–65).

12. Janet certainly believed, and complained loudly (1925), that Freud had stolen many of his ideas and simply renamed them. So, allegedly, what Janet called the "subconscious" Freud would label the "unconscious"; Janet's "function of reality" became Freud's "reality principle," etc. (Ellenberger, 1981, p. 539).

13. So, Schreiner (1998): "[A]ll people possess knowledge of God, even though it has been repressed and is not saving" (p. 87); cf. Calvin's (2008) "sense of deity" (p. 9).

14. Freud (1933) described the unconscious id as a "cauldron full of seething excitations" (p. 73). Evidently, his understanding of human beings was greatly conditioned by Darwinian naturalism and Hobbesian political theory (Mitchell & Black, 2016). So, "Human beings, in Freud's account, are . . . wired the way Freud and his contemporaries understood animals to be, oriented toward pursuing simple pleasures with ruthless abandon. . . . The project of childhood is socialization, the transformation of the infant, with his or her bestial impulses, into the adult, with his or her complex psychic apparatus and its intricate and elaborate system of checks and barriers channeling those impulses and aims into socially acceptable forms of civilized living" (p. 112). This bears little resemblance to Kierkegaard. Evans (1995) notes a further distinction between Freud's and Kierkegaard's respective perspectives, namely, the latter's view of

By questioning the regnant rationalist dogma regarding the intelligibility of human subjectivity, Freud effectively turned modernist anthropological optimism on its head. As his close associate and hagiographer Fromm (1980) concludes,

> [His] theory [of the unconscious] was radical because it attacked the last fortress of man's belief in his omnipotence and omniscience, the belief in his conscious thought as an ultimate datum of human experience. Galileo had deprived man of the illusion that the earth was the center of the world, Darwin of the illusion that he was created by God, but nobody had questioned that his conscious thinking was the last datum on which he could rely. Freud deprived man of his pride in his rationality . . . and discovered that . . . most of conscious thought is . . . a mere rationalization of thoughts and desires which we prefer not to be aware of. (pp. 133–134)

For his temerity, Ricoeur (1977) dubbed Freud, along with Marx and Nietzsche, a "master" in the "school of suspicion" (p. 32).

Just the same, only when one dismisses Christian Scripture and the long history of Christian pastoral writers, can modern psychology—let alone Freud—be regarded as having discovered humanity's capacity for subliminal mentation. What Freud did accomplish, and what Christians may rightly celebrate, was the overthrow of the Cartesian/Kantian self's overweening hubris and its unwarranted pretense at self-knowledge.

Dynamic psychology and the self-concept

In modern psychological writings a divided and conflicted self first appears in James (1961, 2012). To varying degrees of emphasis other contemporary theoretical models make allowances for internal conflict as well. Within the various schools of thought falling under the rubric of psychodynamic psychology, however, the conflictual self is seminal and paradigmatic (Lingiardi & McWilliams, 2017; Summers & Barber, 2010). While all so-called dynamic theories trace their provenance to classical psychoanalysis, most have evolved considerably over the past century from orthodox Freudian thought (Mitchell & Black, 2016; Safran, 2012).

---

the "unconscious" as "something I have formed, and therefore something for which I may be in some ways responsible" (p. 81).

Since Freud, the inner self of dynamic psychologies has been generally characterized in terms of the conflictual relationship between an individual's *conscious* and *unconscious* mind. Just the same, understandings of these terms and the ostensible reasons for the conflict have moved far beyond a classical understanding (Christian, 2017; Eagle, 2010; Mitchell & Black, 2016). What now remains of Freud's contribution to contemporary psychodynamic psychology still bears some resemblance to his early theory. What was centrally important to Freudian classical psychoanalysis—and most problematic, as it happens—has been largely jettisoned.[15]

Perspectives on the dynamic self

With the waning influence of classical psychoanalysis, a diversity of approaches have arisen in its wake. In addition to classical and contemporary psychoanalytic methods, McWilliams (2011) counts the respective schools of ego psychology (see Blanck & Blanck, 1974; Hartmann, 1965), the object relations tradition (see Fairbairn, 1952; Greenberg & Mitchell, 1983; Guntrip, 1973), self psychology (see Kohut, 1977; Wolf, 1988), and relational psychotherapy (see DeYoung, 2003; Stern, 2010) among its major theoretical branches.[16] Taken together these demonstrate the profound contribution to modern psychology and psychotherapy Freud made with his vision of the psychic structures and dynamics of mental life, while simultaneously confirming the inherent instability of his idiosyncratic conceptions of human psychology. Accordingly, Bucci (1997) describes "psychodynamic psychology . . . as a rigorous and focused attempt to apply the methods of empirical science to the propositions of clinical theory, while abandoning the [Freudian] metapsychological framework" (pp. 50–51).

15. For example, few contemporary psychoanalytical theorists hold any longer to Freud's biologically conceived drive/instinct theory of the unconscious. Most have shifted toward a relationally structured understanding of the self (see Fisher & Greenberg, 1996; Greenberg & Mitchell, 1983; Aron & Mitchell, 1999; Mitchell, 2000).

16. Summers & Barber (2010) list six essential features common to all psychodynamic psychotherapies: (1) the use of "exploratory, interpretative, and supportive interventions"; (2) "frequent sessions"; (3) an "emphasis on uncovering painful affects, understanding past painful experiences"; (4) facilitating "emotional experience" and increasing "understanding"; (5) focus on "the therapeutic relationship, including attention to transference and countertransference"; and (6) an openness to "a wide range of techniques" (p. 12).

The "schizoid self"

Every psychodynamic school emphasizes, as an aspect of theoretical and clinical normativity, the "*internal experience*" of the individual (Lingiardi & McWilliams, 2017, p. 6; emphasis original). Dynamic theories of self, as a result, tend to stress the fragmented and conflictual nature of self-consciousness. A second emphasis entails the shared human inclination to distance oneself from awareness of that which is unpleasant or anxiety inducing. The terms by which the diverse schools of thought characterize these phenomena sometimes vary. What each school has in common is their shared perspective on the fragmentary nature of human identity and mentation.

For our purposes, the respective terminology is less important for our purposes than the observation: we think and act in divided, discontinuous ways. Psychoanalytic psychology and its various derivative models often speak in terms of a developmentally split self-consciousness, or "schizoid ego" (see McWilliams, 2011). Regarding the schizoid nature of the human mind, Fairbairn (1952) asserts,

> [E]verybody without exception must be regarded as schizoid.
> . . . The qualification which confers meaning on the concept is that everything depends upon the mental level which is being considered. The fundamental schizoid phenomenon is the presence of splits in the ego; and it would take a bold man to claim that his ego was so perfectly integrated as to be incapable of revealing any evidence of splitting at the deepest levels, or that such evidence of splitting of the ego could in no circumstances declare itself at more superficial levels, even under conditions of extreme suffering or hardship or deprivation. (pp. 7–8)

In other words, while we human beings may pretend to a unitary, contiguous self-awareness reflective of an integrative equanimity, there are segments and compartments of self presently sequestered from each person's present awareness. These dissociated aspects of the self, in otherwise healthy individuals, contribute to the dis-ease of the mind in distressing or disruptive circumstances; whereas, in more seriously disordered minds they can result in severe psychopathology (Bromberg, 1998; Howell, 2005; McWilliams, 2011). According to the theory, "the self" (i.e., one's self-concept) splits in the context of its formative development during childhood. The task of psychodynamic psychotherapy, then, is to bring about the integration of the various aspects of self. The healing or wholeness of the self is the aim of treatment.

Dynamic wholeness

Defined by the unipolar epistemology of modernity, psychodynamic psychology and psychotherapy presume that the schizoid self-consciousness can be made whole through reflective self-knowledge, though substantial differences have arisen as to the role relationship plays in this process (Aron & Mitchell, 1999; Bromberg, 1998; Eagle, 2013; Mitchell, 2000). For psychoanalytic models adhering to a more classical conception of the self, knowledge of self is the sole criterion for psychotherapeutic change. The means of overcoming barriers to self-knowledge is therefore unidimensional. According to Greenberg & Mitchell (1983),

> [T]he goal of [classical] analysis and its therapeutic action [is] . . . enhancing the power of the ego by increasing its knowledge and its hegemony over the drives. . . . By knowing himself better, a knowledge which includes awareness of and respect for previously disavowed aspects of his personality, the patient will be more able to renounce old, impossible, and frustrating aims and to embrace new ones which are attainable and true to himself. . . . Insight alone is curative. (p. 390)

This theory of personality most closely follows Freud's concern to identify infantile and biologically instantiated drives that had become split off and repressed in his patients (S. Freud, 1923).[17] The impulses of the infant self may serve well enough in early life, but are considerably less desirable in otherwise mature adults. Thus, there is a need to construct elaborate internal defenses against their expression in either cognition or overt behavior. As the analyst brings such motives, fantasies, or illicit desires to light, the individual should come to experience personal growth. In other words, through knowledge of self, healing becomes possible. As repressed thoughts and impulses become integrated into conscious awareness, the anxiety they previously induced will be

---

17. Freud believed that a split in the self (i.e., self-consciousness) arises due to conflict between the primitive self—Freud's id—and the self-governing ego. The job of the analyst is, therefore, to assist the adult patient in resolving internal conflict through integrative self-understanding.

resolved over time. The chief role of the analyst, then, is that of an essentially passive expert observer.

Developmental factors

Early psychoanalytic theory held that the environment played little to no role in the development of the self.[18] Freud gave such notions little freight, preferring instead to rely on his organismic conception of human nature. Dissatisfaction with classical theory would eventually lead to more developmentally sensitive theories of the dynamic self (Karen, 1998). According to Freudian orthodoxy, splits in the self-consciousness and the resultant psychological distress are strictly the result of the repression of "the gratification and discharge of sexual instinctual drives as central aspects of adequate functioning" (Eagle, 2013, p. 64). It would not take long, however, for critics of this model to arise from within the field. Early attachment theorist Bowlby (1988) would recall of his own psychoanalytic training,

> Anyone who places emphasis on what a child's real experiences may have been . . . was regarded as pitifully naïve. Almost by definition it was assumed that anyone interested in the external world could not be interested in the internal world, indeed was almost certainly running away from it. (pp. 48–49)

Bowlby's objections to his classical training grew out of an intuition regarding the role socio-developmental factors play in the formation of human persons.

As concerns mounted regarding the dearth of explanatory power in Freud's drive theory of the personality and its unwarranted presumption of autonomous therapeutic action, a number of mid-century psychodynamic theorists would eventually initiate a major conceptual revision (Eagle, 2013; Greenberg & Mitchell, 1983; Mitchell & Black, 2016). The principal basis of the shift in psychoanalytical thinking stemmed from a growing appreciation of the seminal influence of early childhood relationships in the formation of personality and character and the role they continue to play in adults (Karen, 1998; Mitchell, 2000). As a result of this shift toward developmental factors, so also did discussions

---

18. The exception to this is Freud's understanding of the super-ego, which he held to be a function of socialization.

of psychotherapeutic means move from autonomous, cognitive factors toward relationality.

In their summary of what has now come to be known as relational psychoanalysis, Greenberg & Mitchell (1983) observe,

> [S]ince it is the quality of early relationships that are seen as developmentally crucial, . . . it is the quality of the analytic relationship that is seen as fundamentally therapeutic. . . . Although the analyst may interpret, may communicate information, it is not the information alone that is understood as producing change. The nature of the relationship that develops around this communication . . . is essential to cure. (p. 391)

The exchange of information, "communication"—i.e., dialogue—that occurs in the context of the therapeutic relationship effects a benign, constructive knowing and being-known essential for the remediation of the disordered individual (Stern, 2010). The analyst and patient come to understand each other through the dynamic exchange of deep, empathic relatedness commonly known as *transference* and *countertransference*. As self develops an abiding interpersonal connectedness with other, adverse childhood experiences of self come to be reformulated, resolved, and integrated into adult experience.[19] Healthy relationships, so the theory suggests, are key to a healthy human self.

By the 1920s, borne out of his work with the extreme psychopathology of schizophrenic patients, Sullivan (1940, 1953) was beginning to posit an interpersonal structuring of the inner self, wherein, he believed, relationally induced anxiety stemming from early childhood experiences contributes to a divided and discontinuous subjectivity in adults. His developmental perspective on the self has come to characterize much of contemporary dynamic psychology (see Mitchell & Black, 2016). In particular, Sullivan believed that the relationship between mother and child

---

19. Mitchell & Greenberg (1983) unwittingly employ the language of *perichoresis* in describing the relationship of patient and analyst as "transference and countertransference reciprocally generate and interpenetrate each other" (p. 389). Likewise, Pizer (1998) occasionally employs quasi-religious language in descriptive ways: "While engaged in the process of [analysis], the patient experiences his participation in a kind of duet. He uses his voice to render the imperatives and the potentials in his own subjective world and hears the analyst's voice offering other-than-me substance that, in moments of grace, he may find and use to effect transformations in the core of the self" (p. 26). Although devoid of any theological content or reference, such formulations nevertheless accord with the implications of a Christian account of the covenantal self.

critically impacts the development of the self, whether toward a basically whole or schizoid schema.

According to Mitchell & Black (2016), Sullivan "envisioned mind as thoroughly social" (p. 71). External experiences—i.e., what we colloquially refer to as nurture—provide the primary means by which the young develop and grow to become psychologically healthy adults. What distinguishes Sullivan's view of psychopathology from Freud's is the belief that internal splitting develops during childhood as a primary result of bad parenting.[20] Splits in consciousness formed in childhood may persist as schisms in the individual's perception of self. Distress in the context of the parent-child relationship serves to mitigate undesirable qualities in the self in order to maintain the good graces of the other: "I" won't be "me" if who I am results in mom's and/or dad's disfavor. In adulthood, distress in other relational contexts will generate a similar compensatory need to bring about resolution to internal conflicts and to stabilize relational bonds.

Attachment theory

Alongside these developments, Bowlby's (1988) attachment theory provides another vital component to modern dynamic psychology. More so than most contemporary forms of psychoanalysis, Bowlby maintains a biological basis for human relationality that is nonetheless rooted in evolutionary and ethological theory (Eagle, 2013).[21] Bowlby's (1988) evolutionary bias led him to discern a link between animal and human attachment patterns. From this he concluded that social relationships are essentially preprogrammed and develop in predictably linear ways provided the proper conditions. In "[s]tudy after study," he observes, "healthy, happy, and self-reliant adolescents and young adults are the products of stable homes in which both parents give a great deal of time

20. Specifically, Sullivan (1953) held that the alternation of anxiety and calm on the part of the mother, corresponding in the child's mind to "bad mother" and "good mother," effectively conditions the child to view him/herself as either "bad me" or "good me" depending on the response of the mother to the child's behavior. Extreme anxiety might result in dissociation from some aspect of the self—whatever "mother" might disapprove of—as "not me."

21. Although significant divergences between psychoanalysis and attachment theory persist, Fonagy (2001) considers that the initial "bad blood" between the two schools has begun to dissipate (p. 1; see H. Steele & Steele, 2017).

and attention to the children" (p. 5). On the other hand, children who lack the proper nurturing inputs of a healthy relational context develop insecure patterns of attachment that persist in adulthood.[22] The onset of psychopathology in adulthood, again, occurs as the predictable result of lapses in parental efficacy. Respective to self-knowledge, Ainsworth & Bowlby (1991) argue, "What cannot be communicated to the [m]other cannot be communicated to the self" (p. 333).

Object relations psychology

According to the theory of object relations, a child's sense of self develops in relation to his or her primary caregivers, unflatteringly referred to as "objects" (Greenberg & Mitchell, 1983). In what would amount to a major challenge to Freudian orthodoxy, early object-relations theorists (e.g., Fairbairn, 1952; Klein, 1955) would posit that the child's internal experience of self develops in relation to these external objects.[23] Over time, the child's real and, in many cases, fantasized object-relations are organized internally becoming "important building blocks for one's experience of self" (Safran, 2012, pp. 37–38). Since the experience of self is organized around one's experiences of other(s), self-consciousness increases in this relational context. As the theory further suggests, the development of the child's self-consciousness can be arrested or skewed by lapses in healthy relationality. So, Safran concludes, "[T]he depriving or traumatizing aspects of the significant other that provide the raw material for the unconscious fantasy or internal object inevitably end up becoming part of the internal structure or enduring psychic organization" of the developing self (p. 38).

Due to their own ambivalence, parents and other close relations may behave at times in confusing and contradictory ways (see Klebanov & Travis, 2015). Even an otherwise attentive, nurturing parent may respond harshly to the child for a relatively minor infraction. Potentially, this unexpected and intense experience of parental disfavor triggers an internal conflict in the child. On the one hand, there may be a strong

22. Through the lens of psychoanalysis, Eagle (2013) determines that attachment theory evinces a tendency to see human social functioning in terms of mechanistic behavioral systems—something of a "biological instinct theory" of interpersonal relationality (p. 79).

23. Fairbairn (1952) holds that, in the case of the infant's "oral orientation toward the breast," the relation is to a "partial object" (p. 13).

desire to move toward the parent for comfort; yet, since the parent is simultaneously the source of discomfort, the child feels compelled to move away from the parent who has suddenly become unsafe. Depending on the length and severity of such contradictoriness in parental behavior, the child can develop a dysfunctional pattern of object-relations[24] that will then likely be carried into adulthood.

If distressing occurrences are few in number, the child will likely negotiate the meaning of the conflict by dissociating from awareness the parent's "bad" behavior, if only to preserve the relationship (Howell, 2005). The image of the parent may thus be preserved as basically good. Alternatively, the child may come to internalize the parent's disapproving projection of a "bad" child into his/her identity, which the child constructs, over time, as an intrapsychic object in the context of relationship. Within a corrosive relational context, the child's sense of self inevitably develops along predictably disordered and dysfunctional lines. In extreme cases, the relational damage endured by the young self can lead to severe psychopathological sequelae in adulthood (Dutra et al., 2009).

Understanding developmental dissociation

At its most basal level, "[d]issociation means simultaneously knowing and not knowing" (van der Kolk, 2015, p. 123; see also Whitmer, 2001). Notwithstanding the appearance of paradox, by some mysterious means, our human minds have the ability to distance themselves from full awareness of that which disturbs and overwhelms our coping capacity. What is too much to bear, the mind omits from known reality. As the preceding discussion of dynamic psychology suggests, the developing self is vulnerable to disruptions in relational equilibrium, insecure patterns of attachment, and the emotional upheaval associated with psychosocial distress (Dutra et al., 2009). The ability of the self to dissociate from intolerable experiences appears to be a function of an essentially automatic defensive system (Putnam, 1997; Wieland, 2015).

As a refuge from psychological distress, dissociation offers considerable psychological protection to the young mind. According to Carlson et al. (2009), "Dissociation is a complex psychophysiological process" that is most likely "integrally related to the developing self" (p. 39; see

---

24. This mirrors, though differs conceptually from, Bowlby's (1988) "insecure attachment."

also Putnam, 1994). Once the tolerance of the child has been exceeded, dissociation is unconsciously and automatically deployed in defense of the young self. What the child cannot bear to know—of self and other— the mind obfuscates. Given time and circumstances, the form of the child's consciousness of self may become altered to accommodate a now-truncated record of experience. As circumstances go, the most egregious include trauma at the hands of an otherwise trusted, needed caregiver. As Howell (2005) concludes, "Dissociation is one way that the psyche modifies its own structure to accommodate interaction with a frightening, but needed, and usually loved, attachment figure" (p. 3). Unacceptable and unbearable experiences are segmented and compartmentalized in service to the core self.[25]

Pathological dissociation

According to the standard account, dissociation occurs along a spectrum from normal/adaptive responses on the one end to pathological/maladaptive responses on the other (Bromberg, 2009; Chu, 2011; Howell, 2005; Putnam, 1994; van der Hart et al., 2006). In children and adults dissociation is a normal, reflexive response to overwhelming psychological and somatic stimuli typically associated with traumatic events (Briere & Scott, 2014; Lynch, 2012). According to common nosological criteria, "Dissociative disorders are characterized by a disruption of and/or discontinuity in the normal integration of consciousness, memory, identity, emotion, perception, body representation, motor control, and behavior" that are "frequently found in the aftermath of trauma" (American Psychiatric Association, 2013, p. 291). Yet, as Dutra et al. (2009) have observed, traumagenic factors alone do not supply an adequate account of the etiology of pathological dissociation in adults; evidently, additional early developmental deprivations contribute to the breakdown of the normal integrative process.

Trauma is likely not the only etiological criteria for the development of pathological dissociation. Some theorists have suggested a link between attachment style and dissociative tendencies as well. Along these lines, Liotti (1992, 2009) has pointed out research indicating the

25. The remarkable degree to which brain and mind interrelate can be seen in correlations between psychological and neurological compartmentalization of traumatic experience (see van der Kolk, 2015).

likelihood that disorganized infant attachment is predictive of dissociative experiences in adolescents and adults (see Brown, 2009; Carlson, 1998; Ogawa et al., 1997). Evidently, the phenomena associated with pathological dissociation in adults may depend less on traumagenic factors than on a systemic failure to securely attach to parental caregivers during the child's formative years.

Occurrences of severe, chronic childhood sexual and physical abuse correlate very highly with the diagnosis of dissociative disorders in adults (Chefetz, 2015; Howell, 2011; K. Steele & van der Hart, 2009; van der Kolk, 2015). Human beings develop an integrated sense of self over time provided the proper nurture and relational foundation (Cozolino, 2017; Siegel, 2012).[26] Children naturally learn to integrate and regulate disparate states of experience and their associated behaviors, feelings, etc., as they mature and grow (Harter, 2015). Chronically abused and neglected children, on the other hand, unconsciously and reflexively employ discrete experience states as a means of sheltering the delicate psyche from traumatic experiences (Putnam, 1997; Wieland, 2015).

Physical pain and sexual assault perpetrated over the course of weeks, months or even years, betrayal of trust, mandated secrecy often accompanied by threats, and the concomitant feelings of powerlessness, isolation, and shame together undermine any sense of subjective unity or wholeness (see Finkelhor & Browne, 1985). Over time, these lingering divisions can develop from disparate experience states into discrete identities and accompanying frameworks of meaning. Young minds fragmented by betrayal and abuse do not heal so easily as bodies. In adulthood, the unseen damage remains.

Dissociative disorders and dynamic psychology

Serious objections have been raised from within modern psychology concerning the standard nosological account of psychopathology (Colbert,

---

26. Siegel (2012) alternately defines *integration* as the "mind's process of linking differentiated parts" and "the fundamental mechanism of health and wellbeing" (p. A1-40). He essentially describes three levels of integration—the neurobiological, the intrapsychic, and the interpersonal, to which a Christian perspective may reasonably add a fourth, namely, the psychospiritual (i.e., "integration" or union with Christ). Curt Thompson (2010), in synthesizing the findings of neuroscience and Christian spirituality, employs the descriptor "dis-integrated" (p. 4) in speaking of the breakdown of normal integrative development.

2000; Frances, 2013; Gonçalves et al., 2002; Houts, 2002; Paris, 2015). These objections suggest the presence of a contradiction at its conceptual heart. In particular, some have come to question whether mental disorders should be conceived of in similar terms to somatic diseases. As Ingersoll and Marquis (2014) point out,

> In physical disorders the symptom depends on the disease—meaning that when a symptom appears, a medical doctor tries to trace it to an underlying disease process. . . . This is not the case with mental disorders. In mental disorders, rather than symptoms leading to tests that reveal a disease process, *the symptoms . . . are themselves considered the disease.* Of the hundreds of diagnoses in the DSM-5, *not one* qualifies as a specifically identifiable disease process (which has a physiological/neurological marker) underlying the set of symptoms. (pp. 36–37; emphasis original)

Dissociative disorders, more so than most others, highlight the critical shortcoming of the standard descriptive taxonomy of mental disorders as *diseases* or *illnesses* of the mind. The assumption implicit in any nosological model is that diseases—whether physical or psychological—arise causally from organic or physiological conditions (cf. Lingiardi & McWilliams, 2017).[27] Such assumptions are perfectly apropos respective to somatic illnesses. When it comes to many mental disorders, however, the standard nosological account is most consistent with a materialistic model of human beings which disregards the reality of the inner self and discounts its vulnerability to psychospiritual harm.

The medical model of psychopathology possesses very little explanatory power with respect to the etiology of pathological dissociation. What, after all, explicates the connection between insecure attachment and dissociative coping strategies? How is psychological injury—i.e., trauma—to be understood, if not as a wound inflicted upon the self? And from what organic or neurobiological criterion does the development of a split psyche arise? A constellation of thorny philosophical and theological problems accompany post/modern agnosticism concerning

---

27. Medication often offers a reduction in symptomology through the regulation of brain chemistry. Medical interventions of this sort offer no cure for a disordered psyche but can provide an important buttress against overwhelming depression or anxiety. As Christians, we rightly celebrate the benefit such medications may offer while simultaneously supporting higher order interventions. Anesthetic may numb the pain but does not heal the wound; likewise, psychotropic medications may reduce psychogenic distress but without addressing root causes.

the reality of the human self. Similarly, biologically-based nosological approaches to psychopathology simply cannot account for the subjective sense of multiplicity evident in cases of structural dissociation.

Implications for self-knowledge

Dynamic psychology, on the other hand, offers a more penetrating perspective on human subjectivity. As Howell (2011) succinctly articulates, "Relationality, multiplicity, and traumatic dissociation all come together to frame a different way of understanding the human mind" (p. 29). Human subjectivity—and, more specifically, the individual's experience of self—develops in the context of relationship (Harter, 2015), that is, intersubjectively. We first become aware of self and other at a very early developmental stage. Considered globally, self-consciousness bears both a synchronic and diachronic character. In other words, under normal conditions, one's sense of self entails a paradoxical certainty that I-am-the-same-me-as-ever, whereas, simultaneously, I-am-not-who-I-once-was.

Autobiographical memory and human embodiedness appear to play crucial roles in granting one's subjective sense of idiosyncratic personal identity. Crucially, the degree to which one possesses a sense of singularity and continuity appears to depend on whether one's self-perception gains sufficient anchorage at a surprisingly early stage of life. Even before birth, the care and nurture of loving caregivers are vitally important for a child's ability to establish a firm self-concept that is relatively unbroken and discontinuous (Klebanov & Travis, 2015). On the other hand, relational instability and insecurity deprives the child of the necessary prerequisites for a firm and enduring sense of singularity.

Developmental dissociation appears to offer a cognitive cushion, so to speak, against harm inflicted upon the young self (Wieland, 2015). This defensive strategy, however, comes at the cost of genuine subjective unity in that it disrupts the normal integrative trajectory of the self-consciousness, depriving the child of a sense of singularity and continuity. As a species of self-threatening injury, trauma greatly undermines the stability of an individual's self-concept (van der Kolk, 2015). Developmental or "complex" trauma, moreover, can eventually lead to "breakdowns in the most fundamental outcomes of healthy psychobiological development" (J. D. Ford & Courtois, 2009, p. 16). Over time, severe interpersonal evil perpetrated against a young psyche will foment a multiple sense of self—a *we*-ness rather than a *me*-ness.

For minds broken in early life, dissociative disorders interpose significant barriers to self-knowledge later in life. What remains often may appear to the outside observer as a clutter of disorganized bits of a shattered self. As Bromberg (2011) explains, pathological dissociation phenomenologically expresses the individual's "alienation from aspects of *self*" (p. 7; emphasis original). That which in the interpersonal development *of* the self became unbearable results in estrangement *from* the self. It is expressly not *me*, but *not-me*, who endured the horrors of abuse and trauma. Under the threat of annihilation, the self divested itself of any perception of integrity having discarded some degree of its own narratival and autobiographical continuity. What remains of the individual's self-concept is now more or less fragmented and disjunct leaving the path to integrative self-knowledge unclear and uncertain.

A christological response to dynamic psychology

Psychodynamic psychotherapy suggests that the internal resolution of a conflicted self takes place through the integration into conscious awareness of one's disorganized and disordered sense of self in the context of relationship (Summers & Barber, 2010). To the degree that this premise can be sequestered from the shortcomings of post/modern anthropology and epistemology, it may well be compatible with a christological, covenantal perspective on self-knowledge. As a supplement to orthodox pastoral theology, dynamic psychology offers a penetrating analysis of the phenomenon of dissociation and the psychological means by which human beings may persist in intrapsychic conflict.

In their evaluation of psychodynamic psychotherapy from a Christian perspective, Mangis et al. (2011) regard as compatible efforts "to understand the profound impact of early relationships on our character, the mysterious way in which we are shaped by unconscious processes, and the pervasive presence of psychological conflict in our lives" (p. 135). Arguably, the latter two bear considerable consonance with the apostle Paul's own personal experience of inner conflict.

A developmentally sensitive account of psychopathology provides a helpful corollary to a Christian understanding of sin and brokenness. Not all barriers to self-knowledge, we do well to note, bear the moral weight of pride, sloth, or falsehood. To suggest otherwise unjustifiably conflates the agency and responsibility of abuser and survivor. Since pathological dissociation occurs as a sequela of interpersonal evil, structural impediments to veridical self-perception can hardly be regarded as morally blameworthy. Truly, all have sinned and fall short of the glory of God; but children who suffer at the hands of abusers are *not* somehow guilty of the sins perpetrated against them.[28] They tragically suffer the consequences of another's sin, but the guilt of that sin rests squarely on the head of their abuser(s).

Neither strictly nosological nor hamartiological frameworks can offer sufficiently broad explanation for the existence of pathological dissociation. Even healthy, adaptive forms of dissociation occur as automatic creaturely responses to traumagenic dynamics. As Christian psychologist Frank Lake (2005) concludes, "The entire subject of the psychoneuroses, including depression along with hysteria and the schizoid reaction, is a corollary of the dissociation or splitting off of intolerable experiences of the self, either in its deprivations or its depravities" (p. 460). Sin stands as a universal barrier to self-knowledge. Nevertheless, the phenomenon of dissociation implicates a diminished capacity for dipolar self-reflection among victims of interpersonal evil.[29] Christian perspectives on dissociation must give a more nuanced, compassionate response to abuse survivors than to demand they "just get right with God."

The seminal principles for secular psychodynamic remediation of trauma-induced dissociation, including the pathological splitting off of consciousness that follows from complex trauma, are empathic relationship and dialogue (DeYoung, 2003). Pressley & Hoek (2014) explain, "In order to facilitate the necessary conditions for emotional healing and behavioral change, the therapist has to provide a secure and safe enough environment for a client (child or adult) to release internalized 'bad objects' from the unconscious" (p. 254). Within a benign relational context, the externalization of conflict through dialogue aids in integration.

---

28. Howell (2011) observes that "Freud's views on instinctual drives and infantile development for the most part left out exogamous [*sic*; i.e., exogenous] trauma and blamed the child as the guilty one for having incestuous wishes" (p. 31). In fact, purportedly Christian approaches to counseling and caregiving that stress sin and obedience to God to the exclusion of other etiological factors do the same. There is a high risk of retraumatization for survivors of complex trauma by caregivers who do not adequately account for the traumagenic dynamics of abuse.

29. Natural disasters and other deprivations, although impersonal, also contribute to the breakdown of healthy psychological development in innumerable ways.

Caring, compassionate concern for others and a willingness to provide supportive help to the needy are hallmarks of New Testament ethics (Bonhoeffer, 2005; see Gal 6:2). Whether the church can readily perpetuate Jesus' mission to provide "rest" for the "weary and heavy-laden" may depend on its ability to identify and redress the unseen burdens borne by survivors of trauma and abuse (see Simpson, 2013; Stanford, 2017). Relational psychotherapy, in its attempts to ease the burden of the afflicted and heal the broken through empathic relationality, in many ways images the agapic concern of the triune God, if only partially and unconsciously. Final, eschatological remediation of the *curvum in se* self and integration of its fragmented self-consciousness can be finally achieved only through union with Christ. Yet, the principles of dynamic psychotherapy mirror at the psychosocial discursive level the means by which final eschatological healing takes place.[30]

In addition to these points of consonance, at least one serious disjunction with dynamic psychology must also be noted. At the theoretical or metapsychological level, psychodynamic theory rests on a strictly modernist foundation. As such, it eschews the Christian doctrines of the imago dei and hereditary sin, which together point out the basal antinomy of the fallen human condition. Created by God in his image, the original state of human beings was that of sinless perfection and communion with God. Since the fall, though still bearing a vestigial goodness by reason of the constitutive imago, human beings enter the world covenantally estranged from God and thus congenitally broken and *curvum in se* (Bonhoeffer, 1996; see Ps 58:3). At a strictly phenomenological level, this reality only becomes visible in the universally sinful inclination of the human heart (Rom 3:10–11).

Dynamic psychology, as an intellectual heir to modernist anthropology, regards the newborn self as an integral whole. According

30. Yet another reason to stipulate an ontological distinction between self and soul is the rhetorical impression given by referring to counselors as "soul physicians" (see, e.g., Kellemen, 2007; Kemp, 1947). This jargon, though essentially innocuous, nonetheless stems from an overly dualist anthropology that dichotomizes human nature into outer and inner essences claiming the latter as the sole proprietorship of God and the church. To reiterate, Jesus offers salvation not to *souls* but to *persons*. A biblical ecology of the whole person suggests that God's eschatological concern is to redeem the whole person, not just the inner, psychospiritual self (see 1 Cor 15:54). Consequently, creaturely care and concern for the *inner* self may justifiably be termed *psychotherapy* or *soul care*. Since neither label describes the work that only God can do in bringing about final salvation, the former need not bear the polemical weight of association with secular competitors to the Christian faith.

to Fairbairn (1954), "the pristine personality of the child consists of a unitary dynamic ego" (p. 107). Contemporary theorists have built on this thesis arguing that the infant self possesses a "primordial density" (Loewald, 1989, p. 180) or an "original, primal unity" (Mitchell, 2000, p. 4) undivided and undifferentiated by schism. These together suggest that, provided the ideal environment for its development, the adult self can achieve perfect equanimity and wholeness. A covenantal model of the self, on the other hand, rejects the possibility that human beings could achieve psychospiritual unity or wholeness apart from their reconciliation to, and union with, God-in-Christ.[31]

The dialogical relationship of sin and psychopathology

Dynamic psychology, covenantally understood, commends itself as a welcome ancillary to a christological anthropology, though caveats are warranted. As I have already noted, the language of sin and fallenness is conspicuously absent from most modern anthropologies (Menninger, 1973). Although the field of trauma studies regularly engages in implicit probing of the psychospiritual roots of interpersonal evil, most writers refrain from venturing beyond the strictly clinical sphere (though cf. Herman, 2015; Howell, 2005). Whether consciously or not, the impression given is that human nature is perfectible without God: given the proper care and nurture, in other words, people will be—and do—good.

Regrettably, this blind spot has come to characterize much of the Christian psychotherapeutic community at least insofar as it relies on modernist assumptions (J. E. Adams, 1986; McMinn, 2004; Powlison, 2003). As McRay et al. (2016) lament, "There certainly seems to be a fear among Christians [in the field] that if they reference sin they will be associated with those who essentially use the explanatory framework to bully others" (p. 95). On the other hand, as Johnson (2017) notes, Christian

---

31. This crucial point appears lost on Price (2002) who argues, "The anthropological holism that Barth advocates . . . finds a parallel in object relations [theory]. . . . Barth considers the human being as a dynamic and integrated whole, in ordered relation to God, self, and others. In similar fashion, object relations developed to the point where it could not accept the Freudian compartmentalization of the human being" (p. 225). Price is, perhaps, half-right; but the half he gets wrong is the concern Barth (2010) was most keen to emphasize: covenantal human relationality depends entirely on the person and work of Christ and believers' union with him. While object relations psychology corrects Freud in a number of helpful ways, its philosophical commitment to secularism remains expressly Freudian.

theologians rarely accommodate the reality of psychopathology and tend instead to focus exclusively on sin.[32] A dialogical perspective on the self, in contrast, views sin and psychopathology as complementary and interrelated phenomena. Not limited to a single discursive domain or explanatory framework, whether theological or psychological, this dialogical approach promises a more holistic account of the fallen human condition.

The paradox of self-deception

Illustrating the warrant for a dialogical perspective on sin and psychopathology, there is the problem of self-deception. This problem, as I refer to it, bears several related aspects. The first aspect shows up as we examine the close relationship between pathological dissociation and self-deception. Put succinctly, how can we determine which is which? No merely human being stands in a position to adduce whether barriers to self-knowledge stem from personal or interpersonal sin. In other words, determining the respective degrees to which sin and psychopathology are responsible for barriers of self-knowledge can prove difficult.

When it comes to what we can know about God and self, human beings are prone to "hinder the truth in unrighteousness" (Rom 1:19 ASV). In other words, there is a subliminal yet sinful motivation at work beneath agnosticism regarding the respective natures and forms of God and self (Calvin, 2008). Yet, it also seems likely that some limitations to self-knowledge (along with the knowledge of God) stem from factors beyond the personal control of the individual. Pathological dissociation, for example, disrupts one's ability to engage in dipolar self-reflection. Clearly, God does not charge the individual with sin for damage inflicted by others. To the extent that healing for psychopathological barriers like structural dissociation can be effected, self-knowledge is both means and end for the psychotherapeutic enterprise. In contrast, self-deception is both an ethical and a psychopathological problem. In other words, the ability of the individual to engage in self-deception is fomented by *both* sin and dissociation.

---

32. Sin can be understood as a form—indeed the most heinous form—of psychopathology.

A supreme irony of the modern age is the fact that, with the notable exception of Kierkegaard,[33] inquiry into the phenomenon of self-deception has been dominated by *secular* philosophers and psychologists. Since Sartre's (1993) notion of "bad faith" (*mauvaise foi*), in fact, the phenomenon of self-deception has been dominated by post/modern philosophy (see, e.g., Barnes, 1997; McLaughlin & Rorty, 1988; Räikkä, 2014). Fueling secular interest is the second aspect of the problem of self-deception: paradox. The intellectual challenge surrounding self-deception relates to its inherent contradiction.

Whether considered biblically (Gal 6:3; Jas 1:26) or empirically (Lauria et al., 2016), the conclusion is the same: people deceive themselves. What modern philosophy and psychology have wrestled to understand is, how can it be so? Whether we consider the question conceptually or psychologically, how, after all, can self deceive itself? Self-deception requires that the individual be conscious of some truth that has somehow simultaneously been hidden from consciousness. Paradoxically, the one who conceals the truth and the one who believes the lie are one and the same.

In consideration of the problem, Christian theology fares better than secular philosophy in that we can posit a more comprehensive subjective motivation for self-deception. Fallen and sinful, we are inclined toward the active maintenance of our self-blindness. With no such perspective on human sinfulness, Sartre (1993) is left to puzzle over the contradiction at the heart of self-deception:

> The essence of the lie implies in fact that the liar actually is in complete possession of the truth which he is hiding. A man does not lie about what he is ignorant of; he does not lie when he spreads an error of which he himself is the dupe; he does not lie when he is mistaken. . . . Bad faith then has in appearance the structure of falsehood. Only what changes everything is the fact that in bad faith it is from myself that I am hiding the truth. Thus the duality of the deceiver and the deceived does not exist here. (pp. 87, 89)

The well-worn case is often given of the woman with a philandering husband whose adultery is obvious to all but his stubbornly naïve wife. She cannot simultaneously acknowledge his sin *and* evade the resultant fear, shame, and self-hatred she would undoubtedly face. The lie

---

33. See, chiefly, Kierkegaard (1980, 1991).

she believes—that he is innocent—is preferable to the truth she conceals. Sartre implies as much in describing "bad faith" as "hiding a displeasing truth or presenting as truth a pleasing untruth" (p. 89).[34]

Respective to the cognitive *means* of self-deception, the problem is no less complex for Christian or secular psychology. By what mechanism or method can I simultaneously know the truth and believe its opposite? Half a century before Sartre, Freud (S. Freud, 1923) posited a tripartite structure of the self, wherein the ego—the "me" who is conscious and active in reality—is influenced by the id—my unconscious, primitive, self-gratifying impulses—and the superego—acquired social and moral strictures for acceptable behavior frequently in conflict with the impulsive id. In applying classical psychoanalysis to the paradox of self-deception, Spiegel (1999) observes that an individual "may unconsciously know one thing and, due to the impulses of the id, consciously believe something wholly contradictory" (p. 49). Thus, one module or system within the self impinges on another—obfuscating, concealing, placating—all in defense of the whole.

Freudian theory further proposes that defense mechanisms operating separately from the individual's conscious awareness serve to protect the ego from the anxiety induced by unpleasant truths (A. Freud, 1977; see also Bachkirova, 2016, p. 4; cf. Johnson & Burroughs, 2000). The challenge respective to self-deception most often leveled against compartmentalist theories of the self—such as those found in the psychoanalytical tradition—is that they lack coherence (Spiegel, 1999). Despite the apparent explanatory power of such models, their chief weakness lies in their appeal to interpersonal deception. In other words, what appears non-contradictory when there are two individuals—the deceiver and the deceived—descends into incoherence when there is only one person, unless it is assumed that persons are actually (and not metaphorically) made up of discrete systems capable of, and intent upon, deceiving one another.[35]

Probing the nuances of Freudian compartmentalism, Johnston (1988) queries,

---

34. In this case at least, the parallel between self-deception and Freudian repression is clear.

35. An additional problem arises when consideration is made as to how the unconscious can *intend* anything, let alone perpetrate the deception of the conscious self, if it is truly *un*conscious (see Spiegel, 1999, p. 51).

> [H]ow does the deceiving system engage in an extended cam-
> paign of deception, employing various stratagems to alter the
> beliefs of the deceived system, without the deceived system's
> somehow noticing? If the deceived system somehow notices
> then the deception cannot succeed without the collusion of
> the deceived system. However, to speak of the collusion of the
> deceived system in its own deception simply reintroduces the
> original problem [i.e., paradox]. (p. 64)

Moreover, Johnston points out in reference to the details of Augustine's conversion that self-deception often entails an act of the will, a refusal to face the truth.[36] Thus, self-deception, he concludes, is more akin to epistemic cowardice, though he notes that this type of mental activity is frequently "subintentional" (p. 64).[37]

Taking both the cognitive and the volitional aspects into consideration, Spiegel (1999) concludes that there are, perhaps, two related forms of self-deception, differentiation between which

> depends upon the degree of cognitive processing in the for-
> mation of one's belief. The more one is aware of the evidence
> for one's belief (whether bogus or not), the greater the ability
> and willingness to avow or spell out reasons for one's behavior.
> And the less one is aware of evidence for the belief upon which
> one's behavior is premised, the less the ability to avow it. Self-
> deceivers of the former sort are what we call rationalizers, while
> those in the latter case are ignorantly self-deceived. (pp. 64–65)

In other words, not all faulty beliefs are thought out. Sometimes we have an impression of a false but pleasant reality; at other times, the whole body of evidence is stacked against us. In either case, some cognitive process is working against a veridical appraisal. Self-deception implies as much.

---

36. See my treatment of Augustine's conversion in Chapter 2.

37. A "subintentional" act might be akin to a reflexive or habituated response; so, for instance, one person might run from danger while another, perhaps someone trained as a first responder, might, without much reflection, run toward it. In secular philosophy the habituated avoidance of unpleasant truths about oneself is typically viewed as an "adaptive" response—thus, persons who believe the best about themselves are more likely to thrive and, ultimately, reproduce. It is difficult to see how self-deception, according to this naturalistic account, can be a bad thing (see S. E. Taylor, 1989)!

By definition, self-deception is never unmotivated,[38] as this would be a contradiction.[39] Nevertheless, I may not always have a sense of why I believe something that does not correspond to a truth that I, at some level, know. The degree to which I may reasonably be expected to recognize my self-deception will determine the degree to which I may be held responsible for this form of self-"betrayal" (Bachkirova, 2016, p. 6; cf. John 9:40–41). Along these lines, Darwall (1988) concludes, "[S]elf-deception is at least like other-deception in this respect: a person can be charged with and held responsible for it. It is a moral matter in a way that simply believing or thinking something as the causal result of desires may not be" (p. 411).

If all this be true, then the gap between the phenomenon of self-deception may be explained in terms of motivation. The naïve wife of a philandering husband is, perhaps, motivated by fear of shame and loss to trust in her husband's claims to fidelity. She will likely hold out in the marriage, enduring the inner turmoil of willed ignorance regarding his unfaithfulness, until, perhaps, he moves to divorce her and the reason for her self-deceit becomes moot. Augustine, until awakened from his ignorance and unbelief, was motivated, by both fear and pride perhaps to believe he was one thing when in fact he was something else—a sinner (see Gal 6:3). Only when God refused to allow him to shelter any longer in his comfortable delusion was he obliged to confront the painful reality of his sinfulness.

Self-deception, then, is rooted in a motivational bias[40] to protect and provide for the real or imagined wellbeing of the self. This is accomplished by hiding—i.e., dissociating from—unpleasant realities and focusing instead on that which reinforces a more salutary fiction.[41] Given some degree of assistance from others in ignoring or diminishing defeaters for faulty views of self, these beliefs can become reinforced over

---

38. Motivationalist accounts of self-deception (see, e.g., Fernández, 2013) are particularly compatible with a Christian understanding of the deceitfulness of sin.

39. Mistaken belief (i.e., "epistemic failure") does not qualify as self-deception (contra Patten, 2003).

40. Recent empirical studies examining how subintentional cognitive and volitional processes influence self-deception have demonstrated the remarkable degree to which bias can inform conscious belief and avowals (see, e.g., Funkhouser & Barrett, 2016).

41. In his discussion of the psychosocial implications of the noetic effects of sin, Moroney (2000) employs the term "self-serving cognitive distortion" to describe the phenomenon of self-deception (pp. 89–90).

time and habituated so that the likelihood of influencing self-deception becomes increasingly remote. Self-deception is no solo affair; it is a team sport.

As is clear from the two examples—the desperate wife and Augustine pre-conversion—not all forms of self-deception are morally equivalent. Although, generally, the motivation for self-deception seems to be preserving the self from unpleasant truths, Augustine's desire to avoid certain truths—namely, the extent of his sinfulness and his concomitant feelings of guilt and shame—meant that he was consequently deceived about his need for forgiveness and salvation. While the naïve wife's self-deception may, in fact, bear a moral component,[42] Augustine's pre-conversion self-ignorance amounted to moral self-deception precisely because he thought himself better than he actually was.

Self-deception and the relational self

Jesus' warning against hypocrisy among believers suggests our capacity for self-obfuscation remains even after conversion (Matt 7:5). Experience confirms this to be true. Morally blameworthy self-deception, as I have shown, may be defined as the motivated assuagement of the conscience—one's God-given sense of reflexive moral judgment (see Johnson, 2007, pp. 341–342; cf. Rom 2:5; Titus 1:15; Heb 10:22)—resulting in a false personal assurance of goodness or sincerity (Badgett, 2018b). Hypocrisy, by extension, consists of the projection of a false image onto others by means of public moral conduct and speech. It is worth noting that hypocrisy essentially functions to conscript others into the service of a conscience-placating agenda. The more others affirm—and so reinforce—our faulty views of self, the more solid and intractable they become. Whereas, when relationships fail to appreciably reinforce self-deception, we are more likely to be confronted with the difficult truth of who we really are.

In observing the dynamics of moral self-deception, modern social scientists and psychologists have made an additional caveat. A growing body of empirical research has noted the apparent desire of persons, regardless of their worldview, to appear before others to act morally

---

42. Some feminist theologies of sin would hold the wife responsible for the sin of sloth, charging her with "*wilful* [sic] indolence or indifference which is culpable because it involves a free choice" for her, albeit subintentional, decision to perpetuate the sham that is her marriage, thereby enabling her husband's philandering (McFadyen, 2000, p. 139; emphasis original).

(Batson, 2007; Batson et al., 1999; Sie, 2015). For example, one study (Burris & Navara, 2002) demonstrated a positive correlation between moral self-deception and one's perceived social standing within a peer group or community. Based on the results of this study, researchers observed, "[individuals] who bolstered self-deception seemed to perceive disclosure of their faults as risking censure rather than ensuring solace from the religious group" (p. 74). In other words, our inclination toward self-deception is likely to increase as the social risks associated with shame and stigma increase. Fear of being found out, of losing the support of one's community, can impel individuals to conceal truths about self from others, as well as from self. Evidently, the dissociative nature of the fallen human mind makes such subterfuge possible.

Shame and the estranged self

In addition to being a subjective affect, emotion or evaluative criterion, shame is also a state of being inherited from the fall, one that profoundly corrupts the imaging capacities of human beings (Johnson, 2017). According to Bonhoeffer (2005), the source of humanity's endemic shame is our primordial estrangement from God,

> the irrepressible memory of disunion from [humanity's] origin. It is the pain of this disunion, and the helpless desire to reverse it. Human beings are ashamed because they have lost something that is part of their original nature and their wholeness. (p. 303)

Shame is the existential angst that flows from humanity's estrangement. The estranged self longs to be whole but is impotent to autonomously effectuate its own healing. Although Kierkegaard (1980) never directly refers to shame, it is nevertheless implicit in his notion of despair, the "sickness unto death" that characterizes our fallen human condition. In the same way that the fallen self seeks to "tear away" from God and from itself, so also does the shame-prone human self tend toward dissociation and self-deception (p. 20). Moreover, the social structures and dynamics of human society only serve to perpetuate this pathological tendency.

Existential shame, or the despair of the fallen self, drives many of the pathological dynamics of intrapsychic and interpersonal functioning (Johnson, 2017). Nevertheless, the subjective experience of shame, like other expressions of human brokenness, is not always due to some moral failing inherent in the individual (Stump, 2012).[43] Thus, shame can be greatly influenced by horizontal relationality as well (see Harter, 2015; Broucek, 1991; Tomkins, 1987). As recent empirical studies have demonstrated, dysfunctional and dysregulating interactions between self and other appear to fuel the subjective experience of shame (Gilbert & Andrews, 1998). Additionally, numerous social and cultural factors have been shown to exacerbate the perception that one is unworthy and unacceptable (Pulakos, 1996; Silfver-Kuhalampi et al., 2013).

While some forms of shame have even been demonstrated to have a prosocial function in inhibiting behavior that transgresses acceptable moral norms (Gruenewald et al., 2007; Tangney, 2003),[44] most secular theorists tend to emphasize its psychopathological or maladaptive aspects. Additionally, chronic or pervasive shame has been implicated as the underlying psychopathological contributor to dissociation: "unspeakable shame at the affective core of the self soon becomes untouchable and unknowable. As a person finds ways to hide, protect, and compensate for shamed vulnerability, chronic shame itself becomes dissociated" (DeYoung, 2015, p. 140). Arguably, no other intrapsychic dynamic generates greater motivation to dissociate from veridical self-knowledge than does shame.

A covenantal anthropology accounts very well for the findings of secular research regarding the interpersonal dynamics of shame and dissociation. We were created for right relationship with God and with others; and subjective wholeness depends on a being-in-relation that cannot be achieved autonomously. By suppressing knowledge of our estrangement from God, human beings unconsciously defend against the guilt and shame of our dislocation from divine favor and communion. In doing so, we dissociate from the very truth that perpetuates our estrangement. Additionally, breeches in horizontal relationality effect an analogous subjective experience of shame and hiding compounding barriers to self-knowledge by further fueling our self-deceptive inclinations. Most tragic of all, humanity's archetypal dysregulating experience—the

---

43. So, for example, Tamar's feelings of shame following her rape by Amnon, her half-brother, did not arise due to any intrinsic fault or transgression on her part (see 2 Sam 13:19).

44. Focusing exclusively on the subjective experience of shame, McCullough et al., (2003) classify shame as an "inhibitory affect" along with the emotions of fear, guilt, grief, and disgust (pp. 21–22).

fall—from which we universally dissociate until grace intervenes, occurred on account of our rebellion.[45]

Dissociation as a defensive strategy—a divine mercy for the abused and neglected—is only necessary in a fallen world where sin and shame pervade all forms of human relationality. As such, dissociation is the cognitive analogue of the animal skins God used to cover our first parents' nakedness—his shield for the vulnerable inner self. Self-deceptive inclinations, on the other hand, most likely function at some level in the interest of quelling psychospiritual unrest, yet often result in heightened dysfunction and isolation. Shame and the fear of shame typically operate on human cognition and volition at a preconscious and subintentional level greatly problematizing active, perspicuous introspection. The dissociative complexion of human cognition, moreover, fosters a sinful tendency to evade direct apperception of moral faults and weaknesses. To a remarkable degree the human mind demonstrates a resilient resistance to truth that disquiets or disrupts our preferred self-conceptions.

Self-blame and moral stigma

Shame is an intrasubjective reality rooted in rejection and estrangement. Personal shame grows out of interpersonal isolation. Stigma, on the other hand, is a social reality with strong implications for the development of pathological shame. Stigma amounts to any mark of distinction resulting in social isolation or exclusion (Goffman, 1963). Stigma can consist of any indicator of difference from culturally-derived standards of normality, whether physical, mental, characterological, or social (see Ainlay et al., 1986). Whether stigmatizing differences bear a moral aspect or not, their effect is to place individuals beyond the bounds of acceptable norms within a given community or culture. As such, stigma often carries an immense social weight driving persons to conceal or otherwise diminish the visibility of such markers.

Any stigma-conferring attribute, when visible or public, can trigger the disapproval and disavowal of the community of "normals" to which

---

45. Cain's experience of divine disfavor motivated his murder of Abel (Gen 4:1–9; cf. 1 John 3:12). These two serve as archetypal figures respectively representative of the dynamics of interpersonal sin since the fall. Cain, having experienced the dysregulating, dis-integrating shame of rejection, narcissistically inflicted his anger upon the one he held responsible for his failure.

the individual had hoped to belong.[46] So long as deviating markers remain unseen, the pressure to conceal them can further fuel any dissociative and deceptive inclinations (see Coleman, 1986).[47] As we might expect, sin and its concomitant shame carry the weight of moral stigma within morally-sensitive cultures, the fear of which instigates self-deception and self-righteousness among believers. Self-stigma can therefore be defined as an enduring perspective on self as unworthy, unacceptable, and beyond rehabilitation. The relationship between stigma and shame on the one hand and dissociation and self-deception on the other becomes evident in the vital connection between personal and interpersonal wholeness. Human beings were created by God to exist in intimate communion with him and with each other.

Conclusion to Part IV

The possibility of self-deception counts against any supposed "scientific" objectivity respective to God and self. Reasonably minded, otherwise well-meaning individuals may claim freedom from bias and a sole commitment to the facts; yet the realities of sin and psychopathology count strongly against such claims. These two barriers to self-knowledge distort and obscure all that we think we know of self, God, and others with the result that our most sincere and discerning judgments can never be wholly trusted. Unseen and unacknowledged conflicts and schisms persist, even in believers, rendering our determinations suspect.

The dissociative nature of fallen human beings makes it possible, even likely, that unpleasant and shameful truths about the self will remain hidden from view; whereas, the deceitful human heart perpetually supplies conscience-placating fig leaves—cover stories that ignore or explain away what cannot be formulated and integrated into our conceptions of self. In light of these mutually reinforcing dynamics of fallen human

46. Vacek's (2015) survey of American Protestantism, for instance, demonstrates how evangelical attitudes toward mentally disordered persons have shifted over the years.

47. Fear of stigma associated with mental disorders varies from person to person (Corrigan & Watson, 2002) as well as along historical and cultural lines. One empirical study (Ilic et al., 2013) found that fears of stigmatization ran higher among sufferers of schizophrenia than for depression suggesting that certain disorders carry a higher degree of social stigma than others. The tendency to self-stigmatize correlates closely with individuals' beliefs regarding the cause(s) of their condition, whether genetic (i.e., tribal), organic, or environmental (see Larkings et al., 2017).

nature, how can we ever finally know that we are not mistaken and self-deceived about who we really are?

The promise of dynamic psychology, when framed in strictly secular terms, amounts to a recapitulation of the serpent's lie: the promise of veridical knowledge—of self and others—without God. As such, it perpetuates the folly of the fall. Yet, there is also ample consonance between Christian and psychodynamic conceptions of human beings to warrant dialogue. In his skepticism, Freud eschewed both Cartesian and Kantian epistemological frameworks inaugurating a new age of suspicion respective to human self-knowledge. While Freud regarded belief in God to be a delusion, he assisted, albeit unwittingly, in the overthrow of his intellectual forbears' faulty conceptions of the self. Psychodynamic psychology, inasmuch as it examines and explicates the phenomena of the conflicted, schizoid self-consciousness, accords with a biblical conception of human beings.

As anticipated by a covenantally-construed christological anthropology, dynamic psychology affirms the relational nature of the human self, the numerous developmental contributors to psychopathology, and the psychosocial phenomena of dissociation and self-deception. Nevertheless, secular models lack sufficient coherence and explanatory power with respect to self-deception, having failed to emphasize the moral weight and consequences of willed self-ignorance "before God" (Kierkegaard, 1980, p. 82). Only a Christian psychological perspective—one that maintains the sinfulness and deceitfulness of the fallen human heart—can sufficiently explain this universal human inclination.

Part V

A Christological Perspective on Pastoral and Psychotherapeutic Modalities

Chapter 9

Reconciliation, instrumentality, and dialogical self-knowledge

CONSIDERING THE FALLEN NATURE of human beings, it should be no surprise that contemporary social psychology has recapitulated Aristotle's observation of a self-serving attributional bias—a tendency to see the good that is not there and discount the bad that is—in our self-conceptions (Baumeister, 1999). As noted in the previous chapter, psychodynamic psychology still maintains a healthy dose of Freudian skepticism regarding hidden and unformulated aspects of the inner self—the "me" I believe myself to be. Additionally, Harter's (2015) broad survey of developmental psychology supports the conclusion that dissociative and self-deceptive tendencies originate in childhood and adolescence.

For the most part, however, the intuition prevails that unchecked dissociation, self-deception, and hypocrisy effect a corrosive influence on individuals and their relationships (cf. S. E. Taylor, 1989). With few exceptions, the assumption is made that authenticity and transparency to self and others foster psychological wellbeing and interpersonal wholeness. Self-awareness promotes characterological growth so long as it avoids the dangers of self-absorption (see Leary, 2002, 2004).[1] From the time of the ancient Greeks until the present, then, knowledge of self has persisted in secular thought as a worthy, achievable aim. In spite of the innumerable

1. Overly "*ruminative* self-consciousness," Christianly understood, is an expression of our fallen nature and, as such, undermines believers' growth in Christiformity (see Johnson, 2007, p. 441, emphasis original).

challenges and caveats, "Know thyself," still stands as a maxim attendant to human existence.

As borne out by the Christian tradition, knowledge of self should be understood, in its ultimate sense, as coming to perceive oneself in light of who Christ is and what he has done. Though any number of veridical claims may be made about the knowable self—its constitutive nature and formal qualities—merely looking at the mirror of others who are made in God's image, there can be no finally true knowledge of the covenantal selfapart from Christ. Authentic human existence is covenantal (Barth, 2010; Horton, 2006). Created as we have been in the image *of* God, we instantiate the condition of our nature only in proper—that is, agapic—relation *to* God and also to others.

Agapic relationality is the telos of the imago. Through love, we fulfill the end for which we were created in God's image. God's archetypal love is the ethical emanation of his being (1 John 4:8), resulting in an unyielding disposition of favor and faithfulness.[2] The Scriptures attest to what the gospel illustrates: his steadfast love endures forever (Ps 136:1). The triune persons of the Godhead eternally subsist in a covenantal relationality perfectly balanced between self- and other-regard. In creating humanity in his image, God has established in our very nature the extrinsic aim of our existence. Through covenantal union with Christ we access this telic agenda, entering into agapic fellowship with God and others by means of a Spirit-mediated, perichoretic mutuality. As the apostle avers, the autonomous self no longer lives, but Christ-in-self (see Gal 2:20).

By way of prerequisite for our participation in the divine life, human beings possess divinely conferred constitutive capacities through which we relate to God, to others, and to ourselves. Yet, the constitutional aspects of human nature subsist in service to the covenantal character of human life. Whole persons consist of inner and outer essences—noetic, volitional, affective, and somatic—so designed and conferred by God in order that we might fulfill the charter of the imago: to love the Lord

---

2. A biblical perspective on God's love need not temper this conclusion by juxtaposing it with God's justice (cf. Wolterstorff, 2015). The love and justice of God are both ethical aspects of his divine perfection; as such, they do not contradict or "balance" one another. A more salient juxtaposition would be God's love and human freedom: God, in his love, gives freedom to humanity to reject his loving overtures. By spurning God's love, humanity invites the just repercussions of eschewing our only good since all that is holy, righteous, and life-sustaining is found in God alone. God's eschatological wrath, then, may be viewed as both just *and* loving in that, by promulgating sin's punitive consequences, God seeks to motivate human repentance (2 Pet 3:9–10).

God with heart, soul, mind, and strength, and to love neighbor as oneself (Mark 12:30). God has created human beings, in other words, in order that we might mirror him through our dialogical participation in covenantal communion—with him and with each other.

The self, that onto-relational locus of subjectivity, is the vehicle for individual agentic expression of the covenantal image of God. Though every image-bearing person *is* a self, selfhood is nevertheless a calling. And the knowledge of self supports the covenantal agenda of selfhood as the barriers of sin and psychopathology are identified and overcome, specifically within the context of agapic relationality. We can know who we truly are—and, therefore, who we are *not*—as we are well-loved by God and by others. Whereas, sin damages and disrupts self-perception, clouds our judgment, and problematizes all claims of self-knowledge.

The universal human inclination toward dissociation and self-deception bears out the tragic noetic implications of human fallenness. Structural self-ignorance and self-blindness are not merely the consequences of the transcendent, ineffable aspects of the human self and our own creaturely finitude. To the contrary, hereditary and interpersonal sin effects a powerful and pervasive corrupting influence on our ability to self-perceive. We do not see ourselves both because we cannot *and* because we will not. There is a plank, as it were, in all our eyes (Matt 7:5).

As the risk of sounding trite, love is the answer. Love, that is, that has been conditioned and oriented as an expression of the covenantal faithfulness of Jesus Christ. This love provokes and sustains psychosocial processes through which self-knowledge and the knowledge of God and others come to be. Simultaneously, the perichoretic knowing that flows from love enriches, informs, and effects a more genuine agapic regard for others. Love is the relational substratum supportive of mutual interpersonal knowing. It is also the ethical expression of intersubjective apperception: to know is to love. So, knowing and loving relate dialogically and reciprocally. Put another way, we know best when we are well-loved, and we love best what we know most intimately.

For fallen human beings, however, neither veridical knowledge nor genuine love are possible without the initiatory self-revelation of God. Apart from our pistic appropriation of divine discourse—confident assurance in the love and faithfulness of God's Logos—we do not know rightly nor can we ever come to love truly.[3] Again, the relationship between the

3. Drawing on the philosophical writings of Reformed theologian Herman Dooyeweerd, Choi (2006) writes, "If the heart remains closed to God's revelation, the pistic

knowledge of and the love for God is dialogical. For this reason, Jesus adjures his disciples to love him through knowing and keeping his word (John 14:21). We can only love Christ as we maintain a pistic commitment to his word. The reverse is also true: as we become better listeners and doers of his word, our love for Christ can only grow (see 1 John 2:5).[4]

In much the same way, love between human persons is mediated and expressed in the context of agapic dialogue. More than an exchange of intersubjective discourse, agapic dialogue is the mutual, reciprocal interpersonal knowing and keeping of the "word" of other.[5] By contrast, a strictly monological "love"—one that speaks but does not listen—is not love at all, but "self-love," autonomy's bitter ethical fruit. Along both its vertical and horizontal axes, relationality characterized by impaired or asymmetrical dialogue cannot but fail to displace barriers to self-knowledge. Faith must "hear" other/Other in fulfilment of love's imperative. Love that listens without fear receives the "word" of other/Other by faith.

Respective to barriers to self-knowledge, it is precisely in the context of the dialogical exchange of covenantal personhood that these impediments come to nothing. By contrast, an exclusively monological "exchange" is tantamount to interpersonal sin in that it deprives other of a fundamental means by which we become more fully human (see McFadyen, 1990, pp. 122–23). Having been reconciled to God-in-Christ,

---

aspect [of the heart] cannot but seek its alternate absolute ground in the creation itself, an act which results in the idolatrous absolutizing of meaning itself" (p. 27).

4. The self-deceived Christian, as James warns, is the one who knows but does not keep the word of God (Jas 1:22). Echoing the apostolic admonition against objectivist spirituality, Kierkegaard (1991) picks up on this theme inviting Scripture's readers to "think that it is I to whom it [the word] is speaking, I—and incessantly I—of whom it speaks" (p. 36). It may be that the entire English Puritan movement can be summed up as the wholesale rejection of objectivist spirituality (see Packer, 2010). There is a case to be made that a person who knows but does not do the word, does not truly know at all.

5. This understanding of dialogue follows from McFadyen's (1990) understanding of the term: "A relation of mutuality and reciprocity which involves the subjective engagement, and therefore autonomy, of two or more partners. In dialogue there is a sharing of the dialogue roles of I and Thou, so that all partners are given space and time for independent communication and are attended to by the others. Because attending to the independent communication and being of others can change one's own understanding of them, oneself or the world (and potentially one's identity as well), dialogue is also a dialectical process and more like a spiral than a circle" (p. 314). McFadyen's use of "autonomy" in this context is, possibly, somewhat misleading, if not, in fact, a poor word choice. It would seem that his usage is similar to what I have termed personal agency or response-ability.

the self that dialogically self-perceives in agapic communion with another need no longer disavow or evade veridical self-knowledge by means of dissociation and self-deception. Through the mediating influence of Christ's Spirit, the gaze of the loving other facilitates the removal of the epistemic and ethical impediments of sin and psychopathology.

Agapic dialogue: Faith working through love

Autonomy leads to the death of the covenantal self and the obviation of self-knowledge. This conclusion follows from the gospel. Apart from Christ, we are dead in our sins and transgressions. To come to Christ as our sole means of reconciliation to God, we are made alive in him. Our autonomous human effort contributes nothing.

In his admonition to the Galatian churches, Paul decries the folly of pursuing an autonomous righteousness through obedience to the law. In the strongest of terms he remonstrates, "You have been severed [κατηργήθητε, katērgēthēte], from Christ, you who are seeking to be justified by law; you have fallen from grace" (Gal 5:4 NASB). Paul intends that his warning should serve as a rebuke to the "foolish Galatians" (3:1) for having abandoned Christ as the sole means of their salvation (Moo, 2013). Although they began in the Spirit, they are now seeking their perfection—eschatological wholeness or completion—through autonomous means (Gal 3:3).

The path of autonomy, according to Paul, is antipodally opposed to life. To seek one's wholeness apart from Christ is ultimately self-defeating (cf. Rom 7). The pursuit of self-righteousness—the ethical right-standing of the autonomous self—only recapitulates the archetypal self-betrayal of humanity's Edenic rebellion (Gen 3). According to the terms of the gospel, reconciliation is wholly contingent on our submission to God's christocentric agenda. The route the Galatians have chosen, in contrast, ends in eschatological death—ultimate, final alienation and separation from God (cf. Ezek 14:7–11).[6] Evidently, to trust in our autonomous ability only perpetuates the fallen, estranged state brought on by human sin. Paul enjoins the Galatians that their autonomous effort is doomed to fail. The only sure route to God, he avers, is "faith working through love" (Gal 5:6)—a pistic commitment to the "word" of Christ expressed both through one's agapic regard for God and concern for others.

6. See the various meanings of καταργέ- (katarge-) in Danker (2001).

Hermeneutics and ethics in dialogue

As we should expect, the dialogical pursuit of Christian self-knowledge parallels the Pauline soteriological framework. By means of the same ethicospiritual framework, *faith working through love*, the covenantal self comes to know God, self, and other. In other words, covenantal relationality results in veridical self-knowledge insofar as both its hermeneutical and ethical aspects have been grounded in the person and work of Christ.

To further explain, the knowledge of self relates to hermeneutics because of the dialogical nature of knowledge (see Clark & Gaede, 1987). With revelation as its epistemological basis, hermeneutics is eminently programmatic for faith.[7] Faith attests to the warrant of Christian belief, the foundation of which is Christ (1 Cor 3:11). Moreover, self-knowledge relates to ethics due to the dialogical nature of the self. Faith, the apostle attests, is meant to be expressed covenantally *in love*—the supreme ethical calling of image bearers. "Love" that acts not in faith will invariably have self as its object.

An unbalanced, wholly reflexive "self-love," by contrast, is the ethical expression of the autonomous self and finds its basis in an inverted ethic. Autonomous "self-love" places self above other as the supreme object of worth, leading inevitably to a consumptive and abusive disposition toward other.[8] It is the wellspring of interpersonal sin. Love that expresses faith, on the other hand, will find its basis in the good of another, even if it comes at cost to self (see Zachman, 2012). These two aspects, faith and love—respectively, the hermeneutical and ethical causata of the covenantal self—function dialectically and dialogically with regard to self-knowledge. Crucially, these two must balance and inform one another lest barriers to self-knowledge persist.

---

7. As early as the Augustinian formulation of *faith seeking understanding*, the relationship between hermeneutics and Christian belief have been clearly articulated. To wit, "There are two things on which all interpretation of scripture depends: the process of discovering what we need to learn, and the process of presenting what we have learnt" (Augustine, 2008, I.i.1; p. 8). Faith, in other words, entails the hermeneutical dialogue of the text and the reader.

8. Kierkegaard (1998) argues that *all* forms of "preferential love" are actually expressions of "self-love" (p. 53).

Toward a dialogue of dialogues

As we have seen, covenantal self-knowledge is fundamentally dialogical—a dialogue of dialogues even, considering the relation of its hermeneutical and ethical aspects. By way of exposition, we must consider the dialogical character of *faith working through love*. To speak of faith and love is to imply some exchange. With respect to faith, this dialogue is hermeneutical. To speak of love is to imply an ethical exchange. Taken together, the hermeneutical and ethical dialogues interact dialogically in service of the formation of the covenantal self.

Orthodox Christianity maintains that God is a speaking God (Wolterstorff, 1995). Revelation is divine discourse—God's gracious Logos to humanity. Faith entails a hermeneutical dialogue precisely because right interpretation—the exclusive provenance of the Holy Spirit—is faith's epistemic prerequisite. "Faith comes by hearing, and hearing through the word of Christ" (Rom 10:17). As the Scriptures make clear, faith is not merely hearing but *receiving* (v. 14; cf. John 1:12; 1 Cor 15:1; Col 2:6; 2 Thess 3:6). Consequently, revelation relates to faith as locution relates to perlocution: faith is revelation's intended result, its dialogical reply (Vanhoozer, 2014; see John 20:31).

The God who speaks also desires that we should *believe* his word/Word (see Gen 15:6; John 6:29; Rom 1:17; Heb 11:6). The idea of faith presumes a hermeneutical dialogue—an interpretative evaluation or determination made in response to divine discourse—and further, that any pistic commitment to Christian truth be rooted in a right interpretation of its discursive content. Unless the content of one's belief corresponds veridically with its revelatory counterpart, faith is misplaced, mistaken. This hermeneutical exchange is completed or "perfected" as faith comes into increasing veridical correspondence with divine truth.[9]

Faith, then, is the proper dialogical response to divine revelation. Yet, as the New Testament bears out, faith's reply to revelation leads to an even higher, divinely enacted end: the reconciliation of God and the human person brought about through the agapic union of Christ and his people. Peace with God comes through faith in Christ's atoning death on our behalf—his act of agapic self-sacrifice by which divine love speaks (Rom 5:1; Eph 2:8). In the death of Christ the divine Word of truth

---

9. The writer of Hebrews refers to Christ as the "perfecter of . . . faith [τὸν τῆς πίστεως . . . τελειωτὴν, *ton tēs pisteōs . . . teleiōtēn*]" (12:2); see Osborne's (2006) "hermeneutical spiral."

discloses God's work of love (John 3:16). The cross of Christ is God's ultimate speech-act with enough perlocutionary force to overcome sin and death, along with every other barrier to covenantal wholeness. Although numerous impediments and deficits may remain for the present age, the promise of love is God's eschatological bestowal of "every blessing in the heavenly places" (Eph 1:3; cf. Col 1:12).

Following from this, as divine revelation relates dialogically to human faith, so reconciliation relates to love. Love for God-in-Christ is the only proper ethical reply to the loving self-sacrifice of God-in-Christ. Indeed, the divine disclosure of Christ must redound in love for God and other if it is to fulfill the ethical calling of *faith working through love*. As with faith, love also entails a dialogical exchange. Mutual, reciprocal agapic regard is the means by which humanity fulfills the covenantal image—both in relation to God and to others. Let me unpack these two premises a bit further as they relate to covenantal self-knowledge.

Dialogical hermeneutics

Hermeneutics relates to covenantal self-knowledge in a number of ways. For Gadamer (1976), self-knowledge is an expressly hermeneutical enterprise. "To understand a text," he writes, "is to come to understand oneself in a kind of dialogue" (p. 57; see also Bakhtin, 1986). Self-consciousness is, as Gadamer suggests, an experience of the transcendent or what he calls "the self-understanding of faith" (p. 49).[10] He further argues that Christian theology provides the proper hermeneutical frame for the knowledge of self as the subjective center of transcendent human experience.[11] The self is not, as modernity would have us believe, an object that may be subjected to phenomenological scrutiny or scientific systematization. This objectivist error perennially bedevils attempts to grasp the meaning of the self and its proper telic orientation.

10. Gadamer focuses on the hermeneutical implications of self-knowledge, but his conclusions bear strong implications for pastoral theology and Christian psychology as well.

11. According to Zimmermann (2004), Gadamer's recognition of the epistemic value of Christian theology respective to transcendence, regrettably, does not extend to any personal commitment to the exclusive truth claims of the Christian faith. His hermeneutical theory is consistent with Christianity even if his personal belief system is not.

Gadamer recapitulates Augustine in arguing that the knowledge of the transcendent human self comes—as with its converse, the knowledge of God—through faith seeking understanding. Along these lines, he concludes,

> From the theological point of view, faith's self-understanding is determined by the fact that faith is not man's possibility, but a gracious act of God that happens *to* the one who has faith. To the extent that one's self-understanding is dominated by modern science and its methodology, . . . it is difficult for him to hold fast to this theological insight and religious experience. The concept of knowledge based on scientific procedures tolerates no restriction of its claim to universality. On the basis of this claim, all self-understanding is represented as a kind of self-possession that excludes nothing as much as the idea that something that separates it from itself can befall it. (p. 54)

Self-knowledge is a gift but *not* a possession. In other words, it is contingent upon relationship, not on any strictly constitutive or rational capacity. As such, self-knowledge can only arise in the context of covenantal dialogue.

As self dialogically discloses itself with other, a mutual and reciprocal knowing and being known ensues. The hermeneutical exchange that results in veridical self-understanding, however, requires that faith pursue its basis in divine self-disclosure. Every mirror reveals self, but only that mirror which reflects self truly should be wholly trusted (cf. Jas 1:24). It is possible, therefore, to grow in assurance of self-understanding and yet be finally misled.[12] Dialogue that disregards the hermeneutical supremacy of Christ and the epistemic warrant of Scripture will necessarily distort perspectives on self and other.

Interpersonal sin, a defective and destructive form of dialogue, certainly informs a diversity of perspectives on self; yet, the resulting "knowledge" of self will necessarily be characterized by various barriers to veridicality. In order to overcome false images of self resulting from hereditary and interpersonal sin, self's hermeneutical dialogue must first rest in assurance of the epistemic sovereignty of the triune God. God alone knows self as it truly is. Although some psychopathological barriers to self-knowledge may, in fact, yield to a strictly secular dialogue,

---

12. From this we may conclude that self-deception, as an aspect of one's self-consciousness, also arises within a relational context.

self's deepest, most fundamental delusions and deceptions can only be overcome when faith is grounded in divine self-disclosure.[13]

The ethical dialogue

Although Gadamer rightly apprehends the dialogical character of self-knowledge, he nevertheless falls short of a fully Christian approach. This is due to his failure to recognize the hermeneutical significance of the person and work of Christ (Zimmermann, 2004). Though he rightly identifies the nature of the transcendent human self and the dialogical quality of self-knowledge, he nonetheless falters on the most crucial juncture—the ethical imperative of love disclosed in and by God-in-Christ.

The incarnation and subsequent vicarious death of Christ supply the necessary hermeneutical correctives for a more thoroughly Christian discursive framework. Zimmermann (2004), in elucidating the lapse in Gadamer's hermeneutic, elevates the ethical dialogue enacted by the Christ event:

> An incarnational view of relational transcendence puts the ethical demand of the other into the context of the good as a historically embodied act of selfless love. . . . If ethical transcendence is rooted in God's self-revelation, the incarnation (which includes the resurrection) is true exteriority rooted not in some abstract notion of God but in the concrete historical act of self-sacrifice, which defines the ethical as the ultimate good (p. 268).

Knowledge without love puffs up (1 Cor 8:1). Whereas, the love that Christ demonstrates for us completes the dialogical exchange of hermeneutics and ethics. Love, when enacted in service to other, perfects or completes knowledge.

---

13. By way of example, pathological dissociation such as that observed in dissociative disorders like DID may, in fact, be partially overcome in a strictly secular context (see Chefetz, 2015; Chu, 2011). However, the authoritative content in any secular hermeneutical dialogue entails the authority of the psychotherapist and, presumably, the normative standard of subjective singularity. By placing his or her faith in these "texts," the counselee/client engages in a discursive exchange that, other therapeutic preconditions assumed, may eventually result in some degree of remediation. But, understood Christianly, the repair of intrapsychic division should not be confused with covenantal wholeness, the latter being a function of one's union with Christ. Nevertheless, the pursuit of intrapsychic integration should be seen as a clear implication of the gospel (see Badgett, 2018a).

God, in his love for fallen humanity, has spoken definitively in the person and work of the divine Word-made-flesh. Revelation and reconciliation, as Barth (2010) avers, are intractably bound together. Neither is dispensable for the proper appropriation and application of the other. Christ is the ultimate "text" dialogically informing human self-understanding and enacting the agapic telos of selfhood. Jesus himself suggests as much in his hermeneutical formula, "You have heard it said, . . . and/but I say to you . . ." in the Sermon on the Mount (Matt 5:21, 27, 33, 38, 43; see France, 2007). Christ alone is διδάσκαλος (*didaskalos*) for his people, the Church (Matt 23:8).[14]

Genuine faith works itself out in an agapic disposition toward God and other. "Faith," argues Gerrish (2015), "makes moral demands on us" (p. 211). Indeed, Christ's love is a display not only of divine regard for sinful, broken human beings, but also of a proper ethical ideal among the community of believers (see John 13:34).[15] To paraphrase the Apostle, even if we come to understand the mysteries of the self and have sufficient faith to remove all barriers to self-knowledge, but have not love, it counts for nothing (1 Cor 13:2). God's love for sinners is initiatory; as such, it is wholly "imbalanced." And yet, its demand on us is that we respond in kind, both to God and among believers. Human love, therefore, works diachronically toward mutuality and reciprocity in order to avoid the subjective dangers of total self-abdication and -annihilation.[16] The ethical distinction between the two self–other love imperatives found in the New Testament is best understood in this light.

Before the crowd Jesus reifies the original Mosaic command to love one's neighbor "as oneself" (Mark 12:33; cf. Lev 19:18), both summarizing

14. According to Yieh (2004), Jesus' "first task" as Israel's teacher *par excellence* "is to interpret the Scripture" authoritatively (p. 248). We may carry this conclusion even further by averring that Christ's hermeneutical sovereignty applies equally to every "text," including the human self.

15. In speaking of the "ideal" love of believers for God and others, allowance must be made for the discrete agentic and ethical capacities of individuals. More on the realities of ethical asymmetry in caregiving relationships follows below.

16. Balance is key to preserving the ethical demands of self and other. Should balance be lost in favor of self, the result will inevitably be attempts to dominate others. Inversely, the ethical abdication of self can result from overemphasis on the needs of other. Bakhtin's (1986) "architectonic self" can be both an I-for-myself—what Bakhtin elsewhere terms the "carnival self"—as well as an I-for-the-other—his "dialogic self"—granted the proper balance. Emerson (2006) explains that "the architectonic self is the most morally responsible structure in all of Bakhtin, because it balances inner and outer pressures, demands of self and other, perfectly" (p. 39).

the ethical substance of the Old Covenant and confirming the ethical standard for all image bearers (cf. also Luke 6:31). Yet, in private, Jesus gives his disciples a "new command" that elevates the older neighbor-love standard to a higher level: "just as I have loved you, you also are to love one another" (John 13:34; see Michaels, 2010). Evidently, Jesus intends that his sacrificial death should serve as an illustration of this more radical ethic *among believers* (v. 35).[17] But just how radically self-effacing is Jesus' love imperative?

With both imperatives, mutuality and reciprocity supply the necessary means of maintaining dialogical balance. Under the Old Covenant, love for self as one bearing the image and likeness of God implicated a call to an equitable love for one's fellow image bearers as well. Conversely, Christ's loving sacrifice impels the believer, out of love for Christ, to take up one's cross and follow him (Matt 16:24). Ideally, love between human beings is to be mutual and equitable. Among the community of believers love adheres to the more radical standard modeled by Christ, yet the clear implication is that New Covenant love must also work toward reciprocity. Love for one's neighbor as self and love among believers aims at imaging Christ's love in order to fulfill these two distinct ethical imperatives *and at the same time* avoid the possibility of self-abdication.

Love between human persons, therefore, best images God's love when it is dialogically enacted and reciprocally exchanged. An asymmetrical or unidirectional love, by contrast, effaces the worth of the self, in effect, putting the self at risk of annihilation. As illustrated by Christ's resurrection, dying to self among believers does not result in self-abdication, but rather fulfills the ethical calling of the covenantal self.[18] Jesus'

17. Just as evidently, God's love for the two basic human constituencies—the elect and nonelect—can be distinguished according to two analogous differentials. Although God loves humanity without exception, his love for the elect redounds efficaciously in their salvation (Carson, 2000). In Scripture, moreover, election is often described in terms of God's having set his affection on a particular people (see, e.g., Deut 7:7–8; 10:14–15; Mal 1:2–3; Eph 5:25). Although God loves the whole world, only as we love God in kind—by giving up our lives for Christ—does his love redound efficaciously in our salvation.

18. Jesus commands his followers to serve rather than be served, yet he accepts the anointing given to him at Bethany just prior to his death (Mark 14:3–9). He rebukes Judas for censuring as wasteful the woman's gift of a costly flask of ointment even though it could have gone toward providing for the poor. The implication of Judas' criticism is an indictment of Jesus as complicit in the woman's profligacy. Yet, Jesus affirms the woman's agapic act as "good [καλός, *kalos*]" (v. 6). Other-regard for Christians, following Jesus' example, must be balanced by self-regard. In other words, it is not *wholly* selfless as in certain Eastern religions.

call for believers to lose their lives, for his sake, comes with the proviso that, in doing so, they will find them (Luke 9:24). Love for God and for others within the body of Christ demands that we relinquish our pretensions at self-understanding and divest self of its aggrandizing delusions and deceptions.

Furthermore, as Christ's sacrifice illustrates, agapic concern that is christocentrically situated both in terms of its hermeneutical and ethical aspects can effect other's dialogical release from captivity to delusion and self-deception. Christ's love for sinners invites our entry into an agapic spiral, as it were, by which our love for God and others is diachronically "perfected." This is to say that, though we at first lack any capacity to love, he overcomes the fears on account of which we dissociate from the truth of who we are and, as our love for him grows, come to see ourselves in the light of his love. Over time, subjective barriers to self-knowledge will become increasingly permeable in the face of other's simultaneously kenotic self-regard and agapic other-regard.

The power of such barriers—to protect the vulnerable self from harm—and their appeal—the false comfort of delusion—are negated by the gift of genuinely loving regard and concern. In the context of mutual self-denial and self-sacrifice, no individual need evade avenues to veridicality or remain hidden behind false self-conceptions and hypocrisy.

Christ's agapic work of atonement bridges the hermeneutical and ethical aspects of self-knowledge for believers: his act of self-sacrifice demonstrates that agapic concern for others is necessary for undermining the autocentric pull of the fallen self. Only in the presence of self-giving love can the autonomous human self escape its reflexive inertia. With respect to self-knowledge, as the individual imitates the divine program of agapic regard for other archetypally enacted by Christ, self achieves the appropriate covenantal balance necessary for veridicality.

Love is vital if we hope to overcome the pathological dynamics of fallenness and autonomy. Self-deception and hypocrisy are the epistemic and moral fruit of autocentric, monological discourse. Barriers to self-knowledge, moreover, so often constructed and maintained in service to self-protection, can be overcome only in the context of agapic mutuality. Fear of self-discovery naturally attends the life of the fallen self. And the sequelae of interpersonal sin so often metastasize these fears into persistent, structural barriers to veridical self-knowledge. The self that is being made whole in love for God and for other, by contrast, will come to welcome the dialogical dynamics of *faith working through love*. "Perfect love," so says the apostle, "casts out fear" (1 John 4:18).

Evaluating disparate discursive frameworks

Both Christian and secular approaches to self-knowledge, insofar as they apprehend its correlation with individual and relational wellbeing, operate with a similar appreciation of hermeneutical and ethical dialogue. For dynamic and relational psychotherapies, the "cure" for dissociation and self-deception involves coming to regard oneself through the eyes of an empathic other. This therapeutic program entails a course of dialogical self-discovery. Self is guided by another(s) through a hermeneutical exploration of the interpersonal roots of defective and pathological self-schemas. Mitchell (2000) describes this process as one by which "one comes to a sense of oneself as an agentic subject through the experience of oneself in the mind of the other, and the other-as-agentic subject in one's own mind" (p. 101).

Faulty perspectives on self that have accumulated in the context of dysfunctional or even abusive relationship(s) may be reformulated and integrated into a less schizoid and conflictual self-concept. Crucially, the ability to deactivate one's protective defenses, renounce toxic self-evaluations, and embrace a deeper self-awareness will reflect the degree to which hermeneutical and ethical dialogues—often referred to as the "therapeutic alliance"—inform this process (Martin et al., 2000; Muran & Barber, 2011; Norcross, 2011). Indeed, "alliance predicts outcome" stands among the most fundamental assumptions of modern psychotherapy (Barber et al., 2013, p. 29). Accordingly, it is the quality and depth of the therapeutic relationship that accounts for change.

Secular psychotherapeutic dialogue

At first glance, then, such psychotherapeutic approaches to healing the self, though secular in orientation, appear to bear out the apostle Paul's peroration: "Love never fails" (1 Cor 13:8 NASB). Self-regard—one's intrasubjective sense of self—can be favorably modified over time through the "interpenetrating involvement" of self with an empathic other (Bromberg, 1998, p. 157). In other words, the crucial element in the therapeutic process seems to be the relationship between therapist and client. For

DeYoung (2003), a capacity for "change in [the individual's] self-structure" arises out of the hermeneutical and ethical dialogues contextually enacted within a "good relational experience" (p. 173). And Stern (2010) pithily concludes, "[W]hen the mind is locked, relationship is the key" (p. 129). Yet, in spite of any superficial similarity between secular and Christian discursive frameworks, a deeper analysis reveals fundamental distinctions.

As it happens, what qualifies as empathic regard by secular standards proves to be a poor substitute for genuine Christ-imaging love. In examining distinctions between to the two, Holifield (1983) posits, "The contrast between therapeutic acceptance and sacrificial love might tell us more about both love and acceptance than would the quest for analogies between them" (p. 355). This is certainly the case. So, for example, Pizer (1998), in frank examination of the "quality" of the therapeutic relationship, acknowledges that it paradoxically bears both "real" and "unreal" aspects—an apparent "love," yet one that is more accurately characterized as metaphorical and "subjunctive" (pp. 48–49; cf. Freud, 1915). In other words, the transference-countertransference dialogue of dyadic caregiving enactments more accurately bears a symbolic or *as-if* quality.

In essence, the psychotherapeutic caregiver becomes a metaphorical parent of sorts, an antitypal presence symbolically interposing agapic regard and concern in place of defective relational dynamics from the past (cf. Kelly, 1991, II, pp. 14–15). Christianly understood, however, parent–child relational dynamics relate antitypally to the relationship of God as Father with his elect people (see 1 John 3:1). Secular caregiving unconsciously appropriates and approximates both the horizontal and vertical dimensions of therapeutic dialogue, and in so doing potentially perpetuates basal barriers to veridical self-knowledge.

This is not to say that secular empathy will never reach the level of "a deeper caring about the fate the other" (Mitchell, 2000, p. 135).[19] But inarguably, secular expressions of empathy cannot match the liberating, illuminating power of *faith working through love*, the archetypal illustration of which can be seen in the cross of Christ. Moreover, genuine healing and growth in the image of God, at least in biblical terms, amounts to much more than favorable modifications of one's self-schema.

The respective presuppositions of Christian and secular frameworks for self-knowledge differ not so much on its dialogical means—that is, the

19. Barth (2010) holds that caring about the good of other is an irreducible aspect of the image of God in human beings.

hermeneutical and ethical outworking of the self-in-relation—but rather on how to characterize and programmatize these dialogues. In particular, the respective objects of faith and love disclose the most crucial distinctions between the two approaches. For Christianity, the object of faith is the God revealed in his own divine self-disclosure and discoverable in the Bible and in the person and work of Christ. It regards all other faith-objects as idols or false gods by which fallen human beings are led astray from the truth and so become enslaved. Any hermeneutical dialogue that neglects or obviates the truth content of the gospel of reconciliation only perpetuates false images of self and other.

The most insightful and sensitive secular psychotherapeutic approaches to self-knowledge approximate this formulation, if only in an analogous or symbolic way. Secular psychotherapy, insofar as it respects the relational nature of the self, will recognize and enact the hermeneutical and ethical aspects of dialogue: the therapist guides the client into dialogical interactions specifically aimed at building mutual understanding and undermining fears and defenses. To varying degrees, then, postmodern and relational approaches esteem dialogue as a means of self-discovery and -understanding. And yet, since they have no epistemic basis in revelation, they lack hermeneutical "authority."

In the context of any strictly secular therapeutic relationship, either the empathic caregiver effectively serves as the hermeneutical "authority" for the task of self-discovery or else they together assume for themselves a hermeneutical sovereignty. What they say goes. A merely human "logos," has become the object of their shared pistic commitment. Christ's paradigmatic hermeneutical formula, "You have heard it said, . . . but I say to you . . . ," has been appropriated and applied along a strictly horizontal dimension. Together therapist and client consider what has been said and supply their word of "faith." This surely bears diminished efficacy for genuine veridicality. When it comes to the deepest, most salient truths about ourselves, apart from Christ, we are all blindly leading each other we know not where.

Secular "faith" amounts to confidence in humanity's putative potential for reformation and actualization by our own ability and effort alone. We should not expect to get very far this way. Once the hermeneutical dialogue has been dissociated from its preeminent connection with divine discourse, it becomes circular and self-serving. Dialogue, in strictly secular terms, ultimately foments a kind of mutually assured self-deception.

Likewise, the empathic regard of secular frameworks, even when it amounts to a genuine caring about the good of others, inevitably falls short of authentic New Covenant love. In contrast to God's exhibition of agapic regard in the cross of Jesus Christ, in the end, secular approximations of "love" are tragically flaccid and inimitably self-serving. Apart from any anchor in the divine wellspring, love becomes a pale imitation of kenotic self-giving and agapic regard for other (see Kierkegaard, 1998). We ought not wonder, then, at how secular psychotherapeutic formulations of interpersonal regard—expressed in such terms as empathic concern (see Mitchell, 2000),[20] therapeutic relationality (see DeYoung, 2003), or "unconditional positive regard" (Rogers, 1961)—differ from a New Covenantal understanding of love.

According to Jesus, the supreme ethical imperative of all image bearers places God above any other object of agapic regard (Mark 12:30). Love for God, then, must surpass all other loves in order both to fulfill the divine command and to accord with the aesthetic and axiological realities of his beauty and worth. Although mutual regard among image bearers—loving neighbor as one loves self (v. 31)—approximates the ethical dialogue of secular frameworks, the hierarchical imperative can only be fulfilled with God-in-Christ as its supreme object: love for God must come *first* (cf. Luke 14:26).

Furthermore, the implicit ethics of secular psychotherapy holds to a confidence in the basic ethical goodness of the human self. A biblical ethics, in contrast, perceives the dialectical quality of the fallen self—both its image-bearing beauty and its sin-wrought horror—and prescribes an exclusively divine cure. The source of the antinomy inherent in human nature is a love for self that conscripts all other objects as servants of the self (see Kierkegaard, 1998). In giving up his life for sinful humanity, Christ interposes a revolutionary new standard for ethical dialogue: a

---

20. Mitchell (2000) differentiates between secular "caring" and "empathy" in a telling way. Empathy, for Mitchell, is "a methodology, a way of thinking that employs feelings" for the purposes of "vicarious introspection," or "imagining what a situation feels like for someone else" (p. 135). "Caring," on the other hand, is a "complex affective involvement" arising as the subjective response to "interpersonal chemistry" (p. 134). Genuine agapic regard, in contrast to these two secular standards, is vitally connected to Christ's love for the care recipient. It is rooted in the volitive rather than the affective domain—a commitment to love others out of love for Christ. Patently, God's command to love implicates its dependence on the will rather than the affections (see Elliott, 2006). From this we may conclude that genuine agapic concern for others is only indirectly fostered by mutual interpersonal affection.

kenotic regard for God and others that does not cling to the rights of self (see Phil 2:3). This "greater love" consciously, purposefully holds the interests of other *above* the interests of self (John 15:13).[21] Love of this sort "endures all things" (1 Cor 13:7). In this way, Christian love comes to image the multidimensional agapic disposition of Christ in relation to the Father and with others, especially toward one's fellow believers (1 John 3:16). Only in this context does the apostle's Corinthian peroration possess genuine warrant.

The paradox of eudaimonist self-knowing

Orthodox Christian perspectives on self-knowledge have always elevated the principals of faith and love as the proper dialogical expressions of our covenantal nature. Following from the Pauline formulation, *faith working through love* best describes a Christian discursive framework for overcoming barriers to self-knowledge. Especially in regard to undermining sinful tendencies, Christian approaches to self-knowledge helpfully elucidate the hermeneutical and ethical imperatives of human nature. Secular frameworks, by definition, neglect the vertical dimension of dialogue presuming, in effect, that the descendants of Adam and Eve can somehow avoid their first parents' tragic fate while exchanging the same deadly fruit.

The contrast between secular and Christian dialogue, then, could not be clearer. Yet, careful reflection around Christian perspectives on eudaimonist self-knowledge reveals a confounding paradox. As we have seen, true knowledge of self for Augustine—and for Calvin (2008) and Kierkegaard (1991) as well—comes from God by means of divine self-revelation contained in the Scriptures. Consequently, knowledge of self from an eudaimonist standpoint is reciprocal and mutual—the "double"

---

21. New Covenant love is more than a reciprocal "care" through the pursuit of just and ethical treatment for both self and other. Barth (2010), after all holds "care" to be the universal ethical imperative of our shared human nature. In his presentation of "care-agapism" Wolterstorff (2015) evidently seeks to balance the ethical interests of justice with those of love, but in so doing only diminishes the scandalous nature of divine love and grace. As John's Gospel makes clear, Jesus' love ethic will supply the singular distinction by which his followers will be identified (John 13:35; Michaels, 2010). New Covenant love requires much more than "that we decenter the self by caring about the other, not only about ourselves" (Wolterstorff, 2015, p. 141). Jesus' agapic illustration of footwashing—to say nothing of his even more definitive sacrificial death—demonstrates as much (cf. 1 John 3:23). Ethical balance, then, is not achieved by juxtaposing love with justice, but through mutuality and reciprocity.

knowledge of God and self imparted as a gift of the indwelling Spirit of God—yet circumscribed within its vertical dimension.

According to Houston (2000), "True self-knowledge comes only through knowledge of God; knowledge both of self and of God comes only through the Bible" (p. 313). Zimmermann (2004), expressing a similar thought, concludes: "We find thus in the [Christian] theological tradition the assurance that self-knowledge is possible, that it depends on divine revelation, that the nature of this revelation is personal, and that self-knowledge is hermeneutical, obtainable only in dialogue with God" (p. 270). According to eudaimonist perspectives, veridical knowledge of self entails the dialogical appropriation of divine discourse. Though there is also ample consensus that human beings are perennially and pathologically inclined to dissociation and self-deception—Augustine (2009) observed as much subsequent to his conversion to Christianity—presumption is made that barriers to self-knowledge are wholly subject to the strictly intrasubjective application of biblical truth.

What is missing from this framework? For one, relationality appears to be dispensable. Having identified and overcome his own dissociation and self-deception, Augustine appears to disavow any horizontal dimensionality. The conclusion seems to be that human beings overcome their dissociation and self-deception through communion with the word of God as they encounter him *individually* in the pages of Scripture. For another, the ethical telos of eudaimonist self-knowledge is not love—for God and others—but eudaimonia, personal, individual wellbeing.

According to the implications of an eudaimonist formula for overcoming noetic barriers, self-knowledge is procured along a vertical relational axis alone; solely via believers' dialogue with divine revelation does veridical self-knowledge become possible (Houston, 2000). Kierkegaard (1991), in commending the subjective appropriation of divine revelation for self-knowledge, describes this process in unidimensional terms:

> [Y]ou will read a fear and trembling into your soul so that, with God's help, you will succeed in becoming a human being. . . . You will, if you read God's Word in this way, you will (even if it will be dreadful for you, but remember that this is a condition of salvation!) succeed in doing what is required—to look at yourself in the mirror of the Word. Only in this way will you succeed. (p. 43)

His admonition, for all its strengths, suggests that sufficient subjective motivation can be mustered to overcome all internal resistance to self-discovery and -disclosure. Though the process "will be dreadful," the believer will "succeed" in accurately self-perceiving, because God himself offers his aid.

Given the constitutive anthropology upon which eudaimonist ethics is based, Kierkegaard's conclusion seems reasonable enough. If human beings image God individually, relationality is of secondary importance. Yet, according to covenantal anthropology, the imago implicates vertical *and* horizontal correspondence as fundamental and indispensable conditions of self-knowledge. In other words, the eudaimonist proposal for veridical self-knowledge neglects human instrumentality as a critical aspect of effecting divine–human dialogue.[22] Respective to self-knowledge, the truth of divine self-disclosure is indeed sufficient for veridicality, but as Paul helpfully reminds us, "How are they to hear, without someone preaching?" (Rom 10:14).[23]

Eudaimonist frameworks do not sufficiently allow for the human instrumentality entailed in horizontal expressions of covenantal relationality. God "speaks," and we "hear" him, through *instrumental* means. The covenantal self may be veridically known and loved in correspondence along both its vertical *and* horizontal axes. Furthermore, in light of the antinomy of fallen human nature, the paradox of eudaimonist self-knowledge becomes even clearer. Although Christian "double" knowledge assumes the supervening assistance of the Holy Spirit, it is still the schizoid, conflictual human mind that acquires and evaluates subjective knowledge of God and self. Left to ourselves, we alone must identify gaps

22. In both Augustine and Kierkegaard examples of horizontal instrumentality respective to self-knowledge can be found. As Augustine (2009) relates, God instrumentally employed the testimony of Ponticianus as a means of directing him inward, thus allowing him to reconsider his need for the gospel (VIII.vii.16; pp. 144–145). In Kierkegaard's (1991) critique of "impersonality" and "objectivity" respective to Christian truth, he observes Nathan's instrumental role in allowing King David to overcome his dissociation and self-deception, effectively bringing him to his senses (p. 39). In both cases, God effected his discursive ends through human means.

23. On this point it is worth noting that the Christian Scriptures are "God-breathed" (2 Tim 3:16), but they bear a dual—divine and human—authorship. The Bible is not the direct speech of God. God speaks to his through his word, yet, as Paul suggests, it is through the Bible faithfully preached that God is heard. To my thinking, present neglect of a proper perspective on human instrumentality in the authorship of the Bible and necessity of incarnational preaching in the proclamation of the Bible correlates closely with the docetic bent of some modern evangelical Christologies (cf. Macquarrie, 2003b, p. 343).

in our correspondence with biblical truth and make our determinations of veridicality.

As noted in the previous chapters, biblical anthropology maintains that the redeemed self remains in a state of internal conflict. Eschatologically whole in Christ, the believer's self-consciousness and noetic faculties nevertheless remain finite, divided, and conflictual, and thus susceptible to dissociation, delusion, and self-deception. As Augustine (2009) keenly observes, "My mind on examining myself about its strengths does not regard its findings as easy to trust" (X.xxxii.48; p. 207). The authoritative role of the Bible notwithstanding, a covenantal anthropology avers that, respective to self-knowledge, it is not good for human beings to be "alone" (cf. Gen 2:18). Yet in contrast to the divine disapprobation of a strictly vertical correspondence, eudaimonist frameworks suggest the inverse: relationality is dispensable.[24]

Though the Scriptures are a mirror for the self, the fallen human mind exerts a distorting influence on all they reveal. In fallen hands the Bible all too often serves as a "nose of wax, to be turned and bent" (Locke, 1824, p. 295). We selectively employ them according to our tastes. With no relational check, the oracles of God foment self-assurance and self-righteousness.[25] Within an eudaimonist framework, apart from the possibility of direct divine disclosure, there is no mechanism of verifiability for the noetic process or its conclusions regarding self.[26] If self-knowledge

24. One could justifiably argue that Christ himself might effect both the vertical and horizontal dimensions of dialogue respective to individual believers. This certainly appears to be the case in Christ's self-disclosure to Saul of Tarsus (Acts 9:4–19; cf. Gal 1:12). This argument does not, however, obviate the necessity of horizontal correspondence, but rather reinforces the present point: God works instrumentally, that is, through created means, to reveal the human self. As the God-man, Christ instantiates a dual correspondence respective to individual human beings (so, see John 15:14–15). He is humanity's archetypal "helper," thus fulfilling our covenantal need for epistemic and ethical correspondence.

25. This paradox is not in the least ameliorated by Wolterstorff's (1995) otherwise helpful admonition: "to interpret God's discourse more reliably, we must come to know God better" (p. 239). This statement is undoubtedly true, but the question remains: when can individuals rest in a strictly subjective assurance that they have come into a more intimate knowledge of God? We need each other.

26. Augustine's (2009) conversion account suggests the direct involvement of God's Spirit in revealing his sinful state, sounding at times similar to Paul's Damascus road experience (Acts 9:3–8; cf. Gal 1:16). We need not eschew all belief in God's willingness to directly intervene. What is notable about such experiences, however, is their scarcity in the pages of Scripture and in everyday experience. These exceptions prove the rule: God uses human persons to bring human persons to greater knowledge of themselves.

comes only through the Scriptures, even assuming the involvement of the Holy Spirit, what assurance can we have that the barriers of sin and psychopathology have been overcome? Left to ourselves, we will always tend to distort their truthfulness to personal advantage.

Christian eudaimonist self-knowledge presumes that God, through the Scriptures, authoritatively reveals the self as it truly is. And this is assuredly the case; yet, who but the self interprets and evaluates all that God is "saying" therein? Who but the self can call the individual to account for hermeneutical faults? Further, how is the self to overcome persistent barriers to self-knowledge such as those encountered in pathological dissociation? Though God unquestionably knows the self veridically, when can individual human beings rest in any assurance that their self-perception accords with divine truth?

In light of our remaining sin and the deceitfulness of the human heart, for the remainder of the present age believers cannot be certain of any ostensible freedom from self-deception (see Jer 17:9). When limited to its vertical dimension and given the dissociative and self-deceptive tendencies of the fallen self, dialogue may all too readily become monologue with barriers to self-knowledge still firmly in place. This is surely the reason for Jesus' parable of the speck and the plank. These memorable images warn us against making facile determinations of bias-free attribution. They suggest we are far more likely to employ the Scriptures to search out others' faults than our own (Matt 7:5).

Not even believers, it would seem, are immune to error or distortions in their self-conceptions. If this is so, Christian eudaimonist approaches to self-knowledge may, in fact, more readily contribute to self-righteousness and pride. Considering the authoritative bearing of divine disclosure, we become more, not less, vulnerable once we have received the oracles of God. Consider the scribes and Pharisees! How simple and seductive to presume they had wholly rooted out false conceptions of self. They effectively turned their own subjective self-approval into divine approbation. When the mirror, Christ, appeared to reveal them as they were, they smashed it. Like them, we risk self-deception and hypocrisy so long as our dialogue remains closed to any horizontal dimensionality.[27] After all, what more effective support for a false

27. It is far more likely, in fact, that those who possess the keenest knowledge of the oracles of God will be most prone to employ them in searching out the faults of others (Badgett, 2018b). This appears to be the concern against which Baxter (1974) undertook to counsel his fellow Puritan pastors.

confidence in one's transparency and authenticity can there be than the presumption of divine authorization?

Covenantal self-knowledge

By contrast, a covenantal framework for undermining barriers to self-knowledge commends both the vertical and horizontal dimensions of dialogue. As Johnson (2007) concludes, our dialogical nature suggest that human self-knowledge must indeed be Christ-centered and biblically grounded, yet also be "fundamentally social" (p. 433). The covenantal implications of Christ's person and work further crystallize this conclusion. As with the doctrine of the Trinity, so too does Christology implicate and decode the fundamental dialectic of divine self-disclosure. Christ, in his relatedness to the Father through the Spirit, reveals God to be one-and-three—beautifully, mysteriously whole in plurality (John 10:30).

Whether historically or logically, the triune nature of God can be neither disclosed nor apprehended apart from the incarnation of the divine Word-made-flesh. In showing himself to be the Son, so Christ reveals the Father. Through Christ, we may see and know God more fully; apart from Christ, we would never have come to a knowledge of the tri-unity of God. As with the divine nature, so Christ discloses the divine telos of human nature as well. Through the person and work of Christ, in other words, God reveals the full grandeur of his intention for human beings as image bearers—as objects of divine affection and instruments of divine agency.

With the cross in view, the Father sends the Son to redeem sinful creatures. In the likeness of sinful flesh, Jesus dies for sinful flesh. Yet, as scandalous as the cross is, the divine aim for humanity is yet further on and more implausible even than the notion of a crucified God. Through his death, Christ sets aside the sins of his people making broken vessels whole in order that he might employ them as vehicles for his glory—a living "temple," as it were, for his presence on earth (1 Cor 6:19).

As head over this redeemed and reconciled body of sinners *cum* saints, Christ effects his gracious will for the world. Now, those whose rebellion contributed to the death and disorder of the whole world God has transformed, through the work of Christ, into instruments of his glorious dispensation for that world. Though banished from the first garden, this redeemed, reconciled humanity has become for the present age the "place" on earth where the divine presence perichoretically dwells. It is through Christ—his person and his work—that we see, know, and appropriate these blessed realities.

Furthermore, it is *in Christ* that human beings instrumentally, dialogically effect his will "on earth as it is in heaven." Believers, through their union with Christ, come to faithfully embody the truth of the word/ Word in such a way that they may serve, if only contingently and instrumentally, as "mirrors" for the self. Though they bear no revelatory authority in themselves, through the perichoretically indwelling presence of Christ, God may nevertheless employ the redeemed as his instruments to authoritatively reveal others as they truly are.[28]

28. Jesus commends the centurion for his recognition of this truth: namely, that all authority rests in God alone, but that Christ bears an instrumental authority conferred upon him by God (Matt 8:9). As of the resurrection, "all authority" resides in Christ (Matt 28:19), yet in transferring his own apostolic ministry to the church, he confers a contingent authority upon believers to "make disciples . . . in the name," that is, under the authority of the triune God and empowered by Christ's perichoretic presence (v. 20). So, Bucer (2009), in articulating the Reformed perspective, attests, "[I]t has pleased [Christ] to exercise his rule, protection and care of us who are still in this world with and through the ministry of his word, which he does outwardly and tangibly through his ministers and instruments" (p. 17; cf. Adams, 1970, pp. 15–16).

Chapter 10

Redeemed humanity
and the ecological presence of Christ

CHRIST'S PERSON AND WORK—WHO he is and what he does in relation to God and to the world—should define the life and bearing of believers (Bonhoeffer, 2005). The anthropological implication of the perichoretically instantiated dual natures of Christ entails that, though the redeemed are not themselves divine, they share in the divine nature even as the incarnate Christ shares in their human nature. The divine person of the Son took on flesh; as of Pentecost, God's gift to believers is that they might take on the Spirit, so to speak (Gal 4:6; 1 John 3:24). Their perichoretic indwelling by the Spirit is effected by—indeed, it is the effectuation of—their union with Christ. Subsequent to these two analogically related unions, neither the essence of the divine Son nor that of the human person becomes anything more or less that it previously was. Christ remains a divine person in spite of his assumed humanity. The believer remains a human person, yet in Christ has been granted a taste of the triune life and communion.

Christ issues to human persons a share of the divine nature by means of their perichoretic union with his Spirit thereby transforming his people into instruments of his covenantal agenda for the world (see Col 1:11–12). God himself dwells within them, accomplishing his purposes through them as they operate in step with him (Gorman, 2015).[1]

---

1. It is Christ who accomplishes his purposes; yet he does so by means of a dual agency—his own and that of his people. So, for example, Jesus says of himself, "I am the light of the world" (John 8:12). He also declares to his followers, "You are the light

Believers relate to the world instrumentally insofar as they mediate the person and work of Christ to all with whom they come into contact.

The knowledge of self, when the whole-person-that-is-self is understood as the onto-relational locus of Christ's covenantal presence in the world, bears immense semiotic and ecological implications. Under the terms of the Old Covenant, God gave the tabernacle—and later the temple—as a sign of his presence in the midst of his people (Koester, 1989; see Inge, 2003).[2] Where God led them, so the tabernacle was to follow. Though he is the God of all heaven and earth, he had chosen a particular people and place within which to dwell (Exod 19:5). Moreover, his presence among them was a sign not only for Israel, but for the whole world (Exod 33:16). The tabernacle/temple signified God's favor, his election of Israel as his covenant people, and his eschatological agenda to fill the earth with the knowledge of his glory (see Num 14:21; Ps 67:7; Isa 49:6; Hab 2:14).

As the history of Israel bears out, however, the place of God's presence periodically fell into disrepair and desuetude as the people's pursuit of God's presence declined (Provan et al., 2015; see Jer 7). In consideration of the prophetic warnings of impending judgment, the ecological impact of their syncretism and idolatry became clear: their bad behavior had brought scorn to the name of their God before the nations (see, e.g., Isa 57:3–21). The eventual destruction of God's own dwelling place—and the exile of his people—amounted to both a repudiation and an anticipation of the dramatic renovation of God's promise to dwell eternally with his people.

On account of their rebellion Yahweh would forsake his people, raze the temple, and eject them from the land. He would demonstrate to the world that his name would not be mocked, not even by his own people. In the course of time, however, Christ, on behalf of God's estranged

---

of the world" (Matt 5:14). Clearly, the metaphor of light is flexible enough to carry a different sense in these two contexts. One key distinction is that individual believers do not have a light of their own; rather, they bear the light of Christ's presence. But there is also a sense in which the two statements relate analogically and instrumentally. After his resurrection, Christ appoints his disciples to carry on his own mission to the world (John 20:21; cf. Matt 28:19). In conferring this mission upon them, he also pledges to remain with them forever (John 14:23; Matt 18:20; 28:20). The appropriate conclusion appears to be that, on account of their union with Christ, believers both *have* the light and *are* the light of the world.

2. Cf. Block's (2011) insightful analysis of deuteronomic prescriptions for encountering the presence of Yahweh under the Old Covenant (pp. 98–99).

people, would vicariously die their deaths thereby ushering in a new age of union between God and humanity in which there would no longer be any possibility of separation or alienation (Rom 8:38–39; Rev 21:3). In his steadfast love, God would remember mercy and show his covenantal favor again—this time, to all peoples and nations.

With the advent of the New Covenant, the locus and sign of God's presence differs in several remarkable ways (Fee, 2009; Hamilton, 2006). As Jesus predicted, human beings no longer encounter and worship God in structures built by human hands, but rather "in spirit and truth" (John 4:23). Throughout the gospel of John, Jesus suggests that the new "place" where God will meet with his people will be in and through him (Gordon, 2016; see Keener, 2010; Michaels, 2010). He will become the living temple wherein the people of God gather before the Almighty (Wright, 1996).

The Apostle Paul confirms that in Christ, the Ephesian Christians "are being built together," along with all other believers, "into a dwelling place for God by the Spirit" (Eph 2:22). In other words, by means of the Spirit each and every individual believer has access to Christ's penetrative presence. Christ bodily resides within the highest heaven, seated at the right hand of the Father (Matt 26:64; Eph 1:20; Col 3:1; Heb 8:1; 12:2). Yet, Christ spiritually dwells within believers and they may encounter him there (John 14:23; Rev 3:20; cf. Jer 29:13).[3] For the remainder of the present age, therefore, the meeting place of God and humanity is circumscribed to the corporate and particular union of Christ with redeemed human persons. The human self may then be construed as a unique, embodied onto-relational unity upon whom God has conferred his image and within whose formal, phenomenological constituents—i.e., the body–soul composite—he has purposed to reside (see 1 Cor 3:17). The

---

3. This proposition *must* be held in dialectical tension with the second half of the Johannine epistemological formula, "in spirit *and truth*" (John 4:23). The gospel writer precludes the possibility of a *wholly* subjectivized spirituality by pressing the point that believers are sanctified by the truth of his Logos (John 17:17). So, while it is accurate to say that believers are perichoretically indwelt by the Spirit of Christ, human beings do not encounter Christ apart from the truth of all that he has said. Christian traditions and movements that emphasize one or the other side of the dialectic—spirit *or* truth—will inevitably levy a tragically anemic spirituality. On the one side they will fall prey to subjectivist error unjustifiably elevating human experience and insight over divine revelation. On the other side, objectivists, perhaps preferring the relative safety of a strictly canonical "presence" of Christ, effectively rule out of bounds all subjective experience. The result is a functionally deist spirituality.

believer's ecological stewardship, then, entails the knowledge of self *as a locus of the triune God's covenantal presence in the world.*

Covenantal dialogue in caregiving contexts

From the earliest moments of its existence, the human self assumes an asymmetrical, proximal correspondence to other that can only be regarded as prospectively dialogical. A bundle of potentialities and promise, the embryonic person growing within her mother's womb will need time and care to fulfill her telic design. For months to come, as a developing fetus and, later, a nursing infant, she will possess a nominal discursive capacity. Yet, given the proper parental nurture over the course of time, her primordial, inchoate agency will invariably acquire fuller expression. Eventually, through an intersubjectively constructed awareness of self, the healthy child will adopt an increasingly sophisticated, albeit subliminally deployed, array of communicative means, both verbal and nonverbal, which will contribute to her growing ability to engage dialogically with others.

On account of her creation according to God's covenantal imago, she will see herself as she is seen and know herself as she is known. As her agentic faculties—her powers of cognition, affection, and volition—come into full flower in proper relation to God and other, the telos of her covenantal personhood will become increasingly viable. She exists to love and be loved in a fully dialogical communion. God created her, in other words, that she might participate in a mutual, reciprocal agapic dynamic—one reflective of triune self-giving and other-receiving—to which Christ through the Spirit gives her access. By means of her perichoretic union with him, she is able to love and receive love as a fully response-able agent. She best expresses her covenantal design, then, in agapic dialogue that is perfectly symmetrical, balanced, and wholly mediated by Jesus Christ. Yet, all of this will only become possible for her *in time.*

The New Testament's agapic imperatives assume mutuality and reciprocity. Evidently, however, some particular relational contexts allow for—and even demand—a diachronic asymmetry. For example, the transitive parent-child relationship, initially asymmetrical and unbalanced in favor of the child, shifts toward a more equitable correspondence over time as the child develops increasing agentic capacity. As the respective needs and capacities of child and parent change over the course of years and decades, dialogical expressions of agapic concern inevitably shift as well.[4]

Parental love for a newborn in some ways reflects the divine initiative of vertical reconciliation and communion. Yet, as with divine love, parental love cannot remain forever monological, one-sided. The ethical calling under which the child has been born is that she grow to love in reply. According to the apostle, our love for God is properly responsive to divine initiative (1 John 4:19); similarly, then, the child's ethical responsibility to love her parents grows as an expression of her maturing agency. As a mature adult agent, her agapic regard and concern now bears the potential of dialogical symmetry. Love is perfected in the course of time. Perfect love, consequently, is dialogically enacted, yet diachronically capacitated (see vv. 16–17).

Expressions of agapic mutuality and reciprocity between parent and child follow the same telic, diachronic trajectory of the believer's relationship to God. Despite the universality of the New Testament's ethical imperatives, evidently determinations of proper dialogical balance must be informed by the respective agentic capacities of each correspondent. Mature agency—one that fulfills its covenantal imperative and telic design—is mitigated by the persistence of barriers to self-knowledge. To the extent that dissociation and self-deception persist, agency is compromised. God's provision for redeemed humanity assumes the diachronic growth of self's capacity to love other/Other with the eschatological promise of final release from any remaining barriers to agapic expression.

We love and know as we are well-loved and -known. Suggestion of this comes from the psalmist: from "my mother's womb," David reflects, "Your eyes saw my unformed substance" (Ps 139:13, 16). And from this he concludes, "I am fearfully and wonderfully made . . . my *nephesh* knows it very well" (v. 14). The discursive movement of divine initiative is what awakens a reciprocal reply. David has seen the Lord seeing him. From this he determines his own worth.

Patently, David's capacity for mature self-reflection in covenantal dialogue with the God who first knew and loved him could have only

---

4. In a clear reversal of classic parent-child roles, Jesus affirms the necessity of caring for one's elderly parents as an expression an agapic ethics (Mark 7:10–13). On the other hand, children with disabilities may never develop a full agentic capacity to love as they are loved. Thus, dialogical symmetry and equity should be seen as ideals that are perfectly instantiated only among the persons of the Trinity.

grown over time, awaiting the development of an agentic response-ability he could not possibly possess within the womb. Capacity for the sort of penetrative reflection and theological synthesis he demonstrates would await the maturation of his cognitive, affective, and volitive faculties. Even more significantly, David's agentic faculties would need to season and mature through his diachronic experience of the love and favor of the God who sees and speaks. In this way God—like a loving parent—nurtured the growth of David's capacity for pistic and agapic dialogue.

Pastoral and psychotherapeutic dialogue

The relational self develops an increasingly whole self-consciousness provided, over time, the proper agapic care and nurture. As David exemplifies, this care must come along both relational axes, horizontal and vertical. Stated another way, as human beings grow in covenantal intimacy with God and agapic others, barriers to self-knowledge are increasingly susceptible to disruption and displacement. To the extent that dissociation and self-deception may be overcome, self-consciousness will increasingly correspond with God's perception of the individual. As barriers to self-knowledge fall, potential grows that the individual will fulfill the agapic telos of the imago.

Sin's influence is pervasive, its scope universal. It corrupts and skews the telic development of the covenantal self and its accompanying self-schema to the extent that it foments the structural self-blindness of otherwise mature, response-able adults. The most durable and persistent barriers to healthy psychosocial development arise from the debilitating impact of interpersonal sin. How others mistreat the developing self can have untold consequences. Personal sin, moreover, compounds and perpetuates the destructive force of caregiver failings, parental neglect, and abuse. Whatever the source, all forms of inter/personal sin contribute to the propagation and reinforcement of dissociative and self-deceptive tendencies. The more damage to self, the more self becomes self-blind.

The psychospiritual consequences of a child's deprivation of healthy attachment, psychological trauma, and interpersonal violence are frequently enduring and debilitating (see Badgett, 2018a). Although every human being suffers from sin's devastating influence, those who have suffered most are invariably the ones perennially confronted with the pangs of inner conflict and pathological self-ignorance. They are truly "poor in spirit" (Matt 5:3). Held "captive," rendered "blind" to self and other, and "oppressed" by sin's lingering insult upon the image of God within them, they await the proclamation of "liberty," "sight," and "favor" that Christ's coming offers to them (see Luke 4:18–19).

It is Christ who alone can grant them freedom; yet for the remainder of the present age he has purposed to do so through the instrumental means of his redeemed, reconciled people. Through the instrumentality of caregivers' *faith working through love*, mediated by the working of his Spirit, Christ sets these captives free. When he calls believers into agapic fellowship with himself, he does so, in part, that they might become vessels and instruments of his redemptive purposes. Our dialogical response to his agapic word impels and empowers our consent to his covenantal agenda for all who suffer the sequelae of estrangement. In laying down his life for us, he has set for us the ethical example by which we now enact the fulfillment of the covenantal telos with others in the body of Christ.

The imprimatur of pastoral and psychotherapeutic dialogue

Discursive relationality should promote covenantal valence. By this I mean that appropriate and efficacious dialogue will necessarily address the twofold consequences of estrangement without neglecting or overlooking either. Both sin and psychopathology interpose barriers to self-knowledge. For this reason, covenantal dialogue cannot fail to address these two means, both of which can lead to a persistent state of self-blindness. Certainly, personal sin has a more detrimental impact on covenantal self-knowledge in that it perpetuates a disruptive and corrosive dynamic within the believing self's inter/subjectivity. Although secure in Christ, believers must still move in step with Christ in order to find benefit from that union. Further, the psychopathological sequelae of interpersonal sin tend to promote the recapitulation of those sins. Tragically, those who have been sinned against tend to sin against others in similar ways. So, the cycle of damage and disunion is perpetuated and compounded.

Although union with Christ invites agapic submission to Christ, the believer's repentance and obedience will not automatically redress the sequelae of estrangement in toto. Psychotherapeutic healing for past wounds entails separate yet interrelated processes. Consequently, justification—the person's being declared right before God—should be seen as a correlative rather than a preliminary condition of remediation for psychopathological barriers to self-knowledge. In other words, it is not necessary to begin by working toward conversion to faith in Christ. Dialogue must also address the sequelae of inter/personal sin in order to effectively undermine barriers to self-knowledge. Especially as sinful tendencies reflect and recapitulate these sequelae, a dual focus that addresses both sin and psychopathology will prove most efficacious. Very often, faith is only possible after certain barriers have been removed.[5] The conversions of Augustine and Paul serve as exemplars.

By delineating barriers to self-knowledge along these two lines, two types or modes of instrumentality come into focus, namely, the pastoral and psychotherapeutic functions of agapic caregivers. To a significant extent, distinctions between the two should be seen as the result of cultural and historical conditioning. Inarguably, the historical role of the pastor included both expressions of caregiving prior to the advent of the modern psychotherapeutic age (Charry, 1997; Clebsch & Jaekle, 1994; Holifield, 1983; Johnson, 2007; Oden, 1984).[6] Yet, with few exceptions, ostensibly Christian caregiving frameworks tend to emphasize one or the other aspects of the fallen human condition.

In other words, implicit within disparate disciplinary expressions of caregiving, whether pastoral or psychotherapeutic, the assumption seems to be that the most direct route to personal wellbeing and interpersonal wholeness is found, chiefly, in overcoming *either* sin or psychopathology. In very broad strokes, historical pastoral frameworks have tended to emphasize the deleterious effects of sin and the value of obedience for characterological growth while, at times, minimizing psychopathological

5. So long as persistent dissociative barriers remain intact, caregiving that is limited to paraenetic applications of biblical and theological content will prove insufficient. Developmental trauma mitigates agency by compromising one's noetic capacities and reinforcing dysfunctional patterns of intersubjectivity. Christian caregiving that fails to redress the wounds of childhood trauma and abuse, whether ostensibly pastoral or psychotherapeutic, inevitably leaves recipients ill-equipped to walk in faithfulness and obedience to Christ.

6. The ubiquity of secular psychology and psychotherapy is best understood as the fruit of two realities of the modern age: the rise of secularism and the decline of classical pastoral care (Holifield, 1983; Tidball, 1997). Presently, an assumed segmentation of disciplinary purview attends extant expressions and understandings of caregiving in both secular and Christian caregiving. A secondary aim of the present work has been to repair the bifurcation of pastoral and psychotherapeutic considerations while avoiding the presumption that a truly holistic synthesis is either practicable or necessary.

factors beyond the control of the individual.[7] Whereas, psychotherapeutic approaches often focus on psychosocial healing while neglecting the etiological role personal sin plays in fomenting psychopathology.[8] In consideration of the two types of barriers to self-knowledge and their contributory and complementary roles in obstructing covenantal relationality, salutary caregiving interventions should pursue means of supplying both pastoral and psychotherapeutic instrumentality out of agapic concern for the care recipient. Effective care that entails both pastoral and psychotherapeutic dialogue bears the most promise for undermining the two primary barriers to veridical self-knowledge.

Contextually determined hermeneutical and ethical asymmetry

In many ways the relational dynamics that constructively impact barriers to self-knowledge mirror the asymmetrical relationship of parent and child.[9] In the same way a child's understandings of self, other, and the world are appropriated through the instrumental influence of the parent, so persistent dissociative and self-deceptive tendencies in adults will come to be favorably resolved by similar means in the context of the caregiving relationship. The developing self of the child relies on the relative sovereignty of the parent in providing nurture and shelter from excessive stress (Klebanov & Travis, 2015). Over time, and as the child matures, parental sovereignty yields to the burgeoning agency of the child.

Contextual determinations of children's developmental needs include their age and relative capacity for resilience under environmental and relational stress. On the other hand, lapses in healthy development occur when those needs go unmet resulting in persistent dysfunction. The fundamental aim of "good" parenting is the development of the child into a mature agent—a response-able subject capable of functioning in

7. As stated in Chapter 7, sin underlies all forms of psychopathology, but psychopathological sequelae are not always the result of *personal* sin.

8. To the extent that ostensibly Christian psychotherapeutic frameworks rely on secular notions of normativity, they undermine the warrant for their distinction as "Christian." On the other hand, with a fuller appropriation of the hermeneutical and ethical framework of the New Testament, Christian psychology and psychotherapy will provide a more salient complement to orthodox pastoral care.

9. Beasley-Murray (1993) notes the apostle Paul's use of parent–child allusions throughout his epistles as a primary metaphor for pastoral caregiving (see 1 Cor 3:1–3; 4:15, 17; 2 Cor 6:13; 12:14; Gal 4:19; Phil 2:22; 1 Thess 2:7, 11; 1 Tim 1:2, 18; 2 Tim 1:2; 2:1; Titus 1:4).

diverse contexts and, eventually, of recapitulating the process with a new generation (cf. Prov 22:6).[10]

Considered along these lines, the caregiving dyad, whether pastoral or psychotherapeutic, assumes a similar transactional dynamic of care *giving* and *receiving* analogous to the parent–child relationship, though with several significant caveats. Under a covenantal anthropology, the pastoral and therapeutic concern of both caregiver and recipient should be the Christiform wholeness of the latter. As has already been suggested, wellbeing or eudaimonia is a worthy and appropriate aim. Given the covenantal telos of the human self and its eschatological orientation, however, wellbeing should not supersede agapic union with Christ and one's fellow believers (through Christ) as the chief end of all forms of Christian caregiving, whether or not they are primarily pastoral or psychotherapeutic.

The appropriate degree of hermeneutical and ethical asymmetry in any relational dyad follows from several factors. In contrast to secular discursive frameworks, Christian pastoral care and psychotherapy may draw on the truths of divine revelation in determining the proper contextual limits.[11] As McFadyen (1990) rightly concludes, "The ethical limits to communication in a particular relation can only be found, known and understood through the orientation towards a mutuality of understanding which happens in dialogue as relations are in conformity to Christ" (pp. 128–129). Consequently, the primary consideration in achieving dialogical "balance" in any caregiving exchange must be the ultimate hermeneutical and ethical sovereignty of Christ. Jesus is Lord over both caregiver and recipient: he alone knows and believes wholly veridically; he alone has been "perfected" in love.

Both caregiver and recipient, on the other hand, will suffer from remaining sin and the subliminal tendency to deploy dissociative means for avoiding aversive truths and realities. As such, neither is immune to the possibility of self-deception. Although generally pastoral and therapeutic discursive frameworks presume that some degree of interpretative authority must be granted to caregivers, orthodox Christianity recognizes the sole sovereign authority of the Logos. Consequently, Christian caregivers may avoid the pitfalls of self-righteousness and hypocrisy

10. Ostensibly Christian parenting must also recognize the biblical imperative to provide for children's spiritual nurture and discipleship (Eph 6:4; cf. Deut 6:7).

11. This is not to say that Christians may not benefit from the empirical findings of secular transactional analysis (see Jacobs, 1994).

automatically entailed by asymmetrical relational dyads only by acknowledging their own need for agapic dialogue with God and others. There is always a risk that one's status as caregiver could become a refuge from the need for personal introspection. Where better for planks to hide than in the eyes of those who only look outward?

The therapeutic role of the Christian caregiver is to undermine dysfunctional attachment patterns and relational schemata carried forward from childhood through agapic exploration and dialogical enactment of divine and human "texts." For this reason, efficacious therapeutic dialogue—that is, intersubjective communication that effectively undermines intrapsychic barriers—is inevasibly asymmetrical. Christian caregivers will necessarily be afforded greater hermeneutical authority respective to both divine and human "texts" if barriers are to be identified and overcome.

Nevertheless, caregivers' authoritative role must be properly balanced and conditioned by genuine agapic concern for care recipients. This is the dialogue of dialogues—the dialogical dynamic of *faith working through love*—by means of which barriers to self-knowledge become permeable. Together, the authority and the agapic concern of the caregiver provide the dialogical means by which old self-"knowledge" comes to be replaced by new. Secular models will recognize intersubjectivity as therapeutic means while neglecting the self's basal need for vertical reconciliation and dialogue. This grants caregivers an unwarranted degree of hermeneutical sovereignty. Caregiver hermeneutical authority must be balanced by genuine agapic concern for care recipients in order to maximize its efficacy. In emphasizing the metaphorical or subjunctive quality of therapeutic caregiving, secular frameworks deprive recipients of a genuine agapic relationality.[12] Knowledge of and love for God-in-Christ should ground all Christian discursive frameworks.

Christian caregiving, in contrast to secular frameworks, sees the triune God not as any metaphorical or subjunctive "parent," but as our archetypal Father after whom all others are so named (Eph 3:14–15). Further, only in Christ are our greatest attachment needs met. As believers come to relate constructively to Christ, the instrumental dialogue of caregiving assumes its most efficacious bearing. The caregiver is called to function instrumentally by embodying Christ's presence, authority, and

12. According to Weiss (1994), excessive hermeneutic sovereignty improperly balanced by ethical considerations—whether due to the caregiver's aloofness or over-identification with the recipient—undermines favorable psychotherapeutic outcomes.

agapic concern, not in any subjunctive sense, but veritably insofar as she or he is filled with and led by the Spirit. Christ is truly present and work-ing as shepherd, healer, and "father" alongside the person of the caregiver and within the dialogical exchange of caregiver and recipient.

As Isaiah prophesied of the Messiah, Jesus' "name shall be called Everlasting Father" (Isa 9:6) inasmuch as he will never forsake or aban-don his people (cf. Heb 13:5). He will not leave them "as orphans" (John 14:18).[13] Efficacious dialogue, moreover, will include both explicit articu-lations of the caregiver's instrumental role respective to Christ and the care recipient, as well as caregiving practices, such as prayer, instruction, confrontation, and expressions of agapic concern, that implicitly enact and demonstrate the caregiver's Christiform instrumentality.[14]

Diachronic degrees of asymmetry

To the extent that barriers to self-knowledge persist, caregiver and re-cipient must negotiate the degree to which each one assumes contingent hermeneutical sovereignty over questions of veridicality. As discoveries are made and barriers removed, the degree of asymmetry will presum-ably decrease as both come to see and know mutually. Over time, the care recipient will ideally assume a greater degree of hermeneutical sovereignty until, having achieved sufficient covenantal wholeness and response-ability, a provisional symmetry becomes possible. The constant concern confronting Christian caregivers, therefore, will be nurturing the appropriate contextual "balance."

The aim of Christian self-knowledge is never mere self-understand-ing or self-mastery, but the appropriation of a Christiform covenantal agency on the part of the care recipient. The *faith working through love* of the caregiver is purposed toward the maturation of the recipient's full agentic participation. Given time, the care recipient/caregiver dyad may

---

13. There is no conflation here of Trinitarian Persons or functions. Isaiah employs the title, "Everlasting Father," as a recognition of the Messiah's "royal . . . kingship" and signifying that he will be "endowed with enduring life" (Childs, 2000, p. 81). Although Christ's fatherhood is ultimately metaphorical, it better approximates the archetypal fatherhood of God the Father than does any strictly human exemplar (cf. Heb 12:9).

14. By explicitly articulating Christ's sovereignty over caregiving processes and outcomes, the caregiver undermines the possibility that she or he would be seen in that light. It is a helpful check on pride and self-righteousness, and it also guards against unhelpful or countertherapeutic degrees of asymmetry in the relational dyad.

even come to be reversed. In the context of a fully symmetrical dialogue, either side of the relational dyad may assume a caregiving role respective to the other. Considering the agapic imperatives of the New Testament, hermeneutical and ethical symmetry should be regarded as the normative aim of caregiving. In other words, Christian caregiving fulfills the "law of Christ" when it is mutual and reciprocal (Gal 6:2). So long as barriers remain, however, an inverted transactional exchange will prove inefficacious, if not countertherapeutic.[15]

The Christiform person
and work of the Christian caregiver

Christ stands at the center of all effective caregiving, Christian or otherwise (see Col 1:17). He alone makes "all things new" (Rev 21:5). The work of Christ in bringing about intrapsychic reconciliation, however, is enacted through the instrumental person and work of the caregiver. Christ's primary means of shepherding and healing broken and sinful human beings is through his redeemed, reconciled people (Johnson, 2017; Kellemen, 2007; Purves, 2004; Tripp, 2002). They are those whose lives have come to be marked by a "radical commitment to the person of Jesus," both in terms of their communal relation to him and their conformity to his character (Boa, 2001, p. 382). Having received the gift of God's reconciling love through their union with Christ, they become signs and vessels for his glorious dispensation for the world. This corporate vocation serves as the particular calling of caregivers within the body of Christ.

Although Christ calls and commands all believers to "bear one another's burdens" (Gal 6:2), he also sets apart specific individuals for the work of pastoral and psychotherapeutic caregiving (see Eph 4:11; cf. Rom 12:6–8).[16] Those he calls he also equips for their work of caregiving.

15. Outside of caregiving contexts, whether pastoral or psychotherapeutic, the love imperatives apply equally to all believers. It should be regarded as both unwise and unethical, however, for caregivers to invert the caregiving dyad, allowing themselves to become the object of concern. That being said, caregivers who do not allow themselves to receive care in other contexts will eventually undermine their effectiveness.

16. Bucer (2009) recognizes a distinction in what today might be called the hortatory and caregiving functions of pastors finding that Christ imparts necessary gifts for each role in differing degrees to individuals: "To one he gives the skill of teaching clearly and understandably, while not endowing him with so much grace in exhorting; to another he gives ability to exhort warmly and seriously, without also enabling him

Central to his preparation and sustenance of caregivers for their vocation, Christ seeks to influence the form and expression of the Christian caregiver through agapic dialogue. He molds and shapes vessels for his use, remaking them in his image and for his purposes. As living vessels—self-conscious, response-able agents capable of doing otherwise—their full agentic participation as Christ's instruments of agapic care is contingent on the removal of their own barriers to self-knowledge.

Consequently, self-knowledge relates intrinsically to caregiving efficacy in that it allows for the formation of the numerous vital ethicospiritual aspects of effective caregivers. As they pursue their own growth in transparent self-awareness through dialogical communion with God and others, they may become more suitable instruments of agapic care for others (Johnson, 2007). In other words, he helps them to remove planks from their eyes so that they might better help those in their care to do the same (see Matt 7:5).

Hermeneutical dialogue and the pistic work of caregivers

The most vital aspect of the caregiving enterprise is the caregiver's conformity to the person and work of Christ. Through union with Christ, the caregiver's *faith working through love* allows the care recipient to begin to "hear" and "see" around false and corrosive conceptions of self that have accumulated due to sin and brokenness. Through pistic submission to the hermeneutical sovereignty of Christ, the caregiver helps undermine subjective barriers to self-knowledge that are rooted in dissociative processes and self-deceptive tendencies. In pastoral and psychotherapeutic contexts, the caregiver embodies a Spirit-mediated confidence in the word/Word of God and its ability to undermine barriers to self-knowledge. Jesus is Lord over every text. Consequently, divine discourse serves as a mirror for self and a lens for other.

---

to be powerful in the teaching and exposition of the scriptures" (p. 34). His description of the latter entails gifts and activities most commonly associated with Christian caregiving: "There are those whom the Lord has appointed to exercise their ministry conscientiously and usefully to the bruised and wounded, warming and powerfully comforting them and applying the right measure of gravity and discipline, but who are not particularly effective in other aspects of the pastoral office" (p. 34). Likewise, Bonhoeffer (1985) holds that pastoral or "spiritual" care, as a form of *diakonia*, is properly complementary to preaching: "In this process of spiritual care . . . the pastor's task is to listen and the parishioner's is to talk" (p. 31). He further argues that "spiritual care joins with the sermon to enable [believers] to uncover and banish true sin" (p. 32).

The caregiver's hermeneutical task entails "hearing" Christ's word to and about the individual, as well as the individual's dialogical reply. The caregiver listens to Christ's "thou art" and the individual's "I am" in order to facilitate determinations of veridicality. Furthermore, Christ's hermeneutical authority applies to all other texts as well: the Logos is a lens through which they may be read and "translated" (see Johnson, 2007, pp. 226–27). Following from a reformational theory of knowledge, the Scriptures, along with the person and work of Christ, are the "norming norm" by which all other texts are rightly interpreted (Vanhoozer, 2005, p. 234). This is the case whether the "text" in question is the counselor, the counselee, or the discursive content that informs their dialogue. More than a mere counselor or specialist, the caregiver serves as a living hermeneutical bridge between Christ and the recipient and all other discursive sources.[17] Critically, the caregiver's competency for this hermeneutical task depends on the degree to which *every* text has been dialogically balanced by pistic commitment to the supremacy of divine discourse.

Maintaining dialogical balance with secular texts

All frameworks for Christian caregiving relate dialogically to their secular counterparts in a variety of ways, whether constructively or not. On the one hand, secular "edification frameworks" have essentially arisen as modern rivals to the Christian gospel offering wholeness and wellbeing apart from any dialogical engagement with the person and work of Christ (Johnson, 2007). Modern and postmodern psychology and psychotherapy have largely evolved, at least since Freud, as competitors to Christianity (Vitz, 1994). Christian counseling offers an alternative to the tide of secularization presently dominant in Western understandings of mental health and wholeness. To some degree the rise of ostensibly Christian counseling[18] as a fundamental aspect or subset of caregiving may be seen as both a converse and constructive response to secular psychotherapy.

17. E.g., secular texts, but also, significantly, the care recipient's past and present relations.

18. The terms "psychotherapy" and "counseling" are often used interchangeably (Corey, 2017; Day, 2004; Sommers-Flanagan & Sommers-Flanagan, 2015; Tan, 2011; though cf. Collins, 1972). I employ the term "Christian counseling" to refer to a particular caregiving process or context—i.e., person-to-person ministry or "soul care"—which, depending on the intended outcome, may be more properly pastoral or psychotherapeutic (though hard distinctions between the two are difficult to maintain).

On the other hand, the relationship between some secular and Christian frameworks is more dependent than constructive. Having recognized the benefits of the kind of focused, purposeful person-to-person dialogue such as that which is practiced in secular contexts, Christians have adopted many of the forms and strategies learned from secular psychotherapy.[19] As Holifield (1983) rightly observes, whether consciously or not, all forms of contemporary pastoral counseling have been influenced by "psychological modes of thinking" (p. 356). The same is certainly true of Christian psychotherapeutic practice, especially as its standards and best practices rely on secular notions of normativity.

The work of the Christian counselor as caregiver, specifically as it relates to the hermeneutical side of the caregiving dialogue—*faith working (through love)*—is, at present, a locus of serious contention among Christians. Throughout the first half of the twentieth century, uncritical engagement with secular discourse unquestionably contributed to the loss of hermeneutical balance in many Christian edification frameworks (E. L. Johnson, 2007, 2010a). For some time, modern psychological and psychotherapeutic discursive frameworks would encounter minimal resistance from Christian theoreticians and practitioners of pastoral and psychotherapeutic caregiving. Little regard was paid to the hermeneutical primacy of the Bible with the result that Christian counseling came increasingly into conformity with modernist standards (Adams, 1970; Ganz, 1993).

Thankfully, reversals of this accommodating trend can be seen in the rise of pastoral and psychotherapeutic efforts to reassert the Bible's fundamental hermeneutical authority (E. L. Johnson, 2010a). Articulations of avowedly Christian, biblically faithful counseling frameworks increasingly reflect a renewed confidence in the hermeneutical sovereignty of divine discourse. That being said, controversy still attends the pursuit of hermeneutical balance, particularly as regards the theory and practice of Christian counseling.

The principal means of distinguishing between the various Christian edification frameworks is the degree to which they appeal to divine and secular discourse, respectively (see Johnson, 2010b; see also Greggo & Sisemore, 2012). Intramural difference tends to be mapped along a

---

19. Christian rejections of secular psychotherapeutic discursive frameworks typically do not entail the determination that person-to-person edification frameworks— i.e., counseling or "soul care"—are inherently unbiblical or unhelpful (see, esp., Bobgan & Bobgan, 2009).

continuum according to the putative warrant each framework grants to dialogue between divine and secular discourse.[20] The concern of such evaluative efforts appears to be ensuring that Christian caregiving frameworks are situated within a stable and faithful hermeneutic that affords the Bible sufficient authority in any dialogical engagement with secular discourse.

Concern to maintain the "norming" normativity of the Logos is certainly a salutary aim. Christian caregiving frameworks ought not to afford undue hermeneutical authority to secular discourse. Caregiving efficacy, to say nothing of the caregiver's responsibility to God, rests on the presumption of a biblically faithful hermeneutic. According to Christ, faith finds its surest footing only when grounded on divine discourse (Matt 7:24). Yet, just as clearly, faith must work itself out *in love*. Above and beyond the justifiable hermeneutical concern, there is the ultimate ethical aim of all Christian caregiving. Biblical or theological fidelity is not our only standard. When Christiform love is lost, the whole endeavor collapses in on itself. Faith that does not work through love—will not work at all.

Given the emphasis on the hermeneutical aspects of Christian caregiving, the vital *ethical* role of caregivers is at risk of being diminished. Among the key competencies of effective caregivers, Kellemen (2015) cites conformity to Christ as crucial to efficacious caregiving: "We are powerful," he avers, "to the degree that we reflect the loving character of Christ" (p. 84). According to Sbanotto et al., (2016), "[T]he most influential variable in counseling is the person of the counselor and the relationship that is cultivated" between caregiver and recipient (p. 34).

In addition to these affirmations from Christian writers, secular researchers have also concluded that "the best available research clearly supports the healing qualities of the therapy relationship and the beneficial

20. All forms of *Christian* counseling engage, to varying degrees, in dialogue with secular frameworks, whether constructively or not. Along the hermeneutical continuum, differences between disparate frameworks depend on two factors: the degree to which divine discourse is afforded hermeneutical sovereignty, and the relative optimism regarding constructive dialogue between Christian and secular frameworks. According to Johnson (2010b), traditional biblical counseling and Christian psychology concur on the supreme hermeneutical authority of divine discourse yet differ on the potential for constructive dialogue with secular frameworks. It should be patently clear that, any time secular discourse is granted hermeneutical sovereignty over and against divine discourse (as in, say, ostensibly Christian affirmations of same-sex marriage or transgenderism), there has been a breach in hermeneutical balance to the extent that it is more consistent with a modern, secular perspective.

value of adapting that relationship to patient characteristics beyond diagnosis" (Norcross & Lambert, 2011, p. 4). Caregiving efficacy, in other words, cannot be wholly linked to its hermeneutical aspects. It is the person of the caregiver—whether as a pastor, friend, spouse, counselor, psychotherapist, etc.—and the quality of the caregiving relationship, that Christ uses to effectuate the removal of epistemic barriers. Truth alone, it would seem, will prove insufficient for undermining barriers to self-knowledge. For this task, truth must learn to speak in love (Eph 4:15). The love with which caregivers "speak" must be rooted and grounded in a dialogical love for Christ.

Pastoral perspectives on agapic caregiving

The biblical and historical literature outlining the optimal character-ological and relational qualities of Christian caregivers is considerable. The person and work of pastoral caregivers, in particular, while not systematically articulated in the New Testament, are implicated as vital aspects of caregiving effectiveness, most notably in the epistles of Paul. Inarguably, the apostle holds that preaching and teaching should serve as the primary discursive function of pastors (Beasley-Murray, 1993). His self-articulated charter for his own personal ministry includes "admonishing" and "teaching" as the seminal means of believers' growth in Christiformity (Col 1:28).[21] In his so-called "pastoral" epistles, Paul affirms numerous necessary characterological aspects of pastors attendant to their divine calling (W. D. Mounce, 2000).

In his first epistolary missive to the young pastor, Paul exhorts Timothy to distinguish himself by his pursuit of "righteousness, godliness, faith, love, steadfastness, gentleness" (1 Tim 6:11).[22] These virtues, though commonly enjoined for all believers, are especially apropos for Timothy in light of the opposition he has encountered in the Ephesian church (Ellicott, 2010). His pastoral care and concern for Christ's people, as Paul suggests, must embody Christ's own compassionate and virtuous character. The "aim" of pastoral ministry, according to the apostle, is

---

21. O'Brien (2000) sees no need to sharply distinguish, based on Paul's apostolic calling, the work of the pastor from that of the missionary.

22. There are four contrasting imperatives in the present context "reminiscent" of Paul's admonitions to the Ephesians and Colossians to "put off" the old and "put on" Christ (Mounce, 2000, p. 353; cf. Eph 4:22–24; Col 3:8–17).

"love that issues from a pure heart and a good conscience and a sincere faith" (1:5).

Consequently, Timothy is to "command and teach" (4:11; cf. 5:7), but not without concern for the status and station of his listeners. He is not to "rebuke" but to "encourage" his fellow believers as he would a close family member (5:1).[23] Similar instructions found in his other pastoral epistles demonstrate the necessity of agapic regard for others in the church (see 2 Tim 2:22–25; Titus 1:8). In summary, Beasley-Murray (1993) rightly concludes, "Love—as a parent for a child—was the bedrock of Paul's pastoral care" (p. 655). Paul's exhortations to his fellow pastors reflects his own parental concern for the believers under his charge.

The notion of the pastor as "parental" caregiver finds ample warrant in the Pauline oeuvre. For the apostle, however, the dyadic correspondence of caregiver and care recipient follows not so much from the analogical link between parent and pastor, but from caregivers'—whether pastoral *or* parental—antitypal correspondence to Christ (see 1 Cor 11:1). If Paul is like a father or mother[24] to others in the church, it is precisely because he is imaging Christ to them. To the degree that pastors and other caregivers image Christ, then, they become effective instruments of God's agapic concern for *his* children.

Following from this biblical sketch, treatises from classical pastoral care writers provide ample supplement in regard to the caregiver's moral life and caregiving competencies (see, e.g., Augustine, 1978; Benedict, 1998; Bucer, 2009; Chrysostom, 2015; Gregory, 1978). Again, the emphasis on the vital relationship of the caregiver to Christ is evident. According to Gregory (1978), caregivers must be like Christ:

> pure in thought, exemplary in conduct, discreet in keeping silence, profitable in speech, in sympathy a near neighbor to everyone, in contemplation, exalted above all others, a humble companion to those who lead good lives, erect in his zeal for righteousness against the vices of sinners. He must not be remiss in his care for the inner life by preoccupation with the external; nor must he in his solicitude for what is internal, fail to give attention to the external. (p. 45)

23. Admittedly, this command not to "rebuke" applies only to those who do not stand in opposition to right teaching and reverent submission to the gospel (see 1 Tim 5:20; Titus 1:13; 2:15).

24. Paul compares himself to a nursing mother in relation to the Thessalonian believers (1 Thess 2:7–8). To the Galatians, he writes that he is "again in the anguish of childbirth until Christ is formed in you" (Gal 4:19).

As instruments of Christ's agapic work among his people, caregivers effect great influence over others, whether for good or ill.

Likewise, Chrysostom (2015) warns that inconsistencies between "work" and "word" in the life of the caregiver "must needs do much harm" (p. 77). Hypocrisy, for those standing in Christ's stead, is a most condemnable sin (see Matt 23; cf. Matt 18:6; Jas 3:1). Whereas genuine conformity to Christ in one's inner life and outward actions is key in fulfilling the caregiving vocation lovingly and efficaciously.

In many ways, the Puritan pastoral writers renewed and deepened the classical tradition by emphasizing the Pauline themes of union and communion with Christ as the basis of all pastoral caregiving (see Packer, 2010; Yuille, 2013). For the most part, the spiritual and ecclesial reforms of English Puritanism centered on the person and work of Christ as revealed in the Scriptures. Central to their perspective on pastoral caregiving is the caregiver's dependence on and love for Christ.

In his call for renewal and reform among his peers, Baxter (1974) cites the crucial link between vertical and horizontal correspondence: "Our whole work must be carried on under a deep sense of our own insufficiency, and of our entire dependence on Christ" (p. 122). As the caregiver's relationship to Christ deepens, so caregiving dyads bear increasing vitality and potency. Nowhere is this more evident than in the need for genuine agapic concern for care recipients. Boston (1998), for example, considers that an individual's "flame of love to Christ" would "fuel" a heart of genuine compassion for others (p. 42).

The agapic character and concern of the caregiver flows from love for Christ. In his prayer echoing the Pauline theme of the pastor as Christiform "parent," Swinnock (1868) entreats,

> Lord, when I behold wounded, bleeding, dying souls, let my eyes affect my heart with sorrow. May I seek Thy blessing upon my diligent efforts for their recovery. Make me such a tender and affectionate mother that I patiently bear their offenses. . . . Let all my actions toward them flow from sincere affection. May all my counsels and comforts, even my rod of reproof, be dipped in honey. (p. 323)

Perspectives such as the Puritans had on pastoral caregiving can be applied to all Christian caregivers regardless of the role or capacity in which they serve (see Deckard, 2010).

In the modern era, the influence of secular psychotherapeutic frameworks has led to a diversification of perspectives on pastoral care-giving (Holifield, 1983; see, e.g., Adams, 1970; Doehring, 2015; Hiltner, 1949; Kellemen, 2007; Tidball, 1997).[25] As with Christian psychotherapy and counseling, pastoral caregiving frameworks continue to wrestle with vital hermeneutical questions regarding the role of divine discourse and the feasibility of dialogue with secular texts.[26] Significant differences presently persist as to the proper nature of the pastoral caregiver's work, whether it amounts to, for example, providing a supportive "spiritual presence" to hurting individuals (Doehring, 2015, p. xxii), identifying and overcoming psychogenic barriers to wellbeing (see Hilter, 1949), or paraenetic exhortation that fosters obedience to God (Adams, 1970).

Whether any one of these may be identified as the *sole* aim of or-thodox pastoral care and counseling remains to be seen; the Scriptures clearly provide ample warrant for all three, and many others besides. Furthermore, extant aims in contemporary pastoral caregiving can also, to varying degrees, be seen within the classical pastoral tradition (see Charry, 1997; Oden, 1984; Purves, 2001). On the other hand, nearly ev-ery perspective on pastoral caregiving, whether ancient or contemporary, consistently holds that the caregiver's compassionate correspondence to recipients is indispensable for efficacious care. "Without love," we do well to remember, "I am nothing" (1 Cor 13:2).

Compassionate correspondence as key

Empathy is an individual's cognitive and affective capacity to vicariously enter the experience of another (Sbanotto et al., 2016; cf. Norcross, 2011).

25. As to the influence of pastoral caregiving on secular psychotherapy, Clebsch and Jaekle (1994), observe, "[M]uch of what is done today by therapists is recognizable in what has been done before by pastors" (p. xi).

26. The biblical counseling movement, broadly conceived, may reasonably be understood as an attempt at hermeneutical renewal for Christian caregiving (see Lam-bert, 2011; MacDonald et al., 2013; Powlison, 2010). Differences within the movement on the feasibility of dialogue with secular discourse, in many ways, mirror similar dif-ferences among Christian counselors and psychotherapists concerning the role of the Bible in counseling. Again, under a covenantal theanthropology, dialogical "balance" entails a presumption of the supreme hermeneutical authority of divine discourse over all other texts. Loss of balance can occur when secular texts are given hermeneutical precedence over the Scriptures, or whenever discourse becomes excessively or exclu-sively monological.

Purposefully "feeling with" this other person is a crucial skill every caregiver must cultivate. Moon and Crews (2002) cite empathy, along with warmth and genuineness, as the three key traits making up the "golden triad" of effective counselors (p. 185; see Rogers, 1967). Care recipients need to know that someone "hears" them, cares, and can identify with the sin and suffering they have endured. Empathic discourse is the most basic therapeutic means by which caregivers may skillfully communicate understanding and warmth.[27] And yet, as Moon and Crews further conclude, a strict emphasis on skills-based competency in Christian caregiving probably reflects an over-dependence on secular frameworks.

Collins (2006), though keen to stress the need for well-developed discursive skills, exhorts caregivers to pursue a life that first "show[s] evidence of the Holy Spirit's fruit" (p. 67).[28] While empathy, warmth, and genuineness are vital to the task of effective caregiving, they do not supplant the New Covenantal imperative to love. "Competent" Christian caregiving is, above all, agapic. The subjective disposition that most clearly expresses agapic concern and regard for others is not empathy but compassion.

Compassion is evidently a reflection of character rather than any discursive competency (Hunsinger, 2015; Purves, 1989). Less a skill that may be learned, it is a wholly Christiform disposition. A compassionate concern for others, according to Purves (1989), embodies the person and work of Christ:

> [C]ompassion is entirely a messianic reality. Jesus alone is the compassionate person, the one in whom compassion is an actuality. This means that compassionate ministry is possible for us only if we are in a relationship with Jesus Christ. Through our relationship with him we participate in his compassion. Our compassion, or, more accurately, his compassion in which we participate, is an expression of our life in Christ, the result of having died and risen with Christ (2 Cor 4:10), of having been

27. Wachtel (2011) observes that empathy can, in fact, be "aversive" whenever the care recipient is closed to reflective self-perception (pp. 207–8). In such cases, caregivers should strategically titrate discourse that might trigger the hardening of barriers. Over time and given a more durable relationship, empathic concern should become less aversive.

28. Collins further cites the past president of the American Psychological Association, Allport (1961), who identifies love as "incomparably the greatest psychotherapeutic agent," yet candidly confesses, "Psychotherapy knows the healing power of love, but finds itself unable to do much about it" (pp. 81–82).

born again (John 3:3), of having been transformed by the renewal of our minds (Rom 12:2). We recognize that apart from
him we can do nothing (John 15:5). (p. 82)

Christiform compassion, unlike empathy, reflects the multiplex
dialogical dynamic of agapic concern. By dwelling or abiding in the
vertical dimension of Christ's love, caregivers become instruments of
Christ's compassion along a horizontal dimension (1 John 3:17). Genuine
compassion, then, proceeds from Christ, through his caregiving instrument, to the individual in need of agapic care. It depends on the degree
to which the caregiver has cultivated the perichoretic appropriation of
Christ's compassionate disposition toward sinful and broken human beings. Other discursive competencies, such as those outlined in secular
counseling manuals, are rooted in individual skillsets rather than dependence on Christ.

This observation should not in any way detract from the necessity
or helpfulness of counseling skills for pastoral and psychotherapeutic
caregiving. A compassionate disposition toward others, moreover, will
likely impel the caregiver to further develop the discursive skills of empathy, genuineness, and warmth—in the interest of learning to "speak
the language" of suffering individuals.[29] That being said, the appropriate
application of competent discourse does not displace the need for genuine compassion in Christian caregiving. The caregiver's call is to express
Christ's own love to the counselee. There is a clear hermeneutical fault in
any presumption by Christian caregivers that efficacy obtains as a result
of a strictly horizontal dialogue (see John 15:5).

Christiform compassion and vicarious suffering

For the apostle Paul, Christiform correspondence to God and others
within the body of Christ suggests that caregivers will suffer vicariously

29. Oden (1984) rightly identifies a christological basis for empathy: "Empathy
is the process of placing oneself in the frame of reference of another, perceiving the
world as the other perceives it, sharing his or her world imaginatively. Incarnation
means that God assumes our frame of reference, entering into our human situation
of finitude and estrangement, sharing our human condition even unto death" (p. 18).
While, as Oden argues, the two are analogous, the degree of disjunction between them
is made clear in his use of the term, "imaginatively." New Covenantal compassion demands that caregivers love "not . . . in word or talk," or, dare I say, imagining, "but in
deed and in truth" (1 John 3:18). There is an important distinction between empathy
and compassion that Oden fails to make.

with both in the context of agapic dialogue. Generally, Christian suffering images the passion and death of Christ (Gorman, 2001; Tannehill, 2006). In regard to his own suffering "for the sake of" Christ and his people, Paul perceives a direct connection to his faithful "stewardship" of the "mystery" God has called him to disclose (Col 1:24–26). This mystery, he explains to the Colossians, is "Christ in you, the hope of glory" (v. 27). In other words, Paul's suffering as a servant of Christ discloses the otherwise hidden purposes of God to bring about the perichoretic union of his people with the indwelling Christ (see Moo, 2008; O'Brien, 2000; see also Rom 8:10; 2 Cor 13:5; Gal 2:20; 4:19; Eph 3:17). Suffering is a key attendant to Paul's apostolic mission.

As a "minister" or servant of divine discourse, Paul's calling includes his active participation in the death and resurrection of Christ as an embodied sign of this transcendent truth.[30] To the extent that Christian caregivers' appropriate this semiodiscursive calling of *faith working through love*, their pastoral and psychotherapeutic ministry will bear out the reality of Christ's redemptive power over every barrier to self-knowledge. "God alone can bear the sins of the world and not be destroyed by them," says Hunsinger (2015); so, "[w]hile God calls human witnesses [i.e., caregivers] to partake in this ministry, it is first and foremost God's ministry into which human beings are called to participate" (p. 40). Through their Christiform participation in the suffering of others, caregivers partake in God's ministry to broken and sinful human beings. In this way, they fulfill the telos of the imago in a fallen world. So doing, they enact the means by which barriers to self-knowledge become permeable.

The ethical imperative of self-knowledge

To the degree that asymmetry characterizes the transactional dyad of caregiver and recipient, the former must pursue the dialogical appropriation of those subjective qualities of Christ's person that undermine persistent barriers to self-knowledge. Caregivers are signs and images of Christ, whether they accurately disclose him or not. The stewardship inherent in their vocation should impel their pursuit of conformity to Christ through veridical self-knowledge. As Jesus advised his followers,

---

30. So, Campbell (2012): "[S]uffering is to be viewed as a *participio Christi* and not as an *imitatio Christi* only. Believers share in the ongoing force of Christ's death and the power of his resurrection" (p. 381).

they must first remove planks in their own eyes before they attempt to help their fellow believers with their specks (Matt 7:5). Caregivers who have drifted from the center of Christ's loving, perichoretic presence will make a poor showing. The more self-blind the caregiver, the less actual care she or he can give.

Barriers to self-knowledge conceal and obfuscate the true nature of the self. As these barriers are displaced, caregivers may more accurately and adequately evaluate their competency for the agapic work to which they have been called, and for which they are being equipped, by God. Not only this, but insofar as caregiving efficacy depends on caregivers' Christiform correspondence, they must endeavor to "judge" themselves according to their conformity to Christ's image (see Matt 7:1). The work of dialogical self-examination and self-evaluation stands among the cardinal desiderata of the caregiving vocation. To whom much is given, much will be required (Luke 12:48).

Shame, stigma, and the ecclesial environment

Barriers to self-knowledge thrive, as it were, in aversive relational contexts. In particular, personal shame and the fear of stigmatization, both of which are relationally induced and maintained, can critically undermine an individual's ability to accurately self-perceive, let alone self-disclose. Tragically, many Christians struggling with the weight of shame and guilt over sin remain in a state of concealment and self-deception because either their primary relational base—home and family—or their faith communities offer judgment and exclusion rather than agapic regard and concern. Expectations of homogeneity and conformity to communal standards of "righteousness," rather than Christiformity, will drive broken and sinful people into hiding.

Clearly, the New Testament never sanctions a flippant or permissive attitude toward sin; on the contrary, sin is condemned in the strongest terms (Matt 5:29–30; John 8:34; 1 Cor 15:34; 1 Tim 5:20; Heb 10:26; 1 John 3:8). Yet, the implication of the gospel is that human sin and divine grace correspond to each other in a strictly binary relationship: Christ's work cancels all debts. Where sin abounded, the apostle declares, grace abounds all the more (Rom 5:20). Divine reconciliation places the repentant believer within a state of divine acceptance and agapic favor (Eph 2:8–9). What sin destroyed, grace restores. Consequently, condemnation of the contrite—amounting to a form of stigma—is absolutely excluded (cf. Rom 8:1).

Once alienated and estranged from God, by reason of Christ's death on our behalf we have now been welcomed back into the garden. Agapic communion with Christ and one's fellow believers is not simply a function or consequence of our obedience, but of our Spirit-mediated proximity to him. We receive the perichoretic joy of Christ by abiding *in* him, not by performing *for* him (John 15:11). Through our *faith working through love* we avoid the pernicious lie of self-righteousness and, to the degree our Christian communities foster an environment of transparency and grace, we deactivate others' fears of stigma and shame. Through active participation in Christ's agapic mission to "sinners," rather than to the "[self-]righteous," Christian communities foster such an environment (see Mark 2:17).

Conclusion to Part V

In the end, it is the knowledge of the Lord that will finally fill the earth as the waters cover the sea (Hab 2:14). And from now and through all eternity, this knowledge supplies human beings light for genuine understanding (2 Cor 4:6; Eph 1:17; 2 Pet 1:3; 3:18). True knowing comes to us through Christ, whether the knowledge is of God, of ourselves, or of anything else in heaven above or earth below. That God has granted to human beings to know him truly, and in so doing to know themselves as he knows them, is the greatest gift imaginable. To know God and the Son he has sent is, as Jesus pronounced, eternal life. In coming to know themselves *in Christ*, they come to see *him* more clearly, to love him more dearly.

Christian self-knowledge differs from secular self-knowledge, therefore, in at least two fundamental ways. First, by promulgating a covenantal theanthropological understanding of the self, the object and subject of self-knowledge can be seen to be one and the same: the "me" that God-in-Christ sees and knows veridically and invites into perichoretic communion with himself. Although he promises eschatological wholeness and wellbeing to his people, the supreme good he offers them is *himself*. He has disclosed himself as the ultimate source of their life and aim of their existence, and further, through his atoning death has opened to them the way to union with him. Christian self-knowledge, then, can never be an end but only a dialogical means of deepening our union with Christ.

Second, although secular approaches to the self and self-knowledge have rightly observed the disruptive influence of inter/personal evil, whether due to individual sin, bad parenting, or other tertiary factors, they cannot perceive the final cause of all human psychopathology and suffering: estrangement from God and the anticipatory torment of autonomy and isolation. Barriers to self-knowledge not only testify to the developmental and relational needs of human beings, but also disclose our fallen-yet-perfectible condition.

We were made for communion with the triune God. Though presently ensnared by and enslaved to sin, the self that is *curvum in se* may be made whole in Christ. The redeemed self, once formerly estranged from God, is now reconciled to God and estranged from sin and death. Formerly isolated, the reborn self is now incorporated into his eschatological body, the Christiform ἐκκλησία τοῦ θεοῦ (*ekklesia tou theou*). Formerly consigned to eschatological chaos and conflict, the believing, persevering self is now being dialogically perfected in faith and love through union with him. All who seek their eschatological rest in him, though subject for the remainder of the present age to the fallen conditions of a cosmos held captive, will one day see him revealed to eyes that now recognize him only by faith. And until he returns, he has entrusted the instrumental remediation of subjective barriers to self-knowledge to the elect, having called them to serve as semiodiscursive vessels of his ecological presence and power.

Bibliography

Adams, J. E. (1970). *Competent to counsel.* Zondervan.

Adams, J. E. (1986). *The Christian counselor's manual: The practice of nouthetic counseling.* Zondervan.

Adams, M. M. (1999). *What sort of human nature? Medieval philosophy and the systematics of Christology.* Marquette University Press.

Ainlay, S. C., Becker, G., & Coleman, L. M. (Eds.). (1986). *The dilemma of difference: A multidisciplinary view of stigma.* Plenum.

Ainsworth, M. D. S., & Bowlby, J. (1991). An ethological approach to personality development. *American Psychologist, 46*(4), 333–341.

Allport, G. W. (1968). *The person in psychology: Selected essays.* Beacon.

Almon, R. L. (2017). The postmodern self in theological perspective: A communal, narrative, and ecclesial approach. *Ecclesiology, 13*(2), 179–196.

American Psychiatric Association. (2013). *Diagnostic and statistical manual of mental disorders: DSM-5.* American Psychiatric Association.

Anderson, R. S. (1982). *On being human: Essays in theological anthropology.* Eerdmans.

Annas, J. (1985). Self-knowledge in early Plato. In D. J. O'Meara (Ed.), *Platonic Investigations* (pp. 111–138). Catholic University of America Press.

Annas, J. (1993). *The morality of happiness.* Oxford University Press.

Aron, L., & Mitchell, S. A. (Eds.). (1999). *Relational psychoanalysis: The emergence of a tradition.* Routledge.

Athanasius. (2012). On the incarnation of the Word. In P. Schaff (Ed.), *Nicene and post-Nicene fathers: Second series* (Vol. 4, pp. 36–67). Hendrickson.

Augustine. (1978). *The first catechetical instruction* (J. P. Christopher, Trans.). Paulist.

Augustine. (2002). *On the Trinity, Books 8–15* (G. B. Matthews, Ed.; S. McKenna, Trans.). Cambridge University Press.

Augustine. (2008). *On Christian teaching* (R. P. H. Green, Trans.). Oxford University Press.

Augustine. (2009). *Confessions* (H. Chadwick, Trans.). Oxford University Press.

Augustine. (2010). *On the free choice of the will, On grace and free choice, and other writings.* Cambridge University Press.

Augustine. (2012a). *Expositions on the Psalms* (A. C. Coxe, Trans.). Hendrickson.

Augustine. (2012b). On original sin. In P. Holmes & R. E. Wallis (Trans.), *Nicene and post-Nicene fathers: First series—Anti-pelagian writings* (Vol. 5). Hendrickson.

Augustine. (2012c). Soliloquies. In P. Schaff (Ed.), & C. C. Starbuck (Trans.), *Nicene and post-Nicene fathers: First series* (Vol. 7, pp. 531–560). Hendrickson.

Augustine. (2012d). The city of God. In P. Schaff & H. Wace (Eds.), *Nicene and post-Nicene fathers: First series* (Vol. 2, pp. 1–511). Hendrickson.

Axton, P. V. (2015). *The psychotheology of sin and salvation: An analysis of the meaning of the death of Christ in light of the psychoanalytical reading of Paul.* Bloomsbury.

Bachkirova, T. (2016). A new perspective on self-deception for applied purposes. *New Ideas in Psychology, 43*, 1–9.

Badgett, J. P. (2018a). Child sexual trauma, dissociation, and the soul: A Christian psychology conceptualization. *Journal of Psychology and Theology, 46*(1), 119–214.

Badgett, J. P. (2018b). Undermining moral self-deception with the help of Puritan pastoral theology. *Journal of Spiritual Formation and Soul Care, 11*(1), 23–38.

Bakhtin, M. M. (1986). *Speech genres and other late essays* (C. Emerson & M. Holquist, Eds.; V. W. McGee, Trans.; 2nd ed.). University of Texas Press.

Bakhtin, M. M. (1993). *Toward a philosophy of the act* (V. Liapunov, Trans.). University of Texas Press.

Barber, J. P., Khalsa, S.-R., & Sharpless, B. A. (2013). The validity of the alliance as a predictor of psychotherapy outcome. In J. C. Muran & J. P. Barber (Eds.), *The therapeutic alliance: An evidence-based guide to practice* (pp. 29–43). Guilford.

Barclay, J. M. G. (2015). *Paul and the gift.* Eerdmans.

Barker, H. G. (2015). *The cross of reality: Luther's theologia crucis and Bonhoeffer's Christology.* Fortress.

Barnes, A. (1997). *Seeing through self-deception.* Cambridge University Press.

Barresi, J., & Martin, R. (2011). History as prologue: Western theories of the self. In S. Gallagher (Ed.), *The Oxford Handbook of the Self* (pp. 33–56). Oxford University Press.

Barrett, L. C. (2013). Kierkegaard on the atonement: The complementarity of salvation as a gift and salvation as a task. *Kierkegaard Studies, 2013*(1), 3–24.

Barth, K. (1960). *The humanity of God.* Westminster John Knox.

Barth, K. (1979). *Evangelical theology: An introduction.* Eerdmans.

Barth, K. (1991). *The Göttingen dogmatics: Instruction in the Christian religion* (H. Reiffen, Ed.; G. W. Bromiley, Trans.). Eerdmans.

Barth, K. (1995). *The theology of John Calvin* (G. W. Bromiley, Trans.). Eerdmans.

Barth, K. (2010). *Church dogmatics.* Hendrickson.

Barth, K. (2011). *Fragments grave and gay* (M. Rumscheidt, Ed.). Wipf & Stock.

Bartholomew, C. G. (2017). *Contours of the Kuyperian tradition: A systematic introduction.* InterVarsity.

Bartholomew, C. G., & Goheen, M. W. (2013). *Christian philosophy: A systematic and narrative introduction.* Baker.

Batson, C. D. (2007). Moral masquerades: Experimental exploration of the nature of moral motivation. *Phenomenology and the Cognitive Sciences, 7*(1), 51–66.

Batson, C. D., Thompson, E. R., Seuferling, G., Whitney, H., & Strongman, J. A. (1999). Moral hypocrisy: Appearing moral to oneself without being so. *Journal of Personality and Social Psychology, 77*(3), 525–537.

Bauckham, R. (2008). *Jesus and the God of Israel: God crucified and other studies on the New Testament's Christology of divine identity.* Eerdmans.

Baumeister, R. F. (1998). The self. In D. T. Gilbert, S. T. Fiske, & G. Lindsey (Eds.), *Handbook of Social Psychology* (4th ed., pp. 680–740). McGraw-Hill.

Baumeister, R. F. (1999). The nature and structure of the self: An overview. In R. F. Baumeister (Ed.), *The self in social psychology.* Psychology.

Bavinck, H. (2004). *Reformed dogmatics, vol. 2: God and creation* (J. Bolt, Ed.; J. Vriend, Trans.). Baker.

Bavinck, H. (2006). *Reformed dogmatics, vol. 3: Sin and salvation in Christ* (J. Bolt, Ed.; J. Vriend, Trans.). Baker.

Baxter, R. (1974). *The Reformed pastor* (W. Brown, Ed.). Banner of Truth Trust.

Baxter, R. (2010). *On the mischiefs of self-ignorance, and the benefits of self-acquaintance.* Nabu.

Beasley-Murray, G. R. (1973). *Baptism in the New Testament.* Eerdmans.

Beasley-Murray, P. (1993). Pastor, Paul as. In G. F. Hawthorne, R. P. Martin, & D. G. Reid (Eds.), *Dictionary of Paul and his letters* (pp. 654–658). InterVarsity.

Beck, J. R. (2002). *The psychology of Paul: A fresh look at his life and teaching.* Kregel.

Beck, J. R., & Demarest, B. (2005). *The human person in theology and psychology: A biblical anthropology for the twenty-first century.* Kregel.

Becker, J. (1993). *Paul: Apostle to the Gentiles.* Westminster John Knox.

Benedict. (1998). *The rule of Saint Benedict* (T. Fry, Ed.). Vintage Spiritual Classics.

Berkouwer, G. C. (1954). *The person of Christ.* Eerdmans.

Berkouwer, G. C. (1962). *Man: The image of God.* Eerdmans.

Berkouwer, G. C. (1972). *The return of Christ* (J. Van Oosterom, Trans.). Eerdmans.

Biderman, S. (2008). *Crossing horizons: World, self, and language in Indian and Western thought.* Columbia University Press.

Bird, G. (2006). *The revolutionary Kant: A commentary on The Critique of Pure Reason.* Carus.

Bird, P. A. (1981). "Male and female he created them": Gen 1:27b in the context of the priestly account of creation. *Harvard Theological Review, 74*(2), 129–160.

Blanck, G., & Blanck, R. (1974). *Ego psychology: Theory and practice.* Columbia University Press.

Blocher, H. (1999). *Original sin: Illuminating the riddle.* Eerdmans.

Blocher, H. (2005). Atonement. In K. J. Vanhoozer (Ed.), *Dictionary for theological interpretation of the bible* (pp. 72–76). Baker.

Block, D. I. (2011). *How I love your Torah, O LORD!: Studies in the book of Deuteronomy.* Wipf & Stock.

Boa, K. (2001). *Conformed to his image: Biblical and practical approaches to spiritual formation.* Zondervan.

Bobgan, M., & Bobgan, D. (2009). *Person to person ministry: Soul care in the body of Christ.* EastGate.

Boethius. (1978). *The theological tractates and the consolation of philosophy* (H. J. Stewart, E. K. Rand, & S. J. Tester, Trans.; Rev. ed.). Harvard University Press.

Bonhoeffer, D. (1985). *Spiritual care.* Fortress.

Bonhoeffer, D. (1996). *Act and being.* Fortress.

Bonhoeffer, D. (1998). *Sanctorum communio: A theological study of the sociology of the church.* Fortress.

Bonhoeffer, D. (2001). *Discipleship.* Fortress.

Bonhoeffer, D. (2005). *Ethics.* Fortress.

Bonhoeffer, D. (2009). *Berlin: 1932–1933.* Fortress.

Boston, T. (1998). *The art of man-fishing: How to reach the lost.* Christian Heritage.

Bowlby, J. (1988). *A secure base.* Routledge.

Bradbury, R. (2011). *Cross theology: The classical theologia crucis and Karl Barth's modern theology of the cross.* Wipf & Stock.

Bray, G. (2012). *God is love: A biblical and systematic theology*. Crossway.

Brennan, J. F. (2014). *History and systems of psychology* (6th ed.). Pearson.

Briere, J. N., & Scott, C. (2014). *Principles of trauma therapy: A guide to symptoms, evaluation, and treatment* (2nd ed.). SAGE.

Bromberg, P. M. (1998). *Standing in the spaces: Essays on clinical process, trauma, and dissociation*. Psychology.

Bromberg, P. M. (2009). Multiple self-states, the relational mind, and dissociation. In P. F. Dell & J. A. O'Neil (Eds.), *Dissociation and the Dissociative Disorders: DSM-V and Beyond* (pp. 637–652). Routledge.

Bromberg, P. M. (2011). *Awakening the dreamer: Clinical journeys*. Routledge.

Broucek, F. J. (1991). *Shame and the self*. Guilford.

Brown, D. (2009). Assessment of attachment and abuse history, and adult attachment style. In C. A. Courtois & J. D. Ford (Eds.), *Treating complex traumatic stress disorders: Scientific foundations and therapeutic models* (pp. 124–144). Guilford.

Brown, H. O. J. (1988). *Heresies: The image of christ in the mirror of heresy and orthodoxy from the apostles to the present*. Baker.

Brown, P. (2000). *Augustine of Hippo: A biography* (Rev. ed.). University of California Press.

Brown, R. E. (1967). *Jesus—God and man: Modern biblical reflections*. Bruce.

Brown, R. E. (1982). *The epistles of John*. Yale University Press.

Browning, D. S., & Cooper, T. D. (2004). *Religious thought and the modern psychologies* (2nd ed.). Fortress.

Bruce, F. F. (1984). *The epistles to the Colossians, to Philemon, and to the Ephesians*. Eerdmans.

Brunner, E. (2014). *The Christian doctrine of creation and redemption* (O. Wyon, Trans.). Wipf & Stock.

Bucci, W. (1997). *Psychoanalysis and cognitive science: A multiple code theory*. Guilford.

Bucer, M. (2009). *Concerning the true care of souls* (P. Beale, Trans.). Banner of Truth.

Bultmann, R. (2007). *Theology of the New Testament* (K. Grobel, Trans.). Baylor University Press.

Burke, P. (2002). *Reinterpreting Rahner: A critical study of his major themes*. Fordham University Press.

Burris, C. T., & Navara, G. S. (2002). Morality play or playing morality?: Intrinsic religious orientation and socially desirable responding. *Self & Identity, 1*(1), 67–76.

Caluori, D. (2015). *Plotinus on the soul*. Cambridge University Press.

Calvin, J. (1965). *The epistles of Paul the apostle to the Galatians, Ephesians, Philippians and Colossians* (D. W. Torrance & T. F. Torrance, Eds.; T. H. L. Parker, Trans.). Eerdmans.

Calvin, J. (1995). *Epistle of Paul the apostle to the Romans* (R. Mackenzie, Trans.). Eerdmans.

Calvin, J. (2008). *Institutes of the Christian religion* (1559). Hendrickson.

Campbell, C. R. (2012). *Paul and union with Christ: An exegetical and theological study*. Zondervan.

Carlson, E. A. (1998). A prospective longitudinal study of attachment disorganization/disorientation. *Child Development, 69*(4), 1107–1128.

Carlson, E. A., Yates, T. M., & Sroufe, L. A. (2009). Dissociation and the development of the self. In P. F. Dell & J. A. O'Neil (Eds.), *Dissociation and the Dissociative Disorders: DSM-V and Beyond* (pp. 39–52). Routledge.

Carson, D. A. (1990). *The gospel according to John*. Eerdmans.

Carson, D. A. (1999). *Jesus' Sermon on the Mount and his confrontation with the world: An exposition of Matthew 5–10*. Baker.

Carson, D. A. (2000). *The difficult doctrine of the love of God*. Crossway.

Cary, P. (2003). *Augustine's invention of the inner self: The legacy of a Christian Platonist*. Oxford University Press.

Cassam, Q. (Ed.). (1994). *Self-knowledge*. Oxford University Press.

Cassam, Q. (2014). *Self-knowledge for humans*. Oxford University Press.

Chamblin, J. K. (1993). *Paul and the self: Apostolic teaching for personal wholeness*. Baker.

Champion, M. L. (1988). *Knowledge of God as the transformation of human existence in the theology of Dietrich Bonhoeffer* [Unpublished doctoral dissertation]. Princeton Theological Seminary.

Charry, E. T. (1997). *By the renewing of your minds: The pastoral function of Christian doctrine*. Oxford University Press.

Chefetz, R. A. (2015). *Intensive psychotherapy for persistent dissociative processes: The fear of feeling real*. Norton.

Childs, B. S. (2000). *Isaiah*. Westminster John Knox.

Christian, C. (2017). The evolution of modern conflict theory. In C. Christian & M. N. Eagle (Eds.), *Psychoanalytic Perspectives on Conflict* (pp. 21–37). Routledge.

Christian, C., Eagle, M. N., & Wolitzky, D. L. (Eds.). (2017). *Psychoanalytic Perspectives on Conflict*. Routledge.

Chrysostom, S. J. (2015). *Saint Chrysostom on the priesthood* (B. H. Cowper, Trans.). Aeterna Press.

Chu, J. A. (2011). *Rebuilding shattered lives: Treating complex PTSD and dissociative disorders*. Wiley.

Clark, D. K. (2010). *To know and love God: Method for theology*. Crossway.

Clark, R. A., & Gaede, S. D. (1987). Knowing together: Reflections on a holistic sociology of knowledge. In H. Heie & D. L. Wolfe (Eds.), *The reality of Christian learning: Strategies for faith-discipline integration* (pp. 55–86). Wipf & Stock.

Clark, S. R. L. (1989). *Civil peace and sacred order*. Oxford University Press.

Clebsch, W. A., & Jaekle, C. R. (1994). *Pastoral care in historical perspective*. Aronson.

Coakley, S. (2002). What does Chalcedon solve and what does it not? Some reflections on the status and meaning of the chalcedonian "Definition." In S. T. Davis, D. Kendall, & G. O'Collins (Eds.), *The incarnation* (pp. 143–163). Oxford University Press.

Colbert, T. C. (2000). *The four false pillars of biopsychiatry*. Kevco.

Coleman, L. M. (1986). Stigma: An enigma demystified. In S. C. Ainlay, G. Becker, & L. M. Coleman (Eds.), *The dilemma of difference: A multidisciplinary view of stigma* (pp. 211–232). Plenum.

Collins, G. R. (1972). *Effective counseling*. Creation House.

Collins, G. R. (2006). *Christian counseling: A comprehensive guide* (3rd ed.). Thomas Nelson.

Conzelmann, H. (1974). *An outline of the theology of the New Testament*. SCM Press.

Cooper, J. M. (1986). *Reason and human good in Aristotle*. Hackett.

Cooper, J. W. (2000). *Body, soul, and life everlasting: Biblical anthropology and the monism-dualism debate*. Eerdmans.

Corey, G. (2017). *Theory and practice of counseling and psychotherapy* (10th ed.). Cengage Learning.

Corrigan, P. W., & Watson, A. C. (2002). The paradox of self-stigma and mental illness. *Clinical Psychology: Science and Practice, 9*(1), 35–53.

Cortez, M. (2008). *Embodied souls, ensouled bodies: An exercise in christological anthropology and its significance for the mind/body debate.* T&T Clark.

Cortez, M. (2016). *Christological anthropology in historical perspective: Ancient and contemporary approaches to theological anthropology.* Zondervan.

Cozolino, L. (2017). *The neuroscience of psychotherapy: Healing the social brain* (3rd ed.). Norton.

Crisp, O. D. (2007). *Divinity and humanity: The incarnation reconsidered.* Cambridge University Press.

Crisp, O. D. (2012). *Jonathan Edwards on God and creation.* Oxford University Press.

Crisp, O. D. (2016). *The Word enfleshed: Exploring the person and work of Christ.* Baker.

Crisp, T. M., Porter, S., & Elshof, G. A. T. (Eds.). (2016). *Neuroscience and the soul: The human person in philosophy, science, and theology.* Eerdmans.

Cross, R. (2005). *The metaphysics of the incarnation: Thomas Aquinas to Duns Scotus.* Oxford University Press.

Crowe, F. E. (2006). Eschaton and worldly mission in the mind and heart of Jesus. In M. Vertin (Ed.), *Appropriating the Lonergan Idea* (pp. 193–234). University of Toronto Press.

Cushman, P. (1995). *Constructing the self, constructing America: A cultural history of psychotherapy.* Da Capo Press.

Danker, F. W. (Ed.). (2001). *A Greek-English lexicon of the New Testament and other early Christian literature (BDAG)* (3rd ed.). University of Chicago Press.

Darwall, S. L. (1988). Self-deception, autonomy, and moral constitution. In B. P. McLaughlin & A. O. Rorty (Eds.), *Perspectives on self-deception* (pp. 407–430). University of California Press.

Davidson, I. (2001). Theologizing the human Jesus: An ancient (and modern) approach to Christology reassessed. *International Journal of Systematic Theology, 3*(2), 129–153.

Davis, S. T. (2006). "Who can forgive sins but God alone?": Jesus, forgiveness, and divinity. In C. Helmer (Ed.), *The multivalence of biblical texts and theological meanings* (pp. 113–123). Society of Biblical Literature.

Day, S. X. (2004). *Theory and design in counseling and psychotherapy.* Houghton Mifflin.

Deckard, M. A. (2010). *Helpful truth in past places: The Puritan practice of biblical counseling.* Mentor.

DeJonge, M. P. (2012). *Bonhoeffer's theological formation: Berlin, Barth, and Protestant theology.* Oxford University Press.

Delitzsch, F. (1885). *A system of biblical psychology* (R. E. Wallis, Trans.). T&T Clark.

Demarest, B. (2006). *The cross and salvation: The doctrine of salvation.* Crossway.

Dennett, D. C. (1991). *Consciousness explained.* Brown.

DeWeese, G. J. (2007). One person, two natures: Two metaphysical models of the incarnation. In F. Sanders & K. Issler (Eds.), *Jesus in Trinitarian perspective.* B&H.

DeYoung, P. A. (2003). *Relational psychotherapy: A primer.* Routledge.

DeYoung, P. A. (2015). *Understanding and treating chronic shame: A relational/neurobiological approach.* Routledge.

Diller, K. (2014). *Theology's epistemological dilemma: How Karl Barth and Alvin Plantinga provide a unified response.* InterVarsity.

Doehring, C. (2015). *The practice of pastoral care: A postmodern approach* (Rev. ed.). Westminster John Knox.

Dooyeweerd, H. (1984). *A new critique of theoretical thought* (D. H. Freeman & W. S. Young, Trans.; Vol. 1). Paideia.

Doriani, D. (2014). Original sin in pastoral theology. In H. Madueme & M. Reeves (Eds.), *Adam, the fall, and original sin: Theological, biblical, and scientific perspectives* (pp. 251–268). Baker.

Douty, N. F. (1973). *Union with Christ.* Reiner.

Dowey, E. A. (1994). *Knowledge of God in Calvin's theology* (3rd ed.). Eerdmans.

Dunn, J. D. G. (1988). *Romans 1–8* (Vol. 38A). Thomas Nelson.

Dunn, J. D. G. (2006). *The theology of Paul the apostle.* Eerdmans.

Dutra, L., Bianchi, I., Siegel, D. J., & Lyons-Ruth, K. (2009). The relational context of dissociative phenomena. In P. F. Dell & J. A. O'Neil (Eds.), *Dissociation and the dissociative disorders: DSM-V and beyond* (pp. 83–92). Routledge.

Dyke, D. (2013). *The mystery of self-deceiving.* International Outreach.

Eagle, M. N. (2010). *From classical to contemporary psychoanalysis: A critique and integration.* Routledge.

Eagle, M. N. (2013). *Attachment and psychoanalysis: Theory, research, and clinical implications.* Guilford.

Eagle, M. N. (2018). *Core concepts in classical psychoanalysis: Clinical, research evidence and conceptual critiques.* Routledge.

Edwards, J. (1998). The end for which God created the world. In J. Piper (Ed.), *God's passion for his glory: Living the vision of Jonathan Edwards* (pp. 117–251). Crossway.

Edwards, J. (2009). *The works of Jonathan Edwards, volume 2: Religious affections* (J. E. Smith, Ed.). Yale University Press.

Edwards, K. J., & Davis, E. B. (2013). Evidence-based principles from psychodynamic and process-experiential psychotherapies. In E. L. Worthingon Jr., E. L. Johnson, J. N. Hook, & J. D. Aten (Eds.), *Evidence-based practices for Christian counseling and psychotherapy* (pp. 122–145). InterVarsity.

Ellenberger, H. F. (1981). *The discovery of the unconscious: The history and evolution of dynamic psychiatry.* Basic.

Ellicott, C. J. (2010). *The pastoral epistles of St. Paul.* Kessinger.

Elliott, M. A. (2006). *Faithful feelings: Rethinking emotion in the New Testament.* Kregel.

Elliston, C. J. (2016). *Dietrich Bonhoeffer and the ethical self: Christology, ethics, and formation.* Fortress.

Emerson, C. (2006). Building a responsive self in a post-relativistic world: The contribution of Mikhail Bakhtin. In P. C. Vitz & S. M. Felch (Eds.), *The self: Beyond the postmodern crisis* (pp. 25–41). Intercollegiate Studies Institute.

Engel, M. P. (2002). *John Calvin's perspectival anthropology.* Wipf & Stock.

Erdelyi, M. (1985). *Psychoanalysis: Freud's cognitive psychology.* Freeman.

Evans, C. S. (1990). *Søren Kierkegaard's Christian psychology: Insight for counseling & pastoral care.* Ministry Resources Library.

Evans, C. S. (1995). Kierkegaard's view of the unconscious. In M. J. Matuštík & M. Westphal (Eds.), *Kierkegaard in post/modernity* (pp. 76–97). Indiana University Press.

Evans, C. S. (2002). Self and other in Kierkegaard's psychology: God and human relations in the constitution of the self. In T. H. Speidell (Ed.), *On being a person: A multidisciplinary approach to personality theories* (pp. 72–87). Cascade.

Evans, G. R. (1986). *The thought of Gregory the Great*. Cambridge University Press.

Fairbairn, W. R. D. (1929). Dissociation and repression. In E. F. Birtles & D. E. Scharff (Eds.), *From instinct to self: Selected papers of W. R. D. Fairbairn, volume II* (pp. 13–79). Aronson.

Fairbairn, W. R. D. (1952). *Psychoanalytic studies of the personality*. Routledge.

Fairbairn, W. R. D. (1954). Observations on the nature of hysterical states. *British Journal of Medical Psychology, 27*, 105–125.

Fee, G. D. (2009). *God's empowering presence: The Holy Spirit in the letters of Paul*. Baker.

Ferguson, S. B. (1997). *The Holy Spirit*. InterVarsity.

Fernández, J. (2013). Self-deception and self-knowledge. *Philosophical Studies, 162*(2), 379–400.

Feuerbach, L. (1989). *The essence of Christianity*. Prometheus.

Finkelhor, D., & Browne, A. (1985). The traumatic impact of child sexual abuse: A conceptualization. *American Journal of Orthopsychiatry, 55*(4), 530–541.

Fisher, S., & Greenberg, R. P. (1996). *Freud scientifically reappraised: Testing the theories and therapy*. Wiley.

Fitzpatrick, E. M. (2013). *Found in him: The joy of the incarnation and our union with Christ*. Crossway.

Flanagan, K. S., & Hall, S. E. (Eds.). (2014). *Christianity and developmental psychopathology: Foundations and approaches*. InterVarsity.

Flavel, J. (2012). *The touchstone of sincerity: Or the signs of grace and symptoms of hypocrisy*. Nabu.

Fonagy, P. (2001). *Attachment theory and psychoanalysis*. Other.

Ford, D. F. (2007). *Christian wisdom: Desiring God and learning in love*. Cambridge University Press.

Ford, J. D., & Courtois, C. A. (2009). Defining and understanding complex trauma and complex traumatic stress disorders. In C. A. Courtois & J. D. Ford (Eds.), *Treating complex traumatic stress disorders: Scientific foundations and therapeutic models* (pp. 13–30). Guilford.

Frame, J. M. (1987). *The doctrine of the knowledge of God*. P&R.

Frame, J. M. (2002). *The doctrine of God*. P&R.

Frame, J. M. (2015). *A history of western philosophy and theology*. P&R.

France, R. T. (2007). *The Gospel of Matthew*. Eerdmans.

Frances, A. (2013). *Saving normal: An insider's revolt against out-of-control psychiatric diagnosis, DSM-5, big pharma, and the medicalization of ordinary life*. Morrow.

Franks, R. S. (1962). *The work of Christ*. Thomas Nelson and Sons.

Freddoso, A. J. (1986). Human nature, potency and the incarnation. *Faith and Philosophy, 3*(1), 27–53.

Freud, A. (1977). *The ego and the mechanisms of defense* (Rev. ed.). International Universities Press.

Freud, S. (1905). Three essays on the theory of sexuality. In *Standard Edition, 7* (pp. 125–245). Hogarth.

Freud, S. (1915a). Observations on transference-love. In *Standard Edition, 12* (pp. 157–171). Hogarth, 1958.

Freud, S. (1915b). Repression. In *Standard Edition, 14* (pp. 146–158). Hogarth, 1957.

Freud, S. (1915c). The unconscious. In *Standard Edition, 14* (pp. 217–235). Norton, 1990.

Freud, S. (1923). The ego and the id. In *Standard Edition, 19*. Norton, 1990.

Freud, S. (1927). The future of an illusion. In *Standard Edition, 21* (pp. 34–63). Hogarth, 1962.

Freud, S. (1933). New introductory lectures on psycho-analysis. In *Standard Edition, 22* (pp. 1–182). Hogarth, 1964.

Freud, S. (1940). An outline of psycho-analysis. In *Standard Edition, 23* (pp. 144–207). Norton, 1989.

Fromm, E. (1980). *Greatness and limitations of Freud's thought.* Harper & Row.

Funkhouser, E., & Barrett, D. (2016). Robust, unconscious self-deception: Strategic and flexible. *Philosophical Psychology, 29*(5), 682–696.

Gadamer, H.-G. (1976). On the problem of self-understanding. In D. E. Linge (Trans.), *Philosophical hermeneutics* (pp. 44–58). University of California Press.

Gaffin, R. B., Jr. (2013). *By faith, not by sight: Paul and the order of salvation* (2nd ed.). P&R.

Gallagher, S. (Ed.). (2011). *The Oxford handbook of the self.* Oxford University Press.

Galot, J. (1981). *Who is Christ? A theology of the incarnation.* Franciscan Herald.

Ganz, R. (1993). *PsychoBabble: The failure of modern psychology—and the biblical alternative.* Crossway.

Gergen, K. J. (1991). *The saturated self: Dilemmas of identity in contemporary life.* Basic.

Gerhardsson, B. (2009). *The testing of God's Son* (J. Toy, Trans.). Wipf & Stock.

Gerrish, B. A. (1981). The mirror of God's goodness: Man in the theology of Calvin. *Concordia Theological Quarterly, 45*(3), 211–222.

Gerrish, B. A. (2015). *Christian faith: Dogmatics in outline.* Westminster John Knox.

Gertler, B. (2011). *Self-knowledge.* Routledge.

Gilbert, P., & Andrews, B. (1998). *Shame: Interpersonal behavior, psychopathology, and culture.* Oxford University Press.

Gingrich, H. D. (2013). *Restoring the shattered self: A Christian counselor's guide to complex trauma.* InterVarsity.

Godsey, J. D. (1987). Barth and Bonhoeffer: The basic difference. *Quarterly Review, 7*(1), 9–27.

Goethals, G. R., & Strauss, J. (1991). The study of the self: Historical perspectives and contemporary issues. In J. Strauss & G. R. Goethals (Eds.), *The self: Interdisciplinary approaches* (pp. 1–17). Springer-Verlag.

Goffman, E. (1963). *Stigma: Notes on the management of spoiled identity.* Simon & Schuster.

Goldingay, J. (2007). *Psalms, vol. 2: Psalms 42–89.* Baker.

Goldsworthy, G. (2010). *Gospel-centered hermeneutics: Foundations and principles of evangelical biblical interpretation.* InterVarsity.

Gonçalves, Ó. F., Machado, P. P. P., Korman, Y., & Angus, L. (2002). Assessing psychopathology: A narrative approach. In L. E. Beutler & M. L. Malik (Eds.), *Rethinking the DSM: A psychological perspective* (pp. 149–176). American Psychological Association.

González, J. L. (2015). *The history of theological education.* Abingdon.

Gordon, J. R. (2016). *The Holy One in our midst: An essay on the flesh of Christ.* Fortress.

Gorman, M. J. (2001). *Cruciformity: Paul's narrative spirituality of the cross.* Eerdmans.

Gorman, M. J. (2009). *Inhabiting the cruciform God: Kenosis, justification, and theosis in Paul's narrative soteriology*. Eerdmans.

Gorman, M. J. (2015). *Becoming the Gospel: Paul, participation, and mission*. Eerdmans.

Green, C. J. (1999). *Bonhoeffer: A theology of sociality* (Rev. ed.). Eerdmans.

Greenberg, J. R., & Mitchell, S. A. (1983). *Object relations in psychoanalytic theory*. Harvard University Press.

Greenhill, W. (2010). *The sound-hearted Christian*. Reformation Heritage.

Greggo, S. P., & Sisemore, T. A. (Eds.). (2012). *Counseling and Christianity: Five approaches*. InterVarsity.

Gregor, B. (2013). *A philosophical anthropology of the cross: The cruciform self*. Indiana University Press.

Gregory. (1978). *Pastoral care* (H. Davis, Trans.). Newman.

Grenz, S. J. (2001). *The social God and the relational self: A trinitarian theology of the imago dei*. Westminster John Knox.

Grenz, S. J. (2004). Jesus as the imago dei: Image-of-God Christology and the non-linear linearity of theology. *Journal of the Evangelical Theological Society, 47*(4), 617–628.

Gruenewald, T. L., Dickerson, S. S., & Kemeny, M. E. (2007). A social function for self-conscious emotions: The social self preservation theory. In J. L. Tracy, R. W. Robins, & J. P. Tangney (Eds.), *The self-conscious emotions: Theory and research* (pp. 68–90). Guilford.

Gundry, R. H. (2005). *Soma in biblical theology: With emphasis on Pauline anthropology*. Cambridge University Press.

Gunton, C. E. (1991). Trinity, ontology and anthropology: Towards a renewal of the doctrine of the imago dei. In C. Schwöbel & C. E. Gunton (Eds.), *Persons, divine and human: King's college essays in theological anthropology* (pp. 47–61). T&T Clark.

Gunton, C. E. (1997). *Yesterday & today: Study of continuities in Christology* (2nd ed.). SPCK.

Guntrip, H. (1973). *Psychoanalytic theory, therapy, and the self*. Basic.

Hagner, D. A. (1993). *Matthew 1–13* (Vol. 33a). Thomas Nelson.

Hamilton, J. M. H. (2006). *God's indwelling presence: The Holy Spirit in the Old and New Testaments*. B&H.

Hannay, A. (1987). Spirit and the idea of the self as a reflexive relation. In R. L. Perkins (Ed.), *The sickness unto death* (Vol. 19, pp. 23–38). Mercer University Press.

Harding, S. (2016). *Paul's eschatological anthropology: The dynamics of human transformation*. Fortress.

Harré, R. (1998). *The singular self: An introduction to the psychology of personhood*. SAGE.

Harris, M. J. (1992). *Jesus as God: The New Testament use of theos in reference to Jesus*. Wipf & Stock.

Harris, M. J. (2005). *The second epistle to the Corinthians*. Eerdmans.

Harris, R. L., Archer, G. J., Jr., & Waltke, B. K. (2003). *Theological wordbook of the Old Testament* (Rev. ed.). Moody.

Harrison, V. (1991). Perichoresis in the Greek fathers. *St. Vladimir's Theological Quarterly, 35*(1), 53–65.

Harter, S. H. (2015). *The construction of the self: Developmental and sociocultural foundations* (2nd ed.). Guilford.

Hartmann, H. (1965). *Essays on ego psychology.* International Universities Press.

Hatfield, G. (2014). *The Routledge guidebook to Descartes' meditations.* Routledge.

Hefner, P. J. (1984). The creation. In C. E. Braaten & R. W. Jenson (Eds.), *Christian Dogmatics* (Vol. 1, pp. 269–362). Fortress.

Heiser, M. S. (2015). *The unseen realm: Recovering the supernatural worldview of the Bible.* Lexham.

Helm, P. (2011). *Eternal God: A study of God without time* (2nd ed.). Oxford University Press.

Herman, J. L. (2015). *Trauma and recovery: The aftermath of violence—From domestic abuse to political terror* (Rev. ed.). Basic.

Hick, J. (1977). *The myth of God incarnate.* Westminster.

Hiebert, D. (2008). Can we talk? Achieving dialogue between sociology and theology. *Christian Scholar's Review, 37*(2), 199–214.

Hiltner, S. (1949). *Pastoral counseling.* Abingdon.

Hoekema, A. A. (1994). *Created in God's image.* Eerdmans.

Holifield, E. B. (1983). *A history of pastoral care in America: From salvation to self-realization.* Wipf & Stock.

Horton, M. S. (2005). *Lord and servant: A covenant Christology.* Westminster John Knox.

Horton, M. S. (2006). Image and office: Human personhood and the covenant. In R. Lints, M. S. Horton, & M. R. Talbot (Eds.), *Personal identity in theological perspective* (pp. 178–203). Eerdmans.

Houston, J. M. (2000). The "double knowledge" as the way of wisdom. In S. K. Soderlund & J. I. Packer (Eds.), *The way of wisdom: Essays in honor of Bruce K. Waltke* (pp. 308–326). Zondervan.

Houts, A. C. (2002). Discovery, invention, and the expansion of the modern diagnostic and statistics manuals of mental disorders. In L. E. Beutler & M. L. Malik (Eds.), *Rethinking the DSM: A psychological perspective* (pp. 17–68). American Psychological Association.

Howell, E. F. (2005). *The dissociative mind.* Analytic.

Howell, E. F. (2011). *Understanding and treating dissociative identity disorder: A relational approach.* Routledge.

Howell, E. F., & Itzkowitz, S. (Eds.). (2016). *The dissociative mind in psychoanalysis: Understanding and working with trauma.* Routledge.

Hume, D. (1746). *A treatise of human nature* (L. Selby-Bigge, Ed.). Dover.

Hunsinger, D. V. D. (1995). *Theology and pastoral counseling: A new interdisciplinary approach.* Eerdmans.

Hunsinger, D. V. D. (2015). *Bearing the unbearable: Trauma, gospel, and pastoral care.* Eerdmans.

Hunsinger, G. (2004). Mysterium trinitatis: Barth's conception of eternity. In G. Hunsinger (Ed.), *For the sake of the world: Karl Barth and the future of ecclesial theology* (pp. 165–190). Eerdmans.

Ilic, M., Reinecke, J., Bohner, G., Röttgers, H.-O., Beblo, T., Driessen, M., Frommberger, U., & Corrigan, P. W. (2013). Belittled, avoided, ignored, denied: Assessing forms and consequences of stigma experiences of people with mental illness. *Basic and Applied Social Psychology, 35*(1), 31–40.

Inge, J. (2003). *A Christian theology of place.* Ashgate.

Ingersoll, R. E., & Marquis, A. (2014). *Understanding psychopathology: An integral exploration.* Pearson.

Irenaeus. (2012). Against heresies. In A. Roberts & J. Donaldson (Eds.), *Ante-Nicene fathers* (Vol. 1, pp. 315–567). Hendrickson.

Jacobs, A. (1994). Theory as ideology: Reparenting and thought reform. *Transactional Analysis Journal, 24*(1), 39–55.

James, W. (1961). *Psychology: The briefer course.* Harper & Brothers.

James, W. (2012). *The principles of psychology.* Dover.

Janet, P. (1925). *Psychological healing,* vol. 1 (E. C. Paul, Trans.). Macmillan.

Jensen, M. P. (2012). *Martyrdom and identity: The self on trial.* T&T Clark.

Jewett, R. (1971). *Paul's anthropological terms: A study of their use in conflict settings.* Brill.

Johnson, A. R. (2006). *The vitality of the individual in the thought of ancient Israel* (2nd ed.). Wipf & Stock.

Johnson, E. L. (2007). *Foundations for soul care: A Christian psychology proposal.* InterVarsity.

Johnson, E. L. (2010a). A brief history of Christians in psychology. In E. L. Johnson (Ed.), *Psychology & Christianity: Five views* (2nd ed., pp. 9–47). InterVarsity.

Johnson, E. L. (2010b). Gaining understanding through five views. In *Psychology & Christianity: Five views* (2nd ed., pp. 292–313). InterVarsity.

Johnson, E. L. (2010c). *Psychology & Christianity: Five views* (2nd ed.). InterVarsity.

Johnson, E. L. (2011). The three faces of integration. *Journal of Psychology and Christianity, 30*(4), 339–355.

Johnson, E. L. (2017). *God and soul care: The therapeutic resources of the Christian faith.* InterVarsity.

Johnson, E. L., & Burroughs, C. S. (2000). Protecting one's soul: A Christian inquiry into defensive activity. *Journal of Psychology & Theology, 28*(3), 175–189.

Johnson, P. E. (1993). *Darwin on trial.* InterVarsity.

Johnston, M. (1988). Self-deception and the nature of the mind. In B. P. McLaughlin & A. O. Rorty (Eds.), *Perspectives on self-deception* (pp. 63–91). University of California Press.

Jones, S. L., & Butman, R. E. (2011). *Modern psychotherapies: A comprehensive Christian appraisal* (2nd ed.). InterVarsity.

Kaiser, O., & Lohse, E. (1981). *Death and life* (J. F. Steely, Trans.). Abingdon.

Kamtekar, R. (2016). Self-knowledge in Plato. In U. Renz (Ed.), *Self-knowledge: A history* (pp. 25–43). Oxford University Press.

Kant, I. (1991). *Kant: Political writings* (H. B. Nisbet, Trans.; 2nd ed.). Cambridge University Press.

Kant, I. (2007). *Critique of pure reason* (N. K. Smith, Trans.). St. Martin's.

Kapic, K. M., & Gleason, R. C. (Eds.). (2004). *The devoted life: An invitation to the Puritan classics.* InterVarsity.

Karen, R. (1998). *Becoming attached: First relationships and how they shape our capacity to love.* Oxford University Press.

Käsemann, E. (1971a). Some thoughts on the theme "The doctrine of reconciliation in the New Testament." In J. M. Robinson (Ed.), *The future of our religious past: Essays in honour of Rudolf Bultmann* (pp. 51–64). Harper & Row.

Käsemann, E. (1971b). *Perspectives on Paul* (M. Kohl, Trans.). SCM.

Keener, C. S. (2010). *The Gospel of John.* Baker.

Kellemen, R. W. (2007). *Soul physicians* (Rev. ed.). BMH.

Kellemen, R. W. (2014). *Gospel-centered counseling: How Christ changes lives.* Zondervan.

Kellemen, R. W. (2015). *Gospel conversations: How to care like Christ.* Zondervan.

Kelly, G. (1991). *The psychology of personal constructs.* Routledge.

Kemp, C. F. (1947). *Physicians of the soul: A history of pastoral counseling.* Macmillan.

Kierkegaard, S. (1967). *Søren Kierkegaard's journals and papers* (H. V. Hong & E. H. Hong, Eds.; Vol. 1). Indiana University Press.

Kierkegaard, S. (1975). *Søren Kierkegaard's journals and papers* (H. V. Hong & E. H. Hong, Eds.; Vol. 4). Indiana University Press.

Kierkegaard, S. (1980). *The sickness unto death: A Christian psychological exposition for upbuilding and awakening* (H. V. Hong & E. H. Hong, Eds.). Princeton University Press.

Kierkegaard, S. (1981). *The concept of anxiety* (R. Thomte, Trans.). Princeton University Press.

Kierkegaard, S. (1991). *For self-examination / Judge for yourself!* (H. V. Hong & E. H. Hong, Eds.). Princeton University Press.

Kierkegaard, S. (1992). *Concluding unscientific postscript to philosophical fragments, volume 1* (H. V. Hong & E. H. Hong, Eds.). Princeton University Press.

Kierkegaard, S. (1997). *Christian discourses* (H. V. Hong & E. H. Hong, Trans.). Princeton University Press.

Kierkegaard, S. (1998). *Works of love* (H. V. Hong & E. H. Hong, Trans.). Princeton University Press.

Kilborne, B. (1999). The disappearing who: Kierkegaard, shame, and the self. In J. Adamson & H. Clark (Eds.), *Scenes of shame: Psychoanalysis, shame, and writing* (pp. 35–52). State University of New York Press.

Kilby, K. (2000). Perichoresis and projection: Problems with social doctrines of the Trinity. *New Blackfriars, 81*(956), 432–445.

Klebanov, M. S., & Travis, A. D. (2015). *The critical role of parenting in human development.* Routledge.

Klein, M. (1955). *Love, guilt, and reparation: And other works 1921–1945.* Free.

Koehler, L., & Baumgartner, W. (2002). *The Hebrew and Aramaic lexicon of the Old Testament.* Brill.

Koester, C. R. (1989). *The dwelling of God: The tabernacle in the Old Testament, intertestamental Jewish literature, and the New Testament.* Catholic Biblical Association of America.

Kohut, H. (1977). *The restoration of the self.* University of Chicago Press.

König, A. (1989). *The eclipse of Christ in eschatology: Toward a Christ-centered approach.* Eerdmans.

Köstenberger, A. J., & Swain, S. R. (2008). *Father, Son and Spirit: The Trinity and John's Gospel.* InterVarsity.

Kuyper, A. (1968). *Principles of sacred theology.* Eerdmans.

LaCugna, C. M. (1991). *God for us: The Trinity and Christian life.* HarperCollins.

Ladd, G. E. (1993). *A theology of the New Testament* (Rev. ed.). Eerdmans.

Lake, F. (2005). *Clinical theology: A theological and psychiatric basis to clinical pastoral care* (Vol. 1). Emeth.

Lambert, H. (2011). *The biblical counseling movement after Adams.* Crossway.

Langberg, D. (2015). *Suffering and the heart of God: How trauma destroys and Christ restores*. New Growth.

Larkings, J. S., Brown, P. M., & Scholz, B. (2017). "Why am I like this?": Consumers discuss their causal beliefs and stigma. *International Journal of Mental Health*, 46(3), 206–226.

Lauria, F., Preissmann, D., & Clément, F. (2016). Self-deception as affective coping: An empirical perspective on philosophical issues. *Consciousness & Cognition, 41*, 119–134.

Leary, M. R. (2002). When selves collide: The nature of the self and the dynamics of interpersonal relationships. In A. Tesser, D. A. Stapel, & J. V. Wood (Eds.), *Self and motivation: Emerging psychological perspectives* (pp. 119–145). American Psychological Association.

Leary, M. R. (2004). *The curse of the self: Self-awareness, egotism, and the quality of human life*. Oxford University Press.

Lee, S. H. (2000). *The philosophical theology of Jonathan Edwards*. Princeton University Press.

Lewis, G. R., & Demarest, B. A. (1990). *Integrative theology* (vol. 2). Zondervan.

Lewis, P. (1997). *The genius of Puritanism*. Soli Deo Gloria.

Lim, P. C.-H. (2004). The Reformed pastor by Richard Baxter (1615–1691). In K. M. Kapie & R. C. Gleason (Eds.), *The devoted life: An invitation to the puritan classics* (pp. 152–166). InterVarsity.

Lingiardi, V., & McWilliams, N. (Eds.). (2017). *Psychodynamic diagnostic manual (PDM-2)* (2nd ed.). Guilford.

Liotti, G. (1992). Disorganized/disoriented attachment in the etiology of the dissociative disorders. *Dissociation, 5*(4), 196–204.

Liotti, G. (2009). Attachment and dissociation. In P. F. Dell & J. A. O'Neil (Eds.), *Dissociation and the dissociative disorders: DSM-V and beyond* (pp. 53–65). Routledge.

Lippett, J. (2016). Self-knowledge in Kierkegaard. In U. Renz (Ed.), *Self-knowledge: A history* (pp. 205–222). Oxford University Press.

Locke, J. (1824). The reasonableness of Christianity as delivered in the Scriptures. In *The Works of John Locke* (12th ed., Vol. 6). Rivington.

Loder, J. E. (1998). *The logic of the Spirit: Human development in theological perspective*. Jossey-Bass.

Loder, J. E., & Neidhardt, W. J. (1992). *The knight's move: The relational logic of the Spirit in theology and science*. Helmers & Howard.

Loewald, H. (1989). *Papers on psychoanalysis*. Yale University Press.

Long, A. A. (2001). Ancient philosophy's hardest question: What to make of oneself? *Representations, 74*(1), 19–36.

Longman, T. (2015). *Proverbs*. Baker.

López-Larrea, C. (Ed.). (2012). *Self and nonself*. Springer.

Lowery, M. (2006). The trinitarian nature of the transmodern person. In P. C. Vitz & S. M. Felch (Eds.), *The self: beyond the postmodern crisis* (pp. 269–286). Intercollegiate Studies Institute.

Lynch, M. F. (2012). Theoretical contexts of trauma counseling. In L. L. Levers (Ed.), *Trauma counseling: Theories and interventions* (pp. 47–58). Springer.

MacDonald, J., Kellemen, B., & Viars, S. (Eds.). (2013). *Christ-centered biblical counseling: Changing lives with God's changeless truth*. Harvest House.

Macleod, D. (1998). *The person of Christ*. InterVarsity.

Macquarrie, J. (2003a). *Christology revisited*. SCM.

Macquarrie, J. (2003b). *Jesus Christ in modern thought*. SCM.

Madueme, H., & Reeves, M. (Eds.). (2014). *Adam, the fall, and original sin: Theological, biblical, and scientific perspectives*. Baker.

Maier, B. N., & Monroe, P. G. (2001). Biblical hermeneutics & Christian psychology. In M. R. McMinn & T. R. Phillips (Eds.), *Care for the soul: Exploring the intersection of psychology & theology* (pp. 276–293). InterVarsity.

Mangis, M. W., Jones, S. L., & Butman, R. E. (2011). Contemporary psychodynamic psychotherapies. In S. L. Jones & R. E. Butman (Eds.), *Modern psychotherapies: A comprehensive Christian appraisal* (2nd ed., pp. 135–165). InterVarsity.

Marsh, J. L. (1987). Kierkegaard's double dialectic of despair and sin. In R. L. Perkins (Ed.), *The sickness unto death* (Vol. 19, pp. 67–83). Mercer University Press.

Marshall, B. D. (1999). *Trinity and truth*. Cambridge University Press.

Martin, D. J., Garske, J. P., & Davis, K. M. (2000). Relation of the therapeutic alliance with outcome and other variables: A meta-analytic review. *Journal of Consulting and Clinical Psychology, 68*(3), 438–450.

Martin, R., & Barresi, J. (2008). *The rise and fall of soul and self: An intellectual history of personal identity*. Columbia University Press.

Martin, R. P. (1989). *Reconciliation: A study of Paul's theology*. Wipf & Stock.

McCormack, B. L. (1997). *Karl Barth's critically realistic dialectical theology: Its genesis and development 1909–1936*. Oxford University Press.

McCullough, L., Kuhn, N., Andrews, S., Kaplan, A., Wolf, J., & Lanza Hurley, C. (2003). *Treating affect phobia: A manual for short-term dynamic psychotherapy*. Guilford.

McDermott, B. O. (1993). *Word become flesh: Dimensions of Christology*. Liturgical.

McFadyen, A. I. (1990). *The call to personhood: A Christian theory of the individual in social relationships*. Cambridge University Press.

McFadyen, A. I. (2000). *Bound to sin: Abuse, Holocaust, and the Christian doctrine of sin*. Cambridge University Press.

McGrath, A. E. (2006). *A scientific theology: Volume 2, Reality*. T&T Clark.

McKinley, J. E. (2009). *Tempted for us: Theological models and the practical relevance of Christ's impeccability and temptation*. Wipf & Stock.

McLaughlin, B. P., & Rorty, A. O. (1988). *Perspectives on self-deception*. University of California Press.

McMartin, J. (2013). The theandric union as imago dei and capax dei. In O. D. Crisp & F. Sanders (Eds.), *Christology ancient & modern: Explorations in constructive dogmatics* (pp. 136–150). Zondervan.

McMinn, M. R. (2004). *Why sin matters: The surprising relationship between our sin and God's grace*. Tyndale.

McMinn, M. R., & Phillips, T. R. (Eds.). (2001). *Care for the soul: Exploring the intersection of psychology & theology*. InterVarsity.

McRay, B. W., Yarhouse, M. A., & Butman, R. E. (2016). *Modern psychopathologies: A comprehensive Christian appraisal* (2nd ed.). InterVarsity.

McWilliams, N. (2011). *Psychoanalytic diagnosis: Understanding personality structure in the clinical process* (2nd ed.). Guilford.

Megill, A. (1985). *Prophets of extremity: Nietzsche, Heidegger, Foucault, Derrida*. University of California Press.

Melanchthon, P. (2007). *The Loci Communes of Philip Melanchthon* (C. L. Hill, Trans.). Wipf & Stock.

Menninger, K. (1973). *Whatever became of sin?* Hawthorn.

Merriell, D. J. (1990). *To the image of the Trinity: A study in the development of Aquinas' teaching.* Pontifical Institute of Mediaeval Studies.

Mersch, E. (2011). *The whole Christ: The historical development of the doctrine of the mystical body in Scripture and tradition* (J. R. Kelly, Trans.). Wipf & Stock.

Metzinger, T. (2009). *The ego tunnel: The science of the mind and the myth of the self.* Basic.

Metzinger, T. (2011). The no-self alternative. In S. Gallagher (Ed.), *The oxford handbook of the self* (pp. 279–296). Oxford University Press.

Michaels, J. R. (2010). *The Gospel of John.* Eerdmans.

Michener, R. T. (2007). *Engaging deconstructive theology.* Ashgate.

Miell, D. K. (1989). Barth on persons in relationship: A case for further reflection? *Scottish Journal of Theology, 42*(4), 541–555.

Miller, A. (2012). *Healing the unimaginable: Treating ritual abuse and mind control.* Karnac.

Mitchell, S. A. (2000). *Relationality: From attachment to intersubjectivity.* Routledge.

Mitchell, S. A., & Black, M. J. (2016). *Freud and beyond: A history of modern psychoanalytic thought* (Rev. ed.). Basic.

Moloney, R. (1999). *The knowledge of Christ.* Continuum.

Moltmann, J. (1981). *The Trinity and the kingdom of God: The doctrine of God* (M. Kohl, Trans.). SCM.

Moltmann, J. (1993). *The Trinity and the kingdom* (M. Kohl, Trans.). Harper.

Moltmann, J. (1997). *The source of life: The Holy Spirit and the theology of life.* Fortress.

Moo, D. J. (1996). *The epistle to the Romans.* Eerdmans.

Moo, D. J. (2008). *The letters to the Colossians and to Philemon.* Eerdmans.

Moo, D. J. (2013). *Galatians.* Baker.

Moon, G. W., & Crews, F. (2002). The essential helping relationship. In T. Clinton & G. Ohlschlager (Eds.), *Competent Christian counseling.* WaterBrook.

Moran, R. (2001). *Authority and estrangement: An essay on self-knowledge.* Princeton University Press.

Moreland, J. P., & Rae, S. B. (2000). *Body & soul: Human nature & the crisis in ethics.* InterVarsity.

Moroney, S. K. (2000). *The noetic effects of sin: An historical and contemporary exploration of how sin affects our thinking.* Lexington.

Morris, T. (1986). *The logic of God incarnate.* Wipf & Stock.

Mounce, R. H. (1997). *The Book of Revelation* (Rev. ed.). Eerdmans.

Mounce, W. D. (2000). *Pastoral epistles* (vol. 46). Thomas Nelson.

Mullen, J. D. (1988). *Kierkegaard's philosophy: Self-deception and cowardice in the present age.* University Press of America.

Muran, J. C., & Barber, J. P. (Eds.). (2011). *The therapeutic alliance: An evidence-based guide to practice.* Guilford.

Murray, J. (1968). *Epistle to the Romans.* Eerdmans.

Murray, J. (1955). *Redemption: Accomplished and applied.* Eerdmans.

Nazianzen, G. (2012). Epistle 101. In P. Schaff & H. Wace (Eds.), *Nicene and post-Nicene fathers: Second series* (Vol. 7, pp. 439–443). Hendrickson.

Neisser, U. (1997). The roots of self-knowledge: Perceiving self, it, and thou. *Annals of the New York Academy of Sciences, 818*(1), 19–33.

Niesel, W. (1956). *The theology of Calvin* (H. Knight, Trans.). Westminster.

Norcross, J. C. (Ed.). (2011). *Psychotherapy relationships that work: Evidence-based responsiveness* (2nd ed.). Oxford University Press.

Norcross, J. C., & Lambert, M. J. (2011). Evidence-based therapy relationships. In J. C. Norcross (Ed.), *Psychotherapy relationships that work: Evidence-based responsiveness* (pp. 3–24). Oxford University Press.

Norris, R. A. (1996). Chalcedon revisited: A historical and theological reflection. In B. Nassif (Ed.), *New perspectives on historical theology: Essays in memory of John Meyendorff* (pp. 140–158). Eerdmans.

O'Brien, L. (2010). *Self-knowing agents*. Oxford University Press.

O'Brien, P. T. (2000). *Colossians–Philemon* (Vol. 44). Thomas Nelson.

O'Collins, G. (2009). *Christology: A biblical, historical, and systematic study of Jesus* (2nd ed.). Oxford University Press.

O'Collins, G. (2011). The incarnation: The critical issues. In S. T. Davis, D. Kendall, & G. O'Collins (Eds.), *The incarnation* (pp. 1–27). Oxford University Press.

Oden, T. C. (1984). *Care of souls in the classic tradition*. Fortress.

O'Donovan, O. (1994). *Resurrection and moral order: An outline for evangelical ethics* (2nd ed.). Eerdmans.

Ogawa, J. R., Sroufe, L. A., Weinfield, N. S., Carlson, E. A., & Egeland, B. (1997). Development and the fragmented self: Longitudinal study of dissociative symptomatology in a nonclinical sample. *Development and Psychopathology, 9*(4), 855–879.

Oh, P. S. (2006). *Karl Barth's trinitarian theology: A study in Karl Barth's analogical use of the trinitarian relation*. T&T Clark.

Osborne, G. R. (2006). *The hermeneutical spiral: A comprehensive introduction to biblical interpretation* (2nd ed.). InterVarsity.

Oswalt, J. N. (1986). *The Book of Isaiah, chapters 1–39*. Eerdmans.

Otto, R. E. (2001a). The use and abuse of perichoresis in recent theology. *Scottish Journal of Theology, 54*(3), 366–384.

Owen, J. (2006). *Overcoming sin & temptation*. Crossway.

Packer, J. I. (1999). The "wretched man" revisited: Another look at Romans 7:14–25. In S. K. Soderlund & N. T. Wright (Eds.), *Romans and the people of God* (pp. 70–81). Eerdmans.

Packer, J. I. (2000). Theology and wisdom. In J. I. Packer & S. K. Soderlund (Eds.), *The way of wisdom: Essays in honor of Bruce K. Walke* (pp. 1–14). Zondervan.

Packer, J. I. (2007). The heart of the gospel. In J. I. Packer & M. E. Dever (Eds.), *In my place condemned he stood: Celebrating the glory of the atonement* (pp. 29–52). Crossway.

Packer, J. I. (2010). *A quest for godliness: The Puritan vision of the Christian life*. Crossway.

Packer, J. I. (2012). *Puritan portraits: J. I. Packer on selected classic pastors and pastoral classics*. Christian Focus.

Pannenberg, W. (1977). *Jesus—God and man* (L. L. Wilkins & D. A. Priebe, Trans.; 2nd ed.). Westminster John Knox.

Pannenberg, W. (1985). *Anthropology in theological perspective* (M. J. O'Connell, Trans.). Westminster.

Pannenberg, W. (1994). *Systematic theology* (G. W. Bromiley, Trans.; Vol. 2). Eerdmans.

Paris, J. (2015). *The intelligent clinician's guide to the DSM-5* (2nd ed). Oxford University Press.

Pascal, B. (1995). *Pensées* (A. J. Krailsheimer, Trans.). Penguin.

Patten, D. (2003). How do we deceive ourselves? *Philosophical Psychology, 16*(2), 229–246.

Payne, L. (1995). *The healing presence: Curing the soul through union with Christ.* Baker.

Pearcey, N. R., & Thaxton, C. B. (1994). *The soul of science: Christian faith and natural philosophy.* Crossway.

Pelser, G. M. M. (1998). Once more the body of Christ in Paul. *Neotestamentica, 32*(2), 525–545.

Pennington, J. T. (2017). *The Sermon on the Mount and human flourishing: A theological commentary.* Baker.

Percival, H. R. (1991). *The seven ecumenical councils* (P. Schaff, Ed.). Hendrickson.

Pierre, J. P. (2010). *"Trust in the Lord with all your heart": The centrality of faith in Christ to the restoration of human functioning* [Unpublished doctoral dissertation]. Southern Baptist Theological Seminary.

Pierre, J. P. (2016). *The dynamic heart in daily life: Connecting Christ to human experience.* New Growth.

Piper, J., & Edwards, J. (2006). *God's passion for his glory: Living the vision of Jonathan Edwards, with the complete text of The End for Which God Created the World.* Crossway.

Pittenger, W. N. (1959). *The Word incarnate: A study of the doctrine of the person of Christ.* Harper.

Pizer, S. A. (1998). *Building bridges: The negotiation of paradox in psychoanalysis.* Routledge.

Polanyi, M. (1974). *Personal knowledge: Towards a post-critical philosophy.* University of Chicago Press.

Porter, S. E. (1993). Peace, reconciliation. In G. F. Hawthorne, R. P. Martin, & D. G. Reid (Eds.), *Dictionary of Paul and his letters* (pp. 695–699). InterVarsity.

Powlison, D. (2003). *Seeing with new eyes: Counseling and the human condition through the lens of Scripture.* P&R.

Pressley, J. D., & Hoek, K. K. V. (2014). Psychodynamic and attachment-based approaches to treatment. In K. S. Flanagan & S. E. Hall (Eds.), *Christianity and developmental psychopathology: Foundations and approaches* (pp. 247–281). InterVarsity.

Price, D. J. (2002). *Karl Barth's anthropology in light of modern thought.* Eerdmans.

Prochaska, J. O., & Norcross, J. C. (2014). *Systems of psychotherapy: A transtheoretical analysis* (8th ed.). Brooks/Cole.

Provan, I., Long, V. P., & Longman, T. (2015). *A biblical history of Israel* (2nd ed.). Westminster John Knox.

Pulakos, J. (1996). Family environment and shame: Is there a relationship? *Journal of Clinical Psychology, 52*(6), 617–623.

Purves, A. (1989). *The search for compassion: Spirituality and ministry.* Westminster John Knox.

Purves, A. (2001). *Pastoral theology in the classical tradition.* Westminster John Knox.

Purves, A. (2004). *Reconstructing pastoral theology: A christological foundation.* Westminster John Knox.

Putnam, F. W. (1994). Dissociation and disturbances of self. In D. Cicchetti & S. L. Toth (Eds.), *Rochester symposium on developmental psychopathology: Vol. 5. disorders and dysfunctions of the self* (pp. 251–265). University of Rochester Press.

Putnam, F. W. (1997). *Dissociation in children and adolescents: A developmental perspective.* Guilford.

Rahner, K. (1966). Dogmatic reflections on the knowledge and self-consciousness of Christ. In K.-H. Kruger (Trans.), *Theological Investigations* (Vol. 5, pp. 193–215). Helicon.

Räikkä, J. (2014). Adaptive preferences and self-deception. In *Social Justice in Practice: Questions in Ethics and Political Philosophy* (Vol. 14). Springer.

Ramm, B. L. (1985). *An evangelical Christology: Ecumenic and historic.* Thomas Nelson.

Remes, P. (2007). *Plotinus on self: The philosophy of the "we."* Cambridge University Press.

Renz, U. (Ed.). (2016). *Self-knowledge: A history.* Oxford University Press.

Ricoeur, P. (1977). *Freud and philosophy: An essay on interpretation* (D. Savage, Trans.). Yale University Press.

Ricoeur, P. (1995). *Oneself as another* (K. Blamey, Trans.). University of Chicago Press.

Ridderbos, H. N. (1975). *Paul: An outline of his theology.* Eerdmans.

Rist, J. M. (1996). *Augustine: Ancient thought baptized.* Cambridge University Press.

Roberts, R. C. (1993). *Taking the word to heart: Self and other in an age of therapies.* Eerdmans.

Roberts, R. C. (2001). Outline of Pauline psychotherapy. In M. R. McMinn & T. R. Phillips (Eds.), *Care for the soul: Exploring the intersection of psychology & theology* (pp. 134–163). InterVarsity.

Roberts, R. C. (2007). *Spiritual emotions: A psychology of Christian virtues.* Eerdmans.

Roberts, R. C., & Watson, P. J. (2010). A Christian psychology view. In E. L. Johnson (Ed.), *Psychology & Christianity: Five views* (pp. 149–178). InterVarsity.

Robinson, J. A. T. (1952). *The body: A study in Pauline theology.* SCM.

Robinson, J. A. T. (1973). *The human face of God.* SCM.

Rogers, C. R. (1961). *On becoming a person.* Houghton Mifflin.

Rogers, C. R. (1967). *The therapeutic relationship and its impact.* University of Wisconsin Press.

Rumscheidt, H. M. (Ed.). (1986). *The way of theology in Karl Barth: Essays and comments.* Wipf & Stock.

Runia, K. (1984). *The present-day christological debate.* Wipf & Stock.

Ryken, L. (1993). *Words of delight: A literary introduction to the Bible* (2nd ed.). Baker.

Ryle, G. (1949). *The concept of mind.* University of Chicago Press.

Safran, J. D. (2012). *Psychoanalysis and psychoanalytic therapies.* American Psychological Association.

Sanlon, P. (2014). Original sin in patristic theology. In H. Madueme & M. Reeves (Eds.), *Adam, the fall, and original sin: Theological, biblical, and scientific perspectives.* Baker.

Sartre, J.-P. (1993). *Being and nothingness* (H. E. Barnes, Trans.). Washington Square.

Sbanotto, E. A. N., Gingrich, H. D., & Gingrich, F. C. (2016). *Skills for effective counseling: A faith-based integration.* Intervarsity.

Schaefer, K. (2001). *Psalms.* Liturgical.

Schaeffer, F. A. (1998). *The God who is there* (Rev. ed.). InterVarsity.

Schökel, L. A. (1976). The poetic structure of Psalm 42–43. *Journal for the Study of the Old Testament, 1*(1), 4–21.

Schoonenberg, P. J. A. M. (1971). *The Christ: A study of the God-man relationship in the whole of creation and in Jesus Christ*. Herder and Herder.

Schreiner, T. R. (1998). *Romans*. Baker.

Schreiner, T. R. (2008). *New Testament theology: Magnifying God in Christ*. Baker.

Schwarz, H. (2013). *The human being: A theological anthropology*. Eerdmans.

Schwöbel, C., & Gunton, C. E. (Eds.). (1991). *Persons, Divine, and Human: King's college essays in theological anthropology*. T&T Clark.

Seifrid, M. A. (1992). *Justification by faith: The origin and development of a central Pauline theme*. Brill.

Shields, C. (2016). Aristotle's requisite of self-knowledge. In U. Renz (Ed.), *Self-knowledge: A history* (pp. 44–60). Oxford University Press.

Shults, F. L. (2003). *Reforming theological anthropology: After the philosophical turn to relationality*. Eerdmans.

Shults, F. L. (2008). *Christology and science*. Eerdmans.

Sibbes, R. (1658). *The soul's conflict with itself: And victory over itself by faith*. A Puritan at Heart.

Siderits, M. (2016). *Personal identity and Buddhist philosophy: Empty persons* (2nd ed.). Routledge.

Siderits, M., Thompson, E., & Zahavi, D. (Eds.). (2013). *Self, no self?: Perspectives from analytical, phenomenological, and Indian traditions*. Oxford University Press.

Sie, M. (2015). Moral hypocrisy and acting for reasons: How moralizing can invite self-deception. *Ethical Theory & Moral Practice, 18*(2), 223–235.

Siegel, D. J. (2012). *Pocket guide to interpersonal neurobiology: An integrative handbook of the mind*. Norton.

Silfver-Kuhalampi, M., Fontaine, J., Dillen, L., & Scherer, K. (2013). Cultural differences in the meaning of guilt and shame. In J. Fontaine, K. Scherer, & C. Soriano (Eds.), *Components of emotional meaning: A sourcebook* (pp. 388–396). Oxford University Press.

Silverman, A. (2002). *The dialectic of essence: A study of Plato's metaphysics*. Princeton University Press.

Simone, R. T., & Sugarman, R. I. (1986). *Reclaiming the humanities: The roots of self-knowledge in the Greek and biblical worlds*. University Press of America.

Simpson, A. (2013). *Troubled minds: Mental illness and the church's mission*. InterVarsity.

Skinner, B. F. (1976). *About behaviorism*. Vintage.

Solomon, R. C. (1988). *Continental philosophy since 1750: The rise and fall of the self*. Oxford University Press.

Sommers-Flanagan, J., & Sommers-Flanagan, R. (2015). *Counseling and psychotherapy theories in context and practice: Skills, strategies, and techniques* (2nd ed.). Wiley.

Sorg, T. (1979). Heart. In C. Brown (Ed.), *The new international dictionary of New Testament theology* (Vol. 2). Zondervan.

Spence, A. (1991). Christ's humanity and ours: John Owen. In C. Schwöbel & C. E. Gunton (Eds.), *Persons, divine and human: King's College essays in theological anthropology* (pp. 74–97). T&T Clark.

Spiegel, J. S. (1999). *Hypocrisy: Moral fraud and other vices*. Baker.

Stanford, M. S. (2017). *Grace for the afflicted: A clinical and biblical perspective on mental illness* (Rev. ed.). InterVarsity.

Steele, H., & Steele, M. (2017). On conflict in attachment theory and research. In C. Christian & M. N. Eagle (Eds.), *Psychoanalytic perspectives on conflict* (pp. 210–222). Routledge.

Steele, K., & van der Hart, O. (2009). Treating dissociation. In C. A. Courtois & J. D. Ford (Eds.), *Treating complex traumatic stress disorders: Scientific foundations and therapeutic models* (pp. 145–165). Guilford.

Stendahl, K. (1963). The apostle Paul and the introspective conscience of the west. *Harvard Theological Review, 56*(3), 199–215.

Stern, D. B. (2010). *Partners in thought: Working with unformulated experience, dissociation, and enactment.* Routledge.

Stevenson, L., & Haberman, D. L. (2004). *Ten theories of human nature* (4th ed.). Oxford University Press.

Stock, B. (2010). *Augustine's inner dialogue: The philosophical soliloquy in late antiquity.* Cambridge University Press.

Stott, J. R. W. (1978). *The message of the Sermon on the Mount.* InterVarsity.

Stott, J. R. W. (2006). *The cross of Christ.* InterVarsity.

Stratton, S. P. (2006). Self, attachment, and agency: Love and the trinitarian concept of personhood. In P. C. Vitz & S. M. Felch (Eds.), *The self: Beyond the postmodern crisis* (pp. 247–268). Intercollegiate Studies Institute.

Strauss, J., & Goethals, G. R. (1991). *The self: Interdisciplinary approaches.* Springer.

Strongman, K. T. (2003). *The psychology of emotion* (5th ed.). Wiley.

Stump, E. (2002). Aquinas' metaphysics of the incarnation. In S. T. Davis, D. Kendall, & G. O'Collins (Eds.), *The incarnation: An interdisciplinary symposium on the incarnation of the Son of God* (pp. 197–218). Oxford University Press.

Stump, E. (2012). *Wandering in darkness: Narrative and the problem of suffering.* Oxford University Press.

Sullivan, H. S. (1940). *Conceptions of modern psychiatry.* Norton.

Sullivan, H. S. (1953). *The interpersonal theory of psychiatry.* Norton.

Sullivan, J. (1963). *The image of God: The doctrine of St. Augustine and its influence.* Priory.

Summers, R. F., & Barber, J. P. (2010). *Psychodynamic therapy: A guide to evidence-based practice.* Guilford.

Swain, S. R., & Allen, M. (2013). The obedience of the eternal Son: Catholic trinitarianism and Reformed Christology. In O. D. Crisp & F. Sanders (Eds.), *Christology: Ancient & modern* (pp. 74–95). Zondervan.

Swinburne, R. (1994). *The Christian God.* Oxford University Press.

Swinnock, G. (1868). The Christian man's calling, part I. In *Works, volume 1* (pp. 1–362). J. Nichol.

Talbot, M. R. (1997). Starting from Scripture. In R. C. Roberts & M. R. Talbot (Eds.), *Limning the psyche: Explorations in Christian psychology* (pp. 102–122). Eerdmans.

Tan, S.-Y. (2011). *Counseling and psychotherapy: A Christian perspective.* Baker.

Tangney, J. P. (2003). Self-relevant emotions. In M. R. Leary & J. P. Tangney (Eds.), *Handbook of self and identity* (pp. 384–400). Guilford.

Tannehill, R. C. (2006). *Dying and rising with Christ: A study in Pauline theology.* Wipf & Stock.

Tanner, K. (2010). *Christ the key.* Cambridge University Press.

Taylor, C. (1989). *Sources of the self: The making of the modern identity.* Harvard University Press.

Taylor, S. E. (1989). *Positive illusions: Creative self-deception and the healthy mind*. Basic.

TeSelle, E. (1970). *Augustine the theologian*. Wipf & Stock.

Theissen, G. (1987). *Psychological aspects of Pauline theology*. T&T Clark.

Thielman, F. (2010). *Ephesians*. Baker.

Thiselton, A. C. (1995). *Interpreting God and the postmodern self: On meaning, manipulation and promise*. Eerdmans.

Tidball, D. (1997). *Skilful shepherds: Explorations in pastoral theology*. Apollos.

Tietjen, M. A. (2016). *Kierkegaard: A Christian missionary to Christians*. InterVarsity.

Tomkins, S. S. (1987). Shame. In D. L. Nathanson (Ed.), *The many faces of shame* (pp. 133–161). Guilford.

Topping, R. R. (2007). *Revelation, scripture and church: Theological hermeneutic thought of James Barr, Paul Ricoeur and Hans Frei*. Routledge.

Torrance, T. F. (1957). *Calvin's doctrine of man*. Wipf & Stock.

Torrance, T. F. (1996). *Christian doctrine of God: One being three persons*. T&T Clark.

Torrance, T. F. (1998). *Transformation and convergence in the frame of knowledge*. Wipf & Stock.

Tripp, P. D. (2002). *Instruments in the redeemer's hands: People in need of change helping people in need of change*. P&R.

Turner, L. (2008). *Theology, psychology and the plural self*. Routledge.

Turner, L. (2011). Disunity and disorder: The "problem" of self-fragmentation. In J. W. van Huyssteen & E. P. Wiebe (Eds.), *In search of self: Interdisciplinary perspectives on personhood* (pp. 125–140). Eerdmans.

Vacek, H. H. (2015). *Madness: American Protestant responses to mental illness*. Baylor University Press.

van der Hart, O., Nijenhuis, E. R. S., & Steele, K. (2006). *The haunted self: Structural dissociation and the treatment of chronic traumatization*. Norton.

van der Kolk, B. (2015). *The body keeps the score: Brain, mind, and body in the healing of trauma*. Penguin.

van Huyssteen, J. W., & Wiebe, E. P. (Eds.). (2011). *In search of self: Interdisciplinary perspectives on personhood*. Eerdmans.

van Leeuwen, M. S. (1982). *The sorcerer's apprentice: A Christian looks at the changing face of psychology*. InterVarsity.

Van Til, C. (1969). *A Christian theory of knowledge*. P&R.

Van Til, C. (1980). *A survey of Christian epistemology* (2nd ed.). P&R.

Van Til, C. (2015). *Common grace and the gospel* (2nd ed.). P&R.

Vanhoozer, K. J. (1998). *Is there a meaning in this text?: The Bible, the reader, and the morality of literary knowledge* (Rev. ed.). Zondervan.

Vanhoozer, K. J. (2005). *The drama of doctrine: A canonical-linguistic approach to Christian theology*. Westminster John Knox.

Vanhoozer, K. J. (2014). *Faith speaking understanding: Performing the drama of doctrine*. Westminster John Knox.

Via, D. O. (2005). *Self-deception and wholeness in Paul and Matthew*. Wipf & Stock.

Vitz, P. C. (1993). *Sigmund Freud's Christian unconscious*. Eerdmans.

Vitz, P. C. (1994). *Psychology as religion: The cult of self-worship* (2nd ed.). Eerdmans.

Vitz, P. C. (2006). Introduction: From the modern and postmodern selves to the transmodern self. In P. C. Vitz & S. M. Felch (Eds.), *The self: Beyond the postmodern crisis* (pp. xi–xxii). Intercollegiate Studies Institute.

Vitz, P. C., & Felch, S. M. (Eds.). (2006). *The self: Beyond the postmodern crisis*. Intercollegiate Studies Institute.

Von Balthasar, H. U. (1992a). *The theology of Karl Barth: Exposition and interpretation*. Ignatius.

Von Balthasar, H. U. (1992b). *Theo-drama: Theological dramatic theory, vol. III: Dramatis personae: Persons in Christ*. Ignatius.

Vos, G. (1953). *The self-disclosure of Jesus: The modern debate about the messianic consciousness* (2nd ed.). P&R.

Wachtel, P. L. (2011). *Therapeutic communication: Knowing what to say when*. Guilford.

Waltke, B. K. (1980). נֶפֶשׁ. In R. L. Harris, G. J. Archer Jr., & B. K. Waltke (Eds.), *Theological wordbook of the Old Testament* (pp. 587–591). Moody.

Ware, B. A. (2000). *God's lesser glory: The diminished God of open theism*. Crossway.

Ware, B. A. (2012). *The man Christ Jesus: Theological reflections on the humanity of Christ*. Crossway.

Warfield, B. B. (1956). *Calvin and Augustine*. P&R.

Warfield, B. B. (2015). *The person and work of Christ*. Benediction Classics.

Webster, J. (1995). *Barth's ethics of reconciliation*. Cambridge University Press.

Weeks, N. (2014). The fall and Genesis 3. In H. Madueme & M. Reeves (Eds.), *Adam, the fall, and original sin: Theological, biblical, and scientific perspectives* (pp. 289–305). Baker.

Weiss, L. (1994). The ethics of parenting and reparenting in psychotherapy. *Transactional Analysis Journal, 24*(1), 57–59.

Wells, D. F. (1984). *The person of Christ: A biblical and historical analysis of the incarnation*. Crossway.

Wells, M. A. (2007). The necessity of a Christocentric anthropology for Christian psychology: Reflections on Ray Anderson's doctrine of humanity. *Edification: Journal of the Society for Christian Psychology, 2*(2), 57–64.

Wellum, S. J. (2016). *God the Son incarnate: The doctrine of Christ*. Crossway.

Wenham, G. J. (1987). *Genesis 1–15, volume 1*. Zondervan.

Westermann, C. (1984). *Genesis 1–11: A commentary*. Augsburg.

Westermann, C. (1992). *Genesis: An introduction*. Fortress.

White, V. (1996). *Paying attention to people: An essay in individualism and Christian belief*. SPCK.

Whitmer, G. (2001). On the nature of dissociation. *The Psychoanalytic Quarterly, 70*(4), 807–837.

Wieland, S. (2015). Dissociation in children and adolescents: What it is, how it presents, and how we can understand it. In S. Wieland (Ed.), *Dissociation in traumatized children and adolescents: Theory and clinical interventions* (pp. 1–40). Routledge.

Wilkins, E. G. (1979). *"Know thyself" in Greek and Latin literature*. Garland.

Willard, D. (1998). *The divine conspiracy: Rediscovering our hidden life in God*. Harper.

Williams, D. A. (2001). Knowing as participation: Toward an intersection between psychology & postcritical epistemology. In M. R. McMinn & T. R. Phillips (Eds.), *Care for the soul: Exploring the intersection of psychology & theology* (pp. 332–345). InterVarsity.

Williams, J. (2010). *One new man: The cross and racial reconciliation in Pauline theology*. B&H Academic.

Williams, P. A. (2001). *Doing without Adam and Eve: Sociobiology and original sin*. Fortress.

Witherington, B. (2005). *The problem with evangelical theology: Testing the exegetical foundations of Calvinism, Dispensationalism, and Wesleyanism*. Baylor University Press.

Wolf, E. S. (1988). *Treating the self: Elements of clinical self psychology*. Guilford.

Wolff, H. W. (1974). *Anthropology of the Old Testament* (M. Kohl, Trans.). SCM.

Wolpe, J. (1978). Cognition and causation in human behavior and its therapy. *American Psychologist, 33*(5), 437–446.

Wolterstorff, N. (1995). *Divine discourse: Philosophical reflections on the claim that God speaks*. Cambridge University Press.

Wolterstorff, N. (2010). *Justice: Rights and wrongs*. Princeton University Press.

Wolterstorff, N. (2015). *Justice in love*. Eerdmans.

Woodhead, L. (1999). Theology and the fragmentation of the self. *International Journal of Systematic Theology, 1*(1), 53–72.

Wright, N. T. (1996). *Jesus and the victory of God*. Fortress.

Wright, N. T. (2009). *Justification: God's plan & Paul's vision*. IVP Academic.

Wright, N. T. (2011). Jesus' self-understanding. In S. T. Davis, D. Kendall, & G. O'Collins (Eds.), *The incarnation* (pp. 47–61). Oxford University Press.

Wright, N. T. (2013). *Paul and the faithfulness of God*. Fortress.

Yarbrough, R. W. (2000). Atonement. In T. D. Alexander, B. S. Rosner, D. A. Carson, & G. Goldsworthy (Eds.), *New dictionary of biblical theology* (pp. 388–393). IVP Academic.

Yieh, J. Y.-H. (2004). *One teacher: Jesus' teaching role in Matthew's Gospel report*. de Gruyter.

Yuille, J. S. (2012). *Living blessedly forever: The Sermon on the Mount and the Puritan piety of William Perkins*. Reformation Heritage.

Yuille, J. S. (2013). *A labor of love: Puritan pastoral priorities*. Reformation Heritage.

Zachman, R. C. (2012). The bond and critique of social union: John Calvin and Søren Kierkegaard on the image of God. In *Reconsidering John Calvin* (pp. 35–61). Cambridge University Press.

Zimmermann, J. (2004). *Recovering theological hermeneutics: An incarnational-trinitarian theory of interpretation*. Baker.

Zizioulas, J. D. (1975). Human capacity and human incapacity: A theological exploration of personhood. *Scottish Journal of Theology, 28*(5), 401–447.

Zizioulas, J. D. (1985). *Being as communion: Studies in personhood and the church*. St. Vladimir's Seminary Press.

Zizioulas, J. D. (1991). On being a person: Towards an ontology of personhood. In C. Schwöbel & C. E. Gunton (Eds.), *Persons, divine and human: King's College essays in theological anthropology* (pp. 33–46). T&T Clark.

Zizioulas, J. D. (2007). *Communion and otherness: Further studies in personhood and the church*. T&T Clark.